Studies in European Economic Law and Regulation

Volume 18

This series is devoted to the analysis of European Economic Law. The series' scope covers a broad range of topics within economics law including, but not limited to, the relationship between EU law and WTO law; free movement under EU law and its impact on fundamental rights; antitrust law; trade law; unfair competition law; financial market law; consumer law; food law; and health law. These subjects are approached both from doctrinal and interdisciplinary perspectives.

The series accepts monographs focusing on a specific topic, as well as edited collections of articles covering a specific theme or collections of articles. All contributions are subject to rigorous double-blind peer-review.

More information about this series at http://www.springer.com/series/11710

Luca Lionello

The Pursuit of Stability of the Euro Area as a Whole

The Reform of the European Economic Union and Perspectives of Fiscal Integration

Springer

Luca Lionello
Faculty of Political and Social Sciences
Catholic University
Milan, Italy

ISSN 2214-2037 ISSN 2214-2045 (electronic)
Studies in European Economic Law and Regulation
ISBN 978-3-030-28044-4 ISBN 978-3-030-28045-1 (eBook)
https://doi.org/10.1007/978-3-030-28045-1

This Springer imprint is published by the registered company Springer Nature Switzerland AG.
The registered company address is: Gewerbestrasse 11, 6330 Cham, Switzerland

Stability is not immobility
Klemens von Metternich

For Ife and Jade

Contents

Acronyms

AGS	Annual Growth Survey
AMR	Alert Mechanism Report
BEPGs	Broad Economic Policy Guidelines
BICC	Budgetary Instrument for Convergence and Competitiveness
CACs	Collective Action Clauses
CAP	Corrective Action Plan
CCCTB	Common Consolidated Corporate Tax Base
CJEU	Court of Justice of the European Union
CMU	Capital Market Union
COSAC	Conférence des Organes Spécialisés dans les Affaires Communautaire
CSRs	Country-Specific Recommendations
DGS	Deposit Guarantee Scheme
EBA	European Banking Authority
ECB	European Central Bank
ECCL	Enhanced Conditions Credit Line
ECHR	European Court of Human Rights
ECJ	European Court of Justice
ECU	European Currency Unit
EDF	European Development Fund
EDIS	European deposit insurance scheme
EDP	Excessive Deficit Procedure
EFSF	European Financial Stability Facility
EFSI	European Fund for Strategic Investments
EFSM	European Financial Stabilisation Mechanism
EIB	European Investment Bank
EIOPA	European Insurance and Occupational Pensions Authority
EISF	European Investment Stabilisation Function
EMF	European Monetary Fund
EMI	European Monetary Institute
EMS	European Monetary System

EMU	Economic and Monetary Union
ERM	Exchange Rate Mechanism
ESA	European Supervisory Authority
ESBies	European Safe Bonds
ESCB	European System of Central Banks
ESFS	European System of Financial Supervision
ESIF	European Structural and Investment Funds
ESM	European Stability Mechanism
ESMA	European Securities and Markets Authority
ESRB	European Systemic Risk Board
EUCFR	EU Charter of Fundamental Rights
FTT	Financial Transaction Tax
GFCC	German Federal Constitutional Court
GG	Grundgesetz
GNI	Gross National Income
HICP	Harmonised Index of Consumer Prices
IDRs	In Depth Reviews
IFIs	Independent Fiscal Institutions
IGA	Inter-governmental agreement
IMF	International Monetary Fund
MAP	Macroeconomic Adjustment Programme
MIP	Macroeconomic Imbalance Procedure
MFF	Multiannual Financial Framework
MoU	Memorandum of Understanding
MREL	Minimum Requirement for own funds and Eligible Liabilities
MSP	Multilateral Surveillance Procedure
MTO	Medium Term Objective
NCB	National Central Bank
NPLs	Non-preforming loans
NRA	National Resolution Authority
OMA	Optimum Monetary Area
OMTs	Outright Market Transactions
PCCL	Precautionary Conditioned Credit line
RMV	Reverse Majority Voting
RSMV	Reverse Simple Majority Voting
RQMV	Reverse Qualified Majority Voting
SGP	Stability and Growth Pact
SMP	Securities Markets Programme
SPV	Special Purpose Vehicle
SRB	Single Resolution Board
SRF	Single Resolution Fund
SRM	Single Resolution Mechanism
SSM	Single Supervisory Mechanism

TESM	Treaty establishing the European Stability Mechanism
TINA	There Is No Alternative
TSCG	Treaty on Stability, Coordination and Governance
VCLT	Vienna Convention on the Law of Treaties

Chapter 1
General Introduction

1.1 The Need for Stability in the Euro Area

Since its conception in the Maastricht Treaty, the Economic and Monetary Union (EMU) has always been in search of stability. This pursuit has assumed along the years different forms: convergence criteria for the introduction of the single currency, price stability quantified in a specific level of inflation, sound budgetary policy in terms of public deficit and debt, financial stability through banking regulation and supervision, and, eventually, the 'stability of the euro area as a whole'.

The first reference to the objective of 'stability of the euro area as a whole' can be found in several statements of the Heads of State or Governments of the Union and the euro area during the first months of 2010, regarding the management of the Greek financial crisis.[1] Since then, the concept has been widely used by EU institutions and national governments to justify financial assistance to Member States during the sovereign debt and banking crisis in the Eurozone. The increasing prominence of the objective was confirmed by its inclusion in several legal sources and especially in the Treaty on the Functioning of the European Union. Most importantly, the Court of Justice of the European Union recurred to the concept of 'stability of the euro area as a whole' to prove the consistency of some significant reforms of the Eurozone governance with the EU Treaties. By doing so, the Court has also acknowledged it to be the primary objective of the economic union.

---

[1]'All euro area members must conduct sound national policies in line with the agreed rules. They have a shared responsibility for the economic and financial stability in the area.' Statement by the Heads of State or Government of the European Union, Brussels, 11 February 2010. Cf. also Statement by the Heads of State and Government of the Euro Area Brussels, 25 March 2010; Statement on the support to Greece by Euro area Members States, Brussels, 11 April 2010; Statement of the Heads of State or Government of the Euro Area, Brussels, 7 May 2010.

L. Lionello, *The Pursuit of Stability of the Euro Area as a Whole*, Studies in European Economic Law and Regulation 18,
https://doi.org/10.1007/978-3-030-28045-1_1

1.2 Problem Description

The fundamental need of stability of the Eurozone can be understood looking at the unique legal features, which have characterised the creation of the single currency in Europe. By transferring monetary competence at supranational level, Member States gave up a fundamental part of their sovereignty,[2] which is deeply rooted in the concept of statehood itself. Notably, monetary unification and political integration are two interdependent phenomena, as the establishment of a new currency does normally follow a process of state building or a declaration of independence. Unlike all other currencies of the world, however, the Euro does not belong to a state, but to a group of countries, which are bound to each other in an association (*Staatenverbund*)[3] without abdicating their other sovereign prerogatives. Consequently, the EU did not develop a self-defining legal authority, which can decide on its own competences, but it gained only a limited authority in some specific fields. More precisely, the European Court of Justice clarified that Member States have permanently transferred to the EU some specific 'sovereign rights', which allow the supremacy of European law over domestic law only in the relative policy areas.

In accordance with this explanation, the only part of sovereignty, Member States decided to transfer to the Union when they established the EMU was monetary competence, while their authority on economic policy remained substantially unscathed. In particular, fiscal sovereignty has firmly remained an exclusive prerogative of national governments, since it represents the main source of their political power,[4] as well as the most important instrument, they have available in order to reach popular consensus.[5] The rejection of any form of fiscal solidarity between the Member States has been officially sanctioned in the Maastricht Treaty through the introduction of the no bailout clause, according to which every country is responsible for its own debt and cannot rely on the financial support of the Union and the other governments. Aside from fiscal policy, Member States initially refused to give up control of the management of their banking system, whose stability remained a responsibility of domestic authorities. Also in this case, national governments did

---

[2]'On the definition of monetary sovereignty see Lastra (2006), p. 16.

[3]As the German Constitutional Court has specified in the Judgment on the Maastricht Treaty, the introduction of the single currency did not transform the European Union into a federation, because Member States remained 'the masters of Treaties'. See German Constitutional Court, Judgment of 12 October 1993, BVerfGE 89/155, paras. 112, 135.

[4]Fiscal policy consists of the power to decide the revenues and expenditures of a state. This competence is exercised through a budgetary law, which is normally adopted every year by the parliament on proposal from the government. Economic policy is a wider concept, which in addition to fiscal policy covers also other structural policies such as industrial, regional and social policies. Tuori and Tuori (2014), p. 31.

[5]There is a close link between economic policy, tax collection, social welfare systems, employment policy, expenditures for national defense and infrastructure. For this reason, Member States do not want to make any transfer of their ultimate sovereign control over their economic policies as such, but only accept obligations outlined in the Treaties. Goebel (2007), p. 1273.

not want to renounce their power of regulation and supervision on a fundamental part of their economy, especially considering that banks play an important role in the purchase of sovereign debt and the financial stability of the country. Accordingly, the Eurozone has been missing all the instruments that states normally use, next to monetary policy, to take care of their economic stability: a common budget financed by genuine taxes, the ability to borrow resources from the financial markets, effective supervision and resolution tools for the banking system, and, more importantly, a true economic government democratically legitimised.

Evidently, the establishment of a single currency between a group of countries fully sovereign under every aspect other than monetary policy made necessary to balance the management of European interdependence with the protection of national prerogatives. In fact, the contradiction of having a single monetary policy and a decentralised management of economic power has represented a major challenge for the fulfilment of stability in the euro area. Notably, monetary and fiscal competences are two complementary attributes of sovereign states and even when the national central bank is independent, it still makes decisions that are coherent with the economic conditions of the country and the budgetary policies implemented by the government. In the European Union, however, there is no single fiscal authority, nor a common macroeconomic policy. Consequently, the European Central Bank (ECB) is obliged to pursue its own monetary objectives by dealing with the different economic situations of every participating country. As monetary and fiscal sovereignty are detached, the fundamental challenge of the EMU has been to avoid the progressive economic divergence between the Member States, which could raise imbalances within the Union and make it vulnerable towards external shocks. Being aware of these collateral risks, European institutions and national governments have committed since the stipulation of the Maastricht Treaty to developing an economic union in charge of preserving national fiscal rights, while pursuing at the same time stability in the euro area. In order to achieve this balance, they created a governance system based on the regulatory role of financial markets and the European supervision on national macroeconomic policies.[6] While this approach characterised the first 10 years of life of the single currency, the outbreak of the sovereign debt crisis in 2009 has started questioning its effectiveness. Indeed, the serious threats to the survival of the monetary union coming from the fiscal and banking crisis in several countries, obliged Member States and EU institutions to reconsider the need for further sovereignty sharing in the EMU. Accordingly, over the last few years, they started a process of overall reform of the economic union, which has included the creation of a common stabilisation mechanism in case of systemic shocks and stronger supervisory tools on national macroeconomic policies. While these measures have helped to overcome the imminent risks for the stability of the Eurozone, the process of reform remains unfinished. Some lasting fragilities of

[6]See Delors Report on Economic and Monetary Union in the European Community, 17 April 1989, pp. 16–17.

the governance have made necessary to start an important debate on the further actions, the euro area still needs to take in order to exhaust its need of stability.

Evidently, the outcome of this hard work of reform will give an answer to the fundamental dilemma, which has been underlying the project of European economic and monetary union since its conception: is it possible to create a single currency without a state? Or, better, can a monetary union achieve stability without the instruments, states normally use for this purpose, such as a common fiscal policy accountable to the people? Notably, in order to answer these questions, it will be necessary to analyse some related issues. What is stability and how it can be measured? How is it possible to balance fiscal stability with financial solidarity? Does stability require democratic accountability? Can stability in the euro area be achieved without reforming the existing EU Treaties?

1.3 Objectives of the Research

The main purpose of the research is to define a new stability paradigm for the euro area, which may exploit the full potential of the project of economic and monetary union and better serve the interests of the European citizens. By developing the original model of EMU outlined in the Maastricht treaty and taking into consideration the lesson thought by the crisis, the definition of a new stability paradigm will help interpret the ongoing transformations of the Eurozone governance. Accordingly, the work won't simply acknowledge and describe the functioning of the economic union and its possible evolution, but more importantly, it will develop a critical analysis of the existing legal framework and the future reforms.

The monograph joins the vast legal literature on the issue of the reform of the European economic governance, which over the last few years has counted several important contributions. While the research will acknowledge the most relevant findings and legal considerations developed by the doctrine, it also aims to be innovative under at least three profiles.

First, the work aims to clarify the meaning of the objective of the 'stability of the euro area as a whole'. As it was already mentioned, the latter has been formally introduced in art. 136(3) TFEU and has several references in EU secondary legislation, intergovernmental agreements and the case law of the CJEU. Despite its importance, the concept of the 'stability of the euro area as a whole' has not received a clear definition yet, as it is usually confused with the objectives of financial or fiscal stability. The research will instead analyse its specificities and make it the cornerstone for the development of a new stability paradigm for the euro area.

Second, the analysis aims to assess the quality of the reforms adopted over the last few years by identifying the obstacles, which are still preventing the euro area from fully recovering from the crisis. The analysis will try to identify the common ground of these fragilities, in a way as to bring them back to some underlying structural deficits of the governance, which will be clarified. The research will be based on the new stability paradigm built on the exegesis of the objective of the 'stability of the euro area as a whole', which will work as a benchmark of the quality of reforms.

Third, the work will present a number of proposals for the completion of the economic union. Taking into consideration the ongoing political and academic debate on the matter, the research aims to identify the fundamental reforms, the economic union still needs to adopt in order to finally achieve long-term stability. After having provided a description of the proposals, the research will also explain the main legal challenges, their implementation will have to deal with.

1.4 Boundaries of the Research

While stability is an objective regarding the entire project of economic and monetary union, the research will have a more limited focus. As anticipated, the main objective of the analysis will be the transformation of the economic governance and the process of fiscal integration of the euro area. Consequently, the monetary pillar of the EMU will be taken into consideration only incidentally. This choice can be justified for the following reasons.

First, the objective of the 'stability of the euro area as a whole', whose analysis will occupy a significant part of the research, represents the primary objective of the economic union and the CJEU has explicitly distinguished it from the main goal of the monetary union, namely price stability. Even if the distinction between monetary and economic policy may seem sometimes artificial, it still plays an important role in the current EU legal framework, where the first competence belongs to the Union, while the other is still an exclusive prerogative of the Member States. Despite their interdependence,[7] setting some boundaries between economic and monetary policy seems therefore necessary in order to comply with the principle of conferral, as well as the rules of the Treaty regarding the functioning of the governance.

Second, the monetary union represents a mature project, which has been deeply investigated by the academic doctrine over the last three decades. Even if the crisis has recently obliged the ECB to adopt some non-conventional policies,[8] no institutional reform has been necessary to put the monetary union in the condition to pursue its objectives and foster stability in the euro area. Evidently the monetary pillar of the EMU is essentially complete, as it was based on the conferral of full sovereignty to the European Union. Consequently, the ECB does already have all the necessary instruments to contribute to the cause of stability through monetary policy. This does not mean that improvements won't be possible in the future, as several authors have

[7]On the connection between monetary and fiscal policy see Munari (2015), pp. 739–340.

[8]Since 2010, the ECB has adopted some non-conventional monetary policy, including the Securities Market Programme (2010), the Outright Monetary Transaction (2012) and the Quantitative Easing (2015).

suggested for example to turn the ECB into a real lender of last resort.[9] At the same time, these developments of the monetary union may be possible only once the economic pillar of the EMU will be completed.

Finally, in the current momentum of European integration, the research of stability of the euro area must necessarily focus on the economic side of the EMU. The outbreak of the sovereign debt crisis has clearly proven that the fundamental sources of destabilisation for the monetary union were rooted in the fragilities of the economic governance. Notably, the latter was not characterised by the creation of a genuine European fiscal sovereignty and the alternative instruments originally established to pursue stability have not been sufficiently effective. This is the reason why the reforms adopted over the last few years essentially focused on improving the functioning of the economic governance, through the consolidation of European surveillance on national budgets, the introduction of a stabilisation mechanism in case of systemic crisis, the development of common investment tools and the partial establishment of a banking union.

1.5 Methodological Precautions

The monograph will develop a legal analysis of the ongoing reform of the economic union from a critical perspective. Three important methodological precautions will be taken.

First of all, the research does acknowledge that the EMU represents a unique legal phenomenon, which has progressively developed over the years through the contribution of several actors.[10] The progressive emergence of an economic constitution of the euro area provided with its own internal coherence, regulatory principles and institutions, does clearly represent a challenge for the identification of the right methodology to adopt in the legal analysis. Indeed, even if the establishment of the monetary union shifted a significant part of sovereignty from national to the European level, the Union has not developed the features of statehood yet, but it is still complying in wide part with the rules of international law. This is confirmed by the fact that the economic union is not solely regulated by the EU Treaties, but also by other legal sources, including intergovernmental agreements and soft law. Evidently, this hybrid legal nature of the governance prevents the adoption of a methodology exclusively based on one approach. Notably, most of the legal contributions on the analysis of the economic union have been based either on a constitutional or a comparative perspective. The use of legal concepts, theories and categories belonging to either public, comparative or international law may make

[9] De Grauwe (2013) and Steinbach (2016).

[10] Tuori and Tuori speak in this regard of a process of 'constitutionalisation', which has been developing through a number of foundational events and thanks to the contribution of several actors. Tuori and Tuori (2014), pp. 3–4.

sense to define and explain some of the procedures and mechanism overlooking the functioning of the euro area. At the same time, these instruments do always require a work of adaptation to the special features of the EMU and its developments.

Second, the monograph will pay particular attention to the contribution of the European and national courts to the legal development of the economic governance. Notably, the CJEU has exercised an important hermeneutical work to adapt the existing EU legal framework to the evolutionary needs of the governance. The research will take into consideration the legal reasoning of the Court and adopt some of the legal interpretations argued therein for the development of its analysis. Equal attention will be paid also to the judgments of national constitutional judges. Indeed, even if domestic courts do normally embrace a national perspective to European issues, considering their point of view can be extremely important to understanding the impact of economic integration on state sovereignty, thus helping to verify how reforms have been complying with the principle of conferral. The research will specifically focus on the dialogue between the CJEU and the German Federal Constitutional Court, which over the last few years has developed an important legal analysis on the impact of fiscal integration on national sovereignty.

Third, the monograph aims to take part in the rich academic debate on the reform of the economic union. The latter will be fully acknowledged and taken as a reference for the further development of the legal analysis on the matter. Counting on the theoretical and doctrinal insights developed by the constitutional and international legal doctrine, the research will pay particular attention to the role of objectives in the EU legal order, the consistency of secondary law and international agreements with the EU Treaties, as well as the compliance with the democratic principle. While the analysis will essentially adopt a legal approach, it will also take into consideration the contributions of other social sciences on the matter. More precisely, the research will be enriched by several considerations, definitions and arguments developed by the political and economic doctrine. This approach should help in understanding the complexity of the problems underlying the research for stability of the euro area.

1.6 Structure

The research is structured in six chapters, each of which aims to analyse a specific issue.

After the introduction has explained the main objectives, methodologies and structure of the research, the second chapter will focus on the concept of the 'stability of the euro area as a whole'. By considering the relationship with other interpretations of stability such as monetary, fiscal and financial stability, the research will develop an exhaustive definition and qualification of the objective. The analysis will argue that the 'stability of the euro area as a whole' essentially consists of the preservation of the existence and the integrity of the monetary union, whose establishment is a goal of the EU in accordance with art. 3(4) TEU.

The third chapter will analyse the functioning of the economic union assessing its ability to pursue the objective of 'stability of the euro area as a whole' in concrete. After having introduced the concept of economic governance, the research will explain how the latter contributes to the achievement of stability. In particular the analysis will consider the application of European supervisory and corrective instruments on national macroeconomic policies, the introduction of constitutional limits in the national budgetary cycle, the regulatory role of financial markets, the implementation of the conditionality policy in the framework of financial assistance, the development of investment policies in the EU legal framework and the establishment of the banking union.

On the basis of the previous analysis, the fourth chapter will identify the main deficits, which are preventing the economic governance from fully achieving the objective of the stability of the euro area as a whole. These are essentially three. The limits of the existing legal basis for the implementation of necessary reforms has been the cause of the legal incoherence of the reforms, as well as the wide use of intergovernmental agreements beyond EU law (so called 'flight into international law'). Second, the reforms introduced to fulfil consolidation and stabilisation policies in the euro area have proven to be substantially ineffective, meaning unable to contribute to the cause of stability. Finally, the democratic deficit of the governance has prevented the governance from fully taking into consideration the requests and interests of the people affected by its policies. This has undermined the relationship between citizens and institutions and helped the rise of populist parties across the continent.

The fifth chapter will eventually consider the most recent proposals of reform of the economic union taking into account both positions in favour of fiscal centralisation in the euro area and those against: the reform of the European Stability Mechanism, the creation of a separate budget for the euro area, the institution of a European minister of finance, the strengthening of surveillance on national budget and the introduction of a debt restructuring mechanism. After having analysed the content of each proposal, in particular the official ones put forward by the EU institutions, the research will consider the main legal challenges that the future reform of the euro area will have to face.

The conclusions will summarise the results of the analysis and answer the fundamental questions identified at the beginning of the research.

References

De Grauwe P (2013) The European Central Bank as lender of last resort in the government bond markets. CESifo Econ Stud 59:520–535

Goebel RJ (2007) Economic governance in the European Union: should fiscal stability outweigh economic growth in the stability and growth pact? Fordham Int Law J 31:1266–1359

Lastra RM (2006) Legal foundations of international monetary stability. Oxford University Press, Oxford

Munari F (2015) Da Pringle a Gauweiler: i tormentati anni dell'Unione monetaria e i loro effetti sull'ordinamento giuridico europeo. Il Diritto dell'Unione Europea, 723–755
Steinbach A (2016) The lender of last resort in the Eurozone. Common Mark Law Rev 53:361–384
Tuori K, Tuori K (2014) The Eurozone crisis. A constitutional analysis. Cambridge University Press, Cambridge

Chapter 2
The Objective of Stability of the Euro Area as a Whole

2.1 Introduction

Stability is a multiform concept in legal science. The founding fathers of the Economic and Monetary Union (EMU) declined it in different ways by identifying some specific targets of inflation, deficit and public debt, whose achievement would have helped the monetary union to become a 'community of stability' (*Stabilitätsgemeinschaft*).[1] While the latter concept was initially based on the convergence criteria that Member States had to fulfil in order to access the monetary union, the outbreak of the sovereign debt crisis made necessary to reconsider the meaning of stability in euro area. Since 2010 national governments and EU institutions have been reforming the economic governance of the Eurozone by creating new instruments to increase convergence, manage the crisis and avoid its reoccurrence in the future. This process of transformation of the EMU has been characterised by the gradual emergence of a new objective of economic policy, namely 'the stability of the euro area as a whole'. The latter has found a direct reference in primary law thanks to the amendment of art. 136 TFEU, while the CJEU has contributed in the interpretation of its meaning in some important judgments on the consistency of the anti-crisis measures with EU law.

The purpose of the chapter is to define and analyse the objective of 'stability of the euro area as a whole', which is being consolidated throughout the ongoing reform process of the economic union. After having recalled the general role of objectives in the EU legal order, the chapter will explain the structural deficits of the EMU, which are responsible for its fundamental need of stability: the weak convergence between participating Member States and the asymmetry between the

[1] The concept was developed by the German Federal Constitutional Court (GFCC) as a condition of the German participation in the EMU. See German Constitutional Court, Judgment of 12 October 1993, [BVerfGE 89/155], paras 138, 144, 147, 148.

L. Lionello, *The Pursuit of Stability of the Euro Area as a Whole*, Studies in European Economic Law and Regulation 18,
https://doi.org/10.1007/978-3-030-28045-1_2

economic and the monetary union. It follows an analysis of the objective of 'stability of the euro area as a whole' in relation to the other formulations of stability outlined in the EU Treaties, such as price stability, sound public finances and the stability of the financial system. The last part of the chapter will verify whether the 'stability of the euro area as a whole' can be qualified as an objective of the European Union.

2.2 Meaning of Objectives in the EU Legal System

2.2.1 Definition

European primary and secondary law identify a number of objectives that EU institutions and Member States shall pursue in the framework of the Union's legal order. Despite missing a precise definition, the legal doctrine has qualified objectives as directive principles, meaning general rules referring to the achievement of specific results.[2] While values and structural principles explain what the European Union is and stands for, objectives clarify what it does and tries to accomplish.[3]

Since its conception, the European Union has been in 'need of objectives' (*Zielbedarf*).[4] Art. 1 TEU recalls that Member States confer competencies to the EU to achieve the objectives, they have in common.[5] The fundamental role played by objectives in the process of European integration depends indeed on the non-sovereign nature of the organisation and the principle of conferral. As the EU legal order is not original, but derives from those of its Member States, it requires objectives to find its *raison d'être* and exercise the competences conferred by the European Treaties. For this reason, Ipsen has defined the Union as a 'special-purpose association',[6] meaning that, in accordance with the principle of speciality of international organisations, the EU shall exercise the functions conferred upon it by the Member States with the view of achieving the objectives outlined in the founding Treaties. On the contrary, sovereign states don't need objectives, because they have the *Kompetenz-Kompetenz* and can constantly define their course of action through a process of continuous self-determination.[7] The conferral of objectives, for whose

---

[2]See Sommermann (2013), Article 3 TEU, para 3.

[3]See Larik (2016), p. 162. Objective define a desirable condition to achieve (*erstrebeswerter Zustand*) or an element of material perspective (*materiell-prospektives Element*). See Terhechte (2017), Artikel 3 EUV, para 19.

[4]See Ipsen (1972), p. 995.

[5]See Larik (2016), p. 134.

[6]In German 'Zweckverband'. See Ipsen (1972), pp. 197–198, 1055.

[7]See Larik (2014), p. 948.

achievement the EU was given sovereign powers, makes sure that Member States are the real 'masters of the Treaties'.[8]

2.2.2 Functions

The role of objectives in the EU legal order has changed over time. Their initial function has been 'competence-enabling' (*zuständigkeitseröffnende Funktion*), meaning that they provided both a legitimation and limitation of the powers, the EU can exercise in concrete. At the beginning of the integration process this task was evident, as the identification of an objective was considered a sufficient legal basis for the development of a new power.[9] The strengthening of the conferral principle and the clear distribution of competences between the Union and its Member States, however, has gradually reduced the application of the implied powers doctrine according to which *ius ad finem dat ius ad media*.[10] Art. 3(6) TEU stresses indeed that objectives shall be pursued by appropriate means, but they are not able to allow acts of the Union.

Even if the presence of an EU goal does not imply that the Union has all the competences to achieve it,[11] objectives still play an important function in legitimising the actions of European institutions in concrete. Indeed, defining the objectives of the European Union helps to understand whether a specific action falls within the competences of the EU institutions or is *ultra vires*. Furthermore, the flexibility clause offers a margin of expansion of EU powers, when it is necessary to achieve an objective of the Union. Art. 352 TFEU states that if an action is necessary to attain one of the objectives set out in the Treaties, but the EU lacks necessary powers, the Council can adopt the appropriate measures by unanimity on a proposal from the Commission and with the consent of the European Parliament. The

---

[8]See German Federal Constitutional Court, Judgment of 12 October 1993, [BVerfGE 89/155], para 112. In the *Lissabon* judgment the GFCC specified that 'the Basic Law does not authorize the German state bodies to transfer sovereign powers in such a way that their exercise can independently establish other competences for the European Union'. German Federal Constitutional Court, Judgment of 30 June 2009, [2 BvE 2/08], para 233.

[9]In the Gimenez Zaera case the CJEU stated that the aims laid down in art. 2 of the EEC Treaty 'are concerned with the existence and functioning of the Community'. ECJ Judgment of 9 September 1987, Case C-126/86, ECLI:EU:C:1987:395, para 10.

[10]The implied power doctrine should not allow the attribution of new powers to the Union, but clarify the sphere of application of the existing competence. In European Agreement on Road Transport case, the Court explained that the 'authority [of the Community] arises not only from an express conferment by the Treaty [. . .] but may equally flow from other provisions of the Treaty and from measures adopted within the framework of those provisions by the Community institutions.' ECJ Judgment of 31 March 1971, Commission of the European Communities v Council of the European Communities. Case C-22/70, ECLI:EU:C:1971:32, para 16.

[11]Sommermann (2013), Article 3 TEU, para 12; Ruffert (2016), Artikel 3 EUV, para 12.

flexibility clause works therefore as an emergency measure allowing an *ad hoc* conferral of power to the EU in order to better achieve a common objective.[12]

The progressive development of European integration over the last decades has gradually transformed the role played by objectives. The process of constitutionalisation of the EU legal order has turned the Union into a *sui generis* supranational entity,[13] which is more than an international organisation, even if it is still less than a federal state. The level of integration reached so far has indeed made it possible for the Union to exercise limited, but real sovereign rights with direct legal effects on the Member States and their citizens.[14]

This gradual thickening of the European legal order and the identification of a precise list of competences for the EU and the Member States[15] has had an impact on the role played by objectives: they have been gradually exhausting the original function of competence-enabling and have started providing directives to European institutions for the management of their powers. According to Larik, objectives 'have become goals, which shape the exercise of powers defined elsewhere and embedded in a more sophisticated 'thickened' legal order'.[16] Evidently, the setup of a permanent administration of powers at European level, which is in charge of achieving common goals, necessitating that objectives don't only provide a specific competence, but also explain how the latter shall be exercised in concrete. This has occurred because the Union is not a simple international organisation dedicated to the achievement of specific goals, but has become a legal order based on the sharing of common values.[17] In the light of these considerations, objectives of EU law can be assimilated, at least in part, with the *Staatszielbestimmungen* of German constitutional law and the *objectifs de valeur constitutionnelle* of French

---

[12]In the *Maastricht* judgment, the GFCC referred to the flexibility clause as a 'competence extension provision' (*Kompetenzerweiterungsvorschrift*). German Federal Constitutional Court, Judgment of 12 October 1993, [BVerfGE 89/155], para 127. The strict procedure requested for the activation of the flexibility clause proves that there is no automatic correspondence between objectives and competences. See Larik (2014), p. 957.

[13]See Larik (2014), pp. 947–948; Tuori and Tuori (2014), pp. 3–6. In the *Van Gend &Loos* case, the CJEU stated that the 'Community constitutes a new legal order of international law for the benefit of which the states have limited their sovereign rights, albeit within limited fields'. ECJ Judgment of 5 February 1962 C-26/62, *NV Algemene Transport- en Expeditie Onderneming van Gend & Loos v Netherlands Inland Revenue Administration. Reference for a preliminary ruling: Tariefcommissie – Netherlands,* ECLI:EU:C:1963:1, p. 12. In the *Le Verts* case, the ECJ said that 'the European Economic Community is a Community based on the rule of law' and is provided with a 'basic constitutional Charter, the Treaty'. ECJ Judgment of the of 23 April 1986, Case C-294/83, *Parti écologiste "Les Verts" v European Parliament*, ECLI:EU:C:1986:166, para 23.

[14]See Geiger (2014), Article 1 TEU, para 13.

[15]The catalogues of competences are provided in art. 3, art. 4, art. 5 and art. 6 TFEU.

[16]Larik (2016), p. 146.

[17]Larik (2016), p. 143.

constitutional law,[18] which have the function to provide sovereign states with directives for the management of their public powers.[19] Accordingly, objectives have become able to orient and limit the margin of discretion of the Union by providing guidelines and references. This happens not only in regard to political institutions, but also to the CJEU, which shall interpret European law accordingly by recurring to the teleological interpretation.[20] At the same time, objectives are binding also for the Member States when they act within the EU legal framework. The participation of national governments in the pursuit of objectives makes sure that the latter apply not only when the EU exercises an exclusive or shared competence, but also when it coordinates those policies, which are still managed at national level.[21] Member States have indeed the obligation to comply with the rules and guidelines provided at European level in accordance with the principle of loyal cooperation ex art. 4(3) TEU. Domestic judges shall in particular take into consideration objectives in the process of harmonisation of national law.[22] Despite being difficult to assess, the CJEU and national courts can sanction gross violation of objectives, when the latter are completely ignored or unattended by both European institutions and Member States.[23] Objectives don't create instead rights and duties for individuals.[24]

Even if the transition of objectives from 'competence-enabling' to 'policy orientation' is a natural process caused by the progressive development of the European Union, this transformation does not regard all branches of EU law in the same way. The new role of objectives has been consolidated for those policies, where the EU has gained an exclusive competence or where the national legal orders are open to the influence of European law. In other areas, where Member States are instead reluctant to share their sovereign rights and it is difficult to qualify the nature of a specific action, objectives are still an important parameter to verify whether a measure taken by European institutions falls within the competences conferred by

---

[18]The concept of *Staatszielbestimmung* has been developed by the German legal doctrine, while the concept of *objectifs de valeur constitutionnelle* can be identified in the case law of the *Conseil constitutionnel*. See Larik (2016), pp. 23, 27; Ruffert (2016), Artikel 3 EUV, para 2.

[19]The assimilation of EU objectives to *Staatszielbestimmungen* and the *objectifs de valeur constitutionnelle* depends on the fact that they both have the purpose to guide the management of public powers. Despite this significant similarity, some important differences remain. First, while objectives in an international organisation represent a substantial 'need' (*Zielbedarf*), in a sovereign state they represent more of a 'desire' of the public authority to better orientate its policies (*Zielbedürfnis*). See Larik (2016), pp. 149–150. Second, while the *Staatszielbestimmungen* and the *objectifs de valeur constitutionnelle* are self-posed by the sovereign legal order of the State, the objectives of EU law are (etero-) determined by the Member States, in accordance with the principle of conferral. See Ruffert (2016), Artikel 3 EUV, para 2.

[20]See Becker (2012), Artikel 3 EUV, para 7; Ruffert (2016), Artikel 3 EUV, para 9; Terhechte (2017), Artikel 3 EUV, para 12.

[21]See Ruffert (2016), Artikel 3 EUV, para 7.

[22]See Sommermann (2013), Article 3 TEU, para 11.

[23]See Sommermann (2013), Article 3 TEU, para 6; Ruffert (2016), Artikel 3 EUV, para 5.

[24]See Sommermann (2013), Article 3 TEU, para 8; Ruffert (2016), Artikel 3 EUV, para 4.

the EU Treaties or if it consists of an *ultra vires* act.[25] This has recently happened, when the judges of Luxembourg used objectives to distinguish between monetary and economic policies and consequently decided whether a certain measure was adopted by the competent authority. In the Pringle Judgment, the Court qualified the European Stability Mechanism (ESM) as an instrument of economic policy on the basis of the objective it pursues, namely the 'financial stability of the euro area as a whole'.[26] Similarly, the Gauweiler Judgment has confirmed that the 'Outright Monetary Transactions' Programme is an instrument of monetary policy falling within the competence of the ECB, because it aims to ensure the correct functioning of the transmission mechanism of monetary policy, this being a precondition to achieve the goal of price stability.[27]

2.2.3 Classification of Objectives in the EU Treaties

The EU Treaties outline different kinds of objectives, which can be classified depending on their scope.

Particular attention should be paid first of all to the well-known aim of 'an ever-closer Union among the Peoples of Europe', as recalled in the Preamble of the EU Treaties and in art. 1 TEU. This has been qualified as the *finalité* of the integration process,[28] meaning its ultimate objective or destiny. The goal of an 'ever closer union' in reality doesn't mention a clear result to achieve, but rather a method Member States shall pursue in developing their relationship, notably a continuous sharing of national sovereignty in accordance with the principle of subsidiarity.[29] Whether this process should lead to the establishment of a political union, meaning a European federal state, is not clear. Quite interestingly, the original draft of the Maastricht Treaty recalled in art. 1 the 'federal goal' of the Union, but the British opposition obliged Member States to agree on the current formulation.[30]

After art. 2 TEU has defined the common values on which the Union is based, art. 3 TEU identifies the general objectives of the organisation. This norm is usually

---

[25] See Larik (2016), p. 129.

[26] See ECJ Judgment of 27 November 2012, Case C-370/12, *Thomas Pringle v Government of Ireland,* ECLI:EU:C:2012:756, paras 94–97.

[27] See ECJ Judgment of 16 June 2015, Case C-62/14, *Gauweiler (and Others) v. Deutscher Bundestag,* ECLI:EU:C:2015:400, paras 49–50.

[28] See Larik (2016), p. 130.

[29] The principle of subsidiarity can be deduced by the reference to the 'closeness to the citizens' in art. 1 TEU.

[30] The German Constitutional Court in the *Lissabon Urteil* clarified the that *Grundgesetz* would prevent Germany from participating in a future European federation except if, by way of art. 146 of the Basic Law, a new constitution given by the people replaced the existing Basic Law. See German Federal Constitutional Court, Judgment of 30 June 2009, [2 BvE 2/08], para 113. On the matter see also Calliess (2011–2012), pp. 103–104.

considered the programme for integration of the European Union.[31] While the reference to 'an ever-closer union' in art. 1 TEU recalls the vague idea of a political union, art. 3 TEU explains more specifically what the Union shall do in concrete towards the path of integration. In this regard, the final longstanding aims[32] of the promotion of peace, the Union's values and the peoples' well-being (para 1) are pursued through the achievement of four general objectives: area of freedom, security and justice (para 2), the internal market (para 3), the economic and monetary union (para 4) and the external action (para 5). These objectives define the different areas in which the European Union shall act. It is important to stress that the latter cover already most of the fundamental tasks that States exercise in accordance with their constitution.[33]

The achievement of these general goals is ensured thanks to the pursuit of several specific objectives. The latter are recalled throughout the EU Treaties in regard to each policy that the Union shall develop as part of its own competences. Specific objectives are identified for example in relation to the external policy (art. 21 TEU), economic policy (art. 119 and 120 TFEU), monetary policy (art. 127(1) TFEU), employment policy (art. 145 TFEU), social policy (art. 151 TFEU) and environmental policy (art. 191 TFEU). As the EU Treaties are often vague or even silent regarding the exact content of each objective, the CJEU has contributed to define their meaning and field of application by taking into consideration the relevant secondary law.

There is generally no hierarchy between the objectives outlined in the EU Treaties. As they are very diverse, however, it might occur that the pursuit of one objective undermines in concrete the achievement of another one. In this case, a balance will be found by European institutions thanks to the margin of discretion, they can exercise in the management of their tasks.[34] Only sometimes the Treaty identifies a preference between objectives; for example, art. 127(1) TFEU states that the ECB shall support the general economic policies in the Union, as long as this does not undermine the primary objective of price stability.

---

[31]See Ruffert (2016), Artikel 3 EUV, para 1.

[32]According to Tehechte these 'meta objectives' reflect themselves in the other concrete objectives outlined in the following paragraphs of art. 3 TEU. This provision works as a hinge with the Preamble and the values of art. 2 TEU. See Terhechte (2017), Artikel 3 EUV, para 29.

[33]See Larik (2016), p. 140.

[34]See Sommermann (2013), Article 3 TEU, paras. 17–18; Ruffert (2016), Artikel 3 EUV, para 11; Terhechte (2017), Artikel 3 EUV, para 22.

2.3 Stability in Context

2.3.1 The Economic and Monetary Union

The establishment of the Economic and Monetary Union (EMU) is one of the objectives of the European Union ex art. 3(4) TEU. The EMU is fully integrated into the legal framework established by the EU Treaties, in particular Title VIII of the Treaty on the Functioning of the European Union, as well as several Protocols on related issues.[35] Secondary law has developed the discipline on the EMU into details, especially the Stability and Growth Pact (SGP) of 1997 and its later reforms.[36] While the Amsterdam, Nice and Lisbon Treaties have substantially left unchanged the constitutional framework of the EMU,[37] since the outbreak of the sovereign debt crisis in 2009 Member States have engaged in a significant reform process of the economic governance, which is still ongoing. The latter has been implemented by recurring to a variety of legal sources, such as a simplified treaty amendment, secondary legislation and international agreements beyond the EU legal order.

As proven by its continuous transformation, the EMU is the result of an ongoing process of self-improvement and consolidation. Bearing in mind the purpose of this chapter, which is the definition of the new objective of the 'stability of the Eurozone as a whole', it is possible to identify two main deficits in the construction of the EMU, which are responsible for its constant need for stability (*Stabilitätsbedarf*): the weak convergence process between participating Member States and the asymmetry between the economic and the monetary union.

---

[35]These are the Protocol on the statute of the European System of Central Banks and of the European Central Bank (No 4); the Protocol on the on the excessive deficit procedure (No 12); the Protocol on the convergence criteria (No 13) and the Protocol on the Eurogroup (No 14).

[36]The Pact included at the beginning three legal acts: Resolution of the European Council on the Stability and Growth Pact, Amsterdam, 17 June 1997, (1997) OJ L 236/01; Regulation (EC) No 1466/97 of 7 July 1997 on the strengthening of the surveillance of budgetary positions and the surveillance and coordination of economic policies, (1997) OJ L 209/1; Regulation (EC) No 1467/97 of 7 July 1997 on speeding up and clarifying the implementation of the excessive deficit procedure, (1997) OJ L 209/6. The Pact has been subsequently reformed by Regulation (EC) No 1055/05 of 27 June 2005 amending Regulation (EC) No 1466/97 on the strengthening of the surveillance of budgetary positions and the surveillance and coordination of economic policies, (2005) OJ L 174/1, and Regulation (EC) No 1056/05 of 27 June 2005 amending Regulation (EC) No 1467/97 on speeding up and clarifying the implementation of the excessive deficit procedure, (2005) OJ L 174/5.

[37]In 2009 the Lisbon Treaty included the ECB among EU institutions, acknowledged the Eurogroup meetings and partially strengthened the role of the Commission in the process of European supervision on national budgets. See Häde (2009).

2.3.2 *The Incomplete Process of Economic Convergence*

The Maastricht Treaty requested that the introduction of the single currency was preceded by a convergence process to create the economic conditions for a sustainable monetary union in the long run. According to the Delors Report indeed, a monetary union without a sufficient degree of convergence of economic policies would have been unlikely to last and could be damaging the Community.[38] The Maastricht Treaty itself explained that lasting convergence is a prerequisite for a durable monetary union and the achievement of price stability and sound public finances.[39] These initial references are important because they pose immediately the issue of stability in the Eurozone, suggesting that convergence is an essential prerequisite of this.

Art. 109j TEC identified four parameters to measure the process of convergence between participating Member States: a high degree of price stability,[40] sustainability of the government fiscal position in terms of annual deficit and public debt,[41] normal fluctuation margins and durability of convergence in the long-term interest rate levels.[42] In addition to these economic parameters, the Treaty also requested Member States provide their national central banks with a high level of independence.[43] Convergence was monitored by the European Commission and the newly established European Monetary Institute (EMI), a temporary body, which worked as predecessor of the European Central Bank (ECB).[44] After the latter gave a positive assessment of the process,[45] the European Council confirmed that a majority of Member States was respecting the convergence criteria and decided the introduction of the single currency on the 1st January 1999. Looking more into details the economic performances of these countries, however, the process of convergence was only partially successful. For example, only half of the Member States

[38]See 'Delors Report on Economic and Monetary Union in the European Community', 17 April 1989, p. 28.

[39]See art. 109e(2)b TEC.

[40]Member States had to reach an inflation rate, which was close to that of the three best performing Member States in terms of price stability.

[41]Budgetary sustainability consisted of two parameters: 3% of ratio deficit/annual GDP and 60%of the ratio public debt/GDP.

[42]Art. 4 of Protocol No 13 on the convergence criteria specified that a Member State had to present, over the last year, an average nominal long-term interest rate not exceeding 2% points than that of the three best performing Member States in terms of price stability.

[43]See art. 107 TEC and art. 14 of the Statute of the ESCB and the ECB. Except for this obligation, NCBs could conserve their peculiarities and perform other functions.

[44]This body has been active between 1 January 1994 and 31 December 1998. The EMI was in charge of promoting cooperation between NCBs and coordinating monetary policies with the aim of ensuring price stability. The main purpose of the EMI was to verify the convergence process.

[45]The EMI and the Commission presented to the Council favourable reports on the state of convergence. On this basis, the Council adopted a decision by qualified majority in order to prevent a veto from those States not respecting the convergence criteria. See Pipkorn (1994), p. 290.

participating in the monetary union were respecting the debt-to-GDP ratio in 1999. What is even more alarming, countries like Italy and Belgium were indebted at a level of almost twice the limit allowed. More generally several Member States managed to comply with the deficit criterion thanks to the adoption of emergency measures and tax increases, rather than through structural reforms and the rationalisation of public spending.[46]

The limited effectiveness of the convergence process is due to the margin of flexibility allowed by the Maastricht Treaty for the interpretation and the application of the relevant norms. In this regard, it is possible to identify four main vulnerabilities.

First, the application of the convergence criteria presented some important exceptions regarding the assessment of the public debt and deficit ratio. In accordance with art. 104(3) TEC (now art. 126(2) TFEU), the Council could declare non-subsistent an excessive deficit or debt in two situations: if the excess of deficit was only exceptional and temporary remaining close to the reference value; when debt was sufficiently diminishing and approaching the reference value at a satisfactory pace. The vague formulation of these provisions clearly aimed to give the Council a wide margin of discretion in their assessment.

Second, the convergence criteria were not the only parameters taken into consideration to verify whether Member States were fulfilling the 'necessary conditions' to enter the final stage of the EMU ex art. 109 (j) TEC. Even if part of the legal doctrine suggested a mechanic application of the parameters,[47] the concept of 'necessary conditions for the adoption of a single currency' was given a more flexible interpretation. Accordingly, the reports of the Commission and the EMI on the convergence criteria provided only a basis for a political decision of the Council.[48] This is rather logical considering that, if the decision to launch the final stage of the EMU consisted simply of accounting operations, it would not have required the intervention of political institutions through the complex procedure outlined in art. 109 (j) TEC. The exclusion of the Court of Justice and the weak involvement of Eurostat confirmed the logic to make the transition to the last stage of the EMU essentially a

[46] Italy for example adopted an emergency 'tax for Europe', a one-off levy on personal incomes, in order to reduce its deficit and meet the convergence criteria. On the state of convergence see European Monetary Institute (1998).

[47] The *Bundesverfassungsgericht* affirmed that Germany could join the last stage of the EMU only if the latter presented the characteristics of a *Stabilitätsgemeinschaft,* meaning if the convergence criteria were respected. See German Constitutional Court, Judgment of 12 October 1993, [BVerfGE 89,155], para 148.

[48] This could be assumed considering that: (i) art. 109(j)(1) simply TEC states that convergence criteria are parameters the EMI and the Commission shall use to assess the level of convergence achieved between the Member States; (ii) art. 109(j)(2) TEC states that the report of the EMI and the Commission work as a basis for the evaluations of the Council; (iii) art. 109(j)(4) TEC mentions the 'necessary conditions for the adoption of a single currency', which may don't consist of the convergence criteria; iv), Protocol No 11 affirmed that the convergence criteria shall 'guide the Union in taking decisions referred' to the launch of the EMU, implying that this should consider a wider perspective. See Partsch (1998), pp. 58–59.

political choice. Evidently, Member States believed that even if economic parameters were not precisely met, the introduction of the single currency would have eventually produced a spontaneous convergence of national economies. They probably underestimated the danger of accepting in the Eurozone Member States with structural fiscal weaknesses, which would have probably required a longer and more accurate process of structural economic reforms before introducing the single currency.

Third, economic convergence might have failed because of the reference criteria chosen. As the sovereign debt crisis proved later, compliance with the rules on public deficit and debt did not prevent several countries from experiencing severe fiscal difficulties, which were triggered by other sources of instability regarding their financial and productive system. Therefore, the process of convergence should also have had to take into consideration some important factors other than public finances, which can still have an influence on the overall economic stability of the Eurozone countries, notably private indebtedness, the unemployment level,[49] the growth rate, the vulnerabilities of the banking system and the balance of payments.

Last, convergence also failed due to the inefficiency of statistical analysis, which were still managed nationally under the weak European coordination from Eurostat. Governments had indeed the possibility to provide incorrect statistical data, thus preventing European institutions from assessing the real compliance with the convergence criteria. Evidently, the continuous manipulation of economic data in several countries proved the limits of the approach based on cooperation and good practices exchange, rather than on effective monitoring and binding decisions.[50]

The deficits of the convergence process have characterised not only the launch of the EMU, but also its later enlargement. Indeed, compared to the original 11 Member States in 1999, the Eurozone consists now of 19 countries.[51] Despite the many limits identified since the launch of the single currency, art. 140 TFEU, as formulated in the Lisbon Treaty, still provides for a similar procedure to access the monetary union,

---

[49]Regardless of the rhetoric used in the SGP and the introduction of a new *ad hoc* Title in the Amsterdam Treaty, convergence has never taken into consideration the objective of high employment level. This represents a significant vulnerability, as the latter contributes to the achievement of economic stability and sustainable development. See Hansch (2002), p. 56–57.

[50]Due to the difficulties in ensuring the correctness of economic data Regulation (EU) No 679/2010 amended Regulation (EC) No 479/2009 regarding the quality of statistical data in the context of the EDP. Eurostat has been strengthened and entitled with the power to carry out in all Member States regular visits. Directive 2011/85/EU required Member States to put in place a public accounting system comprehensively and consistently covering all sub-sectors of general government and containing the information needed to generate accrual data. More importantly Regulation (EU) No 1173/2011 allowed the Council, acting on a recommendation by the Commission, to impose a fine in case a Member State intentionally or by serious negligence misrepresents deficit and debt data relevant for the application of art. 121 or art. 126 TFEU.

[51]After the first enlargement to Greece (2001), also Slovenia (2007), Cyprus (2008), Malta (2008), Slovakia (2009), Estonia (2011), Latvia (2014) and Lithuania (2015) adopted the Euro. The case of Greece is quite emblematic. The country managed to join the monetary union in 2001 despite presenting a high debt ratio and having manipulated its financial books.

which is based on the compliance with the same four convergence criteria[52] and gives a wide margin of discretion to the Council for their assessment.

2.3.3 The Asymmetry Between the Economic and the Monetary Union

The establishment of a monetary union, based on the complete and irrevocable fixation of national exchange rates and the introduction of a single currency, represented a qualitative leap in the process of European integration. Member States transferred to the European Union an important part of their power, which is the *ius cudendae monetae*. The European System of Central Banks (ESCB), which is composed of National Central Banks (NCBs) acting under the leadership of the European Central Bank (ECB), has become responsible for monetary policy.[53] This significant transfer of sovereignty, however, wasn't matched by a parallel shift of fiscal competence, as Member States refused to lose their exclusive right to collect taxes and spend public resources. The structural asymmetry between a monetary union based on the transfer of sovereignty to the EU, and an economic union consisting of the coordination of national fiscal policies has characterised the EMU since its conception and still represents its distinctive feature.

Evidently, the detachment of monetary policy from economic policy is a unique legal phenomenon as these two policies are both fundamental attributes of sovereign states and even when the national central bank in a country is independent, it still makes decisions, which are coherent with the economic policy of the government. Unlike most other monetary unions, however, the EU does not have the features of statehood, but is part of an ongoing process of integration between an association of independent nations.[54] This is particularly evident in the field of fiscal policy, where governments can in principle act independently from each other and the Union has no means to replace them. Indeed, due to its small size and full dependence on

[52]Art. 140 TFEU requires to take into account also the results of the integration of markets, the situation and development of the balances of payments on current account and an examination of the development of unit labour costs and other price indices.

[53]Only external monetary relationships of the euro area are managed by the Council in accordance with art. 138 and art. 219 TFEU.

[54]The transfer of monetary competence to the European level represents a significant renouncement, as it represents one of fundamental functions of modern states along with security and taxation. While the establishment of monetary unions has normally followed a process of political independence or unification, the European case is rather the opposite. The sovereign rights exercised by the European institutions don't come from an original source of authority, but are conferred by the Member States, which remain the true masters of the Treaty. See German Constitutional Court, Judgment of 12 October 1993, [BVerfGE 89, 155], paras 112, 135.

Member States' contributions,[55] the EU budget can only take care of the limited functions assigned by the Treaties, which are mainly related to the correct functioning of the internal market. By deriving its powers from the national legal orders, the EU does not have the authority to develop an independent fiscal policy to exercise the typical functions of state budgets, namely redistribution, stabilisation and the financing of public goods.[56]

When Member States decided to create the economic and monetary union, they evidently knew that the asymmetry could have posed some threats to the sustainability of the project. In any case, they agreed to support it due to the influence exercised by the dominant economic doctrine of the time, according to which national economies in a monetary union would spontaneously achieve convergence.[57] More importantly, no government was actually ready to transfer part of its fiscal authority to the European Union, as this represents the ultimate bastion of national sovereignty and the most important source of political legitimation.[58]

2.3.4 *The Fundamental Need for Stability in the EMU*

Predictably, the incomplete convergence between participating Member States and, more importantly, the full decentralisation of the fiscal function has exposed the EMU since its very foundation to two major vulnerabilities.

First, a country, which is participating in a monetary union, but is still fully in charge of its fiscal competence, can be easily tempted by moral hazard and increase its indebtedness to unsustainable levels.[59] Fiscal misbehaviours depend on the awareness that the negative consequences of excessive public spending in one country don't only fall on the shoulders of the debtor, but are automatically shared

---

[55] The EU budget is based on a system of own resources: traditional own resources (customs duties on imports from outside the EU and sugar levies); own resources based on value added tax (0.3% on the harmonised VAT base of each Member States); own resources based on GNI. The latter, which essentially consist of national contributions, have gradually become the main source of financing. The budget must be balanced and is not allowed to borrow. The financing and spending of the budget are set in the Multiannual Financial Framework (MFF) agreed every 7 years by the Council. Between 2014 and 2020 the EU budget has been financing the common agriculture policy, the cohesion policy and structural funds, foreign aid and the administration costs of the EU itself. See *infra*. Sect. 5.6.2.1.1.

[56] See Schor (1999), p. 136; Cottarelli and Guerguil (2014), pp. 2–4.

[57] Since 1980s the monetarist paradigm has been prevailing especially among central bankers. See De Grauwe (2016), p. 158. On the debate between 'monetarists' and 'economists' see Tuori and Tuori (2014), p. 42.

[58] Tuori and Tuori (2014), pp. 49–50. See *supra* Sect. 1.2.

[59] On moral hazard behaviours in the Eurozone see De Grauwe (2016), p. 229; Estella (2016), pp. 514–515.

with the other Member States of the monetary union.[60] This happens either immediately, as the high level of national public debt may increase the cost of the government debt in the other countries, or later, when governments on the precipice of bankruptcy request the financial support of the other Member States and of the ECB.[61] Fiscal misbehaviour is therefore extremely harmful not only because it sets the conditions for systematic destabilisation in the monetary union, but also because it undermines the mutual trust between participating countries. As the process of preliminary convergence for the introduction of the single currency was relatively lax, Member States could easily perpetrate fiscal misbehaviours also after the establishment of the EMU.

Second, a monetary union deprived of a fiscal capacity is unable to efficiently absorb economic shocks. The latter are events, which can negatively affect the economy of single Member States (asymmetric shocks) or of the entire Union (symmetric shocks).[62] While sovereign countries can normally react to economic shocks by using several stabilisers, the Member States of the EMU lack most of them, as they are obviously deprived of the national exchange rate mechanism, while labour mobility and price flexibility are still weak in the euro area.[63] As a result, the only available instrument to effectively absorb economic shocks remains fiscal policy. The national exclusive on this stabilisation tool, however, raises several problems. As mentioned before, Member States might lack solid public finances due to protracted excessive public spending, or national fiscal buffers may be insufficient to absorb multiple economic shocks of a significant magnitude.[64]

The analysis developed above helps clarify the central problem of the EMU: a monetary union between states, which are fiscally independent, has a structural tendency towards instability. This analysis complies with the narrative of the 'impossibility trilemmas' developed by the economic doctrine to explain how the creation of supranational common goods is not sustainable with an exclusively

---

[60] This has progressively become ineffective because the threats on which the economic supervision has been based, such as the imposition of sanctions from intergovernmental institutions and the cessation of financial support, have progressively lost their credibility. Adamski (2016), pp. 190–191.

[61] See Schor (1999), pp. 132–133; De Grauwe (2016), p. 225.

[62] The participation in the monetary union increases interdependence between the Member States. Accordingly, the shock in one country may affect also the others. See Tuori and Tuori (2014), p. 31.

[63] The theory of the Optimum Monetary Area (OMA), which was initiated by the economist Robert Mundell in 1961, describes the necessary conditions, which make advantageous (in terms of employment, price stability and balance of payments) for a number of regions to relinquish their monetary sovereignty in favour of a common currency. These conditions are labour mobility, openness of the economies, capital mobility, and high degree of product diversification among members. If all these conditions occur, the monetary area would automatically balance asymmetric shocks affecting its members and avoid macro stabilisation costs determined by the loss of the national exchange rate policy. In the case of Europe, however, the Community lacked some elements to be an OMA, precisely a high level of labour mobility and price flexibility. See Schor (1999), pp. 75–79; Apel (2002), pp. 95–97; Stiglitz (2016), pp. 92–94.

[64] On the weak compliance with the fiscal discipline see Tuori and Tuori (2014), p. 49–51.

national administration of powers. Mundell argued that fixed exchange rate between currencies, a single market of capital and the monetary autonomy of Member States are incompatible with each other, thus being necessary the introduction of a monetary union.[65] Schoenmaker explained that financial stability, financial integration and national financial policies cannot be combined together, but require the transfer of supervision, regulation and stabilisation tools at supranational level.[66] When it comes to the EMU, it is possible to identify a similar trilemma: the creation of the single currency, the stability of the euro area and full national fiscal autonomy are incompatible due to the vulnerability towards economic shocks and moral hazard behaviours of Member States.

2.3.5 *The Adherence to the Surveillance Model*

Being aware of the intrinsic dangers coming from the decentralised model of economic union, the Member States agreed that stability in the EMU would not be automatic, but demanded an active behaviour of national and European authorities. Lacking the political will to provide the EU with some instrument of fiscal policy, the economic governance of the Eurozone has developed towards a 'surveillance model'.[67] The latter means that fiscal policies remain an exclusive competence of Member State, but the EU can intervene by monitoring national economic choices and ensuring budgetary discipline. Member States remained therefore responsible for their own fiscal policy (*Eigenverantwortlichkeit*), but they lost discretion in the way they exercise it. The result is a polycentric management of the governance: the economic policies within the Union are shaped in accordance with the cooperation between European institutions, the governments of the Member States and national parliaments. More precisely the surveillance model has been applied in two ways. Pre-emptive coordination aims to promote convergence and prevent those fiscal behaviours that have been qualified by the EU Treaties as unsound (art. 121 TFEU).[68] Corrective coordination applies when Member States have reached a level of excessive indebtedness and European institutions intervene to demand budgetary adjustments through recommendations and eventually an economic sanction (art. 126 TFEU).[69] In both procedures, decisions are taken by the Council, which acts on proposal from the Commission. The result is some form of

---

[65]Mundell (1963).

[66]Schoenmaker (2011). Rodrik developed a trilemma on the process of globalisation: you cannot have at the same time deep international economic integration, national sovereignty and mass politics. See Rodrik (2000). The same trilemma was adapted by Snell to the EMU. See Snell (2016), p. 158.

[67]In the surveillance model, Member States maintain taxing authority, while the EU has a corrective role as an enforcer of discipline. Hinarejos (2013), p. 1621.

[68]See *infra* Sect. 3.3.2.

[69]See *infra* Sect. 3.3.3.

peer review between national governments. Aside from coordination, the economic governance has been completed by a number of other rules: art. 122(2) TFEU allows the Union to provide temporary financial assistance to Member States in case of natural disasters or exceptional occurrences beyond their control; national governments shall not receive monetary financing (art. 123 TFEU), nor have privileged access to financial institutions (art. 124 TFEU)[70]; finally the no bailout clause ex art. 125 TFEU provides that every government is responsible for its own financial obligations and neither the Union, nor Member States are liable for the commitments taken by the other countries.[71] The latter prohibitions are extremely important, because they aim to make financial markets play a regulatory role on public finances, requesting high risks premiums on national bonds, when Member States do not present sound fiscal policies.[72]

In conclusion, the adoption of the surveillance model had the purpose to ensure sound public finances and economic coordination between Member States, thus correcting the original deficits of the EMU. In this legal framework, the effectiveness of the economic governance relies essentially on the individual responsibility of each country, which shall implement fiscal policies by taking into consideration the European rules and guidelines, as well as the financing costs of its debt on the financial markets.

2.4 The Objective of Stability of the Euro Area as a Whole

2.4.1 Preliminary Remarks: Defining a Stability Paradigm

After having explained the role of objectives in the EU legal order and introduced the fundamental features of the EMU, it is possible to start analysing the concept of stability of the euro area as whole and explain why it has become the primary goal of the economic union.

The following analysis will first of all explain how the concept of 'the euro area as community of stability' has evolved along the years. While the pursuit of price stability has initially monopolised most of the efforts from the Union and the

[70]These provisions have a double intent: on the one hand the ECB shall have the full control over money supply in the Eurozone, thus preventing uncontrolled monetary expansion and inflation; on the other hand, Member States shall rely only on their capacity to collect public resources, thus fostering fiscal responsibility.

[71]On the principal of 'no bailout' see Tufano (2002). The prohibition considers central, regional, local governments or other public authorities, other bodies governed by public law, or public undertakings. The only exception to the prohibition, which is expressly mentioned in art. 125 TFEU, is the mutual financial guarantees for the joint execution of a specific project. The prohibition of bailout does not prevent Member States from purchasing the bonds of other States, as long as this is done at market conditions. See Allemand (2015), p. 261.

[72]See *infra* Sect. 3.4.

Member States, since the outbreak of the sovereign debt crisis the economic union has started defining its own targets and priorities. The implementation of rescue policies for several countries led to the reform of art. 136 TFEU and the formal introduction of the objective of the 'stability of the euro area as a whole' in the EU Treaties. At the same time, the Court of Justice of the European Union provided a fundamental contribution to the clarification and extension of the concept.

Taking into consideration the relevant case law of the CJEU and legal doctrine, the research will then start analysing the objective of the 'stability of the euro area', by identifying its qualification, beneficiaries, applications, as well as the obligations it creates. Accordingly, it will be possible to propose a definition of the objective and distinguish it from the wider goal of financial stability. Finally, the last paragraphs will focus on the ownership of the objective of stability of the euro area as a whole, by explaining why its pursuit is shared by both the Member States and the Union.

2.4.2 The Eurozone as a 'Community of Stability'

The objective of stability had a central role in the discussions, which preceded the creation of the single currency.[73] The political and legal narratives, which surrounded the ratification and implementation of the Maastricht Treaty, made significant efforts to celebrate the new monetary union as a genuine 'community of stability' (*Stabilitätsgemeinschaft*). The latter concept was developed by the German Federal Constitutional Court (GFCC) in the famous judgment on the consistency of the Maastricht Treaty with the German Basic Law. In this judgement, the Court of Karlsruhe clarified that the monetary union shall be a community committed to long-term stability, in particular to price stability,[74] this representing a *condicio sine qua non* of German participation in the EMU.

The initial conception of 'community of stability' consisted of a monetary union where the level of inflation remains under control (internal price stability), this being the primary objective of monetary policy. The fulfilment of this goal was ensured at the same time by a number of other provisions, such as the full independence of the ECB, the prohibition of monetary financings, the principle of individual responsibility of Member States for national fiscal policies and the stability criteria for sound budget management.[75]

[73]This depended on the influence of the ordo-liberal school of economic thinking on the EU economic constitution, according to which market freedom and competition shall be balanced with political decisions and rules pursuing order; this includes price stability. See Tuori and Tuori (2014), pp. 18–21.

[74]See German Constitutional Court, Judgment of 12 October 1993, [BVerfGE 89/155], para 138.

[75]See German Constitutional Court, Judgment, 7 September 2011, [2 BvR 987/10], para 129.

2.4.3 *Price Stability as Primary Objective of Monetary Policy*

The pursuit of price stability represents the *Grundnorm* of the monetary union.[76] Art. 127(1) TFEU qualifies it as the primary objective of monetary policy of the European System of Central Banks (ESCB), meaning that any action of the European Central Bank (ECB) and National Central Banks (NCBs) must be consistent with it. At the same time, the importance of price stability resounds in all the EU Treaties: art. 3(3) TEU defines it as one of the objectives of the single market, which is functional to the sustainable development of Europe, while art. 119(3) TFEU recalls it among the guiding principles of the EMU. Art. 140(1) TFEU mentions it among the convergence criteria, which is necessary to respect, in order to introduce the Euro.

Despite the many references to this objective, the EU Treaties do not provide a clear definition of price stability. Some authors called for rigid inflation targets,[77] while others preferred to take into consideration the variation of the economic context.[78] Regardless of this initial debate, the ECB Governing Council decided to adopt a quantitative definition of price stability. In its Decision on 13 October 1998, it announced that 'price stability is defined as a year-on-year increase in the Harmonised Index of Consumer Prices (HICP) for the euro area of below 2%'.[79] The quantification of the admissible inflation rate, however, does not mean that the ECB would automatically assume responsibility in case it exceeded the limit of 2%, as the EU Treaty recognises a wide margin of manoeuvre in the pursuit of this objective.[80]

The ECB takes care of price stability through the adoption of standard and non-standard monetary policies, like the control of interest rates, exchange rate management and the central bank's supervision of the payments system.[81] At the same time, governments shall refrain from those fiscal behaviours, which might undermine this objective, notably receiving monetary financings[82] and privileged access to financial institutions, as well as presenting excessive deficits. Finally,

---

[76]See Herdergen (1998), p. 21.

[77]Smits considered acceptable less than 2% inflation rate. See Smits (1997), p. 185. Stadler considered acceptable 2–3% of annual inflation. Stadler (1996), p. 104.

[78]See Dutzler (2003), p. 28; Chemain (2005), p. 362.

[79]European Central Bank (1998). The Harmonised Index of Consumer Prices (HICP) is regulated by Council Regulation (EC) No 2494/95 of 23 October 1995 concerning harmonized indices of consumer prices, (1995).

[80]The ECB has discretion in deciding which monetary policy ensures monetary stability. The target of 2% shall take into consideration the bias of economic and statistical measures. See Dutzler (2003), p. 32; Gaitanides (2005), p. 21.

[81]Lupo Pasini (2013), p. 235.

[82]See Whereas (7) Council Regulation (EC) No 3603/93 of 13 December 1993 specifying definitions for the application of the prohibitions referred to in Articles 104 and 104b(1) of the Treaty (1993) OJ L 332/1. The ECB can still buy sovereign bonds on the secondary market.

art. 130 TFEU provides the ECB with full independence, in order to avoid undue pressures, which might undermine the fulfilment of its mandate.

Coming to the reasons why Member States elected price stability as the primary objective of the monetary union, it shall first be analysed the role it plays in the development of European and national economies and then contextualised in the legal framework of the EMU.

Considering its relevance for economic development, price stability can be qualified as an objective in itself (*Selbstzweck*), meaning a goal having an intrinsic and self-standing value. The academic literature has exhaustively explained its importance. Empirical studies prove that price stability contributes to financial stability, encourages the people's confidence in money and price signals, ensures an efficient allocation between lenders and borrowers and improves competition and the level of productivity, thus having a positive impact on the employment rate.[83] On the contrary, high inflation contributes to social injustice eroding savings and salaries and causing an arbitrary redistribution of wealth.[84]

The importance of price stability was sanctioned in the political agreement, which surrounded the establishment of the monetary union. By deciding to relinquish their monetary sovereignty and create a single currency, Member States identified in price stability the fundamental condition to make the new currency stable, potentially as much as the Deutsche Mark was.[85] The importance of this objective is clear considering that monetary stability in countries like Germany is not only part of the economic culture, but has also become a legal obligation.[86] This is the reason why the Court of Karlsruhe stated in the Judgment on the Maastricht Treaty that, if the conditions to ensure price stability faded away, Germany would no longer be allowed to participate in the monetary union (thus automatically undermining its survival). In this way, the GFCC prioritised the stability of the single currency ahead of the existence of the monetary union.

[83]Dutzler (2003), p. 30. On the reasons, why price stability is an objective of monetary policy see Issing (2001).

[84]Dutzler (2003), p. 30.

[85]See Resolution of the German *Bundestag* on the Economic and Monetary Union, 2 December 1992 the German (BTDrucks. 12/3906; Sten.Ber. 12/126 p. 10879). The adoption of the German model of monetary policy is clearly visible in the application of two provisions of the Maastricht Treaty, which directly derive from the German Basic Law: the objective of price stability and the principle of independence of central banking (cf. art. 88 GG).

[86]See art. 109(3) of the German Basic law.

2.4.4 *The Immediate Objectives of Economic Policy*

2.4.4.1 The Difficult Identification of the Objectives of Economic Policy in the Original Maastricht Model

While the monetary policy of the ECB is committed to the pursuit of price stability, the EU Treaties, unfortunately, don't identify a clear objective of economic policy. The provisions regulating the functioning of the economic governance recall some principles and targets, including 'open market economy with free competition', 'sound public finances', 'sustainable balance of payments' and 'efficient allocation of resources',[87] but none of these concepts have been formally qualified as the primary objective of economic policy.

The reason why the Maastricht Treaty could not choose a clear goal of economic policy as it did for the monetary union depends on the asymmetry within the EMU. The monetary union is notably based on the transfer of sovereign rights to the European Union. For this reason, the Treaties were able to decide how the EU shall manage this delegated competence by identifying a 'positive' obligation for the ECB and national central banks, notably the achievement of price stability. As previously explained, the economic union is rather different: as Member States refused to transfer sovereign powers to the supranational level in the field of fiscal policy and the EU budget has limited resources, nothing can be done to develop a genuine European economic policy in the framework of the EMU. In other words, while the conferral of monetary competence was followed by the identification of a mandate for the ESCB, what Member States have to do with their economic competence remains in principle a national matter. Accordingly, Member States can decide how allocating resources and developing their economic strategy without EU institutions being able to put their nose into it. The only limit posed by the membership in the monetary union consists of avoiding certain behaviours, which may damage the other countries and the euro area as a whole. Notably, the adoption of the surveillance model, according to which Member States are still in charge of fiscal choices, but act under the supervision of the EU, complies with a model of negative integration, where the Union intervenes to prevent certain actions, rather than exercising an autonomous power. Two consequences follow. First of all, while the objective of monetary policy is pursued by the EU through the management of a delegated sovereignty, the objective of economic policy is put forward in concrete by the Member States under the supervision of the Union, which shall coordinate national fiscal policies in accordance with art. 5(1) TFEU. Second, due the full adherence to the surveillance model, the objectives of economic policy in the Maastricht Treaty can be identified only through a teleological interpretation of the

---

[87] See art. 119 and art. 120 TEU. In the Lisbon Strategy and the 2020 Strategy, the EU also identified a number of economic targets (regarding employment, research and development, climate change and energy, education, poverty and social exclusion), Member States should have achieved through the Open Method of Coordination.

prohibitions, which regulate the functioning of the Eurozone governance. Indeed, in the decentralised model of economic union, the aim is not to do something using a European power, which does not actually exist, but rather to give EU institutions the instrument to prevent Member States from acting in a way that could damage the euro area as *Stabilitätsgemeinschaft*.

In the light of these considerations, it is possible to recognise *prima facie* two objectives of the economic union in the original Maastricht model. First, the EU Treaties demand economic convergence by limiting national discretion in the management of their budgetary policy; second, the economic governance is based on the pursuit of sound public finances, which is ensured through the prohibition of excessive public spending.

2.4.4.2 Economic Convergence

The objective of economic convergence may be deduced from art. 121 TFEU and the other rules of the SGP providing for coordination of national budgetary and macroeconomic policies.

Economic convergence between Member States could be qualified as the adoption of coordinated economic policies, which shall allow the Eurozone countries to react in a similar way and possibly achieve equivalent performances along the economic cycle.[88] The participation in the EMU notably required Member States to complete a process of substantial convergence between their economies before they could relinquish monetary sovereignty and join the Eurozone. Due to the many deficits of this procedure, however, the economic situation in the euro area has been from the very beginning quite heterogeneous, thus making further coordination necessary.

In the EMU, economic convergence should fulfil several functions. First, if countries systematically experienced diverse economic situations, it would be difficult for the ECB to ensure a coherent monetary policy oriented towards price stability. The correct functioning of the monetary transmission mechanism requires indeed that Member States present homogenous economic conditions to make sure that decisions of the central bank produce the same consequences on the real economy of each country.[89] Second, economic divergence can cause the rise of macroeconomic imbalances within Member States. EU law defines imbalances as 'any trend giving rise to macroeconomic developments which are or may be adversely affecting the proper functioning of the economy of a Member State, the EMU or the EU as a whole'.[90] Examples of imbalances can be excessive public or

[88]On the concept of convergence cf. European Central Bank (2015).

[89]See Ruffert (2011), p. 1793.

[90]Imbalances are considered 'excessive', if they are able to jeopardise or risks jeopardising the proper functioning of the EMU. See art. 2 of Regulation (EU) No 1176/2011 on the prevention and correction of macroeconomic imbalances, (2011), L 306/25.

private indebtedness, housing bubbles, the scarce competitiveness of the productive system, negative balance of payments or declining export market shares. Even if these situations may not represent an immediate threat to fiscal stability, they can undermine the economic solidity of Member States in the longer term, thus having destabilising effects on the rest of the Eurozone.[91] Finally, the development of different economic performances between Member States can also undermine the political cohesion within the EMU, stressing tensions between those countries taking advantage of the participation in the monetary union and those unable to do so.

As the following analysis will explain the pursuit of convergence has not applied in a way to ensure some form of fiscal redistribution between the Member States, but as a process of macro-economic consolidation every country shall put forward in accordance with some common criteria. Rather than achieving the same level of economic development and welfare, convergence has been functional to the avoidance of risks for fiscal destabilisation in the euro area, thus approaching the objective of sound public finances.

2.4.4.3 Sound Public Finances

The objective of sound public finances (fiscal stability) is recalled in a number of provisions of both primary and secondary law. Preventive economic coordination ex art. 121 TFEU already requests Member States to achieve a medium-term objective (MTO) of budgetary policy. The prohibitions of monetary financing (art. 123 TFEU), privileged access to financial institutions (art. 124) and bailout (art. 125 TFEU) also have the purpose to strengthen budgetary responsibility of national governments by easing the regulatory role of financial markets. The most relevant provision in this regard, however, is art. 126 TFEU, which essentially interprets the objective of sound public finances as a prohibition of excessive public deficit and debt. The containment of public spending is quantified in clear thresholds, notably the limit of 3% of ratio deficit/annual GDP and 60% of the ratio public debt/GDP.[92] Over the years, EU institutions have adopted different interpretations of these numbers by taking into consideration both the specificities of each country and the economic situation in the euro area as a whole.[93]

The prohibition of running excessive public spending was introduced for several reasons.[94] First, excessive spending in one Member State is financed through increasing recourse to the EU capital market, thus driving the union's interest rates

[91] This was the cause of the outbreak of the fiscal crisis in Ireland and Spain between 2010 and 2012.

[92] See Protocol No 12 on the on the excessive deficit procedure.

[93] The SGP was reformed in 2005 in order to grant more margin of flexibility to the interpretation of the convergence criteria.

[94] On the necessity to contain public deficit see Gros and Thygesen (1998), pp. 327–329; Schor (1999), pp. 131–133; Padoa-Schioppa (2000), p. 156; De Grauwe (2016), pp. 218–225.

upwards.[95] Furthermore, an important expansion of the money supply may increase the inflation rate in the Member State concerned and in the rest of the Union. More importantly, the continuous rise of public debt in one country can undermine the stability of its national public finances, making sovereign default possible. This is especially true when an external shock hits a country and fresh resources are needed to stabilise the economy. In case the previous abuse of public spending makes the margin of national fiscal action tight, either the concerned Member State faces bankruptcy, or the ECB monetises its debt,[96] or the other countries intervene with last minute bailouts. Evidently none of these options are consistent with the pursuit of stability in the EMU. Sovereign defaults are extremely dangerous due to the unpredictable economic consequences, they can trigger.[97] The monetary intervention of the ECB in favour of countries risking fiscal collapse is clearly inconsistent with the objective of price stability. Finally, continuous fiscal misbehaviours, which make a Member State eventually dependent on the other countries' financial assistance, is unsustainable in a monetary union based on the free participation of sovereign nations and the mutual trust between their governments.

While this brief outline on the functioning of the EMU aims to help defining the objective of the economic union, the next Chapter will provide a more accurate analysis on the matter.

2.4.5 *Looking for an Ultimate* telos *of Economic Policy*

2.4.5.1 Stability Beyond Price Stability

The identification of the goals of economic convergence and sound public finances in the framework of the original Maastricht model does not exhaust the search for objectives of economic policy in the EMU. Indeed, unlike the pursuit of price stability for monetary policy, these two objectives are not self-sustaining, but have been made functional to the achievement of something else. The intermediary nature

---

[95] De Grauwe (2016), p. 225. As the cost of national indebtedness increases for all, the other governments will be obliged to adopt more restrictive fiscal policies in order to stabilise their public finances.

[96] This is what might have happened during the sovereign debt crisis when the ECB introduced some non-conventional monetary policies on the secondary bonds market having the consequence to support Member States, whose public finances were seriously compromised. The consistency of these policies with the monetary mandate of the ECB and the prohibition of monetary financing (art. 123 TFEU) has been the object of a proceeding before the ECJ on request of the German Federal Constitutional Court ex art. 263 TFEU. See ECJ, Judgment of 16 June 2015, Case C-62/14, *Gauweiler (and Others) v. Deutscher Bundestag*, ECLI:EU:C:2015:400.

[97] The possible exit of Greece from the Eurozone started a debate on its opportunity and feasibility. Most of the economic doctrine highlighted the negative effects of such a scenario on both Greece and the rest of the Eurozone. See Petersen and Böhmer (2012), Alcidi et al. (2012) and Dabrowski (2012).

of economic convergence and sound budgetary policies has been suggested by European and national courts, according to which the fulfilment of these objectives must be contextualised in relation to other goals.[98]

The original interpretation of the rules regulating the functioning of the EMU identifies the ultimate objective of economic policy in price stability.[99] This is essentially the position of the GFCC in the Maastricht judgment, when it stated that the EMU shall be first of all committed to monetary stability, otherwise the necessary conditions for the German participation would basically disappear.[100] Taking into consideration the natural interdependence between fiscal and monetary policy, this interpretation suggests that all rules on the Eurozone governance, namely economic coordination, the no bailout clause, as well as the prohibitions of monetary financings and of privileged access to credit, are essentially functional to the containment of the inflation rate, this being the fundamental manifestation of stability in the EMU. Such interpretation has been confirmed in the rules of the SGP, which have initially identified price stability as the main objective of economic convergence and fiscal discipline.[101]

The achievement of this goal has so much monopolised the attention of European institutions and Member States during the first decade since the foundation of the monetary union that other relevant factors for stability, such as the correction of macroeconomic imbalances and the creation of stabilisation tools, were essentially neglected. Even the pursuit of sound fiscal policies, despite being acknowledged as a fundamental condition to ensure price stability, was not effective. Indeed, as long as the ECB could contain the level of inflation through the ordinary measures of monetary policy and the high level of public debt were not posing an immediate threat to the stability of the currency, European institutions could have a more indulgent approach to the application of fiscal rules in the Member States.

Only the outbreak of the sovereign debt crisis[102] showed the limits of the surveillance method and made clear that the equivalence between price stability and stable union was substantially wrong.[103] The significant deterioration of national

[98]See German Constitutional Court, Judgment of 12 October 1993, [BVerfGE 89/155], para 147; ECJ Judgment of 27 November 2012, Case C-370/12, *Thomas Pringle v Government of Ireland*, ECLI:EU:C:2012:756, para 135.

[99]See Hansch (2002), pp. 293–294.

[100]See German Constitutional Court, Judgment of 12 October 1993, [BVerfGE 89, 155], para 148.

[101]See Whereas (1) Regulation (EU) No 1466/1997 and Whereas (2) Regulation (EU) No 1467/1997: 'the Stability and Growth Pact is based on the objective of sound government finances as a means of strengthening the conditions for price stability and for strong sustainable growth conducive to employment creation'.

[102]When the sovereign debt crisis broke out in Greece, some authors suggested sticking with the strict policy of no-bailout. Member States, however, decided to come in aid of the countries experiencing financial difficulties due to the harsh consequences of a default for the country concerned, but also for the other Member States and the euro area as a whole. Hinarejos (2013), p. 1628.

[103]Monetary stability is not the only thing, which counts in a monetary union. Several kinds of stability are needed in a monetary union. See Tuori and Tuori (2014), pp. 57–60; Borger (2016),

public finances and banking system eventually triggered a general destabilisation of the Eurozone as a whole, thus proving that real stability takes more than just complying with the inflation target. While the Euro has generally remained stable, the crisis spread from the more vulnerable countries of the Eurozone to the stronger ones, thus challenging the integrity of the monetary union. The EMU came indeed to the paradoxical situation where it could count on a relatively strong and stable currency,[104] but its Member States risked abandoning the monetary union one after the other.

2.4.5.2 The Deficits of the Surveillance Model

The outbreak of the sovereign debt crisis showed the limits of the Maastricht model of economic governance based exclusively on surveillance. The latter has been unable to address the two major sources of instability coming from the asymmetry between the economic and the monetary union, notably fiscal misbehaviours and the inability to manage macro-economic shocks.

Considering the first challenge, European fiscal discipline lacked effectiveness, because it was based on a peer review system of national political authorities within the Council.[105] In this way, Member States could continue tolerate each other's fiscal misbehaviours. It is important to stress that moral hazard was possible also because of the weak regulatory role of the financial markets: due to the strong interdependence within the Eurozone, even the most indebted countries were granted cheap interest rates on their sovereign debt, as investors knew that the other Member States would come to their aid, if necessary.[106]

At the same time, the outbreak of the sovereign debt crisis showed the inability of the euro area to deal with economic shocks. When in 2008 the global financial crisis put under distress the public finances of the most advanced economies of the world, those EU Member States that had perpetrated a lax management of their public finances for years became unable to finance their debt on the international markets.

pp. 148–149. Experience proves that a monetary union requires other instruments to avoid crisis, such as risk sharing and mechanism to absorb economic shocks. Even the idea that the financial sector can always self-stabilise is wrong; on the contrary, a banking crisis can turn into a debt crisis. See Vallee (2014), p. 54.

[104]The single currency remained relative stable during the crisis, even if the inflation rate started decreasing since 2013. Cf. Draghi (2013) and Neri and Siviero (2015).

[105]This was proven few years after the introduction of the single currency, when the Commission started in 2003 an excessive deficit procedure against Germany and France, but the Council refused to sanction these two countries, despite the clear violation of the convergence criteria. See *infra* Sect. 4.3.2.

[106]On the inefficiency of private capital markets and the weak credibility of the 'no bail-out clause' see Louis (2010), pp. 979–981; Stiglitz (2016), pp. 24–26; Brunnermeier et al. (2016), pp. 99–100; De Grauwe (2016), pp. 225–226, 229. See *infra* Sect. 4.3.3.1.

This triggered vast and uncontrolled financial turmoil in the euro area.[107] The likely insolvency of these countries exacerbated the ongoing banking crisis, as national financial institutions owned a significant quantity of their sovereign debt. While the fiscal crisis of Member States increased the difficulties for those banks owning national public bonds, the management of the banking crisis requested fiscal support, that governments were no longer able to provide.[108] This interdependence created therefore a toxic loop between the banking and the sovereign debt crisis, thus leading to a dangerous process of destabilisation of the monetary union.[109] According to these reactions, the economic collapse of Greece in autumn 2009 caused a progressive destabilisation of the weaker Member States of the monetary union, namely Ireland and Portugal in 2010, Italy and Spain in 2011 and Cyprus in 2012.

2.4.5.3 The Reform of the Economic Governance and the Emergence of the Objective of 'Stability of the Euro Area as a Whole'

The impellent need to ensure the survival of the monetary union pushed national governments and European institutions to look for a better implementation of the 'community of stability' in the Eurozone. This has been done through the adoption of two major sets of reforms.

First, Member States have provided financial help to countries attacked by speculation and risking default. After having created two temporary rescue funds in 2010, namely the ESFM and the EFSF, Eurozone governments set up a new permanent instrument, the European Stability Mechanism (ESM).[110] The latter was introduced on the basis of Decision 2011/199/EU[111] amending art. 136 TFEU and an international Treaty signed on the 2 June 2012 (Treaty on the European Stability Mechanism, TESM). When there is a risk for the stability of the euro area as a whole (indispensability criterion), the ESM can provide Member States with loans in the framework of a macroeconomic adjustment programme, finance direct and indirect recapitalisations of financial institutions, purchase debt in the primary and secondary debt markets and grant precautionary financial assistance in the form of credit lines. The ESM has a subscribed capital of around €700 billions, which corresponds to a

---

[107] On the dynamics of the sovereign debt crisis see Adamski (2012), pp. 1325–1329; Wilsher (2014), pp. 252–254; Pace (2018), pp. 36–68.

[108] The banking and the sovereign debt crisis were therefore 'twin'. See Lastra (2013) p. 1190; Moloney (2014), p. 1622.

[109] See Lupo Pasini (2013), p. 228.

[110] See *infra* Sect. 3.6.1.

[111] European Council Decision of 25 March 2011 amending Article 136 of the Treaty on the Functioning of the European Union with regard to a stability mechanism for Member States whose currency is the euro, (2011) OJ L 91/1. The amendment was adopted on the basis of art. 48(6) TEU. The compliance of the amendment procedure was carefully analysed by the ECJ in the Pringle Case of November 2012. Cf. ECJ Judgment of 27 November 2012, Case C-370/12, *Thomas Pringle v Government of Ireland*, ECLI:EU:C:2012:756, paras 29–76.

lending capacity of €500 billions. The European financial aid is conditional to the signature of a 'memorandum of understanding' (MoU) between the national government and the European Commission in connection with the European Central Bank (ECB) and the International Monetary Fund (IMF) (conditionality criterion). The memorandum foresees all measures the government has to endorse in order to consolidate public finances and appoints the so-called troika (composed by the Commission, the ECB and the IMF) to monitor the application of reforms. Decisions are taken by the Board of Governors, which is composed of the Ministers of Finances of the euro area Member States. In 2013, the Two Pack reform has started a process of 'comunitarisation' of the ESM, by granting European institutions a more active role in the activation of financial assistance.

Second, Member States and European institutions tried to improve the weak economic governance, that was unable to prevent the increase of public deficit and debt in several Member States. In 2011 and 2013, the Six Pack and the Two Pack reforms[112] modified the functioning of European supervision on national public finances. The latter has become more effective thanks to an assisted procedure for the adoption of national budgets (European and national semesters) and the introduction of semiautomatic sanctions in case of non-compliance with European recommendations. Furthermore, next to public indebtedness, EU institutions have started monitoring excessive macroeconomic imbalances in the Member States. Aside from the reform of the SGP, 25 EU Member States signed on 2 of June 2012 the Treaty on Stability, Coordination and Governance (TSCG or Fiscal Compact).[113] The most important innovation of this agreement has been the balanced-budget amendment that Member States are obliged to introduce in their national constitutional system within 1 year of the ratification of the Fiscal Compact. The ratification of the TSCG is a legal condition for Member States to receive financial support from the ESM.

Clearly, the reform of the economic union has acknowledged a new conception of stability in the Eurozone. After being mentioned in relation to the EFSF,[114] the 'stability of the euro area as a whole' has become the objective of the European Stability Mechanism in accordance with new paragraph 3 of art. 136 TFEU. The latter reads that the countries sharing the single currency can establish a stability mechanism subject to strict conditionality, which would be activated if indispensable to safeguard 'the stability of the euro area as a whole'. This objective has been recalled also in other sources of law such as the TSCG, the TESM and the Two

---

[112]See *infra*. Sect. 3.2.

[113]See *infra* Sect. 3.5. The opposition of two Member States, notably the United Kingdom and Czech Republic, prevented the reform of the European Treaties in accordance with art. 48 TEU or the activation of the flexibility clause. Accordingly, the other governments under Franco-German pressure decided to stipulate a separate international agreement. At the same time, the stipulation of an *ad hoc* Treaty aimed also to stress the content of the agreement and make it more effective. Ziller (2015) p. 29.

[114]Cf. Whereas (1) EFSF Framework Agreement of 8 June 2010. Art. 1 of Regulation (EU) No 407/2010 establishing a European financial stabilisation mechanism mentions instead the financial stability of the European Union.

Pack.[115] Last, the CJEU gave a decisive contribution to the definition of the objective in the Pringle and the Gauweiler judgments. Even if it has been sometimes qualified as '*financial* stability of the euro area as a whole', the different sources of law mentioned above essentially refer to the same objective.[116]

2.4.6 *Analysing the Objective of Stability of the Euro Area as a Whole*

2.4.6.1 The Qualification of the Pursuit of 'Stability of the Euro Area as a Whole' as a Primary Objective of Economic Policy

Despite these many references, the content of the objective of 'stability of the euro area as a whole' is still far from having a clear definition. The vagueness, which is surrounding it, depends on the fact that what the Eurozone actually needs to do in order to achieve full stability, is still debated.[117] The following analysis will try to develop a general understanding of the objective on the basis of the available sources of law and the most recent contributions of the legal doctrine.

First of all, it is necessary to highlight that the objective of 'stability of the euro area as a whole' has emerged as primary *telos* of the economic union.[118] This qualification was suggested by the CJEU, in the context of a wider analysis on the consistency of the ESM and the non-conventional monetary policies of the ECB with EU law. In the Pringle case, the Court of Luxembourg had the necessity to distinguish the sphere of monetary policy, which is an exclusive competence of the EU, from the sphere of economic policy, where only Member States exercise sovereign rights and can stipulate intergovernmental agreements, such as the TESM. In the Gauweiler case, the CJEU had instead to verify whether the purchase of sovereign bonds that the ECB was programming to do on the secondary market (notably the OMTs programme) could still be qualified as an instrument of monetary policy, despite having an impact on the refinancing costs of national sovereign debts. In both circumstances, the Court of Luxembourg managed to distinguish monetary and fiscal policies through a teleological interpretation of the relevant provisions,[119]

---

[115]See Preamble of the TSCG, art. 3 TESM and art. 3(7) of Regulation (EU) No 472/2013.

[116]See *infra* Sect. 2.4.7.3.

[117]According to Tuori and Tuori, the concept of the stability of the Eurozone as a whole remains vague, because it is not yet clear what the ESM can do in order to achieve this objective. This was done on purpose in order to give the ESM some margin of action. The ESM can in fact take care of sovereign debt, but also private institutions. See Tuori and Tuori (2014), p. 133.

[118]Tuori and Tuori, qualify it as 'second order telos'. Tuori and Tuori (2014), pp. 132–133.

[119]According to Beck this distinction does not make sense. On the one hand the ESM has a direct impact on the stability of the currency, which depends on the stability of the currency union. On the other hand, the ECB purchase of bonds falls within the domain of economic policy as long as it

rather than focusing on the available tools to develop each policy.[120] While monetary policy is characterised by the pursuit of price stability, as outlined in art. 127 (1) TFEU, economic policy is committed to the achievement of the stability of the euro area as a whole. Furthermore, the Court specified that sound budgetary policy, which has been previously considered as the main aim of the economic governance, is in reality functional to the pursuit of stability of the euro area as a whole, thus assuming the latter shall be prioritised.[121]

The CJEU evidently took advantage of the vagueness left in the formulation of EU law and the TESM to elevate the 'stability of the euro area as a whole' to primary objective of economic policy and make it the distinctive factor between the economic and the monetary union.[122] On the one hand, the Court acknowledged that monetary and economic policies can influence each other,[123] this being a natural effect in an economic system. At the same time, the use of teleological interpretation to qualify the nature of a specific measure is effective, because it recalls the original 'competence enabling' function of objectives in the EU legal system. As it has been already explained in the previous paragraphs,[124] objectives today exercise mainly a directive role on the management of competences, thus approaching to the concept of *Staatszielbestimmungen* and *objectifs de valeur constitutionnelle* of national constitutional law. At the same time, in those areas of the EU legal order where the process of constitutionalisation has just started, objectives can still help with understanding whether a specific measure represents an *ultra vires* act of the Union and distinguishing between policies, when they are strictly interdependent.

---

eases refinancing conditions for the government on the capital market. See Beck (2014), pp. 544–546.

[120]Advocate General Villalon has distinguished the two policies also considering the available tools. See View of Advocate Cruz Villalón delivered on 14 January 2015 (1) Case C-62/14 *Peter Gauweiler (and Others) v. Deutscher Bundestag*, ECLI:EU:C:2015:7, para 132. The doubts on the participation of the ESM in the shaping of monetary policy depend on the fact that financial support is developed through the same instruments used by the ECB (except for the purchase of bonds on the primary markets). See Grimm (2016), pp. 62–63.

[121]'[T]he attainment of a higher objective, namely maintaining the financial stability of the monetary union.' ECJ Judgment of 27 November 2012, Case C-370/12, *Thomas Pringle v Government of Ireland*, ECLI:EU:C:2012:756, para 135.

[122]See ECJ Judgment of 27 November 2012, Case C-370/12, *Thomas Pringle v Government of Ireland*, ECLI:EU:C:2012:756, paras 56, 93–96, 135; ECJ Judgment of 16 June 2015, Case C-62/14, *Gauweiler (and Others) v. Deutscher Bundestag*, ECLI:EU:C:2015:400, para 64.

[123]ECJ Judgment of 27 November 2012, Case C-370/12, *Thomas Pringle v Government of Ireland*, ECLI:EU:C:2012:756, para 97; ECJ Judgment of 16 June 2015, Case C-62/14, *Gauweiler (and Others) v. Deutscher Bundestag*, ECLI:EU:C:2015:400, paras 51, 52.

[124]See *supra* Sect. 2.2.2.

2.4.6.2 Beneficiary of the Objective: The Concept of 'Euro Area as a Whole'

The new objective of stability does not refer to the European Union as a whole, but expressly identifies the euro area as the beneficiary of the goal. The latter consists of the EU countries united by the sharing of the same currency and consequently bound to a number of rules, interests and needs that the participation in the monetary union has necessarily created.

The qualification of the Eurozone as beneficiary of the new objective of stability is rather problematic. Unlike the European Union, the euro area does not own legal personality, nor a separate legal framework.[125] From the point of view of the drafters of the Maastricht Treaty, the derogation to participate in the monetary union was indeed only transitional: except for the UK and Denmark, which gained a right of permanent opting-out, all the other EU countries were meant to introduce the Euro, once they achieved a sufficient level of convergence. Looking at the legal framework provided by the EU Treaties, it is therefore difficult to grant rights or duties to the Eurozone as such. It would be easier instead to refer the objective of stability of the euro area as a whole either to the European Union or to the single Member States, which participate in the monetary union. This has also been the approach followed by the EU Treaties when they regulated the functioning of the EMU: decisions of economic and monetary policy belong either to the EU institutions or to the concerned Member States. The Eurozone has never been qualified as a subject in itself.

Even if the current formulation of the EU Treaties prevents the conferral of legal personality to the euro area, the countries sharing the same currency have been emerging as integrated core within the EU legal framework working as *de facto* one entity. The outbreak of the sovereign debt crisis has been the catalyst of this transformation, as the Eurozone countries, pushed by the necessity to save the single currency, have moved forward on the path towards stronger integration, leaving the other EU Member States substantially behind. Despite lacking an official definition, the Eurozone has gained a specific identity and has been able to determine itself by shaping its own policies and creating its own instruments of crisis management and prevention. The emancipation of the Eurozone from the rest of the EU has also been proven by the progressive consolidation of a separate (unofficial) institutional framework, including for example the Euro Summit and the Eurogroup,[126] as well as by the development of its own specific interests, like the need to prevent national defaults and stop the vicious circle between the banking and sovereign debt crisis.[127]

---

[125] Cf. Cisotta (2018), p. 100.

[126] The Eurozone can count on its own governance for the economy, which is ruled by the Euro Summit and the Eurogroup, as well as a government of the currency, which is managed by the Executive Board and the Governing Council of the ECB.

[127] The crisis has been the detector of a divergence of priorities for example in relation to burdening the costs of the rescue mechanisms for those countries experiencing financial difficulties.

The dichotomy between the state of facts, where the Eurozone works as one *de facto* entity, and the law, where it does not have any legal personality, can be reconciled by interpreting the letter of art. 136(3) TFEU, as introduced in Decision 2011/199/EU. The norm specifies that the stability in the euro area shall consider the 'whole', meaning the interdependence between the countries participating in the monetary union. Real stability is not fulfilled when States are stable on their own, but only when they are stable together, meaning when national public finances are solid enough to prevent the outbreak of economic crisis and common instruments are available to stop contagion and ensure the compactness of the monetary union. For the same reason, the objective of stability in the euro area as a whole necessarily excludes the non-participating countries in the monetary union.[128] This is logical because only the sharing of a single currency creates the interdependences and the spill-over effects, which require a collective pursuit of stability.

2.4.6.3 The Objective of Stability of the Euro Area as a Whole in the Context of the Stabilisation Policies of the ESM

Coming to the effective applications of the objective, the pursuit of stability of the euro area as a whole has first of all emerged in relation to the rescue policies adopted since 2010. Art. 136(3) TFEU expressly states that the ESM shall provide economic assistance to the Eurozone countries experiencing financial difficulties when it is indispensable to ensure the 'stability of the euro area as a whole'. In order to understand the latter concept, it is necessary to clarify what kind of destabilisation art. 136(3) TFEU refers to, meaning what it is actually at stake when the ESM takes care of the stability of the euro area as a whole. Evidently, the concept has been intentionally left vague, in order to give Member States some margin of discretion to decide on the activation of the financial assistance. Nevertheless, some better understanding of the objective can be deduced looking at the type of crisis the ESM is in charge of avoiding and containing.

On the one hand, the ESM can intervene to rescue Member States, which may be experiencing a sovereign default. Credit lines, loans, purchase of bonds on the primary and secondary market have the purpose to address the relevant difficulties and risks that national governments can experience regarding their fiscal autonomy, meaning the ability to finance their sovereign debt on the international markets.[129] The conspicuous amount of resources that the ESM can immediately mobilise (€500 billions) is meant to manage relevant financing difficulties arising in the Member States. Also looking at the history of the rescue mechanisms (the EFSF and the ESM), the assistance programmes adopted in favour of Greece, Portugal and Ireland had the purpose to deal with the severe financing problems of these countries,

[128] Art. 2 TESM.

[129] Art. 3 TESM.

which had lost access to financial markets[130] and whose debt had become unsustainable.[131]

On the other hand, the ESM can intervene to rescue those private financial institutions, whose economic default may trigger a fiscal destabilisation of the Member States, where they are based. The ESM can intervene in two ways: either it provides resources to the national government, which will then use them to support the financial institution concerned; or it provides direct recapitalisation to the financial institution experiencing economic difficulties, when the Member State is not even able to take care of this operation, without experiencing adverse effects on its own fiscal sustainability.[132] In both scenarios, the recapitalisation of the private financial institution is needed to discharge Member States from the costs of a bailout, which may substantially trigger a sovereign default.[133] So far, the ESM has provided economic support to save banks in two countries, Spain and Cyprus, through *ad hoc* loans.

In order to understand the gravity of the crisis, the ESM aims to defuse, it is important to recall an important condition that art. 136(3) TFEU poses for the activation of financial assistance: the indispensability criterion. Indeed, the threat, the ESM is meant to address, shall not regard one country in particular, but the entire monetary union. This means that the sovereign default of a country or the economic collapse of a financial institutions shall be able to start a domino effect spreading the same risks of default to other countries and financial institutions in the rest of the Eurozone.[134] Furthermore, the intervention of the ESM shall be qualified as an *ultima ratio* meaning that the concerned Member State is unable of manage the crisis on its own.[135] In the light of the principle of indispensability, limited crisis, which are circumscribed to one territory and are unable to pass contagion, shall not be eligible for the activation of the ESM because they cannot undermine the stability of the euro area as a whole.[136]

[130]Whereas (13) TESM.

[131]Art. 13(1)b TESM.

[132]The Board of Governors of the European Stability Mechanism (ESM) adopted on the 8 December 2014 the direct recapitalisation instrument for euro area financial institutions. Direct recapitalisation can be granted only if 'the requesting ESM Member is unable to provide financial assistance to the institutions in full without very adverse effects on its own fiscal sustainability, including via the instrument of an ESM loan for the recapitalisation of financial institutions'. Cf. art. 3(2) of the ESM Guideline on Financial Assistance for the Direct Recapitalisation of Institutions, 8 December 2014. See *infra* Sect. 3.6.2.

[133]The project of common backstop in the framework of the European Banking Union aims to prevent banking crisis of systemic relevance, thus being functional to the pursuit of stability of the euro area as a whole. See *infra* Sect. 5.3.3.2.

[134]See Piecha (2016), pp. 62–63; Palm (2017), Artikel 136 AEUV, paras 56.

[135]See Palm (2017), Artikel 136 AEUV, para. 57. For example, the country is not able to finance itself through credit or taxation. Ibid. para. 57.

[136]According to Ohler the purpose of the ESM is not to solve the funding problems of a specific Member State on the capital markets, but to reduce the stability risks for these markets. It follows that that there is no individual right of financial assistance for the Member States. The latter can be provided only when it is indispensable for the stability of the euro area and conditionality applies. See Ohler (2011), pp. 60–63. This may be problematic in reality: the financial difficulty of a small Member State may not reach the magnitude to become a significant problem for the stability of the monetary as a whole. This means that small Member States shall participate in the mechanism without, however, being able to benefit from it. See *infra* Sect. 2.4.7.2.

Following this analysis, it is possible to argue that the type of crisis, which art. 136(3) TFEU shall take into consideration, are those situations where the monetary union might come to some form of termination or breakup. Indeed, while it is not clear whether art. 136(3) TFEU may include other (less serious) forms of crisis, the concept of stability of the euro area as a whole must necessarily take into consideration that extreme case, when the monetary union experiences a collapse, either because one or more Member States leave it or because it is fully dissolved. First, this is a logical consequence deriving from the concept itself of 'stability of the euro area as a whole': if the latter stopped existing, there would be nothing to remain stable and to take care of. Second, this is the scenario the TESM describes when it sets the conditions and the instruments of financial assistance: a vicious circle of private and public defaults throughout the euro area, whose consequence can't be other than the end of the monetary union or the exit of some countries. In the case of uncontrolled defaults, indeed, Member States would be obliged to recall their monetary sovereignty in order to stabilise their economic and financial system by devaluating the new national currency and stopping the flight of capitals from the country.[137] In conclusion, looking at the functioning of the ESM, the hard-core meaning of 'stability of the euro area as a whole' can be qualified as the integrity of the monetary union.

2.4.6.4 The Objective of Stability of the Euro Area as a Whole in the Context of Economic Coordination and Fiscal Discipline

Aside from stabilisation policies, the objective of the stability of the euro area as a whole has also emerged in regard to the coordination rules and fiscal discipline adopted after the outbreak of the sovereign debt crisis. The preamble of the TESM states that '[s]trict observance of the European Union framework, the integrated macro-economic surveillance, in particular the Stability and Growth Pact, the macroeconomic imbalances framework and the economic governance rules of the European Union, should remain the first line of defence against confidence crises affecting the stability of the euro area'. On the same path, the Preamble of the TSCG says that 'the need for governments to maintain sound and sustainable public finances and to prevent a general government deficit becoming excessive is of essential importance to safeguard the stability of the euro area as a whole'.

The importance of economic coordination and fiscal discipline for the pursuit of the stability of the euro area as a whole has been clarified by the CJEU in the Pringle judgment. In this case the Court had the opportunity to reconcile the provision of financial assistance by the ESM ex art. 136(3) TFEU with the prohibition of bailout

[137] Even if default does not automatically determine the exit from the Eurozone, once a Member State is no longer able to repay its debts, it would be *de facto* obliged to restart coining its own currency. On the relationship between default and exit from the Monetary Union see Dabrowski (2015).

ex art. 125 TFEU, according to which every country is responsible for its public finances.[138] The consistency of these norms can be motivated on two main arguments both based on the teleological interpretation of the Treaty.[139] First, the immediate *telos* of art. 125 TFEU consists of fostering sound budgetary policies in Member States, as the prohibition of bailout should make sure that governments remain subject to the regulatory role of financial markets when they assume new debt.[140] The identification of this goal brings the purpose of art. 125 TFEU closer to the one of conditionality policy of the ESM. Even if the CJEU denied that the primary aim of the latter is economic coordination,[141] the academic doctrine has recognised in the conditionality policy of the ESM a hidden function of 'discipline enforcer.'[142] Second, the contribution of the no bailout clause to fiscal discipline has the purpose of pursuing the *ultima ratio* objective of the economic union, namely the financial stability of the euro area as a whole,[143] which is already the goal of the ESM conditional financial assistance specified in art. 136(3) TFEU.[144] By developing these two arguments, it is possible to identify a progression of objectives in the economic union: the pursuit of sound public finances, which is ensured through the regulatory role of financial markets, as well as economic coordination and the conditionality policy of the ESM is not functional to the fulfilment of price stability, as it was implicitly believed before the crisis. The economic union has instead another final objective, namely the stability of the euro area as a whole, which is pursued through both conditional financial assistance and budgetary consolidation.

---

[138] It is doubtful that the introduction of financial assistance of the ESM weakened the principle of individual budgetary responsibility of Member States provided by the no bailout clause. Cf. Ketterer (2016), pp. 254–255.

[139] On the interpretation of art. 125 TFEU see *infra* Sect. 4.2.4.

[140] ECJ Judgment of 27 November 2012, Case C-370/12, *Thomas Pringle v Government of Ireland*, ECLI:EU:C:2012:756, para 135.

[141] Ibid. para 111.

[142] '[W]hilst it is true that loans and credits under the [ESM] aim at substituting the finance that the markets have not been in a position to provide, such assistance is intended to bringing about the budgetary discipline that the logic of the markets—and the Stability and Growth Pact—was not capable to ensuring'. De Gregorio Merino (2012) p. 1627. See also Schwarz (2014), pp. 411–412.

[143] See ECJ Judgment of 27 November 2012, Case C-370/12, *Thomas Pringle v Government of Ireland*, ECLI:EU:C:2012:756, para 135. The Court comes to this opinion also considering the preparatory works relating to the Treaty of Maastricht according to which the aim of art. 125 TFEU is to ensure that Member States follow a sound budgetary policy. See 'Draft treaty amending the Treaty establishing the European Economic Community with a view to achieving Economic and Monetary Union', Bulletin of the European Communities, Supplement 2/91, pp. 24, 54. Borger notes that the Court could not present the objective of safeguarding the financial stability of the monetary union as a new interpretation of art. 125 TFEU following from Decision 2011/199/EU, as this would have led to an implicit modification of the no bailout clause. See Borger (2013), p. 135. In reality, what happened is the application of the 'law of evolution', as highlighted by De Gregorio Merino. See De Gregorio Merino (2012), p. 1615.

[144] '[Fiscal] discipline contributes at Union level to the attainment of a higher objective, namely maintaining the financial stability of the monetary union'. ECJ Judgment of 27 November 2012, Case C-370/12, *Thomas Pringle v Government of Ireland*, ECLI:EU:C:2012:756, 135.

The acknowledgement of the objective in the case law of the CJEU is extremely important: while art. 136(3) TFEU had defined the pursuit of stability of the euro area only in the context of a crisis, the Court of Luxembourg recognised its existence also in a non-pathological situation, namely the ordinary compliance of Member States with the European fiscal rules. According to this interpretation, Eurozone countries and EU institutions shall behave in a way to prevent those crisis that art. 136(3) TFEU aims to solve, notably those undermining the stability (and existence) of the euro area as a whole. This preventive pursuit of stability shall be ensured in a variety of ways. While the governance has been traditionally focused on fiscal discipline and the containment of public deficit, stability in Member States and the euro area also requires other important attentions, such as the correction of macroeconomic imbalances and the implementation of structural reforms. These measures are fundamental to ensure the sustainability of public spending and avoid that countries experience sudden shocks of an endemic nature. This is the reason why the Six Pack reform created in 2011 a new procedure to assess and encourage the correction of macro-economic imbalances.[145]

2.4.7 Defining the Objective of Stability of the Euro Area as a Whole: A Proposal

2.4.7.1 The Obligations Coming from the Pursuit of the Objective

The analysis developed above can help define the content of the objective of 'stability of the euro area as a whole'. Even if the latter is still emerging and will develop in accordance with the further reform of the economic union, it is possible to identify two major obligations, according to which the objective shall be fulfilled.

First, the stability of the euro area as a whole requires the activation of *stabilisation* policies when the economic situation in one or more countries is threatening the survival or the integrity of the monetary union. Even if this may happen in a variety of ways, the only scenario taken into consideration so far consists of multiple sovereign defaults triggered either by a fiscal crisis or a banking crisis. In this situation, the ESM shall intervene to prevent the spread of a crisis, which might undermine the existence itself of the monetary union. European institutions also participate in the achievement of this objective being involved in the activation of financial assistance and monitoring compliance with the conditionality policy. Even if the intervention of the ESM can't be imposed on Member States against their will, Regulation (EU) No 472/2013 creates an enhanced surveillance scheme for

[145]Regulation (EU) No 1176/2011 on the prevention and correction of macroeconomic imbalances sets out the MIP procedure and applies to all EU countries covered by the MIP; Regulation (EU) No 1174/2011 on enforcement measures to correct excessive macroeconomic imbalances specifies a sanction mechanism to enforce MIP recommendations for euro area countries. See *infra* Sects. 3.3.2 and 3.3.3.

countries at risk, which are put in the condition to easily request the ESM assistance programme.[146]

Second, the objective of the stability of the euro area as a whole is ensured through *consolidation* policies, which shall avoid the rise of macroeconomic imbalances and ensure the solidity of public finances. This type of contribution to the cause of stability is given in two ways. On the one hand, European institutions exercise a coordination role ex art. 5(1) TFEU over national economic policies. Fiscal consolidation and correction of macroeconomic imbalances are pursued in accordance with the enhanced surveillance ex art. 121 TFEU, the macroeconomic imbalances procedure and the excessive deficit procedure ex art. 126 TFEU. The conditional assistance in the framework of the ESM also participates in the pursuit of fiscal consolidation by imposing to the recipient country an adjustment programme agreed in the MoU. On the other hand, fiscal responsibility is fulfilled through the regulatory role, financial markets play in normal times on the public finances of Member States thank to the principle of individual responsibility of fiscal policy outlined in art. 125 TFEU.

Stabilisation and consolidation represent therefore the two main sides of the same commitment towards the stability of the euro area as a whole. This double approach to the pursuit of stability has been acknowledged also by the German Federal Constitutional Court. In the judgment on the ratification of the ESM Treaty, the GFCC has updated the traditional stability paradigm developed in the Maastricht judgment by accepting that the 'community of stability' originally based on the pursuit of price stability, the commitment to budgetary discipline and the individual responsibility of national budgets has been completed by the possibility to activate stabilisation measures to ensure the stability of the monetary union.[147]

2.4.7.2 The Meaning of Stability of the Euro Area as a Whole

Once identified the obligations coming from the 'objective of stability of the euro area as a whole', it is finally possible to write some final words about the concrete result, the fulfilment of this goal aims to achieve. The analysis developed above suggested that both approaches to stability, namely stabilisation and consolidation, share the same fundamental ambition to *preserve the existence and the integrity of the monetary union*. Evidently, the objective of setting up an EMU ex art. 3(4) TEU does not consist only of creating the Euro, but also of ensuring its survival.[148] While stabilisation policies (i.e. ESM financial assistance) show the ability to resist economic shocks and avoid the partial or total breakup of the monetary union,

[146]See art. 3 of Regulation (EU) No 472/2013. See *infra* Sect. 3.6.3.

[147]German Federal Constitutional Court, Judgement of 12 September 2012, [2 BvR 1390/12], para 130.

[148]Piecha (2016), p. 129. The stability of the euro area as a whole should be qualified as a 'common good' of the Eurozone. Cisotta (2018), p. 36.

consolidation measures (i.e. economic coordination) focus more on the ability of the Eurozone to achieve economic convergence and fiscal solidity. This interpretation of the objective of economic policy allows us to recover the original meaning of the word stability. Looking at the etymology, 'stability' comes from Latin 'stare', meaning 'stay' and 'stand'.[149] This suggests that the monetary union is stable as long as it is able to stand, meaning to endure over time.

The qualification of the pursuit of the stability of the euro area as a whole as the objective to protect and preserve the existence itself of the monetary union and the single currency is shared by several authors. De Gregorio Merino said that art. 136(3) TFEU endorses a new meaning of 'stability' of the euro area based on the existence of the monetary union, which is one of the objectives of the Union.[150] De Lhoneux and Vassilopoulos believe that the goal of the stability of the euro area demands Member States to do everything in their power to ensure the integrity of the Eurozone.[151] Eventually, also Advocate General Kokott admitted in her view in the Pringle case that the creation of the ESM has the purpose to avoid disruptive events, such as the bankruptcy in a Member State, which may cause severe damage to the other countries sharing the single currency and eventually endanger the survival of the monetary union.[152]

It is important to highlight that the objective of stability of the euro area as whole shall not be pursued only through a technical assessment of destabilisation risks and convergence policies, but also considering the overall integrity of the Eurozone from a political perspective. This has already emerged in the context of the Cypriot crisis, when the ESM intervened to bailout the banking sector of the island, despite several commenters noticing that the situation was not posing a real threat to the stability of the euro area as a whole.[153] Evidently, significant financial difficulties in a small country, which are technically unable to undermine the stability of the euro area as a whole, can still be taken into consideration for an ESM intervention, if it is worth it to ensure the economic and political cohesion of the euro area.[154] This wider interpretation of the concept of stability is consistent also with another rule, which

---

149 Stability does not only means remaining still or the same (static conception), but also self-affirming or self-sustaining through time (dynamic conception). Cf. Hansch (2002), pp. 40–41.

150 De Gregorio Merino (2012), p. 1629.

151 De Lhoneux and Vassilopoulos (2013), p. 25.

152 According to the Advocate General Kokott avoiding this disruptive scenario is part of the sovereign rights of the Member States and it can't be prevented by a restrictive interpretation of art. 125 TFEU. Cf. View of Advocate General Kokott delivered on 26 October 2012, Case C-370/12, *Thomas Pringle v Government of Ireland*, ECLI:EU:C:2012:675, paras 139, 140.

153 The ESM intervention in the Cypriot crisis is a prove of it. See De Witte and Beukers (2013), p. 843. According to Ketterer the ESM intervention in the Cypriot crisis proved that its real objective is not the systemic stability of the euro area, but helping Member States to finance themselves, thus depriving the markets of the regulatory role initially granted by the no bailout role. See Ketterer (2016), pp. 232–233.

154 Cisotta (2015a), p. 87.

has not been fully acknowledged in the Eurozone economic governance yet, namely the principle of solidarity.[155]

2.4.7.3 Irreversibility of the Single Currency

The definition of the stability of the euro area as *the preservation of the existence and the integrity of the monetary union* is strictly connected to the irreversibility of the introduction of the single currency. While the achievements of European integration depend on the permanence of the Member State in the Union, from the point of view of EU law the establishment of the monetary union represents a permanent result.[156] EU institutions, first of all the ECB and the CJEU,[157] as well as most legal doctrines have strongly argued in favour of this principle.[158] Notably, the Protocol annexed to the Treaty on the transition to the third stage of the EMU expressly defined the introduction of the Euro as irreversible.[159] The Treaty did not provide any *ad hoc* procedure to exit the Monetary Union, but on the contrary obliged all EU Member States to introduce the single currency once they reached a sufficient level of convergence.[160]

Evidently, the Monetary Union represents a model of integration radically different from the previous experiments of monetary coordination. While the 'Snake in the Tunnel' and the European Monetary System were based on the voluntary participation of Member States and the periodical realignment of national

[155]Cf. Tuori and Tuori (2014), pp. 134–135; Hinarejos (2015), p. 167; Pilz (2016), pp. 185–214. Even A. G. Kokott in the Pringle judgment recalled the principle of solidarity to support a restrictive interpretation of art. 125 TFEU. View of Advocate General Kokott delivered on 26 October 2012, Case C-370/12 *Thomas Pringle v Government of Ireland*, ECLI:EU:C:2012:675, paras 143, 144. On the principle of solidarity in the EU legal order see Hinarejos (2015), pp. 166–172; Manzini (2017).

[156]The most logical way for a country to withdraw from the Eurozone would have been the adoption of an EU Treaties change by unanimity in order to introduce this option formally. Cf. Athanassiou (2009), p. 30. An alternative to let Greece leave the Eurozone would have been the application of art. 60 (2) (a) of the Vienna Convention on the Law of Treaties (VCLT), according to which if a state commits a material breach of a multilateral treaty, the other parties can by unanimity suspend or extinguish their relations with it. Peroni (2012), p. 144. On the topic cf. also Athanassiou (2009), p. 35. On the possible expulsion of a Member State from the EU cf. Estella (2018), pp. 45–46, 60–63.

[157]The President of the ECB have reputedly reaffirmed the irreversibility of the euro. C.f. President of the European Central Bank (2012).

[158]Most of the legal doctrine argues that the only way to leave the euro area would be leaving the EU ex art. 50 TEU. Cf. Athanassiou (2009), pp. 28–30; Herrmann (2010), p. 417; Hoffmeister (2011), p. 134. Estella instead argues in favour of the right to exit from the euro area in accordance with the 'permissum videtur' principle. Cf. Estella (2018), pp. 56–58.

[159]This Protocol was abolished by the Lisbon Treaty.

[160]Except for the United Kingdom and Denmark, which enjoyed an opting out right.

currencies,[161] the establishment of the Euro was the result of a sovereignty transfer to the EU. The creation of a monetary union relies on a power, which must be at the same time permanent and exclusive, because there is no single currency if participating countries can disregard or escape its authority. Allowing Member States to reintroduce their national currency, where necessary, would make the monetary union 'unsovereign', which is a contradiction in terms. The action of the ECB would automatically lose credibility and effectiveness, if Member States could break away or be kicked out, as they please, transforming the monetary union into a semi rigid exchange rate mechanism. At the same time, even if the irreversibility of the single currency is a necessary consequence of the establishment of the monetary union, such a result can be effectively achieved only if EU institutions and Member States act in a way to foster stability.[162]

2.4.8 *The Distinction of the Objective of 'Financial Stability' from the Objective of 'Stability of the Euro Area as a Whole'*

2.4.8.1 The Financial Character of Stability

The identification of the objective of 'stability of the euro area as a whole' shall be distinguished from the more general goal of the 'stability of the financial system' ('financial stability'). The latter finds several references in EU primary and secondary law. Art. 127(5) TFEU states that the European System of Central Banks (ESCB) shall promote the stability of the financial system by contributing to the smooth conduct of prudential supervision policies pursued by the national authorities. Regulation (EU) No 1092/2010 on the setup of European Systemic Risk Board qualifies the dangers for financial stability as 'a risk of disruption in the financial system with the potential to have serious negative consequences for the internal market and the real economy'.[163] Regulation (EU) No 1024/2013 on the creation of the Single Supervisory Mechanism stresses that the safety and soundness of large

[161] The 'Snake in the Tunnel' was a mechanism introduced with the Resolution of the Council and of the Representatives of the Governments of the Member States of 21st March 1972 on the application of the Resolution of 22 March 1971 on attainment by stages of Economic and Monetary Union in the Community, (1972) OJ L 38/3. It provided for a limited margin of fluctuation between European currencies (the snake) and against the Dollar (the tunnel). The EMS was created with the Resolution of the European Council of 5 December 1978 on the establishment of the European Monetary System (EMS). The EMS was based on the European Currency Unit (ECU), an Exchange Rate Mechanism (ERM) provided with an automatic re-alignment system and a credit mechanism.

[162] Cf. Betbèze (2016), p. 6. On the exit of the monetary union see also Dammann (2013), Peroni (2015), Munari (2015), pp. 731–732.

[163] Art. 2(c) of Regulation (EU) No 1092/2010 of the European Parliament and of the Council of 24th November 2010 on European Union macro-prudential oversight of the financial system and establishing a European Systemic Risk Board, (2010) OJ L 331/1.

and small credit institutions is essential to ensure the stability of the financial system.[164]

Despite the many references to the objective, there is no clear definition of 'stability of the financial system'. According to the ECB, '[f]inancial stability can be defined as a condition in which the financial system – which comprises financial intermediaries, markets and market infrastructures – is capable of withstanding shocks and the unravelling of financial imbalances. This mitigates the likelihood of disruptions in the financial intermediation process that are severe enough to significantly impair the allocation of savings to profitable investment opportunities'.[165] Looking at other definitions provided by the legal doctrine,[166] it is possible to identify two essential components of the objective of financial stability: 'financial system', whose stability is protected, and 'economic shock', which is the cause of instability.

'Financial system' consists of all those subjects, which provide an economic function and are dependent on each other in order to work properly.[167] Among others, banks and sovereigns play a special role, as the first work as main intermediaries in the economy, while the second are the 'indispensable public structure in the economy as a whole'.[168] Evidently, due to their strong interdependence, the Member States, whose currency is the euro, may behave as a single subject within the European financial system.

'Economic shock' consists of a disruption to the normal financial activity of the system. A shock can be qualified as 'systemic' when it may trigger a full collapse of the economic system.[169]

2.4.8.2 The Transversal Application of the Objective of Financial Stability

Elaborating an exhaustive definition of 'stability of the financial system' is difficult because the objective has been pursued so far through the development of different policies.

First, financial stability in the EU has been granted by the European banking governance through the adoption of regulations, supervision and resolution policies. In 2010, the European legislator created the European System of Financial

[164] Whereas (16) Council Regulation (EU) No 1024/2013 of 15 October 2013 conferring specific tasks on the European Central Bank concerning policies relating to the prudential supervision of credit institutions, (2013) OJ L 287/63.

[165] European Central Bank (2012), p. 5.

[166] According to Lastra financial stability refers to the safety and soundness of the financial system and to the stability of the payment and settlement systems. Cf. Lastra (2006), pp. 92–93.

[167] See Lo Schiavo (2017), p. 19.

[168] Ibid., p. 20.

[169] Ibid., p. 20. See also Espinosa et al. (2010), p. 10.

Supervision (ESFS), a network composed of European and national authorities in charge of prudential supervision.[170] At European level the ESFS includes the European Systemic Risk Board (ESRB), responsible for macro prudential supervision, and three European supervisory authorities (ESAs) in charge of micro prudential supervision: the European Banking Authority (EBA), the European Insurance and Occupational Pensions Authority (EIOPA) and the European Securities and Markets Authority (ESMA). In 2012 a more ambitious project of banking union based on four pillars was launched: a Single Supervisory Mechanism (SSM)[171] under the ECB's leadership, a Single Resolution Mechanism (SRM)[172] provided with a Single Resolution Fund (SRF), a common rule book on prudential supervision and a common legal framework for national deposit guarantees.[173] The reform of the banking governance has not only served the stabilisation of the financial market, but has also consolidated the monetary union by helping to break the toxic loop between the sovereign debt crisis and the banking crisis. The banking union project has automatically involved all Members States of the Eurozone, but has also been open to other EU countries.

Second, the ECB has taken care of financial stability through the implementation of non-conventional monetary policies.[174] Initially it provided unlimited liquidity support to the banking system through fixed-rate full-allotments, expansion of collateral, longer-term liquidity provision, liquidity provision in foreign currencies, purchases of covered bonds and emergency liquidity assistance to solvent banks in difficulties. Later, the ECB has adopted programmes for the purchase of sovereign bonds on the secondary market, first through a temporary programme, known as Securities Markets Programme (SMP) since May 2010,[175] and then through the Outright Market Transactions (OMTs) since September 2012.[176] The OMTs consist in particular of a permanent programme providing for an unlimited purchases of short term sovereign bonds of those Member States, which are performing an assistance programme in the framework of the ESM. The purchases of bonds on

---

[170]The reform was based on art. 127 (5) TFEU and art. 114 TFEU.

[171]Council Regulation (EU) No 1024/2013 of 15 October 2013 conferring specific tasks on the European Central Bank concerning policies relating to the prudential supervision of credit institutions, (2013) OJ L 287/63.

[172]Regulation (EU) No 806/2014 of the European Parliament and of the Council of 15 July 2014 establishing uniform rules and a uniform procedure for the resolution of credit institutions and certain investment firms in the framework of a Single Resolution Mechanism and a Single Resolution Fund and amending Regulation (EU) No 1093/2010, (2014) OJ L 225/1.

[173]Directive 2014/49/EU of the European Parliament and of the Council of 16 April 2014 on deposit guarantee schemes.

[174]See Tuori and Tuori (2014), pp. 183–184; Cisotta (2015b), p. 293.

[175]Decision 2010/281 of the European Central Bank of 14 May 2010 establishing a securities markets programme. The plan allowed outright transactions of bond buying in the euro area public and private debt securities markets with a ceiling of €209 billion.

[176]Decisions of the Governing Council of the European Central Bank (ECB) of 6 September 2012 on a number of technical features regarding the Eurosystem's outright monetary transactions in secondary sovereign bond markets.

the secondary market have been justified to address the malfunctioning of the latter and restore an appropriate monetary policy transmission mechanism. Indeed, the increasing spread between the yields paid by Euro nominated bonds prevented the correct functioning of the transmission channel of monetary policy, as sovereign bonds work as benchmarks for private-sector lending rates and for bank balance sheets and liquidity operations.[177]

The last way to ensure financial stability has been the intervention of emergency backstops. During the sovereign debt crisis, the ESM has provided emergency financial support to the Member States, whose currency is the euro, in accordance with the principle of conditionality and indispensability. For countries which are not part of the euro area, the Union has provided financial assistance in accordance with art. 143 TFEU.[178] Considering specifically the stability of the banking sector, the Single Resolution Mechanism (SRM) and the Single Resolution Fund (SRF) are in charge to restructure banks in distress and provide financial assistance.[179] In the event the latter tool was not able to mobilise sufficient resources to deal with a systemic crisis, the fiscal authorities of the Member States could still intervene.[180] As this scenario may reaffirm the toxic loop between sovereigns and banks, Member States are considering providing the SRB with a common backstop. The latter should be financed through a credit line or guarantees from the ESM and parallel credit facilities from non-euro area Member States.[181]

2.4.8.3 Similarities and Differences Between the Objective of Stability of the Euro Areas as a Whole and the Objective of Financial Stability

After having explained the goal of financial stability and its applications, it is necessary to distinguish it from the objective of stability of the euro area as a

[177] See Cour-Thiman and Winkler (2014), p. 774. The legality of this measure has been discussed by the German Federal Constitutional Court and the ECJ in the Gauweiler case. ECJ, Judgment of 16 June 2015, Case C-62/14, *Gauweiler (and Others) v. Deutscher Bundestag,* ECLI:EU: C:2015:400; Order of German Federal Constitutional Court, 14 January 2014, [2 BvR 2728/13]; German Federal Constitutional Court, Judgment of 21 June 2016, [2 BvR 2728/13].

[178] The Hungarian, Latvian and Romanian governments requested financial support from the International Monetary Fund (IMF) and the EU, which was provided in tranches and was conditional to the implementation of economic reforms. Cf. Council Decision of 4 November 2008 granting mutual assistance for Hungary, (2009) OJ L 37/7; Council Decision of 20 January 2009 granting mutual assistance for Latvia, (2009) OJ L 79/37; Council Decision of 6 May 2009 granting mutual assistance for Romania, (2009) OJ L 150/6.

[179] The SRF has a capacity of €55 billion and is financed by national governments in the transitional period and through the contribution of financial institutions at operating speed. Its mandate is to provide guarantees and make loans to banks experiencing financial difficulties, but can't absorb losses or provide direct recapitalisations. See *infra* Sect. 3.8.

[180] See Moloney (2014), p. 1628.

[181] See *infra* Sect. 5.3.3.2.

whole. The two concepts have often been overlapped, probably because some legal sources, notably the Preamble of Decision 2011/199/EU, the TESM, as well as the Pringle judgement expressly qualified the objective of stability of the euro area as a whole as *financial* stability, despite art. 136(3) TFEU not mentioning this qualification.

The concepts of 'stability of the euro area as a whole' and 'stability of the financial system' or simply 'financial stability', however, are not the same thing, even if they present a number of similarities. The analysis of the different applications of financial stability has clarified the strong ties between the two objectives.[182] On the one hand, the stability of the European financial system relies on the stability of the Member States and of the euro area as a whole: multiple sovereign defaults within the monetary union would cause an economic shock of unpredictable size, which could destabilise the entire financial system including the private institutions and the countries, which are not part of the monetary union. The ESM shall therefore intervene as a last resort backstop in order to consolidate the fiscal position of Eurozone Member States and prevent the spreading of the crisis. On the other hand, the solidity of the euro area as a whole needs a sound and stable financial system: its existence would be indeed jeopardised, if the most significant financial institutions of the euro area did not comply with prudential rules or the ECB was unable to provide resources to the banking sector, where necessary. Liquid financial markets, an effective prudential policy and *ad hoc* interventions for banks in financial need are precious elements to ensure the stability of the euro area as a whole.[183]

The existence of a strong interdependence between European financial stability and the (financial) stability of the euro area as a whole does not mean, however, that the two concepts are identical.[184]

The first distinction is formal: the numerous legal sources regulating the functioning of the EMU, as well as the banking governance have never referred to the

[182]Whereas (6) of Regulation (EU) No 1024/2013 on the establishment of the Single Supervisory Mechanism acknowledged the strict interdependence between the two goals: 'The stability of credit institutions is in many instances still closely linked to the Member State in which they are established. Doubts about the sustainability of public debt, economic growth prospects, and the viability of credit institutions have been creating negative, mutually reinforcing market trends. This may lead to risks to the viability of some credit institutions and to the stability of the financial system in the euro area and the Union as a whole, and may impose a heavy burden for already strained public finances of the Member States concerned'.

[183]The interdependence between the two objectives emerges also in relation to the project of future reform of the EMU. The proposals to complete the banking union through the creation of a European deposit guarantee and a common backstop are strictly linked to project of a fiscal union between the Member States of the euro area. See Lupo Pasini (2013), p. 226.

[184]Recalling the Pringle judgment, according to which art. 136(3) TFEU only has a declaratory role, Lo Schiavo denies that 'the stability of the euro area as a whole' owns its one identity apart from the financial stability of the European Union. Lo Schiavo (2017), pp. 48–49. Also other authors consider the stability of the euro area as an equivalent of the stability of the financial system in the Eurozone or the European Union. See Ohler (2011), pp. 60–61; Pilz (2016), pp. 65–67.

two objectives as synonymous. As previously clarified, the stability of the euro area as a whole has been recalled in relation to the establishment of the ESM and the interpretation of the rules on fiscal discipline; the concept of financial stability instead has been widely used in the norms regarding the banking governance and the monetary intervention of the ECB.

Second, financial stability is pursued through a variety of instruments belonging to both economic policy (the ESM financial assistance and fiscal discipline), monetary policy (the non-conventional measures of the ECB),[185] as well as the banking governance. Financial stability is therefore a transversal objective, which is fulfilled through different kinds of policy. The objective of stability of the euro area as a whole instead has been clearly qualified by the CJEU as an objective of economic policy, expressly distinguished from the goal of price stability that the ECB shall pursue in the management of monetary policy.[186]

Third, as previously explained, the objective of the stability of the euro area as a whole is mainly protected through the consolidation and stabilisation of public subjects, meaning those Member States, whose multiple sovereign default might trigger the collapse of the monetary union. The direct and indirect recapitalisation of financial institutions is also taken into consideration, but only when there is a risk of default for a Eurozone country.[187] On the contrary, the stability of the financial sector is protected also by the enhanced liquid support of the ECB and the prudential supervision of the SSM. It is composed not only of public actors, (i.e. the Member States), but mostly of private parties, notably banks, insurances and other intermediaries. Therefore, limited financial crisis involving only the banking system without risk of contagion to the public sector shall not represent a danger for the stability of the euro area as a whole.

Finally, financial stability is an objective of the European Union as a whole, while the stability of the euro area regards only those Member States, which have introduced the single currency. Clearly, the pursuit of financial stability in the Union does not differ on the basis of participation to the single currency.[188] For this reason, while the stability of the financial system in the EU requires the stability of the euro area as a whole, the contrary is not always true. A financial crisis might regard for example only those countries which are not part of the monetary union as it occurred in 2007, when the outbreak of the global financial crisis destabilised the economies of Romania, Latvia and Hungary without these financial difficulties representing a threat for the stability of the Eurozone. The wider sphere of application of financial stability is the reason why the participation in the banking union has been extended

[185] At the same time, also the stability of the euro area as a whole and price stability are complementary objectives and they influence each other, due to the natural interdependence between the economic and the monetary policies. Cf. De Gregorio Merino (2012), pp. 1629–1630.

[186] According to Beck there is no reason why the stability of the Eurozone as a whole may not fall over more competences. Cf. Beck (2014), p. 544.

[187] Tuori and Tuori (2014), p. 133.

[188] Lo Schiavo (2017), p. 65.

to countries, which have not introduced the single currency, while the ESM is composed only of the Member States of the Eurozone.

In the light of the arguments analysed before it is possible to drive some non-exhaustive considerations on the relationship between the objective of 'financial stability' and the objective of 'stability of the euro area as a whole'. First, the two goals are different, both because they are protected in different ways and because they try to achieve two different results: on the one hand, 'financial stability' protects the entire European financial system and market by recurring to a variety of policies (monetary and economic); on the other the 'stability of the euro area as a whole' specifically protects the existence and the integrity of one of the components of the financial system, namely the euro area, by using economic policy. Second, the two goals are interdependent: the protection of one automatically fosters the pursuit of the other. More precisely the protection of 'financial stability' can be qualified as a macro objective, which includes other narrower interpretations of stability, such as the objective of the 'stability of the euro area as a whole' and 'price stability.'[189] For this reason, some of the instruments created to ensure the stability of the financial system in the Union will be also analysed in regard to the pursuit of the stability of the euro area as a whole (in particular the banking governance).

2.4.9 *The Ownership of the 'Objective of Stability of the Euro Area as a Whole'*

2.4.9.1 The Controversial Nature of the Objective

It has been discussed whether the pursuit of stability of the euro area as a whole represents an objective of the Union, rather than an objective of the Member States. As the CJEU has identified this goal in the field of economic policy, the national exclusive on this competence would prevent the Union from participating in its fulfilment.[190] From this point of view, Member States should be the only ones in charge of pursuing stability in the euro area as a whole, because they have full sovereign rights on their budget.

Such interpretation is not completely acceptable, because it ignores the role played by EU institutions in the functioning of the economic governance and the ESM. In order to understand then the nature of the objective of stability of the euro area as a whole, it is necessary to verify who has the ownership of the obligations

[189] According to this interpretation, monetary policy, economic policy and the banking governance would all participate in the pursuit of financial stability, by contributing to its fulfilment in different ways. On the different contribution of each policy to the cause of stability see Lupo Pasini (2013), pp. 235–237.

[190] As art. 136(3) TFEU only has a declaratory role, it does not provide the EU with any new competence. See Lo Schiavo (2017), p. 48.

coming from the concrete application of this goal, notably *stabilisation* and *consolidation*.

2.4.9.2 The Ownership of Stabilisation Policies

Considering first stabilisation policies, the fulfilment of the objective of stability of the euro area falls primarily on the shoulders of Member States. This interpretation has been confirmed by the CJEU in the Pringle judgment. Analysing Decision 2011/199/EU on the introduction of art. 136(3) TFEU, the Court of Luxembourg stated that it is consistent with the amendment procedure ex art. 48(6) TFEU, because it does not extend the competences of the EU,[191] but acknowledges the ability of national governments to create a mechanism of mutual financial support. Art. 136(3) TFEU plays therefore only a declaratory role[192] and does not provide any authorisation for Member States to create a mechanism of financial assistance. In accordance with this interpretation, the real ownership of the ESM does not belong to the Union, but to the countries participating in the mechanism. This is also the reason why the ESM was created through an international agreement rather than on the basis of EU secondary law or a Treaty change. Member States are therefore the main authority in charge of verifying whether there is a danger for the stability of the euro area as a whole.[193]

Once clarified that the ESM is an instrument owned by the Member States, it remains to understand whether stabilisation policies in general could be developed also by the Union. In this regard, two profiles should be distinguished. Considering first the issue of competence, it is not clear whether the Union is entitled with the task of stabilisation. The EU treaties don't provide a clear reference to it. The solidarity clause ex art. 122(2) TFEU allows the Union to provide *ad hoc* financial assistance to absorb limited shocks affecting single countries and not to ensure the stability of the monetary union.[194] In the field of economic policy, the EU treaties only confer the Union a power of coordination ex art. 5(1) TFEU, which does not include the

[191] See ECJ Judgment of 27 November 2012, Case C-370/12, *Thomas Pringle v Government of Ireland*, ECLI:EU:C:2012:756, paras 72–73.

[192] The CJEU stated that art. 136(3) TFEU only has a declaratory role. See ECJ Judgment of 27 November 2012, Case C-370/12, *Thomas Pringle v Government of Ireland*, ECLI:EU:C:2012:756, paras 73, 184–185. Cf. De Gregorio Merino (2012), p. 1629. The GFCC identifies instead a constitutive value in the provision, as it introduces the possibility for voluntary financial support that art. 125 TFEU would otherwise prevent. See German Federal Constitutional Court, Judgement of 12 September 2012, [2 BvR 1390/12], para 129. Cf. on the matter Palm (2017), Artikel 136 AEUV, paras 43–45.

[193] See Cisotta (2015a), pp. 72–74.

[194] Art. 122(2) TFEU was used to set up the European Financial Stabilisation Mechanism (EFSM) in accordance with Council Regulation (EU) No 407/2010 of 11 May 2010. The CJEU in the Pringle case, however, confirmed the doubts on the legality of a European rescue mechanism established under art. 122(2) TFEU. The Court clarified that this norm allows only *ad hoc* assistance to Member States in financial difficulties and cannot legitimise the establishment of a euro-wide stability

authority to absorb economic shocks and implement structural reforms in the Member States. The biggest obstacle for the development of a stabilisation policy of the Union, however, regards the lack of resources. As a logical consequence of the asymmetry between the economic and the monetary union, indeed, the EU lacks fiscal sovereignty and is unable to collect sufficient resources to develop a macro-economic policy in charge of stabilisation. Notably the EU budget is too small to fulfil this scope and any significant increase of its size would require the unanimity of all Member States, including those who are not part of the monetary union.[195] In this situation, the only authorities *de facto* capable of developing stabilisation policies remain national governments.

The structural limits coming from the asymmetry between the Economic and Monetary Union do not prevent EU institutions from playing a supporting role in the management of stabilisation policy of the ESM. In particular the introduction of the Two Pack reform in 2013 had the purpose to integrate the management of stabilisation policy in the sphere of EU law. In this regard, Regulation (EU) No 472/2013 has reduced the margin of discretion, countries can exercise when they 'freely' assume obligations in the framework of European financial assistance of the ESM. First, the European Commission and the Council can launch the enhanced surveillance on a Member State in order to convince it to request European assistance. Second, the Council has assumed a dominant role in the formulation of the conditionality policy, as a Memorandum of Understanding negotiated between the concerned Member State and the Commission shall comply with the Council's decision on the matter. Third, once the economic supervision has started, until the concerned Member State has repaid at least 75% of the capital received, the Commission and the Council apply a post-surveillance programme, which continues implementing enhanced surveillance on national public finances.[196]

In conclusion, the ownership of stabilisation policies belongs primarily to the Member States, but EU institutions participate in their development by exercising a supervisory and coordination role over their choices. The possible setup of a genuinely European stabilisation policy is instead doubtful, especially due to the lack of resources in the EU budget.[197]

---

mechanism. See ECJ Judgment of 27 November 2012, Case C-370/12, *Thomas Pringle v Government of Ireland*, ECLI:EU:C:2012:756, para 65. See *infra* Sect. 4.2.5.

[195] Art. 312(2) TFEU provides that the Council shall adopt a regulation laying down the multiannual financial framework deciding by unanimity after obtaining the consent of the European Parliament.

[196] See *infra* Sect. 3.6.3.

[197] The European Commission has proposed in December 2017 to introduce the ESM in the EU legal framework on the basis of the flexibility clause ex art. 352 TFEU. See European Commission Proposal for a Regulation (2017). Cf. *infra* Sect. 5.3.3.5.

2.4.9.3 The Ownership of Consolidation Policies

On the subject of the obligation of ensuring fiscal stability, art. 5(1) TFEU makes clear that Member States remain fully in charge of their budgetary policies and the Union only has a coordination function. This is also the position of the GFCC, according to which the budgetary competence (*Budgethoheit*) is part of the reserved domain of national constitutions and must necessarily remain a competence of domestic parliaments.[198] For this reason EU institutions have no veto power on national budgets and are unable to replace Member State in the development of fiscal policies, lacking the competence (as well as the resources). In this perspective, being the jealous owners of fiscal sovereignty, it is up to the Member State to comply with the European rules, which ensure the fulfilment of stability in the euro area as a whole.

Even if national governments have most responsibilities in the field of fiscal consolidation it does not mean that the EU has no role to play. On the contrary, the EU Treaties and secondary law confer the Union some fundamental tasks, notably setting and updating rules, monitoring their compliance, giving recommendations and, where necessary, sanctioning governments, which are in a situation of consistent violation. The importance of EU institutions in the functioning of the economic governance has been confirmed by their involvement in the application of the international treaties stipulated beyond the EU legal order. For example, the TESM provides that the Commission and the ECB shall negotiate the MoU and supervise its compliance. At the same time, the TSCG involves the Commission and the CJEU in monitoring the application of the golden rule in national constitutional systems.

In conclusion, EU institutions play a fundamental role in the functioning of the economic governance, although the ownership of fiscal policies remains with national governments.

2.4.9.4 The Pursuit of the 'Stability of the Euro Area as a Whole' as a *sui generis* Objective

In the light of the analysis developed above, the goal of 'stability of the euro area as a whole' can be defined as a *sui generis* objective, in-between European and national objectives. The legal doctrine has distinguished the competence of economic coordination ex art. 5(1) TFEU from both shared competences, where both the Union and the Member States shall make decisions, and supporting competences, where the Union does not have the power of harmonisation of national legislations.[199] The qualification of the pursuit of 'stability of the euro area as a whole' as a *sui generis*

---

[198]See German Federal Constitutional Court, Judgment of 30 June 2009, [2 BvE 2/08] paras 252, 256.

[199]See Kotzur (2014), Article 5 TFEU, paras 1–2; Hinarejos (2012), p. 260.

objective means that the responsibility to ensure the obligations coming from this goal fall primarily on the shoulders of Member States, but the EU institutions are also involved in their fulfilment through a necessary contribution.[200] Indeed, even if the Union is unable to develop an autonomous action in the field of fiscal policy, the coordination, it exercises, over national decisions in the field of stabilisation policy and fiscal discipline is essential to ensure the fulfilment of 'stability of the euro area as a whole'. Only the Union indeed is in the position to identify the risks for stability from a European perspective, assess impartially the compliance of national economic policies with European rules, send warnings and (potentially) sanction Member States.

The qualification of the objective of 'stability of the euro area as a whole' as a *sui generis* objective is consistent with the principle of loyal cooperation ex art. 4 (3) TFEU, according to which the Union and the Member States shall, in full mutual respect, assist each other in the achievement of the objectives outlined in the EU Treaties. The pursuit of stability of the euro area as a whole is clearly one of them. For this reason, national governments and European institutions shall equally participate in their fulfilment, despite playing a different role. Member States shall exercise their budgetary policies by respecting fiscal rules and adopting stabilisation policies in the framework of the ESM; the Union shall instead exercise its power of coordination and supervision making sure that national governments manage their sovereign rights in a responsible way and take into consideration the pursuit of stability of the euro area as a whole.[201]

References

Adamski D (2012) National power games and structural failures in the European macroeconomic governance. Common Mark Law Rev 49:1319–1364

Adamski D (2016) Economic policy coordination as a game involving economic stability and national sovereignty. Eur Law J 22:180–203

Alcidi C, Giovannini A, Gros D (2012) Grexit: who would pay for it? CEPS Policy Brief, Issue No 272

Allemand F (2015) La dette en partage. Quelques réflexions juridiques sur le traitement de la dette publique en droit de l'Union européenne. Cahiers de droit européen 51:235–292

Apel E (2002) European Monetary Integration: 1958–2002. Routledge, London

Athanassiou P (2009) Withdrawal and Expulsion from the EU and EMU: Some Reflections, European Central Bank, Legal Working Paper Series No. 10, 2009

Beck G (2014) The Court of Justice, the Bundesverfassungsgericht and legal reasoning during the euro crisis: the rule of law as a fair-weather phenomenon. Eur Public Law 20:539–566

[200] In favour: Cisotta (2018), p. 36.

[201] The proposal of the Commission to incorporate the ESM in EU law on the basis of art. 352 TFEU (see *infra* Sect. 5.3.3.6) may suggest that the 'stability of the euro area as a whole' has been qualified as an objective of the Union. Indeed, one of the conditions for the application of the flexibility clause is the pursuit of one of the objectives set out in the EU Treaties. Cf. Cisotta (2015b), p. 289.

Becker U (2012) Artikel 3 EUV [Ziele der EU]. In: Schwarze J, Becker U, Hatje A (eds) EU Kommentar. Beck, München
Betbèze J (2016) The euro is irreversible, Robert Schuman Foundation, European Issues, No 380, 2nd February 2016
Borger V (2013) The ESM and the Court's predicament in Pringle. Ger Law J 14:113–140
Borger V (2016) Outright monetary transactions and the stability mandate of the ECB: Gauweiler. Common Mark Law Rev 53:39–196
Brunnermeier MK, James H, Landau J (2016) The euro and the battle of ideas. Princeton University Press, Princeton
Calliess C (2011–2012) From fiscal compact to fiscal union? New rules for the Eurozone. Camb Yearb Eur Legal Stud 14:101–117
Chemain R (2005) L'union économique et monétaire: aspects juridiques et institutionnels. Pedone, Paris
Cisotta R (2015a) Disciplina fiscale, stabilità finanziaria e solidarietà nell'Unione europea ai tempi della crisi: alcuni spunti ricostruttivi. Il Diritto dell'Unione Europea, 57–89
Cisotta R (2015b) Financial stability and the reconstruction of the EU legal order in the aftermath of the crisis. In: European Central Bank Legal Conference (2015) From Monetary Union to Banking Union, on the way to Capital Markets Union. New opportunities for European integration
Cisotta R (2018) L' Unione europea nel sistema delle relazioni economiche e monetarie globali. Un'indagine giuridica, Giappichelli, Torino
Cottarelli C, Guerguil M (2014) Introduction and overview. In: Cottarelli C, Guerguil M (eds) Designign a European Fiscal Union. Routledge, London
Cour-Thiman P, Winkler B (2014) The ECB's non-standard monetary measures: the role of institutional factors and financial structure. Oxf Rev Econ Policy:765–803
Dabrowski M (2012) The need for contingency planning: potential scenarios of Eurozone disintegration. CASE Network E-Briefs, Issue No 11
Dabrowski M (2015) Greece: from default to Grexit?, Bruegel Blog Post, 28th June 2015
Dammann J (2013) The right to leave the Eurozone. Tex Int Law J 48:125–155
De Grauwe P (2016) Economics of Monetary Union. Oxford University Press, Oxford
De Gregorio Merino A (2012) Legal developments in the economic and monetary union during the debt crisis. Common Mark Law Rev 49:1613–1645
De Lhoneux E, Vassilopoulos C (2013) The European stability mechanism before the Court of Justice of the European Union. Comment to the pringle case. Springer, London
De Witte B, Beukers T (2013) The Court of Justice approves the creation of the European stability mechanism outside the EU legal order: Pringle. Common Mark Law Rev 50:805–848
Draghi M (2013) Stable Euro, Strong Europe, Speech at the Wirtschaftstag, Berlin, 25th June 2013
Dutzler B (2003) The European system of central banks: an autonomous actor? Springer, Vienna
Espinosa M, Jobst A, Kahn C, Masaki K, Sole J (2010) Systemic Risk and the Redesign of Financial Regulation, IMF, Global Financial Stability Report (GFSR), April 2010
Estella A (2016) European Union bailouts and credibility: the constitutional dimension. Eur Public Law 22:507–540
Estella A (2018) Legal foundations of EU economic governance. Cambridge University Press, Cambridge
European Central Bank (1998) A Stability-Oriented Monetary Policy Strategy for the ESCB', Press Release, 13th October 1998
European Central Bank (2012) Financial Stability Review, December 2012
European Central Bank (2015) Real convergence in the euro area: evidence, theory and policy implications, ECB Economic Bulletin, Issue No 5, 30–45
European Commission Proposal for a Regulation (2017) On the establishment of the European Monetary Fund, 6th December 2017, COM/2017/0827 final
European Monetary Institute (1998) Convergence Report required by Article 109j of the Treaty establishing the European Community, 14th March 1998

Gaitanides C (2005) Das Recht der Europäischen Zentralbank. Mohr Siebeck, Tübingen
Geiger R (2014) Article 1 TEU [Framework, goals and bases of the European Union]. In: Geiger R, Khan D, Kotzur M (eds) European Union treaties: a commentary. Beck-Hart, Munich
Grimm H (2016) Zur Reform der Wirtschafts-und Wahrungsunion nach der Krise. Nomos, Baden-Baden
Gros D, Thygesen N (1998) European monetary integration. Longman, London
Häde U (2009) Die Wirtschafts- und Wahrungsunion im Vertrag von Lissabon. Europarecht, 200–218
Hansch HM (2002) Gesamtwirtschaftliche Stabilität als Verfassungsprinzip. Duncker & Humblot, Berlin
Herdergen J (1998) Price stability and budgetary restraints in the economic and monetary union. Common Mark Law Rev 35:9–32
Herrmann C (2010) Griechische Tragödie – der währungsverfassungsrechtliche Rahmen für die Rettung, den Austritt oder den Ausschluss von überschuldeten Staaten aus der Eurozone. Europäische Zeitschrift für Wirtschaftsrecht 21:413–418
Hinarejos A (2012) The euro area crisis and constitutional limits to fiscal integration. Camb Yearb Eur Legal Stud 14:243–268
Hinarejos A (2013) Fiscal federalism in the European Union: evolution and future choices for EMU. Common Mark Law Rev 50:1621–1642
Hinarejos A (2015) The euro area crisis in constitutional perspectives. Oxford University Press, Oxford
Hoffmeister H (2010–2011) To bail out or not to bail out? – legal aspects of the Greek crisis. Camb Yearb Eur Legal Stud 13:113–134
Ipsen HP (1972) Europäisches Gemeinschaftsrecht. Mohr Siebeck, Tübingen
Issing O (2001) Why price stability? In: First ECB Central Banking Conference, European Central Bank, Frankfurt, 2001
Ketterer L (2016) Zustimmungserfordernis beim Europaischen Stabilitaetsmechanismus. Mohr Siebeck, Tübingen
Kotzur M (2014) Article 5 TFEU [coordination of economic, employment and social policies]. In: Geiger R, Khan D, Kotzur M (eds) European Union treaties: a commentary. Beck-Hart, Munich
Larik J (2014) From specialty to a constitutional sense of purpose: on the changing role of the objectives of the European Union. Int Comp Law Q 63:935–962, 948
Larik J (2016) Foreign policy objectives in European constitutional law. Oxford University Press, Oxford
Lastra RM (2006) Legal foundations of international monetary stability. Oxford University Press, Oxford
Lastra RM (2013) Banking union and single market: conflict or companionship? Fordham Int Law J 41:1190–1224
Lo Schiavo G (2017) The role of financial stability in EU law and policy. Wolters Kluwers, Alphen aan den Rijn
Louis JV (2010) Guest editorial: the no-bailout clause and rescue packages. Common Mark Law Rev 47:971–986
Lupo Pasini F (2013) Economic stability and economic governance in the euro area. J Int Econ Law 16:211–256
Manzini P (2017) La solidarietà tra gli Stati membri della Unione Europea: un panorama 'costituzionale'. In: Manderieux L, Vellano M (eds) Etique globale, bonne gouvernance et droit international éeconomique. Giappichelli, Torino, pp 137–153
Moloney N (2014) European Banking Union: assessing its risks and resilience. Common Mark Law Rev 51:1609–1670
Munari F (2015) Da Pringle a Gauweiler: i tormentati anni dell'Unione monetaria e i loro effetti sull'ordinamento giuridico europeo. Il Diritto dell'Unione Europea, 723–755
Mundell R (1963) Capital mobility and stabilization policy under fixed and flexible exchange rates. Can J Econ 29:475–485

Neri S, Siviero S (2015) Low inflation in the Eurozone, 15th August 2015
Ohler C (2011) The European stability mechanism. The long road to financial stability in the Euro area. Ger Yearb Int Law 54:47–74
Pace LF (2018) Il regime giuridico dell'euro. La nascita dell'Unione economica e monetaria, la sua crisi e la risposta dell'Unione europea. Cacucci, Bari
Padoa-Schioppa T (2000) The road to Monetary Union in Europe. Oxford University Press, Oxford
Palm U (2017) Artikel 136 AEUV. In: Grabitz E, Hilf M, Nettesheim M (eds) Das Recht der Europäischen Union. Beck, München
Partsch P (1998) De quelques questions juridiques relatives au passage à la troisième phase de l'Union économique et monétaire et au fonctionnement de celle-ci. Revue Trimestrielle de Droit Européen 34:35–74
Peroni G (2012) La crisi dell'euro: limiti e rimedi dell'unione economica e monetaria. Giuffré, Milano
Peroni G (2015) Il recesso dall'Euro: una via percorribile, ma non auspicabile. Studi sull'Integrazione Europea 10:85–108
Petersen T, Böhmer M (2012) Economic impact of Southern European Member States exiting the Eurozone, Bartelsman Stiftung Policy Brief, Issue No 6
Piecha S (2016) Die Rettungsmassnahmen zugunten zahlungsunfahiger EU-Mitgliedstaaten. Peter Lang, Frankfurt am Main
Pilz S (2016) Die Europäische Stabilitätsmechanismus. Mohr Siebeck, Tübingen
Pipkorn J (1994) Legal arrangements in the treaty of Maastricht for the effectiveness of the economic and monetary union. Common Mark Law Rev 31:263–291
President of the European Central Bank (2012) Speech by Mario Draghi at the Global Investment Conference in London 26th July 2012
Rodrik D (2000) How far will international economic integration go? J Econ Perspect 14:177–186
Ruffert M (2011) The European debt crisis and European Union law. Common Mark Law Rev 48:1777–1806
Ruffert M (2016) Artikel 3 EUV [Ziele der EU]. In: Calliess C, Ruffert M (eds) EUV, AEUV, Kommentar. Beck, München
Schoenmaker D (2011) The financial Trilemma. Econ Lett 111:57–59
Schor A (1999) Economie politique de l'euro. La Documentation Française, Paris
Schwarz M (2014) A memorandum of misunderstanding – the doomed road of the European stability mechanism and a possible way out: enhanced cooperation. Common Mark Law Rev 51:389–424
Smits R (1997) The European Central Bank, institutional aspects. Wolters Kluwer, The Hague
Snell J (2016) The trilemma of European economic and monetary integration and its consequences. Eur Law J 22:157–179
Sommermann P (2013) Article 3 TEU [objectives of the EU]. In: Blanke H, Mangiameli S (eds) The treaty on European Union. A commentary. Springer, Berlin
Stadler R (1996) Der rechtliche Handlungsspielraum des Europäischen Systems der Zentralbanken. Nomos, Baden-Baden
Stiglitz JE (2016) The euro and its threat to the future of Europe. Allen Lane, New York
Terhechte JP (2017) Artikel 3 EUV [Ziele der EU]. In: Grabitz E, Hilf M, Nettesheim M (eds) Das Recht der Europäischen Union. Beck, München
Tufano ML (2002) Il principio del no bail-out nel diritto comunitario, Il Diritto dell'Unione Europea, 505–517
Tuori K, Tuori K (2014) The Eurozone crisis: a constitutional analysis. Cambridge University Press, Cambridge
Vallee S (2014) From mutual insurance to fiscal federalism. Int Econ 138:49–62
Wilsher D (2014) Law and the financial crisis: searching for Europe's new gold standard. Eur Law J 20:241–283
Ziller J (2015) Il Quadro Costituzionale della Governance Economica Europea. In: Porchia O (ed) Governance Economica Europea. Editoriale Scientifica, Napoli, pp 13–31

Chapter 3
The Instruments Available to Achieve Stability in the Euro Area: The Current Functioning of the Economic Governance

3.1 Introduction

The previous analysis explained how the outbreak of the sovereign debt crisis pushed Member States and European institutions to define a new stability paradigm centred around the preservation of the monetary union. Aside from the guiding principles outlined in art. 119 TFEU, namely open market economy, stable prices, sound public finances and a sustainable balance of payments, the 'stability of the euro area as a whole' has become the primary objective of economic policy that all existing instruments and procedures of the governance shall try to achieve. While Chap. 2 evocated the reforms implemented over the last few years in order to develop a definition of the objective of 'stability of the euro area a whole', the following analysis will adopt an inverted approach: it will explain more in detail the functioning of the economic governance in order to understand how the stability of the euro area is pursued in the current legal framework.

After having introduced the model of economic integration adopted in the EU Treaties, the Chapter will consider the current instruments available in the governance of the euro area, namely the preventive and corrective coordination procedures on national economic policies, the imposition of budgetary constraints in domestic law, the regulatory role of financial markets, the provision of conditional financial support in the framework of the ESM and the development of a European investment policy for encouraging economic recovery and structural reforms. The last paragraph will analyse the pursuit of the stability of the euro area as a whole in relation to the reform of the banking governance.

L. Lionello, *The Pursuit of Stability of the Euro Area as a Whole*, Studies in European Economic Law and Regulation 18,
https://doi.org/10.1007/978-3-030-28045-1_3

3.2 The Main Features of the Economic Union

Art. 121(1) TFEU qualifies national economic policies as a matter of 'common concern' for the Member States. This is a natural consequence of the interdependence consolidated in more than 60 years of economic integration, which has culminated in the introduction of the single currency. The economic union designed in the Maastricht Treaty complied with a *decentralised model of fiscal integration*, according to which fiscal sovereignty remains an exclusive competence of the Member States. Therefore, the economic and the monetary union maintain an asymmetric structure: while the Union has a single sovereignty in the field of monetary policy, every State is responsible for its own budgetary policy and debts. Despite many reforms, the 'Maastricht paradigm' has passed through the crisis substantially unscathed. The following analysis will summarise some of its distinctive features.

As the previous chapter already touched on,[1] the economic union is based on a *surveillance model*: Member States manage their own economic policies, but their choices shall be made within a common European framework, which limits their margin of action. Accordingly, EU institutions work as 'discipline enforcers' by applying some pre-agreed standards, which are supposed to pursue stability.[2] Evidently, once Member States refused to share fiscal sovereignty, surveillance was the only possible approach to contain the potential disorder and divergence within the monetary union coming from the independent management of budgetary policies in each country. Lacking the authority and the resources to develop a single European macroeconomic policy in charge of absorbing shocks and promoting convergence, stability in the Eurozone has been pursued by limiting the margin of discretion, Member States can exercise when they manage their own public finances and implement structural reforms.

The introduction of the European Stability Mechanism (ESM), which can provide conditional financial support to countries experiencing economic difficulties, does represent an innovation in a model, which would be otherwise exclusively centred on surveillance. For the first time, Member States accepted the use of common resources to help the absorption of economic shocks hitting national economies, which could destabilise the monetary union a whole. Despite improving the pursuit of stability by backing up surveillance mechanisms with a crisis management tool, the establishment of the ESM did not challenge the decentralised model of fiscal integration, as it consists of a purely intergovernmental instrument in the hands of the Member States. At the same time, it is important to stress that the conditionality policy applied by the ESM has become a new instrument of surveillance on national budgetary policies.

---

[1]See *supra* Sect. 2.3.5.

[2]See Hinarejos (2013), p. 1634.

Due to its compliance with the surveillance model, the functioning of the economic union qualifies as a form of *governance*.[3] The latter concept describes a political organisation characterised by the decentralisation of the decision-making process, which involves a network of different authorities, and the lack of genuine sovereign rights, as it is mainly based on non-binding instruments of coordination and political suasion.[4] In order to pursue its own objectives, a 'governance system' relies on the setup of common rules, the supervision of individual behaviours and the possible adoption of countermeasures in case of non-compliance. In this sense, the notion of 'governance' is distinguished from the one of 'government', which refers instead to a model of power administration based on the centralisation of sovereign rights in the hands of a common authority and the use of hard law instruments. Evidently, the asymmetry between the economic and the monetary union is reflected in the structural difference between the economic governance in the hands of the national governments and the European Commission, and the monetary government in the hands of the ECB.

Another important feature of the economic union is the *plurality of the legal basis*, on which it is based. Notably, the stratification of rules, amendments and reforms has been a consequence of the efforts of the Member States and EU institutions to achieve stability in the Eurozone, thus requiring a continuous and unfinished process of self-improvement. Title VIII TFEU provides an *ad hoc* Chapter on economic policy, which was introduced in the Maastricht Treaty and remained substantially untouched over the years.[5] The discipline has been developed by the Stability and Growth Pact (SGP) in 1997[6] and its later reforms in 2005,[7]

---

[3]In the White Paper of 2001 on the European Governance, the Commission defined governance as the 'rules, processes and behaviour that affect the way in which powers are exercised at European level, particularly as regards openness, participation, accountability, effectiveness and coherence'. European Commission Communication (2001), p. 8.

[4]On the concept of 'governance' see Marks et al. (1996), pp. 346–347; Scott and Trubek (2002) pp. 5–6; Shore (2011), p. 298.

[5]See Häde (2009).

[6]Regulation (EC) No 1466/97 of 7 July 1997 on the strengthening of the surveillance of budgetary positions and the surveillance and coordination of economic policies (1997) OJ L 209/1; Regulation (EC) No 1467/97 of 7 July 1997 on speeding up and clarifying the implementation of the excessive deficit procedure, (1997) OJ L 209/6.

[7]Council Regulation (EC) No 1055/05 of 27 June 2005 amending Regulation (EC) No 1466/97 on the strengthening of the surveillance of budgetary positions and the surveillance and coordination of economic policies, (2005) OJ L 174/1, and Council Regulation (EC) No 1056/05 of 27 June 2005 amending Regulation (EC) No 1467/97 on speeding up and clarifying the implementation of the excessive deficit procedure, (2005) OJ L 174/5.

2011[8] and 2013.[9] At the same time, after the outbreak of the sovereign debt crisis, Member States stipulated several intergovernmental agreements beyond the EU legal framework, introducing new rules under international law in the form of either soft law instruments or binding Treaties. This is the case in particular of the Euro Plus Pact,[10] the Treaty on the European Stability Mechanism (TESM)[11] and the Treaty on the Stability, the Coordination and the Governance (TSCG, commonly called Fiscal Compact).[12] Lastly, the case law of the CJEU and national courts has also played an important role in defining the sphere of action that the economic governance can exercise in concrete.

The following paragraphs will explain how the different tools currently available in the governance are contributing to the pursuit of the stability of the euro area as a whole. While Chap. 2 has recalled only the mechanisms and the procedures, which expressly pursue this goal (budgetary discipline and conditional financial support), the following analysis will also take into consideration those other instruments, which contribute to fulfil the same purpose, such as the banking governance and the development of a common investment strategy.

[8]Regulation (EU) No 1173/2011 on the effective enforcement of budgetary surveillance in the Euro area, (2011) OJ L 306/1; Regulation (EU) No 1174/2011 on enforcement action to correct excessive macroeconomic imbalances in the Euro area, (2011) OJ L 306/8; Regulation (EU) No 1175/2011 amending Regulation (EC) No 1466/97 on the strengthening of the surveillance of budgetary positions and the surveillance and coordination of economic policies, (2011) OJ L 306/12; Regulation (EU) No 1176/2011 on the prevention and correction of macroeconomic imbalances, (2011), L 306/25; Regulation (EU) No 1177/2011 amending Regulation (EU) No 1467/1997 on speeding up and clarifying the implementation of the excessive deficit procedure, (2011) OJ L 306/33; Council Directive 2011/85/EU on requirements for budgetary frameworks of the Member States, (2011) OJ L 306/41. Regulations have been adopted with the ordinary legislative procedure, except for Regulation (EU) No 1177/2011, which has been approved with the special legislative procedure. Regulation (EU) No 1173/2011 and Regulation (EU) No 1174/2011 apply only to the Eurozone Member States.

[9]Regulation (EU) No 472/2013 on the strengthening of economic and budgetary surveillance of Member States in the Euro area experiencing or threatened with serious difficulties with respect to their financial stability, (2013) OJ L 140/1; Regulation (EU) No 473/2013 on common provisions for monitoring and assessing draft budgetary plans and ensuring the correction of excessive deficit of the Member States in the Euro area, (2013) OJ L 140/11. They apply only to the Eurozone Member States.

[10]The Euro plus pact was signed on 11 March 2011 by the Eurozone countries and other six EU Member States (Bulgaria, Denmark, Latvia, Lithuania, Poland and Romania).

[11]The Treaty was signed on 2 March 2012 by all the Member States of the euro area.

[12]The EU Member States with the exception of the United Kingdom and the Czech Republic signed the Treaty on 2 March 2012.

3.3 Stability Through Coordination

3.3.1 Purpose

Art. 5(1) TFEU states that the Member States shall coordinate their economic policies within the Union and to this end the Council shall adopt measures. This provision qualifies economic coordination as a *sui generis* competence of the Union, according to which the Member States maintain their sovereign rights, but these are exercised in accordance with a framework defined at European level. While economic coordination does apply to all the Member States of the EU, art. 5(1) TFEU clarifies that specific provisions shall regard only those Member States whose currency is the euro.

The fundamental features of economic coordination are outlined in primary law, notably art. 121 and art. 126 TFEU. The discipline is then further specified in the SGP and a number of intergovernmental acts, including the Euro Plus Pact and the TSCG. These sources of law explain how economic coordination shapes national economic decisions on budgetary policy, structural reforms and the correction of macroeconomic imbalances.

The purpose of economic coordination is to avoid or end situations of current or potential *risk for the stability* of the Member States and of the euro area as a whole. Accordingly, the process of economic convergence between participating countries is not meant to achieve the same level of welfare and economic development, but rather avoiding those situation, which may undermine the pursuit of stability. This result is pursued essentially in two ways. First, economic coordination aims to foster budgetary solidity of the Eurozone countries, by banning the accumulation of excessive deficit and public debt. The latter are particularly noxious in a monetary union, because a fiscal mismanagement in one country increases the financial costs for all the others, as well as the inflation rate in the entire euro area. More importantly, weak public finances limit the margin of fiscal manoeuvre of a Member State to absorb economic shocks, thus making necessary either monetary financing by the central bank or last-minute bailouts by the other countries. Second, economic coordination pursues the stability of the euro area by demanding the correction of structural macroeconomic imbalances. These are negative trends, which are adversely affecting, or have the potential adversely to affect, the economic stability of a Member State or of the EMU, or of the Union as a whole.[13] An imbalance can be qualified as excessive when it is severe and is jeopardising or risks jeopardising the stability of the euro area as a whole.[14]

---

[13]Whereas (11) of Regulation (EU) No 1176/2011 refers to the 'economic stability' of the Member States and the euro area, while art. 2(1) to 'the proper functioning of the economy of a Member State or of the economic and monetary union, or of the Union as a whole.

[14]Art. 2(2) of Regulation (EU) No 1176/2011 refers to 'the proper functioning of the economic and monetary union.'

The contribution of economic coordination to the pursuit of the 'stability of the euro area as a whole' follows a double approach based on *prevention* and *correction*. Preventive procedures represent the physiological side of coordination, as they permanently apply to all countries. Their purpose is to avoid the occurrence of an endemic crisis within the Member States and put them in the conditions to absorb economic shocks. In this regard, European institutions define *ad hoc* guidelines and recommendations for each Member State and monitor their compliance. The latter supervision is not strictly technical, as the political institutions involved, namely the Commission and the Council, can enjoy some margin of flexibility in the interpretation and the application of European rules. The preventive approach to coordination was initially conceived as a form of peer review system based on political pressure. After the crisis, however, new repressive tools, in the form of semi-automatic economic sanctions, were introduced to improve compliance with rules by the Member States. Corrective procedures represent instead an exceptional form of coordination, which intervenes only when a pathological situation has consolidated, in the sense that a Member State has consistently violated European rules on economic coordination, thus jeopardising its own stability and, consequently, the stability of the euro area as a whole. Evidently, the purpose of correction is to end a possible source of destabilisation that the preventive side of coordination has not been able to avoid. This is ensured through a stricter political pressure from EU institutions on national authorities and the possible application of economic sanctions.

Coordination is primarily managed by the Commission and the Council. The first institution monitors the economic policies of the Member States and takes action in case of non-compliance with European rules. The Council is instead in charge of making fundamental decisions regarding the enforcement of rules and the adoption of countermeasures. Over the last few years, two legal trends have modified the institutional balance within the economic union. First, the European Council has developed a political leadership for both the implementation of reforms and the solution of specific emergencies. Second, the Member States of the euro area have set up a separate institutional framework aside from the official one defined in the EU Treaties. The Eurogroup has become a semi-formal body, which reunites the Ministers of Finance of the euro area and coordinates their position before the official meetings of the Ecofin Council.[15] At the same time, since 2010 the Heads of State or Government of the euro area have started meeting regularly to discuss the most important political issues regarding the sovereign debt crisis. The Fiscal Compact has recognised this practice, providing for the creation of a Euro Summit.[16]

---

[15]The EU Treaties refer to the Eurogroup in art. 137 TFEU. Protocol No 14 on the Eurogroup foresees the election of a stable President every two and half years with a renewable mandate and stresses the necessity of stronger cooperation within the Eurozone.

[16]Art. 12 TSCG states that the Heads of State or Government of the contracting parties of the Eurozone shall meet informally together with the President of the European Commission and, if invited, the President of the ECB.

3.3.2 Preventive Arm

Preventive coordination aims to avoid the occurrence of both sources of instability mentioned above: unsound public finances and macroeconomic imbalances.

Sound public finances are pursued through a budgetary discipline outlined in art. 121 TFEU and further regulated by Regulation (EC) No 1466/97.[17] On initiative of the Commission and with the participation of the European Council, the Council adopts and periodically updates broad economic policy guidelines (BEPGs), providing economic goals for every Member State and in particular a Medium-term objective (MTO) towards a balanced budget.[18] Compliance with the BEPGs is ensured through the multilateral surveillance procedure (MSP). Every year Member States submit to the Commission a stability programme,[19] explaining their budgetary developments,[20] as well as a national reform programme, accounting for the other macroeconomic policies. Accordingly, the European Commission consider whether Member States are respecting the BEPGs and in particular the adjustment path towards the MTO. In case of a significant deviation,[21] after the Commission has addressed an early warning to the concerned Member States, the Council can recommend, on initiative by the Commission, to take appropriate action within a certain timeframe and make this recommendation public. The latter decision has the purpose to impose some form of penalty to the concerned Member State by stimulating higher interest rates on its sovereign bonds.

In regard to the following steps of the MSP, the Six Pack introduced two significant reforms. First, the decision-making process has shifted from standard

---

[17]According to art. 1 the purpose of the regulation is 'to prevent, at an early stage, the occurrence of excessive general government deficits and to promote the surveillance and coordination of economic policies thereby supporting the achievement of the Union's objectives for growth and employment'.

[18]The SGP demands a structural deficit of maximum 1% GDP as MTO, while the Fiscal Compact has tightened this parameter up to 0.5% of GDP except for the countries presenting a debt level below 60% and where risks in terms of long-term sustainability of public finances are low. The adjustment path toward the MTO shall pursue the annual improvement of its cyclically-adjusted balance with 0.5% of GDP as a benchmark, but if the country faces with a debt level exceeding 60% of GDP or general risks of debt sustainability, the improvement can be higher. Evidently, the tightening of budgetary target in the preventive arm of coordination aims to provide Member States with a safety margin of manoeuvre to deal with normal cyclical fluctuations and keep the government deficit within the reference value of 3% of GDP, while considering also the need for public investment. The MTO shall be updated every 3 years. See art. 2a and art. 5(1) of Regulation (EC) No 1466/1997.

[19]Similarly, Member States not participating in the euro area submit a convergence programme, which also takes into consideration price and exchange rate stability, in order to verify if they present the conditions to adopt the single currency.

[20]Member States taking part in the Euro Plus Pact shall also explain their progress in the fulfilment of four specific targets: competitiveness and employment, the stability of financial market, the sustainability of public finances and coordination of fiscal policies.

[21]The deviation shall be considered significant in accordance with the criteria outlined in art. 6(3) of Regulation (EC) No 1466/1997.

qualified majority voting to reverse majority voting (RMV). Accordingly, the Commission shall recommend the Council to pass a decision confirming a persistent situation of non-compliance in the concerned Member State by standard qualified majority voting; if the latter is not taken, after 1 month, the Commission may recommend the Council to take the same decision, which this time is adopted unless the simple majority does not reject it within 10 days (reverse simple majority voting or RSMV).[22] Second, after having adopted the decision establishing that a Member State failed to take appropriate action, the Council shall immediately impose economic sanctions in the form of interest-bearing deposits.[23] The latter are adopted also in accordance with a reverse qualified majority voting (RQMV), thus becoming *de facto* semi-automatic.[24] Evidently, the aim of the RMV is to reduce the margin of discretion of the Council, in particular for the adoption of those decisions that it may be more 'unwilling' to take.

Macroeconomic imbalances are prevented in accordance with the Macroeconomic Imbalances Procedure (MIP) outlined in Regulation (EU) No 1176/2011, which was introduced after the outbreak of the sovereign debt crisis in accordance with art. 121(6) TFEU. Unlike excessive deficit and debt, macroeconomic imbalances can't be quantified in one precise limit, but must be contextualised in relation to the economic situation of each country. Regulation (EU) No 1176/2011 presents a scoreboard with a set of indicators, which shall help the identification of imbalances.[25] At the end of the previous year, the Commission develops an Alert Mechanism Report (AMR) analysing the general economic situation in the EU and the euro area and considering imbalances within the Member States.[26] After the Council and the Eurogroup have discussed the AMR, the Commission shall undertake 'In-Depth Reviews' (IDRs) for each Member State, which may be

---

[22]Only the euro area Member States can participate in the voting except for the country concerned by the procedure.

[23]See art. 4 of Regulation (EU) No 1173/2011. The latter was adopted on the basis of art. 121(6) and art. 136(1) TFEU.

[24]This decision shall be deemed to be adopted by the Council unless it decides by a qualified majority to reject the Commission's recommendation within 10 days of the Commission's adoption thereof. The interest-bearing deposit amounts to 0.2% of the Member State GDP in the preceding year. The Council, acting by a qualified majority, may amend the Commission's recommendation and adopt the text so amended as a Council decision.

[25]Imbalances are divided in three groups. External Imbalances/Competitiveness Indicators (current account balance as percent of GDP; net international investment position as percent of GDP; export market shares; nominal unit labour cost; real effective exchange rates based on HICP/CPI deflators, relative to 41 other industrial countries); Internal Imbalances Indicators (private sector debt (consolidated) in % of GDP; year-on-year changes in house prices relative to a Eurostat consumption deflator; credit flow (consolidated); general government sector debt in % of GDP with a threshold of 60%; total financial sector liabilities (non-consolidated); unemployment rate), Employment Indicators (activity rate; long-term unemployment rate; youth unemployment rate).

[26]In accordance with art. 3(2) of Regulation (EU) No 1176/2011, the Commission shall take into consideration 'if necessary, on other relevant economic and financial indicators when assessing the evolution of imbalances'.

affected by imbalances, by specifying whether the latter are standard or excessive. On the basis of the IDRs, the Council on recommendation from the Commission may address the necessary recommendations to the concerned governments and make them public.

In order to improve efficiency, the Six Pack and the Two Pack reforms have organised the existing preventive procedures of economic coordination in one legal framework, which shall continuously assist Member States throughout the year for the adoption of national macroeconomic policy. The process can be divided more precisely in two parts.

The *European Semester* has the purpose to synchronise surveillance on budgetary, structural and employment policies concentrating it in the first part of the year before national parliaments adopt their budgets.[27] The *preparatory phase* is based on the analysis of the situation consolidated in the previous year: in November the European Commission adopts both the Annual Growth Survey (AGS) and the Alert Mechanism Report (AMR), and drafts a recommendation on the economic policy of the euro area.[28] At the beginning of the year, during the *policy guidance phase*, the Council studies these documents, adopts conclusions and passes the recommendation for the euro area, while the European Parliament provides an opinion on employment guidelines. In March, the Commission publishes a country-specific report for all Member States, which is functional to the correction of macroeconomic imbalances. On the basis of the AGS and the conclusions of the Council, the European Council can then provide guidelines for the drafting of the stability programmes and the national reform programmes. In the *country-specific phase*, governments submit these documents to the Commission by the end of April, specifying the adjustment path towards the MTO and the correction of macroeconomic imbalances. Based on the assessment and the proposals by the Commission, the Council in June discusses country-specific recommendations (CSRs) and agrees on their final version. Taking into consideration the conclusions of the European Council in June, the Council approves the CSRs in July and invite the Member States to comply with them.

The second part of the year consists of the *national semester* (or *implementation phase*), when domestic parliament adopts the budgetary law in accordance with the programmes agreed at European level.[29] Member States shall submit to the Commission and the Eurogroup a draft budgetary plan[30] for the forthcoming year by

---

[27]The European Semester was introduced by Regulation (EU) No 1175/2011 amending Regulation (EC) No 1466/97 on multilateral surveillance. For a deeper analysis of the functioning of the European Semester see Costamagna (2015).

[28]On this basis, it can decide to conduct IDRs and passes draft recommendation on the economic policy of the euro area.

[29]The procedure is disciplined by Regulation (EU) No 473/2013.

[30]The draft budgetary plan shall contain a set of information for the forthcoming year specified in art. 6(3) of Regulation (EU) No 473/2013. On 1 July 2013, the European Commission has published the 'Guidelines on the format and content of draft budgetary plans, economic partnership programmes and debt issuance reports'.

15 October. The latter is made public and the Commission shall provide an assessment by 30 November.[31] In the event gross violations of the budgetary policy obligations come to light from the examination, the Commission shall issue an opinion demanding a revision of the draft and explaining publicly the reasons behind this request.[32] After the revised draft budgetary plan has been submitted, the Commission shall adopt a new opinion, which is made public and presented to the Eurogroup together with an overall assessment of the budgetary situation and prospects in the euro area as a whole.[33] The Eurogroup shall then discuss these opinions and evaluations and make the results of these discussions public, where appropriate. Evidently, in the event a Member State does not comply with the opinions of the Commission, European institutions cannot exercise a veto power on the national budget. The latter is a logical consequence of the principle of conferral, according to which economic policy remains a competence of Member States. If violation persists, EU institutions can only move to the corrective side of coordination.

3.3.3 Corrective Arm

The purpose of the corrective arm of coordination is to end a pathological source of instability in the form of either excessive indebtedness or excessive macroeconomic imbalance.

The *excessive deficit procedure* (EDP) is outlined in art. 126 TFEU and developed by the Protocol on the excessive deficit, Regulation (EC) No 479/09 on the application of the Protocol on the excessive deficit,[34] Regulation (EC) No 1467/1997 and Regulation (EU) No 473/2013. The EDP is activated in case of violation of one of the two stability criteria: public deficit and public debt.[35] The *deficit criterion* consists of the 3% for the ratio of the planned or actual government deficit to gross

[31]See art. 7 of Regulation (EU) No 473/2013.

[32]This happens in exceptional cases, when after consulting the Member State concerned within 1 week of submission of the draft budgetary plan, the Commission identifies particularly serious non-compliance with the budgetary policy obligations laid down in the SGP.

[33]At the request of the parliament of the Member State concerned or of the European Parliament, the Commission shall present its opinion to the parliament making the request.

[34]Regulation (EC) No 479/2009 of 25 May 2009 on the application of the Protocol on the excessive deficit procedure annexed to the Treaty establishing the European Community, (2009) OJ L 145/1.

[35]The introduction of thresholds aims to protect the autonomy of Member States in the management of their fiscal sovereign rights: as long as they don't violate the stability criteria, national parliaments can make their own choices of budgetary policy. Cloos et al. (1993), p. 193. At the same time, the quantification of these thresholds in numerical values is supposed to facilitate their assessment. Allemand et al. (2016), p. 121.

domestic product at market prices.[36] The threshold does not consist of an absolute parameter. European institutions shall verify whether deficit has declined substantially and continuously reaching a level close to the reference value also in the light of the adjustment path towards the MTO, as defined in the prevention arm of coordination. Furthermore, the EDP is not activated when the excessive deficit is only exceptional and temporary. In this regard, Regulation (EC) No 1467/97 identifies two possible cases: an unusual event outside the control of the State, which has a major impact on its financial position, and a severe economic downturn for the euro area or the Union as a whole.[37] The *public debt criterion* consists of the 60% for the ratio of government debt to gross domestic product at market prices.[38] At the same time, there is no violation if the level of debt is higher, but Member States are sufficiently diminishing it and approaching the reference value at a satisfactory pace. After the outbreak of the sovereign debt crisis, the pace for the reduction of public debt has been specified: every year it shall decline by 1/20 of the differential between the 60% debt ceiling and the actual level of debt, averaged over a three-year period.[39] Also in this case, however, rules have been interpreted with indulgence. Evidently, what matters in the eyes of the EU institutions is the sustainability of public finances, meaning the ability of national governments to finance themselves in the long term and repay their debts. Therefore, rather than demanding a static compliance with the parameters, it is more important to look at the dynamics of public finances: if the level of public spending and debt is on a decreasing trajectory, EU institutions shall not activate an EDP.[40]

The EDP is developed in three stages.[41] First, the Commission monitors whether Member States respect the stability criteria and draws out a report in case an

---

[36]The containment of current public spending is already a target of the preventive arm of coordination. Regulation (EC) No 1466/1997 demands Member States to present a structural deficit within 1% of GDP. See art. 2a Regulation (EC) No 1466/1997, as amended by Regulation (EU) No 1175/2011.

[37]The first situation consists normally of natural disasters or terrorist attack that art. 122(2) TFEU already takes into consideration for the activation of the solidarity clause. An economic downturn is considered instead exceptional when the annual GDP volume growth rate is negative or the annual GDP volume growth is very low relative to its potential during a protracted period of time. The relevant factors to be considered in the assessment of the excessive deficit are specified in art. 2(3) of Regulation (EC) No 1467/1997.

[38]The values of 3% for deficit and 60% for public debt were chosen because they were the average of level, Member States presented when the Protocol was drafted. Cf. De Grauwe (2016), pp. 148–149.

[39]See art. 2 (1a) Regulation (EC) No 1467/1997 as amended by Regulation (EU) No 1177/2011 and art. 4 TSCG. For a Member State that is subject to an EDP and for a period of 3 years from the correction of the excessive deficit, the requirement shall be considered fulfilled if it makes sufficient progress towards compliance as assessed in the opinion adopted by the Council on its stability programme.

[40]Cf. Allemand et al. (2016), p. 123.

[41]Decisions are adopted by majority vote without the participation of the Member State concerned. The voting rights of States that did not adopt the euro are suspended for the adoption of recommendations to those members whose currency is the euro.

excessive deficit or debt exists or arises. In the second stage, the Council, on initiative of the Commission[42] and voting by qualified majority opens the procedure towards the Member State presenting an excessive deficit and recommends its correction within a specific deadline. Since the introduction of the Six Pack, the Council can also decide by reversed qualified majority voting (RQMV)[43] to charge a Member State of the euro area with a non-interest-bearing deposit amounting to 0.2% of its GDP in the preceding year.[44] If no effective action is taken to correct an excessive deficit or debt, the Council may decide by qualified majority on initiative from the Commission to make its recommendations public, thus triggering a shaming effect from the markets and the public opinion. Furthermore, the Council can decide by RQMV to turn the deposit previously lodged into a fine or impose a new one. In the last stage,[45] the Council, following recommendations from the Commission, gives notice to the Member State to take, within a specified time period, the necessary measures to reduce the level of indebtedness. This request is legally binding. In the event the government still fails to comply, the Council may decide by standard qualified majority, on recommendation from the Commission, to apply economic sanctions.[46] Finally, it is worth remembering that art. 7 TSCG introduces an important innovation in the EDP: in order to ease the application of the corrective arm of coordination, the RQMV shall apply for the adoption of all decisions under the EDP regarding the Eurozone Member States.[47]

In order to facilitate the correction of excessive deficit, the Fiscal Compact and the Regulation (EU) No 473/2013 foresee the setup of an economic partnership between European institutions and countries subject to the EDP. The purpose of the partnership is to prioritise the necessary structural reforms to ensure a sustainable

---

[42]The Council decides, on a proposal from the Commission, whether an excessive deficit exists and recommends the concerned Member State, on a recommendation from the Commission, to implement a correction.

[43]Qualified majority is calculated ex art. 238(3)b TFEU.

[44]This decision can be taken when (i) a Member State has been lodged an interest-bearing deposit with the Commission in accordance with the preventive arm of coordination; (ii) where the Commission has identified particularly serious non-compliance with the budgetary policy obligations laid down in the SGP. See art. 5 of Reg. (EU) No. 1173/2011.

[45]This stage applies only to the Member States of the euro area.

[46]The Council can (i) require the Member State to publish additional information before issuing bonds and securities, (ii) invite the EIB to reconsider its lending policy towards the country, (iii) require the government to make a non-interest-bearing deposit of an appropriate size until the excessive deficit has been corrected, which will become a fine if 2 years after the decision the excessive deficit has not been corrected. In order to reduce the margin of discretion of the Council, applicable fines have been quantified in a fixed value of 0.2% of national GDP plus a variable value of 1/10 of the gap from the reference value up to 0.5% of national GDP. Fines applying to Eurozone Member States shall be paid to the ESM. In case of correction of the excessive deficit, the Council abrogates, on recommendation from the Commission, some or all of its decisions taken in advance, including sanctions. If the Council has previously made its recommendations public, it shall make a public statement that the excessive deficit in the Member State concerned has been corrected.

[47]Like in Regulation (EU) No 1173/2011, the RMV under art. 7 TSCG applies only to situations of excessive deficit, not excessive debt. See Calliess (2012), p. 108.

and long-term containment of public deficit. The introduction of these new obligations in the framework of the EDP has the merit of reducing the margin of discretion Member States can exercise in the process of budgetary consolidation and the adoption of structural reforms. The purpose is evidently to replace obligations of result, notably the compliance with numeric thresholds, with obligations of conduct, such as the implementation of specific reforms.

Finally, the *Excessive Imbalance Procedure* is disciplined by Regulation (EU) No 1176/2011 and Regulation (EU) No 1174/2011, which were adopted in accordance with art. 121(6) TFEU.[48] The latter represents the possible continuation of the MIP. In the event no sufficient action being taken to tackle the excessive imbalances in the framework of the preventive arm of coordination, the Council, on initiative from the Commission, may pass a recommendation acknowledging the situation of non-compliance and demanding Member States submit a corrective action plan (CAP). The Commission and the Council shall evaluate the CAP and decide whether to endorse it or request the submission of a new one. On recommendation from the Commission, the Council will then adopt a recommendation listing the required corrective actions and the deadlines for taking them. The Commission monitors the implementation of the corrections and, for this purpose, the concerned Member State shall regularly present reports. When it considers that the Member State has not taken sufficient corrective actions, the Council, on a recommendation from the Commission, shall acknowledge the existence of a situation of non-compliance and recommend corrections. If no action is taken, the Council, on recommendation from the Commission, shall eventually apply economic sanctions in the form of an interest-bearing deposit or a fine.[49] Both decisions are taken by RQMV.[50]

3.4 Stability Through the Regulatory Role of the Financial Markets

3.4.1 Purpose

The adoption of a decentralised model of fiscal integration does not only have the purpose of protecting national sovereignty, but also of entrusting financial markets with budgetary discipline. According to the drafters of the Maastricht Treaty, as Member States need to finance themselves on the bonds market, they are encouraged

[48]Regulation (EU) No 1174/2011 was introduced also on the basis of art. 136 TFEU.

[49]Fines can be imposed, in two cases: (a) after the CAP has been qualified insufficient for two successive times, the Council still considers that the Member State has submitted an insufficient CAP; (b) the Council decides for two successive times in the same imbalance procedure that a Member States has not complied with the recommendation listing the corrective actions.

[50]The interest-bearing deposit or the annual fine recommended by the Commission shall be 0.1% of the GDP in the preceding year of the Member State concerned.

to pursue sound fiscal policies. This happens because investors around the world purchase the sovereign bonds of a Member State by requesting an interest rate, which is proportional to the safety of the asset, meaning the macroeconomic stability of the issuing country.[51] While governments presenting solid public finances will easily get credit, a riskier investment in an excessively indebted country will be accepted only in return for a higher interest rate. In this way, financial markets represent a counter-power to the fiscal sovereignty of Member States, by limiting their factual ability to excess public spending.[52]

3.4.2 Market Regulation

The correct functioning of market regulation is not automatic. The drafters of the Maastricht Treaty knew that market perceptions on the credit-worthiness of official borrowers can be easily manipulated and their reaction may result too slow and weak or too sudden and disruptive.[53] Consequently, the EU Treaties have introduced a number of rules, which shall avoid distortion in the assessment of countries' stability and encourage a rational behaviour of financial markets.

First, Member States shall finance themselves at market conditions without using undue privileges. For this purpose, art. 123 TFEU forbids the ECB and NCBs to provide overdraft facilities or any other type of credit facility in favour of national governments. This norm prevents the monetisation of public deficit, which is a practice, Member States use to artificially finance their debt. The norm is strictly formulated and self-executing in the national legal system. The possibility for the ECB to operate on the secondary market shall not be used to bypass the prohibition of art. 123 TFEU, financing indirectly Member States' debt.[54] At the same time, art. 124 TFEU precludes also financial institutions from providing any measure, not based on prudential considerations, establishing privileged access to Member States.

Second, national governments shall be able to finance themselves counting on their own forces and credibility, without relying on the backstop of other members of the monetary union. For this purpose, art. 125 TFEU introduces the no bail-out principle, according to which every country is responsible for its own obligations and neither the Union, nor other Member States are liable for its commitments. The no bailout clause is strictly formulated and applies to all obligations assumed by the Member States. The introduction of this provision intends to warn financial markets

[51]Delors 'Report on Economic and Monetary Union in the European Community', 17 April 1989, p. 20.

[52]Allemand et al. (2016), p. 114.

[53]Delors 'Report on Economic and Monetary Union in the European Community', 17 April 1989, p. 20.

[54]See Whereas (7) Council Regulation (EC) No 3603/93 of 13 December 1993 specifying definitions for the application of the prohibitions referred to in Articles [123 TFEU] and [125(1) TFEU], (1993) OJ L 332/1.

that, regardless of the strong economic tights within the EMU, countries will have to pay their own debts without external support, thus encouraging investors to assess the trustworthiness of each borrower. In this regard, it is important to recall that several coordination procedures foresee the publication of EU recommendations confirming a situation of non-compliance as a form of 'sanction' against Member States violating EU rules.[55] The consequence of this measure should be to warn financial markets that the country concerned has not been able to pursue sound public finances or correct macroeconomic imbalances, thus stimulating higher interest rates on its sovereign debt (shaming effect). Art. 125, as well as art. 123 and art. 124 TFEU are directly applicable.[56] In the event of a breach, the Commission may start an infringement proceeding under art. 258 TFEU.

3.4.3 Debt Restructuration

While the regulatory role of financial markets should essentially play a preventive function and discourage Member States from endorsing lax budgetary policies, private investors can also intervene *ex post* in the event a country has developed an unsustainable fiscal position and its debt needs to be restructured. This is exactly what happened in Greece in March 2012, when bondholders agreed a haircut on their credit with the Hellenic government through an exchange as old bonds for new ones with lower principal and interest rate and longer maturity.[57] The restructuration was eased by the fact that the majority of bonds were governed by Greek law, and the Hellenic Parliament could simply introduce a retroactive law in February 2012[58] to introduce CACs allowing debt restructuration by majority of the bondholders.[59] In the light of this experience, the TESM introduced a new regime regarding debt restructuration in the euro area. Two provisions should be recalled in this regard.

First, art. 12(3) TESM states that Member States shall issue as of 1 January 2013 sovereign bonds with more than 1 year of maturity provided with common 'collective action clauses' (standardised euro-CACs). The latter have been formulated following a model developed by the Sub-Committee of the Economic and Financial Committee in 2011 in consultation with market stakeholders.[60] The main innovation of the euro-CACs is the authorisation to amend the contractual terms of the loan by

[55]See art. 121(4) TFEU and art. 126(8) TFEU.

[56]See Whereas (1) Council Regulation (EC) No 3603/93. Cf. Häde (2016), Artikel 125 AEUV, para 2; Bandilla (2017), Artikel 25 AEUV, para. 5.

[57]See Hofmann (2013), p. 552. Notwithstanding the important adjustments and reforms adopted over the last few years, the sustainability of Greek public finances is still debated. Zettelmeyer (2018), p. 71.

[58]Greek Bondholder Act, 4050/12, 23 February 2012.

[59]Martinelli (2016), pp. 2–3.

[60]The Sub-committee was composed of members from the Member States, the European Commission, the ECB, the EIB and the ESM.

qualified majority of the bondholders.[61] The purpose of the reform is to reduce the bargaining power of 'holdouts' and making debt restructuration easier.[62]

Second, art. 13(1)(b) TESM provides that the European Commission, in liaison with the ECB, shall verify the sustainability of public debt. Wherever appropriate and possible, such an assessment is expected to be conducted together with the IMF.[63] Only on the basis of this evaluation, the Board of Governors of the ESM may decide to grant, in principle, stability support to the Member concerned in the form of a financial assistance facility. In the event the fiscal position of the country was considered unsustainable, the Council of Governors can request to implement a process of partial debt restructuration before agreeing on the concession of economic support.

3.5 Stability Through Self-Limitation of National Budgetary Sovereignty

3.5.1 Purpose

While economic coordination and market discipline were initially the exclusive instruments to foster sound public finances in the Member States, the outbreak of the sovereign debt crisis convinced EU institutions and national governments to pursue new ways to achieve budgetary stability. For this reason, the Six Pack and the TSCG introduced the legal obligation for the Member States of the euro area to provide in their national legal systems numerical fiscal rules, setting specific targets of budgetary policy. The obligation evidently aims to shift the ownership of budgetary surveillance from European to domestic authorities. In this way, the Council and the Commission are no longer the exclusive institutions in charge of monitoring the presence of excessive deficit in the Member States. National governments, parliaments and courts share with them this responsibility and are called to create their own mechanisms of supervision and correction. Evidently, Member States and EU institutions hoped that the introduction of numerical fiscal rules in the national legal order would force Member States to respect budgetary discipline, by limiting *ab initio* their ability to excess public spending.

---

[61]More precisely the 'double-limb CACs' require two separate majorities to approve a reform of the bond terms: one at the level of each 'series' of bond and one at the level of all 'series' combined.

[62]In the event holdouts refuse to take part in the restructuring, there are two options. Either the state refuses to pay the holdouts, thus accepting the possibility of protracted legal battles and future restriction to issue debt, or it can repay them, thus making more difficult the restoration of debt sustainability. Zettelmeyer (2018), p. 71. The reform of bond obligations by majority represents a derogation to the principle of consent of contract law. Hofmann (2013), p. 548.

[63]On the coordination of the ESM with the IMF see Adinolfi (2013), p. 10.

3.5.2 Application

The introduction of budgetary constraints in national law has been a priority for the Member States since the beginning of the sovereign debt crisis. The Euro Plus Pact has forced national governments to translate EU fiscal rules, as set out in SGP, into national legislation. Directive 2011/85/EU turned this provision into a legal obligation, while Regulation (EU) No 1175/2011 specified the value of the constraint by demanding a structural deficit within 1% of GDP. Despite the innovative profile of these provisions, the Six Pack left a significant margin of discretion to national legislators regarding both the formulation of the fiscal rules, the source of law in which they are incorporated, as well as the introduction of exceptions.[64] The Fiscal Compact has filled some of these deficits.

Art. 3(1) TSCG obliges the contracting parties to introduce in their national legal system a balanced budget rule, meaning that the budgetary position of the general government of the contracting parties shall be balanced or in surplus. This rule shall be deemed to be respected if the Member State presents an annual structural budget deficit in relation to its country's specific MTO under 0.5% of GDP. Art. 3(2) TSCG specifies that Member States shall enshrine the balanced budget rule in their national legal order 'through provisions of binding force and permanent character, preferably constitutional,[65] or otherwise guaranteed to be fully respected and adhered to throughout the national budgetary processes'. The golden rule shall therefore be implemented in a supra-legislative source of law, which is able to bind the national legislature. This prescription is extremely important because it creates an effective limit of budgetary autonomy for the Member States.

The golden rule outlined in art. 3(1) TSCG is not an absolute obligation, but provides for some element of flexibility.[66] First, Member States presenting a public debt under 60% of their GDP are allowed to reach a maximum structural deficit of 1%, instead of 0.5%, according to the principle that consolidation efforts shall be proportional to the current state of public finances. Second, the 'rapid convergence towards' the MTO shall respect a timeframe proposed by the Commission, which shall take into account the 'sustainability risks' and a general assessment of the structural balance. Third, deviations from the golden rule are admissible in the event of exceptional circumstances (escape clause).[67] Finally, the automatic correction

---

[64] Allemand et al. (2016), p. 139.

[65] This is an unusual provision for an international treaty, which normally does not specify how international obligation should be implemented in domestic law. See Ruotolo (2012), p. 453.

[66] The provision of some flexibility complies with the fact than Member States remain in charge of fiscal sovereignty. See De Sadeleer (2012), pp. 371–372; Martucci (2012) p. 728.

[67] The problem is that neither the TSCG, nor EU law provides a definition of 'unusual event outside the State control', 'major impact on the financial position of the general government' or 'fiscal sustainability in the medium term'. As a consequence, there is more margin of discretion. See Peers (2012), p. 417.

mechanism shall intervene only in the event of significant deviation from the thresholds.[68]

The shift in the ownership of budgetary surveillance from European to national authorities, is completed by the obligation for Member States to set up surveillance procedure on the compliance with fiscal rules. Art. 3(1)(e) of the Fiscal Compact and art. 5 of Regulation (EU) No 473/2013 demand Member States put in place at national level an automatic correction mechanism, which shall intervene in the event of significant deviations from the MTO or adjustment path towards it. Independent fiscal institutions (IFIs) shall be set up with the task of monitoring compliance with numerical fiscal rules at national level and activate the correction mechanism, where necessary. The mechanism shall be established in a supra-legislative source of law and take fully into account European budgetary rules. The principle 'comply or explain' should make sure national governments do not avoid amending their budgetary policies, where necessary. In order to strengthen the surveillance from the Commission and the efforts of Member States to comply with the numerical fiscal rules, the Commission set up in 2015 an independent advisory body on fiscal matters, the European Fiscal Board.[69] While it does not implement policies, the Board shall contribute, in an advisory capacity, to the practice of the Commission's functions in the multilateral fiscal surveillance as far as the euro area is concerned. In particular, it can evaluate the implementation of EU fiscal rules, cooperate with national IFIs, advise the Commission on the fiscal stance appropriate for the euro area as a whole and, upon request, provide advice.

In order to ensure the effective compliance by the Member States, the Fiscal Compact commits the CJEU to supervise the implementation of the golden rule and the automatic correction mechanism within the domestic legal order. The competence of the Court to judge on the application of the TSCG, which is an international agreement external to the EU legal framework, is founded on the arbitration clause ex art. 273 TFEU. The European Commission shall present in due time a report on the measures adopted by each Member State to comply with the obligation ex art. 3(2) TSCG.[70] In the event the Commission or another country notices a breach, the matter shall be brought to the Court, which will decide whether the concerned country has violated the TSCG. In this case, the Court will adopt the necessary measures to force compliance with the judgment within a specific deadline. If the Court finds that the Member State concerned has not complied with its judgment, it

---

[68]Provided that the Fiscal Compact does not specify what 'significant' means, it should apply the definition given by art. 6(3) of Regulation (EC) No 1466/97.

[69]Commission Decision (EU) 2015/1937 of 21 October 2015 establishing an independent advisory European Fiscal Board, (2015), OJ L 282/37.

[70]This agreement has been necessary as art. 273 TFEU allows only Member States and not the Commission to bring a dispute before the CJEU, making the application of the norm more difficult because of the reluctance of national governments to act against their peers. In the event the Commission's report confirms a situation of non-compliance, one or more Member States may bring the matter before the CJEU.

may impose on it a lump sum or a penalty payment.[71] The involvement of the CJEU aims to reduce the margin of discretion of national parliaments in the implementation of the golden rule in order to ensure its effective application in the future. It is important to notice that the CJEU can only verify whether Member States have introduced the golden rule and the automatic correction mechanism in their national law, not how they comply with these obligations afterwards. Indeed, the shift of ownership of budgetary constraints from the Union to the Member States implies that surveillance is now in the hands of domestic (constitutional) courts and national IFIs.[72]

3.6 Stability Through Conditional Financial Support

3.6.1 *Purpose*

The outbreak of the sovereign debt crisis obliged national governments to face the contradiction of the surveillance model, according to which fiscal policy is an exclusive national competence, but it is also a matter of common concern due to the existing interdependence within the monetary union. More precisely, when the fiscal and banking crisis of several countries of the euro area started spreading panic in the financial market due to the imminent risk of multiple sovereign defaults, Member States had to choose between two options: they could either leave countries experiencing financial difficulties to go bankrupt in accordance with a strict application of the no bailout clause, or they could adopt last minute bailouts in order to avoid the unpredictable consequences of a sovereign default on the stability of the other Member States and of the European banking system.

The fear of contagion and the possible systemic effects of a sovereign default on the euro area as a whole convinced EU institutions and the governments of the monetary union to support the rescue strategy. Despite this representing the most reasonable choice, it also posed some relevant challenges: national governments had to establish new mechanisms of crisis management able to mobilise a significant amount of resources, without violating both the conferral principle, according to which the EU does not have fiscal sovereignty, as well as the rules regulating the functioning of the economic union, in particular the no bailout clause.

[71]The financial sanction shall consist of a lump sum or a penalty payment appropriate in the circumstances and shall not exceed 0.1% of its GDP. The amounts imposed on a contracting party whose currency is the euro shall be payable to the ESM.

[72]At the same time, the CJEU might receive a preliminary ruling regarding the interpretation of the national rules implementing the golden rule. See Porchia (2013), pp. 607–608.

After the setup of two temporary rescue mechanisms, notably the European Financial Stabilisation Mechanism (EFSM)[73] and the European Financial Stability Facility (EFSF),[74] the Member States of the euro area created a permanent instrument of stabilisation, the European Stability Mechanism (ESM). The latter was introduced through an intergovernmental treaty, after having expressly foreseen this possibility in a Treaty amendment on the basis of art. 48(6) TEU. More precisely, Decision 2011/199/EU added a new paragraph to art. 136 TFEU on the enhanced integration of the euro area, according to which the Member States of the Eurozone may establish a stability mechanism subject to strict conditionality, which is activated if indispensable to safeguard the 'stability of the euro area as a whole'. On 2 March 2012, the governments of the euro area signed the Treaty establishing the European Stability Mechanism (TESM), which replaced the EFSF and the EFSM on 1 July 2013. As with the temporary mechanisms, European countries decided to request the participation of the International Monetary Fund (IMF). This depended not only on the opportunity to share the costs of the bailouts, but also due to the necessity to count on its technical expertise for the definition and application of conditional financial assistance.

3.6.2 Financial Assistance

The objective of the ESM is safeguarding the 'stability of the euro area as a whole'. This result is achieved in two complementary ways: the provision of financial assistance and the application of the conditionality policy (art. 3 TESM).

Financial assistance requires the mobilisation of a significant amount of resources. For this purpose, the ESM is entitled to raise funds by issuing financial instruments or by entering into financial agreements with its members, financial institutions or other third parties. The ESM has a subscribed capital of around €700

[73]The EFSM was created within the EU legal framework on the basis of the solidarity clause ex art. 122(2) TFEU. It consisted of an emergency funding programme introduced by Regulation (EU) 407/2010 and financed by borrowing secured against the EU Budget up to €60 billions.

[74]The EFSF consisted of special purpose vehicle (SPV) under Luxembourgish law that could guarantee on a pro-rata basis lending up to €440 billion to euro area Member States. Despite having a different legal nature and resources available, both mechanisms could provide financial support under strict conditionality and at an interest premium.

billions, which corresponds to a lending capacity of €500 billions.[75] The contribution of Member States is proportional to the subscription of the ECB's capital.[76]

As Chap. 2 has already explained, the financial assistance of the ESM aims to defuse two sources of systemic destabilisation. On the one hand, the mechanism aims to avoid sovereign defaults, which may happen when a country has lost access to the financial markets and becomes therefore unable to finance itself. This scenario is clearly devastating for the stability of the euro area as a whole: due to the strict economic and financial interdependence, a sovereign default may trigger a domino effect on the stability of the banking system and the public finances of the other Member States of the monetary union. In order to prevent national defaults, the TESM can provide resources to countries experiencing financing difficulties by using different instruments: loans, precautionary credit lines,[77] purchasing government bonds on the primary and secondary markets. On the other hand, the TESM takes into consideration another scenario of potential destabilisation for the euro area as a whole: the default of a financial institution of systemic importance, which may trigger multiple banking and sovereign defaults. In order to avoid this scenario, the mechanism can grant loans to governments and, since November 2014, provide direct recapitalisation to financial institutions.[78] The latter instrument is particularly relevant because it allows the sharing of the risks of a bank restructuration between Member States.[79] Unfortunately the margin of action for direct recapitalisation is narrow, as the ESM can use only €60 billions for this purpose and several conditions apply for its activation.[80]

---

[75]The ESM can count on €80 billion paid-in capital, while the rest is callable at any time. Art. 8(5) TESM provides that the liability of each ESM Member shall be limited to its portion of the authorised capital stock. No country shall be liable, by reason of its membership, for obligations of the ESM. The obligations of ESM Members to contribute to the authorised capital stock in accordance with this Treaty are not affected if any such ESM Member becomes eligible for, or is receiving, financial assistance from the ESM. Cf. Ohler (2011), p. 71.

[76]In the event a country requests the ESM assistance, its portion of callable capital is shared among the other guarantors (art. 25(2) TESM). The contribution to the ESM is not counted in the public deficit under the SGP.

[77]These are Precautionary Conditioned Credit line (PCCL) and the Enhanced Conditions Credit Line (ECCL). The PCCL shall support Member States which have a sound economic and financial situation and are respecting some *ex ante* eligibility criteria. ECCL should support those countries whose economic and financial situation is still sound but that do not comply with the eligibility criteria for the PCCL.

[78]See Board of Governors Resolution No. 4 of 8 December 2014 (SG/BoG/2014/05/04). The resolution was approved under art. 19 of the ESM Treaty.

[79]Allemand et al. (2016), p. 189. It is not a case that it was introduced after the set-up of the Single Supervisory Mechanism and the Single Resolution Mechanism. Regulation (EU) No 1024/2013 and Regulation (EU) No 806/2014. See *infra* Sect. 3.8.

[80]The conditions are the following: (i) the institution(s) is, or is likely to be in the near future, in breach of the capital requirements established by the ECB in its capacity as supervisor, is unable to attract sufficient capital from private sector sources to resolve its capital problems and the bail-in is not expected to address fully the capital shortfall; (ii) the institution(s) concerned should have a systemic relevance or pose a serious threat to the financial stability of the euro area as a whole or of

The activation of the ESM is decided by the Board of Governors, which takes all fundamental decisions, and the Board of Directors, which ensures that the mechanism runs in accordance with its Treaty and by-laws. Both bodies are composed of representatives of the governments of the euro area,[81] while the Commission and the ECB can send observers without voting rights. The most important decisions are taken by unanimity vote, including the granting of financial help to Member States and increasing of the ESM capital. Quite important, the Treaty provides two main exceptions to the unanimity rule. First, the voting rights of any ESM member are suspended, if it fails to pay any part of the amount due in respect to its obligations. Second, in the event of an emergency, decisions are adopted by qualified majority of 85% of the votes cast. These exceptions produce a significant limitation of national sovereignty, as some Member States may have to contribute to an assistance plan, they did not agree to.[82]

As it was already mentioned, before agreeing on the provision of macroeconomic financial assistance, the European Commission and the ECB shall verify that the fiscal position of the country concerned is sustainable. The latter institutions notably may enjoy a significant margin of discretion in this analysis.[83] At the same time, in the event the debt was not sustainable, the government might negotiate some form of debt restructuration with its creditors before accessing the financial support of the ESM.

---

the requesting ESM Member; (iii) the requesting ESM Member is unable to provide financial assistance to the institutions in full without very adverse effects on its own fiscal sustainability, including via the instrument of an ESM loan for the recapitalisation of financial institutions; iv) providing financial assistance to the benefit of the requesting ESM Member is indispensable to safeguard the financial stability of the euro area as a whole or of its Member States. Cf. art. 3 of the ESM Guideline on Financial Assistance for the Direct Recapitalisation of Institutions, 8 December 2014.

[81]The Board of Governors is the highest decision-making body of the ESM. It comprises the Ministers of Finance of the 19 ESM Member States. Representatives of the European Commission and the ECB may participate in its meetings as observers. The Board of Governors is chaired by the President of the Eurogroup. The Board of Directors consists of representatives from each of the 19 ESM Members. Each Governor appoints one Director and one alternate Director.

[82]The German Federal Constitutional Court declared that Germany shall make sure to pay its contribution to the mechanism, otherwise the activation of the ESM, while its voting rights are suspended, would violate the budgetary autonomy of the *Bundestag* and consequently it would be illegal from the point of view of national constitutional law. German Federal Constitutional Court, Judgment of 18 March 2014 [2 BvR 1390/12], paras. 158–161.

[83]The rigorous analysis of debt sustainability should consider several elements including: growth of deficit and debt, development of the primary deficit, maturity of the debt incurred, interest rates paid, prospects of economic growth, political and social range for austerity measures. Ohler (2011), p. 66.

3.6.3 Conditionality Policy

The purpose of the conditionality policy is to ensure budgetary consolidation in the Member States and, consequently, the 'stability of the euro area as a whole'.[84] The Court of Justice in the Pringle case denied it shall 'constitute an instrument for the coordination of the economic policies of the Member States, [as it] is intended [only] to ensure that the activities of the ESM are compatible with, inter alia, Article 125 TFEU and the coordinating measures adopted by the Union'.[85] In reality, the countries, which have requested financial assistance from the ESM, are subject to wider and more intrusive supervision than what the standard EU rules of economic coordination provide.[86] The interdependence between fiscal consolidation and the provision of financial assistance is the reason why the ESM can intervene only in favour of countries, which have previously ratified the Fiscal Compact.[87]

Conditionality may range from a macro-economic adjustment programme to continuous respect of pre-established eligibility conditions. The conditions attached to the financial assistance are contained in a macro-economic adjustment programme detailed in a Memorandum of Understanding (MoU) that the concerned Member State shall negotiate with the *Troika* composed of the Commission, the ECB and the IMF. Afterwards, the Board of Governors of the ESM shall adopt by unanimity a Financial Facility Agreement on the basis of the MoU. The European Commission, in liaison with the ECB and the IMF, is entrusted with monitoring compliance with the conditionality. In the event the concerned Member State does not respect the MoU, the disbursement of financial assistance shall be suspended.

Regulation (EU) No 472/2013 in the framework of the Two Pack introduced some important rules on the preparation, application and assessment of the conditionality policies. First, Member States experiencing severe difficulties with regards to their financial stability or receiving financial assistance on a precautionary basis by the ESM shall be subject to enhanced surveillance on decision by the Commission.[88] If this happens, the government has to comply with a set of obligations to verify the presence of real or potential financial risks to the country and adopt measures aimed at addressing them.[89] Second, in the event a Member State has

---

[84]The concept of 'conditionality' was unknown in EU law before the financial crisis of 2008. Cf. Estella (2018), p. 204.

[85]See ECJ Judgment of 27 November 2012, Case C-370/12, *Thomas Pringle v Government of Ireland*, ECLI:EU:C:2012:756, para. 111.

[86]The countries, which have accepted the conditional financial assistance of the to the ESM, are *de facto* placed in 'temporary receivership ('commissariamento'), meaning that their economic sovereignty has been strongly reduced. Munari (2015), pp. 737–738. See *infra* Sect. 4.2.6.

[87]See Whereas (5) TESM; Preamble TSCG.

[88]The precautionary assistance provided by the ESM consists of credit lines.

[89]The Commission shall conduct regular review missions to verify the progress made in the implementation of these measures. On this basis of the review missions, the Council may recommend to the Member State concerned to adopt precautionary corrective measures or to prepare a draft MAP.

requested financial assistance to the ESM, the government shall prepare a draft macroeconomic adjustment programme (MAP), which shall identify the specific risks emanating from that country for the financial stability of the euro area and decide the measures to re-establish a sound and sustainable economic and financial situation. Art. 7(2) provides that the Council, acting by a qualified majority on a proposal from the Commission, shall pass a decision approving the MAP. On this basis, the Commission will ensure, the MoU signed by the Commission on behalf of the ESM is fully consistent with it. In this way, Regulation (EU) No 472/2013 has modified the decision-making process on the adoption of the MoU, requesting its consistency with the former Council's decision. The introduction of this obligation aims evidently to reduce the margin of discretion, the *Troika* and the Board of Governors of the ESM can exercise in the formulation of the conditionality policy.[90] Regulation (EU) No 472/2013 also foresees that the application of the MAP shall substantially suspend the application of the other monitoring procedures under the SGP, in order to avoid possible overlaps and inconsistences. Regulation (EU) No 472/2013 then provides that the Commission, in liaison with the ECB and, where appropriate, with the IMF, shall monitor the progress made by a Member State in the implementation of the MAP.[91] Finally, in order to ensure the durability of fiscal consolidation, Regulation (EU) No 472/2013 provides a post-programme surveillance for those countries which have received financial support, until they repay at least 75% of the capital received.

3.7 Stability Through a Common Investment Policy

3.7.1 Purpose

The necessary consolidation of national public finances in the context of the European sovereign debt crisis demanded the application of austerity policies in most Member States, which plunged their economy into recession. Since 2007, the level of investments within the Union has significantly lowered, thus slowing down economic recovery and negatively affecting job creation, long-term growth

[90]Ioannidis noticed that considering the early experience with MAP conditionality, such programmes may cover the complete spectrum of economic and social relations of the recipient Member States, including labour law and public healthcare. MAPs are not only broad in scope, but also regulate details of economic and social activity in the beneficiary countries. See Ioannidis (2014), p. 18.

[91]In case of deviance, the Council, acting by a qualified majority on a proposal from the Commission, may formally declared existing a situation of non-compliance. In this case, the concerned Member State, in close cooperation with the Commission, the ECB and, where appropriate, the IMF, shall take measures aimed at stabilising markets and preserving the good functioning of its financial sector. Evidently the European Union is not provided with any legal means to enforce the adjustment programmes, but it can only exercise a political pressure by threatening to interrupt financial assistance.

prospects and competitiveness.[92] National governments have been stuck in the difficult position where they had to respect budgetary constraints, in order to ensure the sustainability of public debt and the stability of the EMU, while looking at the same time for the necessary resources to relaunch economic growth and employment policies. The difficulty for Member States in complying with recommendations, as well as the political and social costs of austerity policies eventually persuaded EU institutions to reorganise the available resources at European level in a way to increase investments and better stimulate economic recovery. Evidently, these intentions had to deal with the structural limits of the economic union, notably the limited size of the EU budget[93] and the lack of a European fiscal sovereignty.

Even if these measures did not have the formal objective to pursue fiscal stability or economic convergence and were developed in the framework of the EU as a whole, investment policy had the purpose to recover national economies consumed by austerity, thus facilitating the process of budgetary consolidation and structural reforms.

3.7.2 *Application*

In June 2012, the European Council took for the first time some solemn commitments to reorganise the growth and employment strategy at European level. This was done through the agreement on a 'Compact for Growth and Employment', which was introduced in an Annex to the Conclusions of the European Council. After having reaffirmed their commitment to achieve the objectives of the Europe 2020 Strategy through the implementation of structural reforms and the deepening of the single market, the Heads of State or Government decided to mobilise €120 billions, equivalent of around 1% of EU GNI, for fast-acting growth measures. Despite the efforts made by EU leaders to emphasise the importance of these new tools, the Compact did not deploy new resources, but simply reorganised the existing funds in the framework of the European Investment Bank (EIB), the Structural Funds and European Investment Fund. As a consequence, the impact of the Compact on Growth and Employment on the recovery of European economy has been modest.

After the European elections, the new European Commission chaired by Jean-Claude Juncker decided to set up a new mechanism to remedy the investment gap in the EU and increase competitiveness with the intention of speeding up economic recovery. On the 26 November 2014, the European Commission presented an 'Investment Plan for Europe' aimed at supporting economic recovery at European

[92]See Whereas (1) Regulation (EU) No 1017/2015 of the European Parliament and of the Council of 25 June 2015 on the European Fund for Strategic Investments, the European Investment Advisory Hub and the European Investment Project Portal.

[93]The resources of the EU budget for the regional cohesion policy are €351.8 billion to be distributed among all 28 EU countries between 2014 and 2020.

level. The fundamental idea has been to use a small fraction of the EU budget as a guarantee for projects that would be riskier and more innovative of those usually financed by the EIB.[94] Following the endorsement of the European Council in December 2014, the Commission launched together with the EIB Group (European Investment Bank and the European Investment Fund) the European Fund for Strategic Investments (EFSI).[95] EFSI is an innovative financial instrument, according to which the Union shall provide an irrevocable and unconditional guarantee to the EIB for financing and investment operations.[96] The purpose of the EFSI is to help resolve the difficulties in financing and implementing strategic, investments 'with high economic, environmental and societal added value contributing to achieving Union policy objectives'.[97] The latter is not a genuine 'fund', but consists of a guarantee instrument that enables EIB to invest more resources in strategic projects.[98] More precisely, the EFSI has been financed by the EU budget and the EIB group for a total of €21 billions,[99] which however, should be able to attract private investments of up to the promised sum of €315 billions thanks to a leverage factor of 1 to 15. Investments can be granted to companies of all sizes, public entities, investment funds, utilities and promotional or intermediating banks. Projects are chosen in accordance some eligibility criteria: they may be economically viable according to a cost-benefit analysis, comply with Union policies, provide additionality[100] and maximise where possible the mobilisation of private sector capital. The EFSI works in strict coordination with the European Structural and Investment Funds (ESIF) foreseen by the multiannual financial framework.[101]

---

[94]See Clayes and Leandro (2016).

[95]Regulation (EU) No 2015/1017 of the European Parliament and of the Council of 25 June 2015 on the European Fund for Strategic Investments, the European Investment Advisory Hub and the European Investment Project Portal.

[96]See Tovo (2016), p. 360.

[97]Whereas (13) Regulation (EU) No 1017/2015.

[98]That governance structure is composed of a steering board, a managing director and an investment committee. See Whereas (29) Regulation (EU) No 1017/2015. There is also a European Investment Advisory Hub between the European Union and the EIB.

[99]EFSI was originally financed with € 16 billion from the EU budget (in particular from Horizon 2020 and innovation and research), combined with € 5 billion provided by the EIB. The plan has been recently extended until 31 December 2020. The investment target has been raised to €500 billion. It can count on €26 billions of EU budget guarantee and €7.5 billion contribution from the EIB.

[100]This means that a project should be supported only if it would not have been realised without the contribution of EFSI.

[101]ESIF consists of five European funds: the European Regional Development Fund, the European Social Fund, the Cohesion Fund, the European Agricultural Fund for Rural Development and the European Maritime and Fisheries Fund. They are managed together by the European Commission and the Member States. Within the Multiannual Financial Framework 2014–2020, ESIF has been provided with €450 billion. See 'ESIF/EFSI complementarities. Maximising synergies and complementarities', 13 October 2015, EGESIF_15-0032-00.

In December 2017, the European Parliament and the Council adopted a new Regulation providing for the extension of the EFSI until the end of 2020, and increasing the level of investment to €500 billions.[102]

3.8 The Pursuit of the Stability of the Euro Area and the Reform of the Banking Governance

Chapter 2 highlighted some important distinctions between the objective of 'financial stability' and the objective of the 'stability of the euro area as a whole'. Even if part of the legal doctrine considers the two concepts as identical, they present some significant differences. Financial stability has been qualified as a macro-objective, which takes care of the entire financial system, including both public and private actors either within or outside the euro area; the objective is pursued through different policies in the banking, monetary and fiscal sectors. The stability of the euro area as a whole, instead, is a more specific goal, which regards only economic policy and focuses on one subject of the financial system in particular: the Eurozone.

Aside from these important distinctions, the two objectives have a strong influence on one another. As the stability of the euro area as a whole is included in the objective of financial stability, the pursuit of the first contributes to the achievement of the latter. For this reason, some (even if not all) instruments created to ensure financial stability do also play a special role in the pursuit of stability in the euro area. This is the case of the banking union, which has started being set up since 2013. The project is composed of different pillars and is still under construction. It has involved almost all Member States of the Union except for the United Kingdom and Sweden. While its main objective is to pursue the stability of the European financial system, in order to do that it shall pay particular attention to the interdependence within the monetary union and, more precisely, between the banking system and the fiscal policies of the Member States, whose currency is the euro. As the sovereign debt crisis has proved, fiscal crisis in one or more countries can destabilise those financial institutions owning a significant quantity of their sovereign bonds; at the same time, the bailout of banks on the edge of default may demand a significant mobilisation of resources that national governments are unable to provide.[103] The toxic loop between banking crisis and sovereign debt crisis can therefore trigger a dangerous process of destabilisation of the European financial market and pose some serious threats to the survival of the monetary union. In the light of these considerations, the following analysis will explain how the project of banking union, whose main

[102]Regulation (EU) No 2017/2396 amending Regulations (EU) No 1316/2013 and (EU) 2015/1017 as regards the extension of the duration of the European Fund for Strategic Investments, (2017) OJ L 345/34.

[103]The banking and the sovereign debt crisis were therefore 'twin'. See Lastra (2013) p. 1190; Moloney (2014), p. 1614.

purpose is to protect the stability of the financial system, does also contribute to the pursuit of stability of the euro area as a whole.

The *Single Supervisory Mechanism* (SSM), introduced by Regulation (EU) No 1024/2013,[104] is a 'mechanism' composed of the ECB and national competent authorities of the participating Member States. It should be noted that, even if the ECB has a primary role in the mechanism, decisions are not taken by those bodies in charge of monetary policy (i.e. Executive Board and Governing Council) but by new Supervisory Board, which enjoys a significant autonomy in the execution of its tasks.[105] The mandate of the SSM, is to 'contribute to the safety and soundness of credit institutions and the stability of the financial system within the Union and in each Member State, with full regard and duty of care for the unity and integrity of the internal market based on the equal treatment of credit institutions with a view of preventing regulatory arbitrage'.[106] The SSM shall exercise direct supervisory competence only in respect of significant credit institutions, financial holding companies and mixed financial holding companies, which are established in participating Member States.[107] The supervision of the other banks remain in principle under the responsibility of national authorities.[108] However, the SSM can take charge of direct

[104]Council Regulation (EU) No 1024/2013 of 15 October 2013 conferring specific tasks on the European Central Bank concerning policies relating to the prudential supervision of credit institutions, (2013) OJ L 287/63.

[105]Art. 25 of Regulation (EU) No 1024/2013 has introduced the formal separation of monetary and supervisory functions within the ECB. The ECB shall carry out the tasks conferred on without prejudice to and separately from its tasks relating to monetary policy and any other tasks. This distinction is ensured in concrete through a number of precautions. First, the decision-making process in the field of supervision is managed by the Supervisory Board, while the Governing Council of the ECB only provides for a formal endorsement of its proposals through the silent assent procedure. In order to keep some distance from monetary issues, the Supervisory Board presents only a limited number of ECB representatives and its members shall act 'in the interest of the Union as a whole'. Second, during the meeting dedicated to supervisory issues, the Governing Council shall not make decisions regarding monetary tasks. Monetary summits have been therefore formally distinguished from supervisory summits. Third, the ECB has adopted an internal division of its personnel between officers in charge of monetary policy and those responsible for supervisory tasks. The rigid division of work between the two branches of the ECB should prevent conflicts of interests. Cf. Verhelst (2013), p. 17.

[106]See art. 1 of Regulation (EU) No 1024/2013.

[107]A bank is considered 'significant': (i) if the total value of its assets exceeds €30 billion; (ii) if the ratio of its total assets over the GDP of the five participating home Member State exceeds 20% (unless the total value of its assets is below €5 billion); (iii) if national authorities notify the ECB, they consider a bank to be of significant relevance with regard to the domestic economy; (iv) if the ECB decides on its own initiative that a bank is significant, taking into consideration that it has banking subsidiaries in more than one participating Member States and its cross-border assets or liabilities represent a significant part of its total assets or liabilities; (v) if the bank has granted financial support from the EFSF or the ESM; (vi) if the bank is one of the three most significant credit institutions in each of the participating Member States, unless justified by particular circumstances.

[108]The ECB can still exercise an indirect supervision on them, by instructing national authorities, which have to report to the ECB on the implementation of their tasks.

supervision also *ex post*, where it considers that, due to the developments of the financial situation, a certain financial institution has gained a 'significant character'.

The *Single Resolution Mechanism* (SRM) is in charge of providing uniform rules for the resolution of banks in distress. It is a complementary instrument to the SSM, as 'a supervisor can only credibly do his job, if liquidation is possible without undue risks to financial stability'.[109] As long as each country remained responsible for their bank resolution, capitals would flow to those States more able or willing to protect their own banks and savers,[110] undermining in this way the stability of the European financial market. The SRM was created on the basis of Regulation (EU) No 806/2014[111] covering the main aspects of the mechanism and an Inter-governmental agreement (IGA)[112] disciplining some specific aspects of the Single Resolution Fund (SRF). Like the SSM, the SRM is a mechanism composed of European and national authorities. National Resolution Authorities (NRAs) act under the supervision of the Single Resolution Board (SRB). The latter is an EU agency in charge of intervening in relation to bank resolutions. The SRM has a competence on resolution over all banks established in the Member States and falling under the supervision of the SSM. The SRB is responsible for the resolution of banks directly supervised by the ECB, while NRAs maintain their competence in relation to the resolution of all other banks. The SRB, however, takes over in the event it believes the resolution requires the consistent application of high resolution standards, the Single Resolution Fund shall intervene or a NRA has requested so. If a bank experiencing financial difficulties fulfils the relevant conditions outlined in the Regulation, the SRB places the bank under resolution. A resolution scheme identifies the applicable tools to restructure the financial institution and if it is necessary the intervention of the SRF. More precisely the SRF has the mandate to provide financial support to resolution in order to make sure that banks operate normally, while they are under renovation. The SRF can provide guarantees, make loans, purchase assets and pay compensation to shareholders or creditors, but it cannot absorb losses or provide direct recapitalisation. The fund has a capacity of around €55 billions, which is equal to 1% of the covered deposit of banks in the participating Member States.[113] Before the implementation of resolutions, the capital instruments of the bank must be written down or converted. Regulation (EU) No 806/2014 provides for different resolution

[109]Mersch (2013).

[110]See Hennessy (2014), p. 164.

[111]Regulation (EU) No 806/2014 of the European Parliament and of the Council of 15 July 2014 establishing uniform rules and a uniform procedure for the resolution of credit institutions and certain investment firms in the framework of a Single Resolution Mechanism and a Single Resolution Fund and amending Regulation (EU) No 1093/2010, (2014) OJ L 225/1.

[112]The Intergovernmental Agreement signed in Brussels on 21 May 2014.

[113]The IGA disciplines the transfer and mutualisation of contributions to the Single Resolution Fund (SRF). The fund will be built up in 8 years on the basis of bank contributions. The SRF will be filled in 10 years through bank levies of 1%. National resources will be required in the transition period in order to ensure the effectiveness of the mechanism. On the financing of the SRF cf. Clauss (2013), p. 73.

tools: sale of business, setup of a bridge institution, asset separation and bail-in. The bail-in tool is particularly important because it aims to write down or covert equity and debt by shifting the costs on shareholders and creditors rather than taxpayers.[114]

The *Single Rulebook* consists of a unified regulatory framework for the EU financial sector. This has been a longstanding objective for the European legislator since the establishment of the single market in financial services. Indeed the process of integration in this field requires a harmonised set of rules to provide similar standards and procedures in the banking and financial sectors throughout the Union. The Single Rulebook evidently does not consist of one legal text, but rather of a collection of applicable directives, regulations, recommendations, and guidelines in the banking field. The process of legal harmonisation and the creation of common standards has accelerated after the outbreak of the sovereign debt crisis.[115] Binding legislations have been adopted on the basis of art. 114 TFEU on the harmonisation of national rules to ensure the correct functioning of the internal market. The European Banking Authority (EBA) has played an important role in the development of the Single Rulebook, as it has the mandate to adopt binding regulatory and technical standards to ensure a consistent implementation of EU banking legislation.[116]

References

Adinolfi G (2013) Il Sostegno Congiunto UE-FMI: è necessario un ripensamento della politica di condizionalità? In: Adinolfi G, Vellano M (eds) La crisi del debito sovrano degli stati dell'area Euro. Giappichelli, Torino, pp 3–27

---

[114]The purpose of the bail in instrument is to make the shareholders and private sector creditors share the costs of a bank rescue or recapitalisation. In a way, shareholders, creditors, bondholders and uncovered depositors are punished for the losses suffered by the financial institution, where they invested. Lo Schiavo (2017), p. 239.

[115]Regulation (EU) No 575/2013 of the European Parliament and of the Council of 26 June 2013 on prudential requirements for credit institutions and investment firms and amending Regulation (EU) No 648/2012, (2013) OJ L 176/1; Directive 2013/36/EU of the European Parliament and of the Council of 26 June 2013 on access to the activity of credit institutions and the prudential supervision of credit institutions and investment firms, amending Directive 2002/87/EC and repealing Directives 2006/48/EC and 2006/49, (2013) OJ L 176/338; Directive 2014/17/EU of the European Parliament and of the Council of 4 February 2014 on credit agreements for consumers relating to residential immovable property and amending Directives 2008/48/EC and 2013/36/EU and Regulation (EU) No 1093/2010, (2014) OJ L 60/34; Directive 2014/59/EU of the European Parliament and of the Council of 15 May 2014 establishing a framework for the recovery and resolution of credit institutions and investment firms and amending Council Directive 82/891/EEC, and Directives 2001/24/EC, 2002/47/EC, 2004/25/EC, 2005/56/EC, 2007/36/EC, 2011/35/EU, 2012/30/EU and 2013/36/EU, and Regulations (EU) No 1093/2010 and (EU) No 648/2012, of the European Parliament and of the Council, (2014) OJ L 173/190; Directive (EU) 2015/2366 of the European Parliament and of the Council of 25 November 2015 on payment services in the internal market, amending Directives 2002/65/EC, 2009/110/EC and 2013/36/EU and Regulation (EU) No 1093/2010, and repealing Directive 2007/64/EC, (2015) OJ L337/35.

[116]For a deeper analysis of the project of Single Rulebook see Alexander (2015).

Alexander K (2015) The EU single rulebook: capital requirements for banks and the maximum harmonisation principle. In: Hinojosa-Martmez LM, Beneyto JM (eds) European Banking Union. The new regime. Wolters Kluwer, Alphen aan den Rijn, pp 21–31
Allemand F, Bion M, Sauron J (2016) Gouverner la zone euro après la crise: l'exigence d'intégration. Gualino, Paris
Bandilla R (2017) Artikel 25 AEUV. In: Grabitz E, Hilf M, Nettesheim M (eds) Das Recht der Europäischen Union. Beck, München
Calliess C (2011–2012) From fiscal compact to fiscal union? New rules for the Eurozone. Cambridge Yearb Eur Legal Stud 14:101–117
Clauss M (2013) The Dynamics of the European Banking Union, CESifo Forum Issue No 4
Clayes G, Leandro A (2016) Assessing the Juncker Plan after one year, Bruegel Blog Post, 17th May 2016
Cloos J, Reinesch G, Vignese D (1993) Le Traité de Maastricht: genese, analyse commentaires. Bruylant, Brussels
Costamagna F (2015) Il coordinamento delle politiche economiche nell'ambito del Semestre europeo. In: Porchia O (ed) Governance economica europea. Strumenti dell'Unione, rapporti con l'ordinamento internazionale e ricadute nell'ordinamento interno, Editoriale Scientifica, Napoli, 127–140
De Grauwe P (2016) Economics of Monetary Union. Oxford University Press, Oxford
De Sadeleer N (2012) The new architecture of the European economic governance. Maastricht J Eur Comp Law 19:354–382
Estella A (2018) Legal foundations of EU economic governance. Cambridge University Press, Cambridge
European Commission Communication (2001) European Governance. A White Paper, C 287/01
Häde U (2009) Die Wirtschafts- und Währungsunion im Vertrag von Lissabon, Europarecht, pp 200–218
Häde U (2016) Art. 125 AEUV. In: Calliess C, Ruffert M (eds) EUV, AEUV, Kommentar. Beck, München
Hennessy A (2014) Redesigning financial supervision in the European Union (2009–2013). J Eur Publ Policy 21:151–168
Hinarejos A (2013) Fiscal federalism in the European Union: evolution and future choices for EMU. Common Mark Law Rev 51:1621–1642
Hofmann C (2013) A legal analysis of the Eurozone crisis. Fordham J Corp Financ Law 18:519–564
Ioannidis M (2014) EU financial assistance conditionality after "two pack". Zeitschrift für ausländisches öffentliches Recht und Völkerrecht 74:1–44
Lastra RM (2013) Banking Union and single market: conflict or companionship? Fordham Int Law J 36:1190–1224
Lo Schiavo G (2017) The role of financial stability in EU law and policy. Wolters Kluwer, Alphen aan den Rijn
Marks G, Hooghe L, Blank K (1996) European integration from the 1980s: state-centric v. multi-level governance. J Common Mark Stud 34:341–378
Martinelli T (2016) Euro CAC and the existing rules on sovereign debt restructuring in the Euro area: an appraisal four years after the Greek swap, Ademu Working Paper Series, No 43
Martucci F (2012) Traite sur la Stabilité, la Coordination et la Gouvernance, Traite instituant le Mécanisme Européen de Stabilité. Le Droit International Public au secours de l'UEM. Revue des Affaires Européennes – Law & European Affairs:717–731
Mersch Y (2013) The Euro and the ECB: Perspectives and challenges ahead. Keynote address by Yves Mersch, Member of the Executive Board of the ECB, Journée Boursière, Luxembourg, 6th May 2013
Moloney N (2014) European Banking Union: assessing its risks and resilience. Common Mark Law Rev 51(6):1609–1670

Munari F (2015) Da Pringle a Gauweiler: i tormentati anni dell'Unione monetaria e i loro effetti sull'ordinamento giuridico europeo. Il Diritto dell'Unione Europea, pp 723–755
Ohler C (2011) The European stability mechanism: the long road to financial stability in the euro area. Ger Yearb Int Law 54:47–74
Peers S (2012) The stability treaty: permanent austerity or gesture politics? Eur Const Law Rev 8:404–441
Porchia O (2013) Il ruolo della Corte di giustizia dell'Unione europea nella governance economica europea. Il Diritto dell'Unione Europea, pp 593–611
Ruotolo GM (2012) La costituzione economica dell'Unione europea al tempo della crisi globale. Studi sull'integrazione europea 7:433–461
Scott J, Trubek DM (2002) Mind the gap: law and new approaches to governance in the European Union. Eur Law J 8:1–18
Shore C (2011) European governance or governmentality? Anthropological perspectives on governance and sovereignty in the European Union. Eur Law J 17:287–303
Tovo C (2016) Il Fondo europeo per gli investimenti strategici: statuto giuridico, profili istituzionali e funzionamento. Il Diritto dell'Unione Europea:357–400
Verhelst S (2013) The Single Supervisory Mechanism: a sound first step in Europe's Banking Union? Egmont European Affairs Paper, 20th March 2013
Zettelmeyer J (2018) Managing deep debt crises in the euro area: towards a feasible regime. Global Policy 9:70–79

Chapter 4
Longstanding Sources of Instability: The Current Deficits of the Economic Union

4.1 Introduction

The efforts made by the Member States and European institutions to ensure the stability of the euro area as a whole during the crisis managed to contain the emergencies, which were undermining the very existence of the monetary union. The reforms created an instrument of crisis management in charge of absorbing economic shocks of systemic relevance, and strengthened the procedures of economic coordination and budgetary surveillance by improving their efficiency. Consolidation and stabilisation have therefore been the two main approaches used to pursue the stability of the euro area as a whole, thanks to which the currency union did not collapse, but started a process of gradual economic recovery. This was also facilitated by the non-conventional monetary measures adopted since 2010 by the ECB.[1]

Clearly, even if the measures adopted so far ensured the survival of the euro area, the economic union that emerged after the crisis still presents some major vulnerabilities. The reforms indeed did not question the foundations of the EMU set out in the Maastricht Treaty, but only tried to adapt the existing legal framework to the many challenges, which were undermining the survival of the monetary union. As a consequence, the consolidation of the governance stalled against some fundamental obstacles, which are rooted in the decentralised model of fiscal integration. These can be summarised in three main deficits: lack of legality, limited effectiveness of the legal tools and weak democratic accountability of the decision-making process.

[1]See Decision 2010/281 of the European Central Bank of 14 May 2010 establishing a Securities Markets Programme; Decisions of the Governing Council of the European Central Bank (ECB) of 6 September 2012 on a number of technical features regarding the Eurosystem's outright monetary transactions in secondary sovereign bond markets (the OMT decisions); Press Release of the ECB, 22 January 2015 (Quantitative Easing decision).

L. Lionello, *The Pursuit of Stability of the Euro Area as a Whole*, Studies in European Economic Law and Regulation 18,
https://doi.org/10.1007/978-3-030-28045-1_4

The following analysis will highlight the existing flaws of the decentralised model of economic union, by explaining why they can represent a threat to the pursuit of the stability of the euro area as a whole.

4.2 The Deficit of Legality

4.2.1 Preliminary Remarks: Changing the Governance Without Changing the EU Treaties

Having no intention to start a difficult process of Treaty amendment, Member States tried to overcome the limits posed by the current formulation of primary law in two ways: stretching the available legal basis as much as possible by embracing a flexible interpretation of the norms, and stipulating intergovernmental agreements beyond EU law. While this double approach seemed the only way forward during the crisis, it also weakened the consistency and integrity of the legal system regulating the functioning of the economic governance. The following analysis will consider the most relevant doubts regarding the legality of the economic governance.

The first paragraphs will focus on the legal basis used for the introduction of several important reforms, including new sanctions in the Multilateral Surveillance Procedure (MSP), the Macroeconomic Imbalance Procedure (MIP) and the Excessive Deficit Procedure (EDP), as well as the application of the reverse majority voting in the decision-making process.

Secondly, the research will verify whether the content of some reforms are in contrast with EU primary law. This is the case for example of the financial support provided in the framework of the ESM, which may be violating the no bailout principle ex art. 125 TFEU and the solidarity clause ex art. 122(2) TFEU. Similarly, the conditionality policy regulated by the TESM and Regulation (EU) No 472/2013 may be partially inconsistent with the norms of economic coordination, as well as the EU Charter of Fundamental Rights (EUCFR) and even the principle of conferral. This obliged the Court of Justice to adopt a new interpretation of the relevant Treaty provisions to accommodate them with the instruments of crisis management and economic coordination introduced during the crisis. The Pringle Judgment in particular has provided for a new reading of the no bailout principle and the solidarity clause. The many efforts made by the Court in the process of adaptation of primary law confirmed, once again, how difficult it is for the economic union to depart from the original paradigm defined in Maastricht.

Finally, the analysis will focus on the so called 'flight into international law', meaning the more and more frequent use of international agreements to reform the economic governance. It is discussed whether the latter process has weakened the legal coherence and integrity of the European legal order. Indeed, economic coordination is now regulated by several sources of law, which are partially overlapping and contradictory to each other and present different forms of enforcement.

Furthermore, the use of international law has created a parallel system of governance in the hands of national governments and undermined the institutional balance within the Union.

4.2.2 The Conferral Principle and the Limited Margin of Extension of EU Powers in the Economic Governance

The reform of the economic governance during the crisis had to deal with the principle of conferral, according to which European institutions act only within the powers expressly attributed by the EU Treaties. The possibility to operate in those areas, where the Union wasn't initially given a clear competence, is essentially limited to few options.

The flexibility clause ex art. 352 TFEU potentially offers an unlimited source of expansion of EU powers. Several authors argued in favour of its application to complete the reform of the governance within the EU legal framework and the European Commission chose it as a legal basis to draft a proposal of European Monetary Fund in December 2017.[2] Despite its significant potential, however, the use of the flexibility clause remains difficult in concrete due to the procedural requirements requested by the EU Treaties for its activation: the Council must decide by unanimity on a proposal from the Commission and after obtaining the consent of the European Parliament. Evidently, art. 352 TFEU behaves as a special amendment procedure of the EU treaties for an *ad hoc* conferral of powers to the Union.

Other authors have suggested the use of enhanced cooperation ex art. 20 TEU to introduce specific measures regarding the euro area, such as for example the incorporation of the ESM in EU Law.[3] Notably, the latter provision can be activated by smaller groups of countries to further the objectives of the Union, protect its interests and reinforce its integration process. In reality, the relevance of the norm is dubious, as art. 20 TEU allows the adoption of a legislative act relying on the existing legal basis of the EU Treaties and within the framework of the Union's non-exclusive competences. Accordingly, the enhanced cooperation does not provide for any transfer of power to the EU.[4]

In light of the limits identified so far, national governments preferred to reform the economic union, by recurring to the existing enabling clauses in the EU Treaties. The latter allow European institutions to develop regulations or extend their powers in regard to a specific matter and under certain conditions. Title VIII TFEU presents

---

[2]European Commission Proposal for a Council Regulation (2017).

[3]Schwarz (2014), Ziller (2015), p. 28; Lo Schiavo (2017), p. 143.

[4]See ECJ Judgment of 27 November 2012, Case C-370/12, *Thomas Pringle v Government of Ireland*, ECLI:EU:C:2012:756, para. 167. On the use of enhanced cooperation see Tuori and Tuori (2014), p. 175.

three enabling clauses in relation to economic policy. The most important one is probably art. 136(1) TFEU, according to which the Council shall adopt measures specific to those Member States whose currency is the euro to strengthen the coordination and surveillance of their budgetary discipline.[5] The activation of this provision is clearly conditional to the compliance with the other norms of the Treaty on the economic union. A more limited room for reform is provided by art. 121(6) TFEU, according to which the European Parliament and the Council, acting by means of regulations in accordance with the ordinary legislative procedure, shall adopt detailed rules for the multilateral surveillance procedure. Similarly, art. 126(14) TFEU allows the Council, on a proposal from the Commission and after consulting the European Parliament, to lay down detailed rules and definitions for the application of the provisions of the Protocol on the excessive deficit procedure.

4.2.3 Flaws in the Legal Basis of Semi-Automatic Sanctions

Strengthening the governance by using the available legal basis has proven problematic. The clearest example in this regard consists of the establishment of semi-automatic sanctions in the framework of European surveillance. More precisely, Regulation (EU) No 1173/2011 and Regulation (EU) No 1174/2011 recurred to the legal basis offered in art. 121(6) TFEU and art. 136 TFEU to set up new early sanctions in the coordination procedures, which the Council shall adopt in accordance with a reverse majority voting (RMV). The reform is extremely relevant from two points of view.

On the one hand, it strengthens the corrective side of coordination. Notably, the Multilateral Surveillance Procedure (MSP) and the Macroeconomic Imbalance Procedure (MIP) have been based on paras (3) and (4) of art. 121 TFEU, which do not foresee sanctions against the Member States violating EU recommendations. The only form of 'penalty' conceived in the norm is the publication of a Council decision confirming a situation of non-compliance, which in the mind of the Treaty drafters should stimulate a sanctioning effect from the markets through higher interest rates on the sovereign bonds of the concerned country. At the same time, the Treaty rules on the EDP ex art. 126(11) TFEU do foresee penalties, but only at the end when it has been certified that a Member State has consistently ignored European requests of correction. Evidently, the introduction of sanctions in procedures, which either do not conceive penalties or only as a last resort instrument, does represent a substantial innovation in the process of economic coordination. The hardening of the procedures is also testified by the fact that, while the Council instrument specified in art. 121 TFEU is normally a recommendation, the Six Pack and the Two Pack do

[5]Art. 136 TFEU may represent the 'locus of true expansion' for new competences to the EU. See Ioannidis (2016), p. 1270. Accordingly, the norm may behave similarly to art. 114 TFUE for the setup of the single market. See Beukers (2013), pp. 11–12.

also provide for the use of Council decisions, notably to establish that national measures have not been sufficient and, consequently, to impose sanctions.[6]

The second important reform of the coordination procedure regards the use of reverse majority voting (RMV) for the adoption of the new economic sanctions. According to this procedure, a proposal of the Commission is automatically adopted unless the Council decides by (simple or qualified) majority to reject it within a specific deadline from the submission. The impact of this rule on the functioning of the governance is extremely relevant, because it modifies the relationship between majority and minority and the role of abstention in the decision-making process. Indeed, in accordance with the standard qualified majority rule ex art. 16(4) TEU and art. 238(3) TFEU, if Member States want to pass a proposal, they shall perform a positive action and the votes in favour must prevail on those against. Accordingly, abstentions don't ease the adoption of the act. The RMV instead reverses this approach: a recommendation from the Commission is approved unless a majority of Member States vote against. This means that abstentions make the adoption of a decision easier and a minority of countries can make sure a Commission proposal is adopted. In this sense reversing the majority rule in the decision-making process may potentially represent a Copernicus revolution in the functioning of the economic governance, by shifting the real balance of powers from the Council to the Commission.[7]

Even if the following analysis on the deficit of effectiveness will explain that semi-automatic sanctions did not manage to consolidate the leadership of the Commission in the functioning of the governance as much as expected, part of the legal doctrine has correctly criticised the choice of the legal basis used to adopt the regulations,[8] namely art. 121(6) and art. 136 TFEU, thus arguing a possible violation of the principle of conferral.[9]

First of all, the provision of new semiautomatic sanctions in the MSP and MIP can be hardly considered as one of those specifications of the coordination procedures, the Council and the Parliament can regulate in accordance with art. 121(6) TFEU. The introduction of economic countermeasures is not a simple

[6]Leino-Sandberg and Salminen (2017), p. 77. Notably recommendations are non-binding and their legality cannot be reviewed by the ECJ. It is nevertheless unlikely that the mandate under art. 121 TFEU, also in combination with art. 136 TFEU, allows to pass from non-binding instruments to binding instruments. Ibid., p. 78.

[7]On the innovative nature of the reverse majority voting see Bauer and Becker (2014), pp. 219–220; Seikel (2016), pp. 1405–1408.

[8]Häde (2010), p. 921; Ruffert (2011), pp. 1800–1806; Calliess (2011–2012), p. 116; Fischer-Lescano and Oberndorfer (2013), p. 12; Ohler (2014), p. 128; Palmstorfer (2014), pp. 201–202; Tuori and Tuori (2014), pp. 170–171; Grimm (2016), pp. 132, 145.

[9]Notably art. 16(3) TEU states that the Council shall always act by standard qualified majority, except where the Treaties provide otherwise. Also, the Court of Justice has interpreted the principle of conferral in the sense that EU institutions shall not modify the norms regulating their own functioning, except if the Treaty expressly allows them to do so. See ECJ, Judgment of 6 May 2008, Case C-133/06, *European Parliament v Council of the European Union*, ECLI:EU:C:2008:257, para 54.

detail, but it has a huge impact on the effectiveness of coordination: the consequence of non-compliance moves from nothing to the possibility of an economic sanction. The result is an extension of the corrective arm of coordination also to those procedures, which were supposed to work only on the preventive side through soft law and non-binding measures.[10] At the same time, the innovation taken by the RMV is even more important. The new voting rule rewards passive attitudes in the decision-making process and reverses the balance of powers between majority and minority. In this context, the adoption of a Commission recommendation requires either a silent behaviour of the Member States or the manifestation of a minority block. For all these reasons, the setup of semiautomatic sanction shall not be qualified as a simple clarification and specification of the existing procedure of preventive coordination.[11]

The use of art. 121(6) TFEU for the introduction of new semiautomatic sanctions in the EDP is also controversial. First of all, primary law foresees that the correction of excessive deficit shall be developed in steps and penalties may apply only at the end of the procedure, as a last resort measure, after the adoption of recommendations has failed to obtain corrections. Such decision needs the assumption of a serious political responsibility, which shall be carried by the Council. In this perspective, the provision of new semiautomatic sanctions in the EDP does modify the structure and the spirit of the procedure by expanding the use of repressive tools and, potentially, reducing the margin of discretion of the Council in favour of the Commission.[12] Furthermore, the reform of the EDP should not have been implemented by using art. 121(6) TFEU,[13] but the *ad hoc* legal basis of art. 126(14) TFEU, according to which the discipline of the Protocol on the excessive deficit procedure shall be detailed by the Council with the participation of the European Parliament.[14]

At first glance, art. 136 TFEU may seem a more promising legal basis, as the introduction of semi-automatic sanctions does help strengthen economic coordination and budgetary discipline in the euro area. In reality, the principle of consistency recalled in para 1 tightens the room for innovation: the norm gives the possibility to improve the functioning of the governance, but without twisting the fundamental rules outlined in the EU Treaties.[15] In this perspective, art. 136 TFEU may allow additions and improvements in the existing procedures, but it shouldn't modify the 'quality of surveillance'. This is instead what happened when the introduction of new sanctions extended the corrective arm of coordination in procedures, which

---

[10]See Leino-Sandberg and Salminen (2017), p. 78.

[11]Palmstorfer (2014), p. 197.

[12]In this regard, it should be noted that art. 126(13) TFEU refers specifically to the use of standard qualified majority to be defined in accordance with art. 238(3) TFEU.

[13]Palmstorfer (2014), p. 201.

[14]The choice of art. 121(6) TFEU depended on the fact that art. 136(1) TFEU expressly excludes the procedures set out in art. 126(14) TFEU from its margin of action. On this topic see Antpöhler (2012), p. 378.

[15]Cf. Palmstorfer (2014), pp. 196–197.

were supposed to work only on the preventive side, and the RMV modified the institutional balance between the Council and the Commission in the decision-making process. Due to the clear reference to the consistency principle, art. 136 TFEU cannot be interpreted as a special flexibility clause for the euro area on the model of art. 352 TFEU. Evidently, the principle of conferral does not allow the attribution of new powers to EU institutions without an express consent of all Member States of the European Union.[16]

The criticism expressed toward the adoption of semiautomatic decisions in accordance with the Six Pack[17] can be extended by analogy to art. 7 TSCG. The latter applies the RMV to all stages of the EDP, by stating that Member States shall commit themselves to supporting the proposals and recommendations of the Commission, assessing a violation of the deficit criterion by a Eurozone Member State. This obligation, however, does not apply when a qualified majority of the contracting parties opposes such initiative. In the light of the arguments analysed before, this 'intergovernmental version' of semiautomatic sanctions may challenge the consistency clause ex art. 2 TSCG, according to which the Fiscal Compact shall comply with the existing EU primary and secondary laws. More precisely art. 7 TSCG may undermine the principle of institutional balance and conferral by giving to the Commission powers, which find no reference in the Treaty. In reality, the ambiguous legal status of art. 7 TSCG may help overcome these criticisms. Several authors denied the norm is legally binding and qualified it as simple political commitment.[18] Accordingly, within the Council, the qualified majority rule should still apply.

In conclusion, the consistency of the semiautomatic sanctions in the framework of the SGP is rather controversial. The EU legislator tried to overcome the boundaries posed by the existing legal framework by adapting the meaning of primary law and altering the original institutional balance defined in the Maastricht Treaty.

---

[16]Some authors tried to argue the legality of the RMV on the fact, they apply only to new sanctions, which are not mentioned in primary law, thus avoiding any direct conflict with the EU Treaty. Others suggested, semi-automatic sanctions might be qualified as implementing acts of the Commission, which might be justified on the basis of art. 291(2) TFEU. Cf. Palmstorfer (2014), pp. 199–201. More in general, even if semi-automatic sanctions aim to change the nature of coordination, thus posing a potentially threat to the conferral principle, their introduction should still be accepted as long as they succeed making budgetary discipline more effective. See Allemand and Martucci (2012), p. 72; Beukers (2013), p. 15.

[17]If the norms of the Six Pack are not consistent with primary law, they may be subject to an action for annulment ex art. 263 TFEU. However, such perspective has now become impossible, because art. 263(6) TFEU sets a deadline of 2 months from the publication of the act to start an annulment procedure. A preliminary-reference procedure is unlikely, but not impossible. See Palmstorfer (2014), p. 202.

[18]See Calliess (2012), p. 108; Allemand and Martucci (2012), p. 78; De Streel and Etienne (2012), pp. 184–185; Baratta (2013), p. 52.

4.2.4 *The Compliance of Rescue Mechanisms with the No Bailout Clause*

4.2.4.1 The Possible Violation of Art. 125 TFEU

The deficit of legality can be identified also in regard to the conflict between the establishment of rescue mechanisms and some important legal provisions outlined in EU primary law. Notably, the main obstacle to the establishment of the ESM was represented by the no bailout clause outlined in art. 125 TFEU. The latter provision says that the Union and the Member States 'shall not be liable for or assume the commitments of central governments, regional, local or other public authorities, other bodies governed by public law, or public undertakings of any [other] Member State, without prejudice to mutual financial guarantees for the joint execution of a specific project'.[19]

Criticism on the compatibility of art. 125 TFEU with the conditional financial support of the ESM was expressed by several lawyers, especially in Germany.[20] From their point of view, the no bailout clause is first of all a natural consequence of the asymmetry between the economic and the monetary union: as Member States refused to share fiscal sovereignty between each other, it is normal, they shall remain responsible for their own debts.[21] Art. 125 TFEU has therefore the primary function to protect national fiscal sovereignty and avoid the Eurozone to become a transfer union.[22] At the same time, the no bailout clause does also encourage the compliance of Member States with budgetary discipline, by promoting the regulatory role of financial markets.

In the light of these observations, the consistency of conditional financial support with the no bailout clause is dubious due to the distortive effects, it may have on the effective ability of each country to fulfil its own financial obligations.[23] Indeed, when Member States are independent in the assumption and payment of their debts, markets are able to demand an interest rate, which is effectively proportional to the

---

[19]The fact that the ESM is an autonomous legal entity with legal personality, distinct from the participating Member States does not make it fall outside art. 125 TFEU. The ESM is in fact an emanation of the participating Member States, which are its owners. Like the EFSF, the ESM is assimilated to the Member States in the sense of art. 125 TFEU and fall within its scope of application *ratione personae*. See View of Advocate General Kokott delivered on 26 October 2012, Case C-370/12, *Thomas Pringle v Government of Ireland*, ECLI:EU:C:2012:675, para. 110; De Gregorio Merino (2012), p. 1626; Tuori and Tuori (2014), p. 123.

[20]See Ruffert (2011), p. 1785; Hoffmeister (2011), pp. 120–123; Hentschelmann (2011), p. 286; Ruffert (2013), p. 258; Manzini (2013), pp. 38–40; Häde (2016), Artikel 125 AEUV, paras 11, 12; Grimm (2016), pp. 81–83; Ketterer (2016), p. 248.

[21]In this sense, the principle of no-bailout follows the principle of subsidiarity. See Tufano (2002), p. 508.

[22]According to art. 25(2) TESM, if a Member State fails to meet the required payment under a capital call, a revised increased capital call shall be made to all the other countries. This may be in contrast with the no bailout principle. See Beck (2014), pp. 548–549.

[23]See Ketterer (2016), pp. 217–218.

investment risk. Instead, when governments are supported by their partners, this regulatory role is undermined: markets will demand cheap interest rates also to the most indebted country, if they believe that the other Member States of the euro area will in any case intervene to put the debtor in the conditions to repay its obligations. In the light of this concern, art. 125 TFEU should be given a strict interpretation and ban all forms of assistance, which may help Member States to carry their own debts. What matters then is not who has the formal liability for an existing obligation, rather who is substantially taking the risk for its fulfilment.[24]

According to the same reasoning, a derogation from art. 125 TFEU can't be justified considering the objective of the 'stability of the euro area' outlined in art. 136(3) TFEU and the TESM. Indeed, the intervention of the ESM in favour of small countries, such as Cyprus,[25] whose financial difficulties do not pose a real threat to the survival of the Eurozone, proves that the objective of financial assistance is not the stability of the monetary union, but the transfer of risks.[26] In this way, by granting resources to every country willing to comply with a MoU, the ESM undermines the principle of individual responsibility for budgetary policy.

In the light of the former arguments, part of the legal doctrine believes that the ESM is in contrast with art. 125 TFEU. Accordingly, by considering a systematic interpretation of the EU Treaties, art. 125 TFEU should represent an absolute prohibition, the same way as art. 123 and art. 124 TFEU.[27]

4.2.4.2 The Reinterpretation of Art. 125 TFEU in the Pringle Judgment

The former arguments did not convince the European Court of Justice, which in the Pringle case spoke in favour of the consistency of the no bailout clause with the ESM conditional financial assistance.[28] Rather than considering art. 136(3) TFEU as an amendment or an exception to art. 125 TFEU, the Court developed a number of arguments to explain why the two provisions are substantially compatible.

First of all, according to the CJEU, the formulation of art. 125 TFEU does not refer to an absolute prohibition of financial assistance among the Member States of the euro area. This can be deduced by the literal interpretation of the Treaty, as the no

---

[24] See Ruffert (2013), p. 258; Tomkin (2013), p. 75; Beck (2014), pp. 547–548; Ketterer (2016), pp. 229–231; Grimm (2016), pp. 66–69.

[25] On the sovereign debt crisis in Cyprus cf. Vellano (2013).

[26] See Ruffert (2011), p. 1786; De Witte and Beukers (2013), pp. 842–843; Ketterer (2016), pp. 232–233.

[27] See Hoffmeister (2011), p. 122. Furthermore, art. 125 TFEU consists of a *lex generalis*, against the *lex specialis* of art. 122(2) TFEU, which allows the provision of financial support in exceptional circumstances. If financial support could be always given, there was no need for art. 122 (2) TFEU. See Ketterer (2016), pp. 223–224.

[28] Most academic doctrine does not share an absolute interpretation of art. 125 TFEU. See Tosato (2010), Herrmann (2010), p. 415; Della Cananea (2011), Thymes and Wendel (2012), pp. 743–748, 754; Smits (2012), p. 828; Bandilla (2017), Artikel 25 AEUV, paras 31–32.

bailout clause only prevents the direct assumption of commitments of other Member States and does not exclude in general the provision of mutual economic support. As long as the assistance from the ESM is voluntary and does not replace existing obligations of the beneficiary Member State, but it simply creates a new loan, there is no violation of the no bailout clause.[29] Such interpretations of art. 125 TFEU is confirmed by the systematic reading of the Treaty. Indeed, the no bailout clause has not been formulated as strictly as other rules, such as art. 123 and art. 124 TFEU on monetary financings, which expressly refer to a 'prohibition'.[30] Moreover, if art. 125 TFEU meant to totally prevent mutual financial support within the EU, the Treaty would not foresee the solidarity clause ex art. 122(2) TFEU.[31]

Second, a teleological interpretation of the Treaty suggests that the no bailout clause shall prohibit financial assistance between countries only when the latter undermines the objective of art. 125 TFEU, namely the conduct of a sound budgetary policy.[32] Notably national governments would be encouraged to mismanage their public finances, if they knew, they could always rely on the financial support of their partners. This is not the case of the ESM, as its financial assistance is granted only in return for compliance with strict conditions, which shall foster budgetary discipline in the Member States.[33] It is in particular up to the MoU to define the economic reforms and targets, the concerned Member State has to meet under the supervision of the *Troika* in order to receive financial assistance.[34]

Third, in accordance with the *ultima ratio* interpretation, the Court identifies a higher (second-order) 'telos' for art. 125 TFEU[35]: the application of the no bailout clause makes Member States subject to the regulatory role of financial markets and in doing so, ensures the 'financial stability of the euro area as a whole'.[36] The emergence of this higher objective helps the reconciliation of art. 125 TFEU with the

---

[29]ECJ Judgment of 27 November 2012, Case C-370/12, *Thomas Pringle v Government of Ireland*, para. 130.

[30]Ibid. para. 132.

[31]Ibid. para. 131.

[32]Ibid. paras. 135–136. Beck strongly criticised the Pringle judgment for the exasperation of the teleological approach and extreme literal interpretation, which leads it to absurdity. See Beck (2014), pp. 548–549.

[33]ECJ Judgment of 27 November 2012, Case C-370/12, *Thomas Pringle v Government of Ireland*, para. 136.

[34]Cf. *supra* Sect. 3.6.3.

[35]See ECJ Judgment of 27 November 2012, Case C-370/12, *Thomas Pringle v Government of Ireland*, ECLI:EU:C:2012:756, para. 135. On the *ultima ratio* interpretation see Tuori (2012), pp. 24–25.

[36]The Court comes to this opinion also considering the preparatory works relating to the Treaty of Maastricht according to which the aim of art. 125 TFEU is to ensure that Member States follow a sound budgetary policy. See ECJ Judgment of 27 November 2012, Case C-370/12, *Thomas Pringle v Government of Ireland*, ECLI:EU:C:2012:756, para. 135. Borger noticed that the Court could not present the objective of safeguarding the financial stability of the monetary union as a new interpretation of art. 125 TFEU following from Decision 2011/199/EU, as this would have led to an implicit modification of the no bailout clause. See Borger (2013b), p. 135.

conditional financial support of the ESM, which pursues the same goal in accordance with art. 136(3) TFEU.[37] Accordingly, the Court observes that the ESM is consistent with art. 125 TFEU, as long as financial support is necessary for the stability of the monetary union.[38]

Unfortunately, the Court did not pick up some of the arguments developed by Advocate General Kokott in her view on the Pringle case. In particular, the latter noticed that an absolute interpretation of art. 125 TFEU preventing the provision of financial support between euro countries would go against two equally important principles of EU law: the principle of sovereignty of Member States and the principle of solidarity. On the one hand, national governments must be granted the authority to avoid default of another country, if this risks putting in danger the survival of the currency union.[39] If art. 125 TFEU forbid any financial support addressed to this objective, it would also deprive national governments of the ability to avert damage to themselves.[40] On the other hand, financial support should be allowed in the light of the principle of solidarity,[41] which is recalled in art. 3(3) TEU and art. 122(1) TFEU. Even if solidarity in the EU is not so strong to create an automatic obligation of mutual financial support, an absolute interpretation of art. 125 TFEU would also forbid the voluntary granting of assistance in case of emergency, including the serious economic and social effects associated with a state bankruptcy.[42]

4.2.4.3 Softening the No Bailout Clause: From Market Discipline to the Pursuit of the Stability of the Euro Area as a Whole

The debate on the consistency of mutual financial assistance between Member States and the no bailout clause has been extremely important in identifying the margin of evolution, the economic union had during the crisis. In this regard, it is possible to draw some conclusions.

The development of a permanent rescue mechanism between Member State does represent a break from the original Maastricht paradigm of economic union based on

---

[37]Tuori and Tuori call it the 'two-level teleology'. See Tuori and Tuori (2014), p. 129.

[38]See ECJ Judgment of 27 November 2012, Case C-370/12, *Thomas Pringle v Government of Ireland*, ECLI:EU:C:2012:756, para. 136.

[39]View of Advocate General Kokott delivered on 26 October 2012, Case C-370/12, *Thomas Pringle v Government of Ireland*, ECLI:EU:C:2012:675, para 139.

[40]Ibid. para 140.

[41]In favour of the consistency of rescue mechanism with the principle of solidarity see Borger (2013a), pp. 25–26; Bandilla (2017) Artikel 25 AEUV, para 31.

[42]View of Advocate General Kokott delivered on 26 October 2012, Case C-370/12, *Thomas Pringle v Government of Ireland*, ECLI:EU:C:2012:675, paras 142–143.

the principle of individual responsibility for budgetary policy.[43] The introduction of art. 136(3) TFEU acknowledges the fact that, when sharing the same currency, Member States can't be left on their own, as the financial difficulties in one country may have an impact on the others and on the monetary union as a whole. For this reason, the ESM creates a system of mutual guarantees for the repayment of individual debts, which shall help to avoid sovereign defaults, thus protecting the stability of the monetary union. Regardless of the silence from the CJEU on this topic, the solidarity of fact created by the interdependence between Member States is starting to develop some form of normative solidarity,[44] even if the legal mechanism, which regulates it, is still intergovernmental and subject to conditions. Indeed, despite the ESM not formally assuming the debts of the recipient Member State,[45] it *de facto* takes the risks for their fulfilment. From the point of view of the creditor, it doesn't make much difference whether the payment is made directly by the ESM or by the debtor using the resources of the ESM.

The rejection of the absolute interpretation of the no bailout clause depends on the assessment that financial markets are not always able to foster budgetary stability in the euro area, but they can also turn into a source of destabilisation.[46] This occurred during the crisis, when several countries were attacked by international speculation: in that moment, the intent of investors wasn't demanding an interest rate proportional to the effective risks of their investment, but making their financings more and more expansive, betting that the stronger countries would have come to pay the bill of those under attack or the monetary union would eventually come to an end. Also, the CJEU expressed its criticism on the ability of financial markets to rationally calculate the interest premium on sovereign bonds. In the Gauweiler case, the Court

[43]According to some authors, the Court supported a new interpretation of art. 125 TFEU with the intention to provide a judicial legitimation to a political decision. See Kerber (2013), pp. 10–11; Beck (2014), p. 550.

[44]Borger identifies two concepts of solidarity. 'Factual solidarity' is a result of the mutual interdependence between Member States of the Union. The introduction of a single currency has indeed strengthened integration within the euro area, making the default of one Member State dangerous for the economic stability of the others. On the other hand, 'normative solidarity' derives from the belonging of Member States to the same community and the pursuit of the common good. Evidently both dimensions of the principle apply in relation to the rescue strategy adopted to deal with the sovereign debt crisis. See Borger (2013a), pp. 10–11.

[45]The CJEU indeed stressed that assistance granted by the ESM does not consist of subsides, but of loans, which must be paid to the ESM, including an appropriate margin. See ECJ Judgment of 27 November 2012, Case C-370/12, *Thomas Pringle v Government of Ireland*, ECLI:EU:C:2012:756, para. 139. Iaonnidis noticed, however, the credit provided by the ESM contains 'subsidized interest rates that are significantly lower than market rates'. Ioannidis (2016), p. 1260. The purchase of bonds on the secondary market is legally controversial, as it sorts the effect of discharging the issuing state's commitment to the former creditor and to upset normal market conditions. See Tuori and Tuori (2014), p. 126; Schepel (2017), p. 88.

[46]The crisis might have determined an 'Abirrung der Markte' (aberration/mistake of the markets), which prevents it from having a regulatory role. See Nettesheim (2012), p. 63. Markets have not always been able to exercise an effective regulatory role. Cf. De Gregorio Merino (2012), p. 1627; Tuori and Tuori (2014), pp. 127–128.

analysed the reasons why during the debt crisis the government bonds of various states were characterised by high volatility and extreme spreads. The judges argued that the latter phenomenon was not solely due to macroeconomic differences between Member States, but in (large) part to the demand for excessive risk premia for the bonds issued by certain countries. The reason why markets requested higher interest rates than what it should have been rational to request depended on the fear (or hope) for the possible collapse of the euro area.[47] Reading this interpretation in connection with the Pringle ruling, the assistance of the ESM should not be considered in contrast with the prohibition of bailout, as long as it does not have the scope to rescue Member States at all costs, thus encouraging moral hazard, but pursuing budgetary consolidation in a way to replace the regulatory role of the financial markets. Rather than being dictated by the interest rates requested by investors, sound public finances result from the conditionality attached to the financial assistance programmes of the ESM.[48]

Following this analysis, the Pringle and Gauweiler judgments confirm the emergence of a new paradigm of stability, which has emancipated from the original market logic outlined in the Maastricht Treaty and relies on the active behaviour of both EU institutions and Member States, which pursue together consolidation and stabilisation policies. In this regard, it should be noticed that the regulatory role of financial markets and the budgetary discipline imposed through the conditionality policy are not equivalent. On the one hand, the influence of financial markets on national economic policy is mediated: the judgment of investors on the economic situation in a country is essentially based on perceptions, forecasts and external analysis, rather than on a direct collection and assessment of information; furthermore, markets are not able to demand precise reforms and corrective measures, but they simply acknowledge that the investment risk in a country's debt has changed, thus demanding a different interest rate on its bonds. On the contrary, the budgetary consolidation pursued by the ESM through conditional financial support is much more intrusive and effective, as it is based on the careful analysis of economic data collected by the *Troika*, as well as on precise requests regarding budgetary policy and structural reforms defined in the MoU. Evidently, the CJEU allowed the shift from one model of surveillance to another assuming that they both pursue the objective of 'stability of the euro area as a whole'.[49]

---

[47] ECJ, Judgment of 16 June 2015, Case C-62/14, *Gauweiler (and Others) v. Deutscher Bundestag*, ECLI:EU:C:2015:400, paras 72, 74.

[48] 'Spreads always only result from the market participants' expectations and are, regardless of their rationality, essential for market-based pricing. To single out and neutralise supposedly identifiable individual causes would be tantamount to an arbitrary interference with market [..]. Ultimately, the distinction between rational and irrational is meaningless in this context and can in any case not be operationalised'. Order of German Federal Constitutional Court, 14 January 2014, [2 BvR 2728/13], para 98.

[49] Cf. Ioannidis (2016), p. 1259.

4.2.4.4 The Longstanding Limits Posed by the No Bailout Clause to the Process of Fiscal Centralisation

The reinterpretation of art. 125 TFEU developed by the CJEU in the Pringle judgment is extremely important because it acknowledges that the stability of the monetary union shall prevail on the rigid protection of national fiscal sovereignty and the sharing of risks can be acceptable at certain conditions. The complex legal debate on the consistency of the no bailout clause with the setup of rescue policies, however, showed the struggle to overcome the Maastricht paradigm and provide the economic union with the right instruments to govern the interdependence between the Member States. The CJEU had the merit to exclude an absolute interpretation of the no bailout clause, which would have prevented the fulfilment of stabilisation policies in the Eurozone.[50] The softening of art. 125 TFEU was evidently possible thank to an eclectic reading of the clause in the light of the new objective of the 'stability of the euro area as a whole'. At the same time, what the CJEU could not do was eradicate the no bailout clause from the TFEU. While the trust in market discipline is no longer absolute, art. 125 TFEU still provides an important protection to national fiscal sovereignty. This may pose some limits to the future development of the economic union.

First, governments shall not directly assume the existing debts of the other countries, but only provide them with new fresh resources to fulfil their obligations (new debt criterion). From the formal point of view, debtors shall not be relieved from their liabilities. The CJEU expressly stated that every form of mutualisation of sovereign debt shall be excluded. For this reason, the introduction of Eurobonds within the EU legal framework should be excluded.[51] Similarly, any form of debt relief cancelling part of national public debt would be in contrast with the no bailout clause. In this regard, it is opportune to recall the doubts raised on the legal nature of resources granted to Greece by the other Member States in the framework of the ESM/EFSF financial assistance. Despite having been formally qualified as 'loans', the terms according to which resources have been provided are rather peculiar: more precisely, the maturity of loans is very long, in average more than 30 years, and the interest rate, they enjoy, is extremely low, definitely much cheaper than what market conditions can offer.[52] For this reason, several commenters have started arguing that the government will probably never repay its debt and that the resources transferred to Greece should be better qualified as a form of 'hidden transfer'.[53] These doubts increased after the agreement in June 2018 on the new terms of the assistance

[50]See Richter (2013), Article 125 TFEU, para 5.

[51]A number of economists and think tanks have already developed some detailed analysis on the project, highlighting the technical options and the legal challenges of the so called 'Eurobonds'. The European Commission itself endorsed the idea of Eurozone-joint stability bond in a Green Paper published in 2011. See European Commission Communication (2011).

[52]See Adamski (2012), p. 1331; Craig (2013), p. 9.

[53]In this regard Adamski believes that Greece received 'funds on preferential terms'. Adamski (2012), p. 1331. On the sustainability of Greek debt cf. *infra* Sects. 4.3.3.2 and 5.3.2.1.2.

programme to Greece, which provides a form of 'debt relief' in the sense of further maturity extension, additional grace periods, new cash injections and even cheaper interest rates on the existing loans.[54]

Second, the grant of financial support is subject to the application of a strict conditionality policy, which shall ensure the application of budgetary discipline and prevent moral hazard, (conditionality criterion). Accordingly, the Eurozone shall not create a mechanism providing automatic financial support. The pursuit of stability requires the simultaneous activation of both financial assistance and the conditionality policy, thus fostering budgetary stability both in the short and the longer term. Therefore, the ESM shall transfer capitals to the beneficiary Member State only in tranches, after the Commission has carefully verified its ongoing compliance with the MoU.

Third, financial support shall be activated only when it is indispensable to fulfil the stability of the euro area as a whole (indispensability criterion): minor shocks which are not able to cause a threat to the survival of the EMU or can be managed autonomously from the concerned Member State fall out of the range of the ESM. The latter criterion, however, is not purely technical. The financial difficulties of a smaller country for example do still matter, when, despite not posing a systematic threat to the survival of the euro area as such, may jeopardise its individual membership in the monetary union and consequently the integrity of the euro area.[55] This explains why the ESM could intervene also in support of small economies, such as Cyprus or Greece.

The fulfilment of these conditions must always be verified in concrete and the CJEU has jurisdiction on the alleged violation of the criteria. At the same time, the Commission and the ECB have some room for discretion for the technical evaluation of financial assistance and conditionality policy.[56]

4.2.5 Consistency of the ESM Financial Assistance with the Solidarity Clause

The establishment of the ESM posed some concerns also on the possible violation of art. 122(2) TFEU, according to which the Union shall provide financial assistance to its Member States, when they are seriously threatened with severe difficulties caused

[54]See Eurogroup statement on Greece, 15 June 2018. Greece officially concluded its ESM financial assistance programme in August 2018. It should be noted that in May 2019 the EFSF decided to the return to Greece €103 million euros paid between January 1 to 17 June 2018, in relation to an interest rate hike provided by the MoU, and to suspend a similar increase related to the period June 17, 2018-June 17, 2019, which will save the Greek government € 226 million. See Press Release, 'ESM formally approves more than 970 million of debt relief for Greece', 2 May 2019.

[55]De Witte and Beukers (2013), pp. 839–840; Cisotta (2015), pp. 291–292; Palm (2017), Artikel 136 AEUV, para. 57.

[56]Thymes and Wendel (2012), p. 748.

by natural disasters or exceptional occurrences beyond their control (solidarity clause). Notably, while art. 122(2) TFEU was used to legitimise the creation of a temporary instrument, such as the European Financial Stabilisation Mechanism (EFSM) in 2010, when Member States decided to set up a permanent mechanism, they stipulated an intergovernmental agreement beyond EU Law.[57] Evidently, this choice was dictated in the first instance by a material contingency: as the size of the necessary bailouts to stabilise the euro area passed the available resources in the EU budget, rescue operations of significant size could be financed only by national budgets.

Aside from the issue of resources, it has been discussed whether art. 122(2) TFEU could have offered an alternative legal basis for the formation of a permanent stabilisation mechanism and whether the creation of the ESM through an intergovernmental agreement is consistent with the solidarity clause. The legal doctrine[58] and the CJEU in the Pringle judgment tried to answer these questions. In particular, the Court of Luxembourg argued that both the Member States and the Union are allowed to provide financial assistance, even if they shall fulfil different conditions to comply with the EU primary law.[59] While the ESM has a permanent character, art. 122(2) TFEU allows only the adoption of temporary measures. Consequently, long-term assistance programme to Member States experiencing serious financing difficulties could not be introduced on the basis of the solidarity clause. At the same time, while the new stability mechanism aims to safeguard 'the stability of the euro area as whole', art. 122(2) TFEU has a more restricted objective, which is to deal with exceptional occurrences beyond the Member State's control. Therefore, the purpose of the solidarity clause is to manage circumscribed emergencies, rather than ensuring the integrity and the solidity of the currency union through critical times. Furthermore, while the ESM consists of a mechanism created by and for the Eurozone countries, the financial help envisaged in art. 122(2) TFEU should be offered to all EU Member States, without distinction. Therefore, the TFEU does not allow to differentiate the application of the assistance instruments between Member States or create *ad hoc* mechanisms only for the euro area. In the light of these considerations, the ESM could correctly be introduced through an international treaty, this being consistent with the solidarity clause.

Evidently, as for art. 125 TFEU, the Court of Justice developed a new interpretation of the solidarity clause to make room for the creation of the ESM. While art. 122(2) TFEU looked initially like the only legal basis to provide financial support within the EMU, after the crisis the CJEU was obliged to acknowledge the

---

[57] In Decision 2011/199/EU amending art. 136 TFEU the European Council clearly stated that art. 122(2) TFEU shall not be applied to safeguard the financial stability of the euro area. See Whereas (4) European Council Decision 2011/199/EU.

[58] The fiscal crisis in countries like Greece does not fit definition as it is the consequence of chronical budgetary mismanagement. See De Gregorio Merino (2012), p. 1634; Vogel (2012), pp. 463–464; Tosato (2012) p. 687; De Witte and Beukers (2013), p. 810.

[59] ECJ Judgment of 27 November 2012, Case C-370/12, *Thomas Pringle v Government of Ireland*, ECLI:EU:C:2012:756, paras 65, 120.

structural limits of this provision. Aside from the letter of the norm, which reasonably refers to local emergencies beyond the State's control, the fundamental obstacle to its application regards the ownership of financial assistance, which art. 122 (2) TFEU specifically confers to the Union. As the EU budget cannot carry the weight of sovereign bailouts, it was then necessary to narrow the application of the solidarity clause to allow the creation of intergovernmental rescue mechanisms.

4.2.6 *The Ambiguous Nature of the Conditionality Policy and Its Compliance with the EU Treaties*

As the TFEU and the TESM do not provide any clear reference on the matter, the function of the conditionality policy in the economic governance is controversial. In the Pringle case, the CJEU adopted a reductive interpretation according to which the purpose of conditionality shall be 'to ensure that [the] mechanism will operate in a way that will comply with European Union law, including the measures adopted by the Union in the context of the coordination of the Member States' economic policies'.[60] From this point of view conditionality would not provide any addition to the existing rules of economic coordination, but simply ensure their correct application. The reason why the Court of Luxembourg suggested such a minimalist reading, was to avoid a possible legal conflict between the new mechanisms created through an intergovernmental agreement and EU primary law.[61]

Such interpretation, however, is not consistent with the concrete application, which has been given to conditionality policies over the years, as well as the opinion of most legal doctrine, according to which the conditionality policy is a *sui generis* instrument of economic governance and surveillance.[62] Indeed, the conditions fixed in the MoUs don't simply replicate ordinary economic coordination under the EU Treaties, but provide for new specific requests, the concerned Member State has to fulfil in order to receive financial assistance. These can be updated and modified taking into consideration the economic development of the country, in the framework of the supervision enforced by the *Troika*. The existence of a difference between the conditionality policy and standard economic coordination is confirmed by the fact that Regulation (EU) No 472/2013 foresees that the application of a macroeconomic adjustment programme under the ESM shall suspend the enforcement of almost all monitoring procedures under the MSP, the EDP and the MIP in order to avoid inconsistences.[63]

---

[60]See ECJ Judgment of 27 November 2012, Case C-370/12, *Thomas Pringle v Government of Ireland*, ECLI:EU:C:2012:756, para. 69.

[61]Ibid. paras 112–113.

[62]See De Lhoneux and Vassilopoulos (2013), p. 44; Schwarz (2014), p. 412; Poulou (2017), pp. 996–997.

[63]See art. 10, art. 11, art. 12 and art. 13 of Regulation (EU) No 472/2013.

Looking at the legal nature and the ownership of conditionality, formally the EU does not have any legal authority to oblige a Member State to start an assistance programme under the ESM and comply with its conditionality policy, meaning that the primary responsibility for the adoption and application of conditionality falls on the shoulders of the Member State concerned. As long as the EU countries conserve their budgetary sovereignty, conditions can't be imposed, but only accepted. For this reason, the adjustment programmes attached to the MoUs recognise that 'the ownership of the programme and all executive responsibilities in the programme implementation remain with the [national] Government'.[64]

The prevalent interpretation, according to which the ownership of conditionality belongs exclusively to the recipient Member States, can be doubted for two main reasons.

First of all, some important legislative reforms have been introduced, which give EU institutions some voice in the definition of conditionality. The latter shall be negotiated by the Commission according to the TESM rules, but also taking into consideration the Council Decision adopted in accordance with art. 7(2) and (5) of Regulation (EU) No 472/2013.[65] The latter is a unilateral act of the Union, which approves and updates the Macroeconomic Adjustment Programme (MAP) for the Member States, which has requested the financial support of the ESM, by defining the main elements of conditionality.[66] Furthermore, the introduction of an 'enhanced surveillance' procedure towards countries, which may experience some form of financial difficulty, has narrowed their margin of discretion when they 'freely' decide to demand the intervention of the ESM. Finally, the binding nature of MoUs under EU law has been implicitly acknowledged by the CJEU in the *Ledra Advertising* case, when the Court recognised that the EUCFR is applicable to EU institutions when they act under the ESM.[67]

Second, aside from the legal formality, the state of necessity, in which a country requesting the activation of the ESM finds itself, reduces *de facto* its autonomy to negotiate and agree on the MoU. This is the paradox of 'conditionality': even if, from a legal point of view, the ownership of policy is national, in concrete European authorities and creditor countries are in a position of strength, which gives them the

[64]Memorandum of Understanding on Specific Economic Policy Conditionality (Second Economic Adjustment Programme for Greece), March 2012.

[65]Before 2013, the measures directed to countries that received assistance from the EFSF or the ESM, except from formally non-binding Memoranda of Understanding, also took the form of decisions of the Council ex art. 126(6) or (9) TFEU together with art. 136 TFEU. See Ioannidis (2016), p. 1269.

[66]The Council decision approving the MAP is binding and its legality can be reviewed by the ECJ. See Leino-Sandberg and Salminen (2017), p. 78. Looking more into details, they have a similar content, but not identical. In particular, the MoUs are longer and more detailed than the decisions of the Council. The loan agreement between the recipient country and the ESM recalls both documents, by acknowledging they have the same legal status. See Poulou (2017), p. 1002.

[67]ECJ Judgment of 20 September 2016, Joined Cases C-8/15 P to C-10/15 P, Ledra Advertising Ltd. and Others v European Commission and European Central Bank (ECB), ECLI:EU:C:2016:701. Cf. Estella (2018), pp. 226–231.

chance to demand and obtain the acceptance of any conditions, they want.[68] Evidently, the force of conditionality is more political, than legal: Member States must respect European requests, if they do not want to end up dealing with their financial troubles on their own.

Once qualified the nature of the conditionality policy as hybrid, it is possible to analyse its consistency with EU law and, more precisely, with the conferral principle. Significant concerns in this regard depend on the fact that the application of conditionality policy, even if it must be formally accepted by the recipient Member State, is *de facto* imposed by the creditor countries and, since the entry into force of Regulation (EU) No 472/2013 also by the Council. The influence of the ESM and the EU institutions involved on the shaping of national economic policy is even more intrusive considering that the TESM and Regulation (EU) No 472/2013 do not provide any criteria to define the contents of conditionality.[69] Such vagueness allows Memoranda to touch upon all a wide range of issues, from the restructuration of the welfare system, to the reform of the labour market and the imposition of new taxes.[70] Evidently, as the ESM can now advance any kind of requests to national authorities by taking advantage of their situation of need, the fiscal rights of Member States are undermined.[71] In the light of these observations, the concrete application of the conditionality policy in the framework of the ESM seems overcoming the limits set out in EU primary law, which conceives economic coordination only in terms of compliance with common rules, thus leaving wide autonomy to each government for their compliance, rather than as an instrument to shape every aspect of national economy. Once the conditionality policy is able to order Member States what to do with their internal policies, national fiscal sovereignty may be irredeemably undermined.[72]

[68]Ioannidis (2014), pp. 34–35. Conditionality policy consists of a form of 'imposition', rather than coordination. Munari (2018), p. 362.

[69]Art. 12 (1) TESM states that conditionality may range 'from a macro-economic adjustment programme to continuous respect of pre-established eligibility conditions' and 'it should reflect the severity of the weakness to be addresses and the financial assistance chosen. According to art. 7(1) of Regulation (EU) No 472/2013, 'macroeconomic adjustment programme shall address the specific risks emanating from that Member State for the financial stability in the euro area and shall aim at rapidly re-establishing a sound and sustainable economic and financial situation and restoring the Member State's capacity to finance itself fully on the financial markets'.

[70]Cf. Rossolillo (2018), p. 141.

[71]See Tuori and Tuori (2014), p. 189; Ioannidis (2016), pp. 1271–1272.

[72]The influence that the ESM can exercise on the budgetary policy of Member States depends on their financial strength, and indirectly on their populations (as decisions are taken on the basis of capital contribution). See Dawson and de Witte (2013), p. 838.

4.2.7 Consistency of the ESM Financial Assistance with the EUCFR

Another problem arising from the creation of intergovernmental rescue mechanisms regards the compliance of conditionality policy with the EU Charter of Fundamental Rights (EUCFR).[73] More precisely, the terms of financial assistance defined in the MoU normally demand the introduction of structural reforms, whose concrete implementation in domestic law may undermine some fundamental economic and social rights protected by the Charter. This happens when the concerned Member State pursues budgetary consolidation through austerity measures, which may consist for example of tax increase, cuts in the welfare state and restructuration of public offices. Therefore, the CJEU was referred several times for the violation of the Charter following the application of the conditionality policy in the Member States under an ESM's financial assistance programme.

Looking at the less recent case laws, the judges of Luxembourg initially dismissed the claims on the basis of two arguments. On the one hand, they argued that the decisions adopted by the Union referring to the conditionality policy consist of informal acts, which leave a significant margin of discretion for the negotiation of the MoU and its implementation in domestic law. In the *Adedy* case, the General Court rejected an action ex art. 263 TFEU against a Council Decision regarding the management of public assets, reduction of family allowances and the limitation of recruitment in the public sector in Greece, based on the fact that the latter provision was indeterminate and provided the national government with a significant margin of action on its effective implementation.[74] For this reason, the Court stated that the applicants were not directly concerned by the Council Decision. On the other hand, the Court argued that the decisions to impose austerity measures do not belong to the Union, but to an intergovernmental body, namely the ESM, whose owners are the national governments. Accordingly, in the *Pringle* case the Court denied the TESM was in contrast with the EUCFR, noticing that the ESM is an international agreement falling out of the scope of the Charter and that Member States are not acting implementing EU law.[75] In the *Mallis* Case, the Court could easily reject the claims against a statement of the Eurogroup referring to the conditions of the Cypriot bailout by arguing that the latter cannot be considered as a decision-making body of the Union and its decisions are not legally binding measures.[76] The arguments put

---

[73]Munari (2015), pp. 741–743.

[74]Order of the General Court, 27 November 2012, Case T-541/10, Anotati Dioikisi Enoseon Dimosion Ypallilon (ADEDY) and Others v Council of the European Union, ECLI:EU:T:2012:626.

[75]ECJ Judgment of 27 November 2012, Case C-370/12, *Thomas Pringle v Government of Ireland*, ECLI:EU:C:2012:756, para.180.

[76]ECJ Judgement of 20 September 2016, Joined Cases C-105/15 P to C-109/15 P, Konstantinos Mallis and Others v European Commission and European Central Bank (ECB), ECLI:EU:C:2016:702. For an analysis of the case cf. Cafari Panico (2017), pp. 295–296.

forward by the Court are not completely convincing. Even if some acts adopted through the process of granting financial assistance are not legally-binding and cannot be contested, the application of the EUCFR to the conditionality policy in the framework of the ESM can be argued in the light of several considerations.

First of all, decisions providing for conditionality are not foreign to EU law. The domestic measures applying austerity are not taken spontaneously by the Member States, but follow a MoU negotiated with the European Commission, which according to art. 7(2) of Regulation (EU) No 472/2013 shall be fully consistent with the macroeconomic adjustment programme approved by the Council. There is therefore a direct link between a binding act of the EU institutions and the (austerity) measures adopted by the Member States.[77] Furthermore, art. 13(3) TESM provides for a consistency clause, according to which the MoU shall be fully consistent with the measures of economic policy coordination provided for in the Treaties. As the acts of EU institutions under Title VIII of the TFEU are subject to the jurisdiction of the EUCFR, the latter should be extended also to the MoUs adopted in accordance with them. In the light of these argumentations, the nature of conditionality policy can be qualified as a hybrid,[78] falling at least partially within the EU legal order and consequently under the jurisdiction of the EUCFR.[79]

The participation of EU institutions in the management of the ESM also confirms the applicability of the EUCFR to the definition of conditional financial support.[80] Notably, even if the TESM is an intergovernmental agreement, the Commission and the ECB play a primary role in both negotiating the MoUs and monitoring their application. As the Pringle judgment implicitly admitted, EU institutions are still subject to EU law when they act for the implementation of intergovernmental

---

[77]In Åklagaren case the CJEU clarified that 'the fundamental rights guaranteed by the Charter must [..] be complied with where national legislation falls within the scope of European Union law'. ECJ judgment of 26 February 2013, Case C-617/10, Åklagaren v Hans Åkerberg Fransson, ECLI:EU:C:2013:105, para 21. Accordingly, the EUCFR should be applied when there is direct link between a national (austerity) measure and an act of the Union, meaning any lacuna in the implementation of the austerity measures may cause a violation of both the MoU and the Council Decision ex art. 7(2) of Regulation (EU) No 472/2013, thus leading to a suspension of financial assistance. On the relevance of the Åklagaren case law see Pistoia (2018), pp. 83–84.

[78]On the hybrid nature of conditionality policy cf. Sect. 4.2.6.

[79]On the connection between conditionality and EU law see Hinarejos (2015), pp. 134–135; Craig (2017), p. 245. Poulou recalls the *Wachauf* judgment (ECJ Judgment of 13 July 1989, Hubert Wachauf v Bundesamt für Ernährung und Forstwirtschaft, C-5/88, ECLI:EU:C:1989:321), according to which Member States act like agents of the Union, why they apply regulations, directives or decisions of the Council. Poulou (2017), pp. 1021–1022. In the *Florescu* case, the Court has qualified a MoU stipulated between the European Commission and Romania in the framework of financial assistance ex art. 143 TFEU, as an act of EU law. The latter can be therefore subject to an action of annulment. The Court based its decision on the fact that the MoU has a clear legal basis in the EU Treaties and it was concluded with the European Union. See ECJ Judgment of 13 June 2017, Case C-258/12, *Eugenia Florescu and Others v Casa Județeană de Pensii Sibiu and Others,* ECLI:EU:C:2017:448. On the analysis of the case cf. Markakis and Dermine (2018).

[80]Bernard (2013), p. 267.

agreements.[81] Accordingly, they should still take care of the protection of human rights as defined in EU law, when they participate in the definition of conditionality policy. This argument has been eventually accepted by the CJEU in its most recent case law. In the *Ledra Advertising* case, the applicants started an action for damages ex art. 340 TFEU after the MoU agreed by the Cyprian authorities with the European Commission decided to take a haircut on their own bank deposit.[82] In this regard, the Court recognised that the Charter is applicable to EU institutions when they act under the ESM. Accordingly, the ECB, the Commission and the Council[83] should not propose or impose conditions to the Member States, which may cause damages to individuals.[84] In relation specifically to the Eurogroup, even if the latter does not adopt attackable decisions under art. 263 TFEU, the General Court affirmed in the *Chrystotomides* and the *Bourdouvali* judgments that its statements can give rise to the non-contractual liability of the Union.[85]

Evidently, even if the CJEU recognised the applicability of the EUCFR in the framework of the ESM, the protection of fundamental rights from the concrete application of the conditionality policy is not automatic, but it must follow the general rules on jurisdiction. For example, an action ex art. 263 TFEU against a Council Decision adopted ex art. 7(2) of Regulation (EU) No 472/2013 will be accepted only if the applicants prove, they own a direct and individual interest to annul the act concerned.[86] Furthermore, a balancing test shall always be fulfilled in concrete to decide whether the protection of the fundamental rights protected by the EUCFR shall prevail on other interests or objectives pursued by the EU Treaties through the conditionality policy. In the *Ledra Advertising* case, for example, the Court stated that the limitation of the right of property determined by the MoU is

[81] '[T]he Member States are entitled, in areas which do not fall under the exclusive competence of the Union, to entrust tasks to the institutions, outside the framework of the Union, [..] provided that those tasks do not alter the essential character of the powers conferred on those institutions by the EU and FEU Treaties'. ECJ Judgment of 27 November 2012, Case C-370/12, *Thomas Pringle v Government of Ireland*, ECLI:EU:C:2012:756, para 158.

[82] ECJ Judgment of 20 September 2016, Joined Cases C-8/15 P to C-10/15 P, *Ledra Advertising Ltd and Others v European Commission and European Central Bank (ECB)*, ECLI:EU:C:2016:701.

[83] The applicability of the EUCFR to the Council should be less controversial as it participated in the definition of conditionality policy through a decision adopted in accordance with Regulation (EU) No 472/2013.

[84] For an analysis of the case cf. Poulou (2017), pp. 1008–1009, 1013–1014; Cafari Panico (2017), pp. 293–295.

[85] ECJ Judgement of 13 July 2018, Case T-680/13, *Dr. K. Chrysostomides & Co. LLC and Others v Council of the European Union and Others*, ECLI:EU:T:2018:486, paras 109–110; ECJ Judgment, Case T-786/14, 13 July 2018, *Eleni Pavlikka Bourdouvali and Others v Council of the European Union and Others*, ECLI:EU:T:2018:487, paras 105–106. It should be noted that the Council has appealed both rulings. See C-597/18 P; C-598/18 P). An action of annulment is excluded because the Eurogroup is not an EU body within the meaning of art. 263 TFEU. Ibid. para. 105.

[86] Poulou (2017), pp. 1012–1013.

acceptable as long as the conditional financial assistance aims to protect the 'stability of the banking system of the euro area as a whole'.[87]

4.2.8 *Flight Into International Law*

Due to the limited competence of the EU, national governments decided to use intergovernmental agreements to introduce some important reform in the economic governance. The two most significant applications of this approach have been the Treaty on the European Stability Mechanism (TESM) and the Treaty of the Coordination, the Stability and the Governance (TSCG). This 'flight into international law' (*Flucht in Völkerrecht*)[88] has comprehensibly raised some serious concerns on the constitutional integrity of the EMU.[89] As it was already argued in the Delors Report, the monetary union and the economic union 'form two integral parts of a single whole'.[90] The wide use of international law may jeopardise therefore the unitary development of the EMU, the internal coherence of the EU legal framework, as well as its institutional balance.[91] The development of parallel procedures beyond EU law has indeed encouraged the marginalisation of supranational institutions and strengthened intergovernmental bodies, such as the Council and the European Council, by providing them with an intrusive power of control on national policies. At the same time, the stipulation of intergovernmental acts, either binding or of soft law, may escape the jurisdiction of the CJEU, as it was the case for the MoUs defining ESM conditionality policy.

Being aware of the implicit risks for the EU legal framework, European institutions tried to pose some limits to the flight into international law of the governance. The Two Pack has notably translated some provisions of the Fiscal Compact in EU law and dictated some new rules on the concession of conditional financial support by the ESM.[92] At the same time, the CJEU explained in the Pringle judgment the

[87]ECJ Judgment of 20 September 2016, Joined Cases C-8/15 P to C-10/15 *P, Ledra Advertising Ltd and Others v European Commission and European Central Bank (ECB)*, ECLI:EU:C:2016:701, para. 71. The strengthening of economic integration has determined a compression of social rights of EU citizens. It is regrettable the CJEU has normally preferred to privilege the sustainability of public finances over the protection of fundamental individual rights. On the relevant case law cf. Cafari Panico (2017), pp. 306–311. On the possible ways to balance fiscal stability with the protection of the fundamental rights in the EU legal system cf. Condinanzi (2016), pp. 249–252.

[88]See Häde (2012), pp. 15–16.

[89]See Craig (2012), pp. 238–241; Tomkin (2013), pp. 79–81, Dimopoulos (2014), pp. 62–63.

[90]Delors 'Report on Economic and Monetary Union in the European Community', 17th April 1989, p. 14.

[91]Miglio (2015), pp. 157–158.

[92]In perspective, the TSCG does foresee an incorporation clause, according to which within 5 years of the date of entry into force of the Treaty, the Member States shall take the necessary step to incorporate its substance into the legal framework of the EU.

conditions that Member States must fulfil when they decide to stipulate an intergovernmental agreement *inter se* beyond EU law: the external treaty shall regard non-exclusive competences of the EU and it must respect the *acquis communautaire.*[93] Looking at the fulfilment of these criteria in concrete, it has been possible to analyse whether the TESM and TSCG are legitimate.

The compliance with the first condition has been notably clarified by the Court. Both Treaties set procedures and mechanisms, which fall within the management of economic policy.[94] This can be deduced looking at the goal that both treaties pursue, namely the 'stability of the euro area as a whole', which the Court has qualified as an objective of economic policy.[95] As the latter is a national competence, on which the Union has only a coordination role ex art. 5(1) TFEU, intergovernmental agreements shall not be forbidden.[96] Even considering the competence of providing financial assistance, which is the main task of the ESM, the Court denied, it represents an exclusive task of the EU. Indeed, while the solidarity clause ex art. 122(2) TFEU gives the Union the possibility to grant financial assistance to the Eurozone countries at certain conditions, nothing in the EU Treaties may suggest that Member States should not also be able to do the same, in case of necessity.[97]

Considering the second condition, the compliance with the *acquis communitaire* is formally ensured by the consistency clause ex art. 2 TSCG and art. 13(3) TESM by virtue of which the agreement applies insofar as it is compatible with EU law. In reality, the situation is more complicated. Considering the TESM, the application of conditionality has a significant impact on the definition of national fiscal policies, thus posing a problem of consistency with the existing EU rules of economic

---

[93]See ECJ Judgment of 27 November 2012, Case C-370/12, *Thomas Pringle v Government of Ireland*, ECLI:EU:C:2012:756, paras 92, 101. According to Munari, in the Pringle case the CJEU allowed Member States to sign intergovernmental agreements that overlap EU competences but are external to the Union, as long as these international obligations respect EU law. This represents a step backwards with regards to the parallelism of internal and external competences affirmed in in the *ERTA* case law. Munari (2015), p. 735; Munari (2018), p. 360.

[94]Art. 1 TSCG explains the Fiscal Compact aims to 'strengthen the economic pillar of the Economic and Monetary Union by adopting a set of rules intended to foster budgetary discipline through a fiscal compact, to strengthen the coordination of their economic policies and to improve the governance of the euro area'. Art. 3 TESM states that 'the ESM shall be to mobilise funding and provide stability support under strict conditionality, appropriate to the financial assistance instrument chosen, to the benefit of ESM Members which are experiencing, or are threatened by, severe financing problems'.

[95]Art. 3 TESM recalls the objective. The TSCG explains in the Preamble that the strengthening of fiscal consolidation, which is the formal objective of the agreement, aims to pursue the stability of the euro area as a whole.

[96]Calliess (2012), p. 105.

[97]See ECJ Judgment of 27 November 2012, Case C-370/12, *Thomas Pringle v Government of Ireland*, ECLI:EU:C:2012:756, paras. 120–121.

coordination.[98] Similar concerns regards the TSCG, as the agreement covers several policy areas, which are already subject to the EU rules of economic coordination.

Focusing specifically on the involvement of EU institutions in the ESM, the Court of Justice took the opportunity in the Pringle case to clarify when this is legitimate. While the involvement of the CJEU has been justified on the basis of the 'arbitration clause' ex art. 273 TFEU,[99] the participation of the Commission and the ECB in the ESM has been motivated by recalling the case law of the Court in the *Bangladesh* and *Lomé* cases.[100] In these judgments the CJEU explained that the involvement of EU institutions in an external Treaty is allowed as long as it does not impinge upon the exclusive competences of the Union and does not alter the powers conferred to them.[101] The Court believes these conditions are fulfilled, as the EU institutions involved in the mechanism do not hold any power to make decisions of their own, nor exercise tasks, which may alter the essential character of their powers under the EU Treaties. More precisely, as the financial conditional assistance of the ESM pursues the stability of the euro area as a whole, the contribution given by the Commission should be in line with its duty to promote the general interest of the Union. Similarly, the tasks of the ECB shall represent a form of support to the general economic policies in the Union, which is one of its objectives in accordance with art. 127(1) TFEU.

The arguments developed by the Court to justify the involvement of the EU institutions in the TESM are not completely convincing. First of all, even if the Commission acts in accordance with the instructions received by the national governments, its contribution to the negotiation and implementation of the MoU is not completely marginal, but it helps shape the material content of conditionality, especially due to its technical expertise. Considering instead the participation of the ECB in the *Troika*, even if art. 23 of the Statute of the ECB and ESCB allows it to 'establish relations [..] with [other] organizations',[102] its involvement in the enforcement of the conditionality policy may jeopardise the principle of independence in the management of monetary policy outlined in art. 130 TFEU.[103] Unfortunately, the

[98]Notably the 'comunitarisation' of the intergovernmental procedures started by the Two Pack aimed to avoid inconsistencies between the MoU and EU law. See *supra* Sect. 3.6.3.

[99]ECJ Judgment of 27 November 2012, Case C-370/12, *Thomas Pringle v Government of Ireland*, ECLI:EU:C:2012:756, paras 170–177. On the role of the CJEU in the TESM cf. Miglio (2015), pp. 162–166; Pistoia (2018), pp. 92–96. According Ziller the conferral of this task to the CJEU is the only provision of the TSCG, which could not have been adopted on the basis of secondary law. Ziller (2015), p. 29.

[100]See ECJ Judgment of 30 June 1993, Joined Cases C - 181/91 and C-248/91 *Parliament v Council and Commission*, ECLI:EU:C:1993:271; ECJ Judgment of 2 March 1994, Case C-316/91 *Parliament v. Council*, ECLI:EU:C:1994:76.

[101]ECJ Judgment of 27 November 2012, Case C-370/12, *Thomas Pringle v Government of Ireland*, ECLI:EU:C:2012:756, para 158.

[102]See ECJ Judgment of 27 November 2012, Case C-370/12, Thomas Pringle v Government of Ireland, ECLI:EU:C:2012:756, para. 165.

[103]As the ECB is provided with strong independence, the Advocate General has highlighted that the TESM cannot oblige it to perform specific tasks, but these must be accepted voluntarily. See See

Court did not have the chance to analyse the role played by the Council in defining conditionality under the ESM, as the Reg. (EU) 472/2013 was adopted 1 year after the issue of the Pringle judgment. The main concerns about its involvement regard the new tasks of the Council, which shall approve the macroeconomic adjustment programme (MAP) prepared by the Member State requesting financial assistance in accordance art. 7(2) of Reg. (EU) No 472/2013. As the Commission shall ensure that the MoU signed by the Commission is fully consistent with the MAP approved by the Council, the latter can now give an important contribution in the definition of the conditionality policy. It is not clear whether the conferral of this power to the Council is legitimate. The fundamental problem regards clearly the intrusiveness of conditionality, which doesn't only reduce the margin of action of Member States, but can shape in detail the economic policy of the countries under financial assistance. The participation of the Council in the management of such an intrusive power of economic supervision may hardly find a justification in the EU Treaties. The legal basis chosen for the adoption of Reg. (EU) No 472/2013, namely art. 121(6) and art. 136 TFEU, does not seem sufficient for this purpose. Indeed, the latter provisions allow only the specification and strengthening of European rules of economic coordination and they cannot modify the quality of the governance, which is exactly what the conferral to the Council of such an intrusive power of control on national economic policies might determine.[104]

4.2.9 The Deficit of Legality: Conclusive Remarks

The previous paragraphs explained the limits posed by the existing legal order to the reforms of the economic union aimed at ensuring the stability of the euro area as a whole. In light of the analysis developed so far, it is possible to draw some conclusive remarks on the matter.

First of all, the available legal basis does not allow the adoption of measures, which may emancipate from the original governance model outlined in Maastricht. The implementation of the most innovative reforms, for example the introduction of semi-automatic sanctions in the process of supervision on national budgets, has been

View of Advocate General Kokott delivered on 26 October 2012 (1) Case C-370/12, *Thomas Pringle v Government of Ireland*, ECLI:EU:C:2012:675, paras 180–181.

[104]The involvement of EU institutions in the TSCG is less controversial. The Fiscal Compact does not modify the competences of EU institutions, but only integrates their functions. See Peroni (2012), p. 182. The tasks granted to the Commission are fully in line with its function of supervisor of European fiscal rules under the SGP. The involvement of the CJEU is also acceptable under the arbitration clause ex art. 273 TFEU being the object of the TSCG in wide party falling within the scope of the EU Treaties. More controversial is the setup of the Euro Summit, which may *de facto* undermine the prerogatives of the Ecofin Council and European Council in the process of economic coordination. On the involvement of EU institutions in the TSCG cf. Pistoia (2018), pp. 134–142.

possible only through a controversial extensive interpretation of the Treaty provisions. Their legality remains therefore controversial.

Second, the efforts to improve the efficiency of the governance crashed with some relevant legal provisions of EU law (i.e. the no bailout clause). The Court of Justice of the Union has been therefore committed to mending the legal fractures caused by the introduction of the reforms through an eclectic exegesis of the EU Treaties.

Third, the creation of intergovernmental instruments involving EU bodies had the purpose to obviate the limits of the legal basis, but it also undermined the institutional balance in the Union and challenged the compliance with the principle of conferral.

In conclusion on the matter, the pursuit of the stability of the euro area as a whole requested Member States and EU institutions to commit themselves in preserving the existence of the monetary union both in ordinary times and during a crisis. Unfortunately, the limited legal basis prevented the governance from developing through an organic and coherent project of reforms. The measures adopted so far consisted more of a process of difficult and partial adaptation of the existing economic governance to the upcoming needs imposed by the crisis. This is one of the reasons why, as the following analysis will explain, the deficits of legality prevented the reform of the economic governance from being sufficiently effective.

4.3 The Deficit of Effectiveness

4.3.1 Preliminary Remarks: An Ineffective Governance

The reforms adopted during the crisis were supposed to strengthen the Eurozone governance and provide it with effective instruments to pursue the stability of the euro area as a whole. Dealing with the available legal basis agreed before the beginning of the crisis, the challenge has been to update and adjust the functioning of the economic union in a way to make it fulfil some new tasks regarding both stabilisation and consolidation policies. The result is a hybrid system, in which Member States have accepted an indirect mutualisation of risks and a more intrusive supervision by EU institutions without, however, losing the formal ownership of fiscal policy.

The following analysis will study whether the economic union can ensure the stability of the euro area as a whole. Measuring the effectiveness of the governance means verifying whether the existing tools can manage those tasks, which are functional to the fulfilment of stability. It will therefore be necessary to consider the results that the Eurozone governance has achieved over the last few years in the development of both consolidation and stabilisation policies. The analysis will test each component of the governance introduced in Chap. 3, namely the preventive and corrective arms of economic coordination, the regulatory role of financial markets, the available procedures for debt restructuration, the implementation of budgetary constraints in domestic law, the stabilisation mechanisms in charge to absorb economic shocks, the development of European investment strategy and the project of banking union.

4.3.2 Weak Economic Coordination

As the previous analysis has widely explained, the strengthening of European surveillance on national fiscal and structural policies has been a priority for European institutions and national governments since the outbreak of the sovereign debt crisis. The reforms aimed to renew the governance based on soft law and political suasion through the addition of new hard law tools.[105] This notably happened with the introduction of semi-automatic sanctions in the MSP, the EDP and the new EIP, which were supposed to strengthen the prerogatives of the Commission and limit the political discretion of Member States in the Council.

Unfortunately, the effectiveness of surveillance remains still unsatisfactory. It is enough to look at the enforcement rate of recommendations issued by the EU institutions over the last few years to realise that Member States are still reluctant to respect European rules on budgetary and macro-economic stability. Looking for example at the country specific recommendations (CSRs) adopted in the framework of the European Semester, data show that since 2013 the implementation of reforms by EU countries has constantly worsened.[106] Also economic convergence between the Member States and budgetary consolidation is not proceeding at the envisaged path,[107] as full compliance with fiscal rules remains more an exception than the norm in most countries. This situation is quite alarming because it shows that national governments have not taken advantage of the relatively favourable macroeconomic environment after the crisis to create fiscal buffers and reduce high debt.[108] The following analysis will identify some of the reasons why the stiffening of economic coordination has been ineffective.

First, economic coordination is based on some 'non-credible threats'.[109] The lack of credibility doesn't depend only on the form and size of the penalties, which consists of a deposit or a fine amounting to few tenths of GDP and may therefore not represent a sufficient deterrent.[110] The main problem is instead that governments are

[105]See Hinarejos (2015), p. 75.

[106]See Darvas and Leandro (2016), Efstathiou and Wolff (2018), European Parliament Briefing (2018), European Commission Communication (2018b) and European Commission Press Release (2019).

[107]See Castaneda and Schwartz (2017); Eurostat, 'Provision of deficit and debt data for 2017 - first notification', 69/2018 – 23 April 2018.

[108]See Haroutunian et al. (2018).

[109]According to Adamski, a non-credible threat is a 'threat that the player making it would not find optimal to actually undertake if called upon to do so'. Adamski (2016), p. 190.

[110]On the scarce effectiveness of sanctions, see Amtenbirik and De Haan (2003), p. 1091; Louis (2004) pp. 577–579.

aware, European institutions will never sanction a Member State, which does not respect the budgetary discipline outlined in the EU Treaties. Indeed, the application of sanctions to countries violating fiscal rules due to an economic downturn or a low growth rate would be counterproductive: resources would be taken away, exactly when the country needs them for either budgetary consolidation or public investments.[111] Furthermore, in a situation of open conflict with the EU institutions where a Member State clearly refuses to comply with European recommendations, the Union would have no means to enforce the payment of a deposit or a fine.

Second, the functioning of the governance is essentially based on political decisions taken by intergovernmental bodies. The inability of the Council to synthetize the different national interests and enforce budgetary discipline is the main reason why several countries have been able to protract fiscal mismanagement in the first decade since the introduction of the euro and now struggle to complete budgetary consolidation in a reasonable amount of time.[112] The prevalence of politics on the law is expressly foreseen by the EU Treaties.[113] Art. 126(10) TFEU forbids actions ex art. 258 and art. 259 TFEU on the application of the EDP, thus excluding the CJEU from the enforcement of budgetary discipline. At the same time, the wide use of recommendations in the coordination procedures does also aim at excluding the Court from the application of budgetary discipline, as the latter are non-legally binding acts and cannot be enforced before the Court.[114] Finally, also the case law of CJEU granted the Council a wide margin of discretion in the assessment of European fiscal rules, in particular the budgetary thresholds and the scoreboard on macroeconomic imbalances.[115] Since the well-known case *Commission v. Council* (C-27/04)[116] on the excessive deficit procedure against Germany and France,[117] the Court of Luxembourg made clear that supranational institutions have no authority to implement corrective measures against the will of the governments.[118] In this

[111]See Adamski (2012), pp. 1341–1342; Adamski (2016), pp. 191–192; Adamski (2018), p. 44.

[112]See Chiti and Teixeira (2013), p. 689.

[113]See Palmstorfer (2014), pp. 190–191; Allemand et al. (2016), p. 159.

[114]Ibid.

[115]This is especially true if we take into consideration secondary indicators, which have not been clearly specified. Although the choice of indicators is in some cases innovative, it still lacks a clear methodology. Most probably, the elaboration of the scoreboard has been more the result of a political compromise within the Council, than a coherent analysis of economic imbalances and their causes. See Solomos and Koumparoulis (2012), pp. 300–301; Kegels and Verlinden (2013), pp. 58–59, 62. On the weak application of the MIP see Adamski (2018), pp. 63–65.

[116]ECJ Judgment of 13 July 2004 on the affair C-27/04, *Commission v. Council*, ECLI:EU: C:2004:436, para 80.

[117]Council Decision of 21 January 2003 on the existence of an excessive deficit in Germany—Application of Article 104(6) of the Treaty establishing the European Community, (2003) OJ L 34/16; Council Decision of 3 June 2003 on the existence of an excessive deficit in France—application of Article 104(6) of the Treaty establishing the European Community, (2003) OJ L 165/29. On the case see Adamski (2018), pp. 38–41.

[118]On the analysis of the case see Palmstorfer (2014), pp. 190–191; Tuori and Tuori (2014), pp. 105–106.

judgment, the CJEU explained that the application of the stability criteria is not automatic, but consists of a political valuation. The Council therefore has *full discretion* to decide on the existence of an excessive deficit and the application of sanctions.[119]

Even the introduction of new semi-automatic sanctions did not produce the desired effects to strengthen economic coordination. Beyond the important legal debate on the consistency of RMV with the EU Treaty, the Commission did not completely take advantage of the new rules to impose its lead in the process of budgetary surveillance.[120] This was in fact rather difficult due to a number of reasons. Looking more carefully at the procedures, sanctions can normally be taken by RMV only after they are preceded by an act of the Council acknowledging a situation of non-compliance with EU law, which must be adopted by standard qualified majority.[121] In this perspective, the normal balance of forces between the Commission and national governments is re-established before passing to the application of sanctions. The new voting procedure therefore does facilitate the application of penalties, but only after Member States have decided to activate the procedure by standard qualified majority. Furthermore, the automaticity imposed by the RMV is only partial. Minority blocks can still be achieved especially through the cooperation of bigger countries. This may become a probable scenario, when several governments find themselves in a situation of non-compliance and might feel reluctant to create an inconvenient precedent.[122]

In conclusion on this point, despite the many reforms adopted in the last 10 years, economic coordination still consists, at least in wide part, of a 'wishful thinking' or a 'barking dog that never bites'. In this regard, it is important to recall the 'paradox of centralisation' highlighted by Fabbrini,[123] according to which the more EU law tries to pursue budgetary discipline by stiffening surveillance and coordination, the more these constraints are ineffective because the Member States are unwilling or unable to respect them. In this situation, the rules of economic coordination look more like a procedural formality, than a substantial constraint: Member States must somehow account for their economic decisions, but EU institutions don't have a real power of coercion. Evidently, the reason why the Commission does usually prefer a soft approach in the application of coordination rules is the awareness to be powerless. The only occasions, when EU institutions can raise their voice in the framework of

---

[119]A sanction effectively adopted in the framework of the SGP was the fine imposed to Spain for the manipulation of statistics in accordance with art. 8 of Regulation (EU) No 1173/2011. Spain challenged the fine in the Case C-521/15. Cf. Chamon (2018).

[120]On the soft approach adopted by the European Commission in the enforcement of the new rules of economic coordination see Adamski (2018), pp. 59–63.

[121]See Council Recommendation for the necessary policy measures based on art. 121(4); Council Decision based on art. 126 (6) on the existence of an excessive deficit.

[122]See Adamski (2012), pp. 1341–1342. On the possible equilibria within the Council for a RMV voting cf. Seikel (2016), pp. 1405–1408.

[123]Fabbrini (2016), p. 61.

economic surveillance is when a country is presenting longstanding fragilities of its public finances and may be obliged to ask soon the financial support of the ESM.

4.3.3 Limits of the Market Model

4.3.3.1 The Failure of the Regulatory Role of Financial Markets

Another substantial failure of the economic governance has regarded the regulatory role, financial markets were supposed to play on the budgetary policies of the Member States. In an asymmetric EMU, where national governments refuse to share fiscal sovereignty and European surveillance is mainly based on soft law mechanisms, financial markets shall sanction Member States by stopping financing their sovereign debt, when they realise, fiscal mismanagement has made their investment excessively risky. This market approach to budgetary discipline complies with the well-known narrative on monetary integration accepted in Maastricht, according to which a single currency does not require a centralisation of fiscal authority to pursue stability, as actors are able to self-regulate. The effectiveness of the market discipline proved weak for two main reasons.

First of all, the commitment of national governments to respect the no bailout clause ex art. 125 TFEU has never been credible. Before the crisis, most authors supported an absolute interpretation of the norm, according to which no financial support of any kind would have been allowed towards the Member States of the euro area. Nevertheless, in the light of the strict interdependence within the monetary union, no investors thought that the clause would have actually been respected in case of fiscal destabilisation of significant importance. Evidently, it is not enough to say that countries will respond alone of their own obligations and no rescue will ever occur in case of need, if no measure is taken to make this scenario realistic.[124] As the EU did not create any tool to manage sovereign defaults and reduce contagion within the monetary union, no one believed that Member State would have been left alone by the others in the event of serious financial difficulties. Consequently, the lack of credibility of the no bailout clause convinced markets to ignore the economic disparities within the euro area and offer cheap credit also to the most indebted governments, thus abdicating their regulatory role.[125] The scarce trust in the no-bail out clause was confirmed after the outbreak of the sovereign debt crisis, when national governments realised, they could not comply with a strict no bailout policy, due to the unpredictable consequences of a sovereign default on the stability of the monetary union as a whole.[126] As a consequence, the reform of the economic

---

[124] In order to work, the logic of the market needs that creditors are afraid of losing their money. Schepel (2017), pp. 81, 85.

[125] See Louis (2010), p. 979; Estella (2016), p. 525. In this regard Menendez recalled Lon Fuller's law: 'you shall not pass laws impossible to comply with'. See Menendez (2014), p. 136.

[126] See Hinarejos (2015), p. 57.

governance preferred to take some distance from the genuine market model and pursue budgetary consolidation through conditional financial assistance and stronger coordination on national economic policies.

The second reason why the regulatory role of financial markets proved ineffective is because they do not always behave as rational actors. Indeed, investors rely on expectations and the creditworthiness of official borrowers, which are based on a number of changeable factors regarding the political and economic developments in a country. Furthermore, markets may react to new events in an abrupt and drastic way: when a major financial institution, a big investment fund or a rating agency stops trusting the ability of a government to repay its own debt, all the other economic actors may automatically follow, thus preventing the country from accessing market financing. Finally, as noticed by the ECB in its opinion in the *Gauweiler* case, the request of higher interest premium on the sovereign bond of some Member States does not always depend on a good faith assessment of their macroeconomic situation, but it can consist of excessive reactions dictated by the fear for a possible breakup of the euro area as a whole.[127] In the light of these limits, rather than enforcing budgetary discipline, the 'aberration of markets' may lead to the worsening of the economic situation in the Member States, by completely destabilising their public finances. In order to avoid this scenario, the setup of the ESM aimed to replace the function of financial markets in two ways: economic assistance offered another source of financing to countries under attack by speculation, while conditionality aimed to replace the regulatory role, markets were no longer able to play.[128]

4.3.3.2 The Fragilities of the Existing Debt Restructuration Regime

Aside from the preventive effect, the regulatory role of financial markets also applies *ex post*, when the sovereign debt of a country is not under control, and private actors must accept some form of losses, which should restore its sustainability. Evidently, as the debt of a Member State was assumed under private law, the latter should also regulate its restructuration.[129] Notably the current legal regime on the matter is rather basic, as it provides only two tools: the Commission can ask the government, whose debt has been assessed as unsustainable, to restructure its debt before the ESM grants financial support; standardised euro Collective Action Clauses (CACs) in all long-

[127] ECJ Judgment of 16 June 2015, Case C-62/14, *Gauweiler (and Others) v. Deutscher Bundestag*, ECLI:EU:C:2015:400, para. 72.

[128] Schepel strongly criticised the correction of the market logic through the intervention of the ESM and the ECB. Schepel (2017), p. 96. On the transformation of the economic constitution from the market paradigm to conditional financial assistance see Ioannidis (2016), pp. 1263–1274. Tuori and Tuori speak of 'constitutional mutation' of the economic union also due to the strengthening of coordination, the widening of surveillance to macroeconomic imbalances and the setup of crisis management tools. See Tuori and Tuori (2014), p. 192.

[129] Ohler (2011), p. 69.

term sovereign bond issued since January 2013 do allow reform of the contractual terms of the loan by qualified majority of the creditors.

The evaluation of debt sustainability in the framework of the ESM financial assistance consists of a complicated task, which presents some significant margin of error. In order to complete this analysis, it is necessary to take into consideration not only the specific situation of the country concerned, but also the consequences of a debt restructuration on the other Member States and the stability of the euro area as a whole, as well as the contribution of a possible financial assistance from the ESM to the sustainability of the sovereign debt. Evidently, due to the difficulty in assessing the economic forecasts and estimations, the decision on debt restructuration ends up being more political than technical.[130]

The application of euro CACs has the purpose instead to reduce the margin of holdout behaviours and ease the restructuration of sovereign debt in a Member State. The main innovation of standardised euro CACs is notably to replace the principle of unanimity with the one of majority on the reform of the loans conditions. Accordingly, creditors are aware that when they buy sovereign bonds, the terms of their loan may change in the future if the majority of investors agree on some amendments. Also, the application of CACs may be complicated. First of all, despite being standardised, clauses will have different applications depending on the national legislation of the country, which has issued them. Different domestic rules, both substantial and procedural, may lead to different outcomes in the negotiation of debt restructuration. Second, CACs apply only to a single bond issuance, meaning that the Member States should start as many negotiations as the tranches of bonds it has sold so far. Lacking some form of coordination mechanisms, holdout behaviours between different groups of creditors are rather likely.[131] In this situation, either creditors decide to resist holdouts by starting a series of litigations and accepting to have their ability to issue debt internationally undermined, or they repay them in full by reducing debt relief, as well as the credibility of future debt restructuration.[132] Third, the application of a debt restructuration may trigger a contagion in financial markets as the application of CACs does essentially consist of a partial default of the debtor.[133] In this sense, the application of debt restructuration will require the intervention of monetary, banking and fiscal authorities in order to avoid the counter effects on the stability of the financial system and the euro area as a whole. Finally, it is doubtful whether CACs are consistent with EU and national law, in particular consumer legislation.[134]

---

[130]Ibid. p. 69. For example, despite the IMF having declared that Greek debt had become unsustainable in 2016, the creditor countries of the ESM decided to continue financial assistance without demanding debt restructuration. Zettelmeyer (2018), p. 72.

[131]Panizza (2014), p. 5; Audit (2014), pp. 218–220; Fuest et al. (2014), p. 311–312. According to Zettelmeyer the fact that the Greek debt restructuration was only partially successful proves the scarce effectiveness of CACs. Zettelmeyer (2018), p. 72.

[132]Ibid., p. 71.

[133]Ohler (2011), p. 69.

[134]Audit (2014), p. 219.

4.3.4 Weak Implementation of EU Budgetary Constraints in National Constitutional Law

Art. 3(2) TSCG has created the obligation for the Member States of the euro area to introduce in domestic law a balanced budget rule, as well as automatic correction mechanisms to ensure its application. The effective compliance with the TSCG is a preliminary condition to access the financial assistance of the ESM, thus anchoring the principle of solidarity to the effective application of fiscal responsibility. The reform aimed to make Member States interiorise the principle of budgetary responsibility in national law and reduce the need for European surveillance. This operation has only partially succeeded. An important contribution to analyse in this regard is the Report on the compliance of Member States with the provisions of the TSCG issued by the European Commission on 22 February 2017.[135] Even if it does not identify any formal violation of the pact, the report acknowledges a significant heterogeneity in the implementation of art. 3(2) TSCG among the Member States. Evidently, national governments took advantage of the inherent flexibility of the pact and chose the most convenient application of the treaty for their national interests.[136]

Considering first of all the *legal status* of the balanced budget rule, only a minority of countries implemented it in constitutional law, as expressly recommended by the Fiscal Compact, in particular Germany, Spain, Italy, Austria and Belgium. A second group of countries preferred to use special laws of higher hierarchical status to reform the internal procedures on the budgetary process, which are still compulsory for the legislator. The majority of Member States instead, simply transposed the balanced budget rule in ordinary law. Some of them, including France, argued that the supra legislative force of international treaties in their legal systems shall grant the effective prevalence of the golden rule.[137] In reality, it could be questioned whether the latter form of implementation is completely satisfactory, as the effective application of art. 3(2) TSCG shall require judicial remedies, which are not automatically granted to all international agreements ratified by the Member States.[138] Even if the governments of these countries have solemnly promised to respect the Fiscal Compact and created national independent institutions in charge of monitoring compliance, this may not be enough to ensure an efficient application of the golden rule in the budgetary process.

---

[135]European Commission Report (2017).

[136]See Fromage and Dermine (2017). For an overlook of the different implementation of the TSCG see the EUI euro-crisis project report. www.eurocrisislaw.eui.eu.

[137]'[A]s soon as France has ratified the Treaty and it has entered into force, the rules laid down in paragraph 1 of Article 3 will apply to it; [...] pursuant to Article 55 of the Constitution, it will be hierarchically superior to legislation; [...] it will be for the different organs of State to monitor the application of this Treaty, within the scope of their respective competences; [the] Parliament will be in particular required to comply with its provisions when enacting finance laws and social security financing laws'. Decision No 2012-653 DC of the Conseil Constitutionnel on 9 August 2012, para. 18.

[138]European Commission Report (2017), p. 4.

Member States adopted different approaches also in regard to the formulation of the *escape clause*. Notably the TSCG allows the introduction of exceptions to the application of the golden rule, in particular in case of ‘an unusual event outside the control of the contracting party concerned, which has a major impact on the financial position of the general government or to periods of severe economic downturn’. While the majority of Member States simply transposed these definitions when drafting the golden rule in domestic law, others added new exceptions. Spain and Latvia for instance refer to social sustainability or social processes, while Italy, Greece and Portugal mention structural reforms, as allowed in the SGP. This wider formulation of the escape clause may be helpful to justify the use of deficit, at least from the point of view of national (constitutional) law.

When it comes to the implementation of the correction mechanism in the hands of independent fiscal institution (IFIs), Member States made different choices in regard to the statutory regime, independence, capacity to communicate and nomination procedures. First of all, only a minority of IFIs are institutionally independent, as many of them are placed within the structure of the government, the parliament, the national central bank or the Court of Auditors.[139] Their tasks can vary from the minimum attributions requested by EU law and the TSCG to wider and stricter supervisory functions.[140] The most important aspect of diversity, however, regards the *activation of the correction mechanism*. For most countries, the identification of a violation by the IFIs does only oblige governments to respect the principle of ‘comply or explain’: the fiscal authority must obey the recommendation of the IFI, or alternatively explain publicly why it is not following its assessments. Only a minority of countries, including Austria, Germany and Spain, opted instead for a more effective application of the correction mechanism. They decided that a significant deviation from the MTO assessed by the IFI shall automatically create the obligation for the domestic parliament to adopt a correction of public finances on the following budgetary year. The latter procedure is based on the assumption that every departure from the process of budgetary consolidation is in principle in contrast with the golden rule, thus encouraging the automaticity of correction.

After having recalled the heterogeneity in the implementation of the golden rule and the automatic correction mechanisms among the Member States, it is possible to consider the effective state of compliance with the TSCG. Unfortunately, looking at the individual performances of the Euro countries, the results are still not satisfactory. Seven years since the entry into force of the Fiscal Compact, only a minority of countries have been reaching its MTO, while the majority is still trying to comply with an adjustment path agreed with the European Commission. What is even more alarming, the translation of the balanced budget rule in the constitutional law of countries presenting structural financial difficulties does not seem producing the hoped result to bring down public spending and debt.[141] There are different reasons

[139]See Fromage (2017), p. 124.

[140]Ibid. pp. 128–130.

[141]See Adamski (2018), pp. 66–69.

for this partial failure. The most immediate explanation, in the light of the analysis developed above, is that different implementations in domestic law provide different results. In this regard, the IFIs of several Member States have already reported some difficulties, they are experiencing in the fulfilment of their mandate, such as the limited access to relevant information, the little amount of time available to develop legal opinions before the budgetary law is passed, the scarce financial resources, they can count on, as well as the weak relationship with the legislature and the government.[142] These problems have clearly undermined the ability of several IFIs to ensure effective corrections of budgetary policies and may explain the different results in the process of budgetary consolidation between the Member States. More in general, the fundamental problem of the automatic correction mechanism is that the IFIs are not allowed to pass binding decisions, but they can only exercise an advisory function,[143] meaning that national parliaments can ignore their opinion, if they want. The 'comply or explain' rule, even when it is applied properly, may not represent a sufficient deterrent to prevent fiscal mismanagement.

Looking at other possible explanations of the weak implementation of the golden rule in domestic law, Gros and Alcidi argue that the TSCG is based on the uncertain concept of 'structural deficit,[144] which cannot be observed *ex ante* and calculated with precision. Furthermore, the lack of a universally accepted method to adjust structural fiscal balances and the several country-specific factors to take into consideration, make the effective assessment of structural deficit rather difficult. Another reason why the TSCG has been scarcely effective may depend on the difficulties that constitutional judges may experience when the deal with the technical analysis of economic policies. Evidently, the lack of expertise and special knowledge on this matter may prevent them from efficiently evaluating compliance with the fiscal rules.[145]

Finally, some observers believe that the imposition of external constraints is not effective for countries, which don't possess a 'strong stability culture'.[146] In this regard, the adoption of the TSCG worked essentially as a 'placebo' to reassure markets in the short term, while it did succeed to change the approach of the most lax national governments to the management of public finances.[147] In fact, the many loopholes of the procedures allowed countries to find a way to escape the hard process of budgetary consolidation.

In conclusion on this matter, the transfer of ownership from European to national authorities does not seem to be producing the desired effects. Evidently, it is difficult to frame fiscal policy in tight legal constrains, especially when they demand the

[142]See Fromage (2017), pp. 133–136; Horvath (2018), pp. 517–518.

[143]See Fromage (2017), p. 138.

[144]Gros and Alcidi (2014), p. 2. On this topic cf. also Chalmers (2012), pp. 682–683; Menendez (2014), pp. 136–137.

[145]See Fabbrini (2016), pp. 45–46.

[146]Boggero and Annicchino (2014), p. 260.

[147]Ibid. See also Adamski (2018), pp. 66–69.

application of strict austerity measures and Member States are experiencing an economic slowdown.[148]

4.3.5 *Fragilities of the ESM Interventions*

4.3.5.1 The Limits of Financial Assistance

The provision of financial assistance by the ESM has been the most important instrument set up by the Member States of the euro area to contain the spread of the sovereign debt crisis. When governments realised that the consequences of a sovereign default in one country could trigger a full destabilisation of the monetary union, they decided to implement a rescue strategy mainly based on an intergovernmental agreement and financed by national budgets. Since 2010, Member Sates disbursed through the EFSF and the ESM more than €380 billions to five countries to avoid their default and help consolidate their banking system.[149] Despite the important results achieved so far, the ESM presents some important weaknesses, which may partially undermine its effectiveness.

Under the profile of resources, the ESM has a limited size, as it can only count on €80 billions of paid-up shares and of around €700 billions of callable shares. These sums may be sufficient to manage limited crisis of one middle-size or several small countries, but they would be clearly unable to absorb economic shocks in major economies, such as Italy or France.[150] Also, the liability regime disciplined in art. 8(5) TESM proves the fragility of the mechanism, as every country is responsible only for its portion of the authorised capital stock and it shall not be liable, by reason of its membership, for obligations of the ESM. The obligations of each country to contribute to the authorised capital stock in accordance with the TESM are not affected if any such Member State receives financial assistance. If one or more countries struggled to pay their own contributions, the ESM may lack sufficient resources to intervene in case of necessity. Even if it is possible to increase the capital of the ESM, the decision must be taken by unanimity and it may be difficult to be accepted by all the Member States in a reasonable amount of time.

Considering the available assistance tools, the ESM has a limited margin of action. Aside from the standard assistant instruments, including loans, credit lines and bonds purchase, since 2016 the ESM can adopt direct recapitalisations of financial institutions in the euro area. This tool is extremely important, because it could help contain banking crisis in a Member State without increasing its public debt, thus helping to break the toxic loop between sovereigns and banks.

---

[148]See Gros and Alcidi (2014), p. 3.

[149]The costs of the approved bailout consist of Ireland €40.2 billion; Greece €308 billions; Spain €100 billions; Portugal €52 billions; Cyprus €9 billions. See Estella (2016), pp. 507–508.

[150]See Peroni (2012), pp. 167. See *infra* Sect. 5.6.3.1.

Unfortunately, the limited resources destined to this instrument (only €60 billions), as well as the many conditions necessary for its activation,[151] make its use rather hypothetical. Furthermore, some regret that the ESM is not able to provide loans for investment to the Member States or private entities.[152]

Finally, the effectiveness of the ESM is also undermined by the decision-making rules. Indeed, the activation of financial assistance can't be decided unilaterally by the Board of Governors of the ESM, but it requires a formal request of the concerned country. More importantly, the disbursement of resources shall be approved by the unanimity of Member States, except in case of emergency, when it applies the qualified majority of 85% of the capital subscribed. This gives Germany, France and Italy a veto power on every decision of this kind. Evidently, the intergovernmental functioning of the ESM has the consequence to give more power to the creditor states, which may easily stop the activation of the ESM and any further disbursement of resources.[153] In this regard, it should be also remembered that several Member States need the previous authorisation from their parliament before authorising the activation of the ESM.[154] This requirement may pose new obstacles to the intervention of the mechanisms, as domestic parliaments discuss issues through a nationally focused political debate, which may miss the full understanding of the European interdependence. The procedural and substantial difficulties for the activation of the ESM prove that the disbursement of financial assistance has been conceived as an exceptional circumstance, which shall take place only on rare occasions, when there is a wide consensus for the support of a Member State experiencing economic difficulties. The intrinsic rigidity of the mechanism may instead prevent it from working efficiently in case of unpredictable and changeable crisis scenarios, when a country requests precautionary financial assistance, and, more in general, in all those situations, where national governments may have different opinions on what to do.

The limits of the current size, tools and functioning of the ESM explain why intergovernmental rescues have been *de facto* backed up by the non-standard monetary measures of the ECB.[155] While formally ensuring the correct functioning of the monetary transmission mechanism and fighting against deflation, programmes like the OMTs or the Quantitative Easing created the monetary conditions to foster the stabilisation process of the euro area as a whole.

---

[151] See *supra* Sect. 3.6.2.

[152] Lo Schiavo (2017), pp. 140–142. More in general on the direct recapitalization instrument see Corti Varela (2015).

[153] The empowering of creditor States was also encouraged by the introduction of RMV in the decision-making process regulating the MSP and the EDP. Menendez (2014), p. 135.

[154] These are Germany, Estonia, Austria, Slovakia, Finland and the Netherlands.

[155] See Hinarejos (2013), pp. 1632–1633.

4.3.5.2 The Strength of the Conditionality Policy and Its Counter Effects

In order to understand the effectiveness of the conditionality policy, it is necessary to recall its hybrid legal nature. Even if the ownership of the adjustment programme formally belongs to the recipient Member State, the latter has no choice than to accept the conditions imposed by the creditor countries and comply with them, if they want to continue enjoying the financial support of the ESM. The state of financial necessity that the beneficiary country is experiencing represents evidently the strongest guarantee for the effectiveness of the ESM conditionality: the threat of stopping financial assistance gives the Eurozone governance an incredible 'blackmailing power', which can be used to shape national budgetary policies and request structural reforms. Evidently rather than coming from the law, this 'power' comes from the balance of forces between creditor and debtor countries, according to which the more compelling is the need, the stronger is the effectiveness of conditionality.

Despite gaining its strength from the weaknesses of the recipient Member States, the process of stabilisation pursued by the conditionality policy has not always been smooth and successful. Looking at its concrete application, the results of financial assistance programmes in countries experiencing the ESM financial assistance is quite heterogeneous: while Ireland, Spain, Cyprus and Portugal have ended the programme after a few years and are now experiencing a solid economic recovery,[156] Greece has been struggling to exit the economic crisis and implement the necessary structural reform to consolidate its public finances. The recent completion of the assistance programme in June 2018 does not represent the end of external supervision, as the country still presents several economic fragilities, which will be strictly monitored in the framework of a 'post-surveillance programme'.[157]

The experience developed over the last few years has shown that an efficient application of the conditionality policy shall take into consideration two opposite needs: pushing the implementation of corrective measures in the beneficiary Member State, in order to make its economy independent from external aid as soon as possible, while maintaining a positive and cooperative relationship with the government, which assumes the responsibility of the reforms. This is not an easy balance to find in concrete.

On the one hand, exceeding the request of structural reforms and austerity measures might produce negative consequences on the economy of the concerned country. Following the economic recipes of the IMF, the *Troika* demanded from the

---

[156]'Cyprus successfully exits ESM programme', ESM Press Release, 31 March 2016; 'Post-Programme Surveillance report. Ireland, Autumn 2017', 16 February 2018; 'Statement by the staff of the European Commission and the European Central Bank following the ninth post-programme surveillance visit to Spain,' 16 April 2018; Statement by European Commission and European Central Bank staff following the Eight Post-Programme Surveillance mission to Portugal, 15 June 2018.

[157]'Eurogroup statement on Greece', 15 June 2018. On the current economic situation in Greece see Avgouleas et al. (2018).

Greek government a number of measures based on the privatisation, marketization and flexibilisation of the national economy, aside from a significant cut of its welfare state. This approach plunged the Greek economy into a deep recession for several years, and the social costs were paid by the most fragile part of the society.[158] Consequently, the people's trust in EU institutions and traditional parties was strongly undermined.[159] Part of the legal doctrine even argued that lender countries acted in a way to intentionally hurt Greek economy, by exercising a form of economic coercion.[160] The application of the conditionality policy has been even more brutal, because conditionality policy has escaped so far, the judicial control of the CJEU.

On the other hand, deteriorating the relationship between the creditor and the debtor countries is risky because it would prevent the success of economic consolidation in the recipient Member State, thus putting in danger the stability of the euro area as a whole. Evidently, the strong interdependence existing within the monetary union makes the pursuit of stability in each country a fundamental interest for both creditors and debtors. In this perspective, the termination of financial assistance to a Member State refusing to comply with the MoU, may be more difficult to do than what it looks like. As the second Greek debt crisis proved in 2015, creditor Member States may still feel tempted to keep providing financial assistance to countries, which do not substantially respect conditionality. This is a consequence of the 'TINA' ('There Is No Alternative') principle (*Alternativlosigkeit*)[161]: the economic consequences of a sovereign default in the monetary union are so unpredictable and potentially so devastating for the stability of the euro area as a whole, that it is not worth the risk of letting a country go bankrupt, even if it is not respecting conditionality rules.[162]

4.3.6 Limited Resources for Investments

Another important limit of the governance regards the weak European support to economic recovery. The recent experience has clearly showed how governments are still struggling to recover from the crisis due to the difficulty of investing fiscal resources to relaunch national economy, while consolidating at the same their public finances and implementing structural reforms. This made compliance with European

[158]On the violation of human rights in the Member States following the application of austerity measures see Salomon (2015), Hinarejos (2016), p. 243; O'Gorman (2017).

[159]On the negative consequences of austerity measures on the public opinion, social conditions and the economy see Tuori and Tuori (2014), pp. 235–236; Wilkinson (2015), p. 1072, Estella (2016), pp. 534–535.

[160]See Bantekas and Vivien (2016), pp. 562–563.

[161]See Tuori and Tuori (2014), pp. 189–190; Adamski (2016), p. 198; Murswiek (2016), pp. 51–52.

[162]Hinarejos (2013), p. 1628.

rules very difficult: the strict application of austerity measures may have recessive effects on the economy and produce unsustainable social costs, while the implementation of structural reforms outlined in the MoU request strong political efforts that most national governments have not been able to make.[163] The governance has tried to balance fiscal consolidation and structural reforms with economic recovery and social care, in two ways.

First of all, the rules on economic coordination have been interpreted in a way to grant some room for investments. As the previous analysis has already explained, the EU Treaties and secondary law provide a wide margin of discretion for the application of coordination rules. Furthermore, the SGP expressly foresees that budgetary consolidation shall keep an eye on some criteria other than fiscal thresholds. Regulation (EC) No 1466/1997 and Regulation (EC) no 1467/1997 for example explain that the pursuit of the sound public finances shall consider the need for public investment for growth and structural reforms and that Member States implementing pension reforms shall be allowed to deviate from the adjustment path to their MTO (structural reform clause).[164] Regulation (EU) No 1176/2011 states that the corrective action plan adopted in the framework of the corrective side of MIP shall take into account the social impact of the policy actions and shall be consistent with the employment guidelines.[165] In order to clarify better the available margin of discretion in the application of economic coordination, the European Commission adopted in 2015 a Communication,[166] which explains how to make the best use of the flexibility within the SGP and achieve a better balance between investment, structural reforms and budgetary consolidation. At the same time, the European Semester has also tried to take into consideration some social element, even if this is not sufficient.[167] Looking at the results achieved so far, the wide use of flexibility has only been partially effective. Over the last few years, the Commission and the Council granted several governments a wide margin of fiscal manoeuvre to foster economic growth and implement structural reforms, but they could not determine how extra-resources have actually been used in concrete.[168] The previous analysis on the implementation of coordination procedures by the Member States has already explained that, even if the euro area as a whole has experienced some moderate

[163]Indeed, governments imposing heavy budget cuts are likely to lose the next general elections. Leino-Sandberg and Salminen (2017), p. 102.

[164]See se art. 5(1) of Regulation (EC) No 1466/1997 and art. 2(5) of Regulation (EC) No 1467/1997.

[165]See se art. 8(1) of Regulation (EU) No 1176/2011.

[166]The communication in particular gives orientation to the application of the SGP by taking into account the cyclical fluctuation of the economy and giving margin of manoeuvre for the implementation of structural reforms and investments. European Commission Communication (2015). Cf. Pace (2018), pp. 109–110.

[167]Costamagna (2015), pp. 132–138; Hinarejos (2016), p. 245.

[168]In a new Communication adopted in 2018, the Commission gave a positive review of the use of flexibility in the last 3 years. See European Commission Communication (2018a).

growth rate, budgetary consolidation and economic convergence between Member States is unfortunately proceeding too slowly.[169]

The second way by which European institutions and Member States have tried to balance fiscal consolidation and structural reforms with economic recovery has been the strengthening of the investment policy in the framework of the EFSI. The latter instrument has mobilised since 2015 more than €335 billions of investment in almost one thousand projects across the European Union. Formally, the EFSI appears close to reaching its targets regarding the total resources invested, the economic sectors covered by the projects, as well as the geographical distribution of the funds. For this reason, the Commission managed to gain the approval of a Regulation in December 2017 to extend the duration of the EFSI up to 2020 and increase its margin of investments.[170] At the same time, the role and the results achieved by EFSI have not been immune to criticism. Some scholars noticed for example that the projects financed so far are in most part not additional to the ones, which would have been supported in any case by the EIB.[171] Thanks to the wide formulation of Regulation (EU) No 1017/2015, the EFSI Committee has been able to select projects with wide discretion, as it was enough to prove the existence of a market failure or sub-optimal investment situation to allow a financing.[172] Another important weakness of the EFSI is that, even if the allocation of funds should not follow country quotas, resources have been mainly distributed to the bigger economies of the EU. More precisely the wide majority of investments have been received by western European countries, with the top beneficiaries being the UK, Spain, France, Germany and Italy.[173] Furthermore, the investment plan produced different results depending on the economic, political and legal situation of the country, in which it tried to operate. For example, it has been difficult to attract private investments in those Member States presenting regulatory uncertainty and poor infrastructures. This is clearly the consequence of the market logic beyond the plan: the most advanced actors find themselves in a better position to attract resources.[174] Finally, another important criticism on the investment strategy pursued by the EFSI so far consists of the scarce

[169]'Figures illustrate how in Europe 'speaking German' is not necessarily 'acting German'. Leino-Sandberg and Salminen (2017), pp. 102–103.

[170]Regulation (EU) No 2017/2396 amending Regulations (EU) No 1316/2013 and (EU) 2015/1017 as regards the extension of the duration of the European Fund for Strategic Investments.

[171]See Clayes and Leandro (2016), Rubio et al. (2016), p. 19.

[172]Art. 5 of Regulation (EU) No 1017/2015 explains that projects shall be considered additional (i) if they 'could not have been carried out in the period during which the EU guarantee can be used, or not to the same extent, by the EIB, the EIF or under existing Union financial instruments without EFSI support'; (ii) they 'shall typically have a higher risk profile than projects supported by EIB normal operations.

[173]This result can be partially explained considering the competition with the European Structural and Investment Funds and the weaker capacity to develop bankable projects and organise private public partnership, as well as the excessively small size of the projects. Cf. Rinaldi and Nuñez Ferrer (2017), p. 11.

[174]Rinaldi and Nuñez Ferrer (2017), p. 10.

attention paid to social issues: projects aiming to help the most disadvantaged part of the society have received little attention by the fund.[175]

Aside from the way the EFSI has operated over the last few years, the fundamental limit of the fund depends on the size of public capitals invested. Indeed, it is difficult to promote growth and structural reforms, when the public resources initially mobilised are only € 21 billion, which are supposed to attract 15 times more private capitals and then be distributed between all the Member States of the EU, including those which are not part of the monetary union. Evidently, the development of an effective strategy for economic growth can't rely almost exclusively on the mobilisation of private capitals. It is not a case that a significant part of global spending in investments is carried by state budgets.[176] Considering this structural limit, the European Commission has envisaged some solutions to provide EFSI with more public resources. For example, the Communication on the best use of flexibility within the SGP of 2015 states that the conferral of additional financial contributions by the Member States to EFSI or the co-financings of project with EFSI shall not be automatically counted in the calculation of public deficit;[177] furthermore the fiscal parameters should be interpreted with some flexibility in regards to the Member States, which decide to contribute more to EFSI.[178] The Commission also clarified that the EFSI financings do not represent a State aid within the meaning of the EU Treaties and consequently they shall not be approved by the European Commission under EU State aid rules.[179] Unfortunately, regardless of the efforts of the European Commission, the offer to confer additional financial contributions to the EFSI has not been appealing to the Member States. The problem here is that countries committed in budgetary consolidation, which would be more in need of European investments to recover their economy, are reluctant to transfer resources to a European fund, they do not directly control, even if they could benefit from it.

In conclusion, the current functioning of the EFSI only allows the financing of small size and middle risk projects, which can easily find support by market investors. In this situation, EFSI risks to work only as a limited pro-cyclical financial instrument. The management of large economic shocks or the reversion of negative economic trend in the euro area do definitely fall out of the fund's capability.[180]

---

[175] Huguenot-Noël and Zuleeg (2016) and Fernandes (2017).

[176] See Inderst (2013), pp. 6–7; Tovo (2016), p. 387.

[177] European Commission Communication (2015), pp. 7–8.

[178] Ibid., p. 8.

[179] European Commission Analytical Grids (2015), pp. 1–2.

[180] Tovo (2016), p. 399; Rinaldi and Nuñez Ferrer (2017), p. 21.

4.3.7 The Incomplete Construction of the Banking Union

The creation of the banking union has represented a major step forward in the process of stabilisation of the euro area as a whole. The main purpose of this project has been to stop the toxic loop between fiscal and banking crisis, meaning ensuring that debt restructuration does not automatically trigger bank defaults, while banking distress does not generate large sovereign debt crisis. The centralisation of supervisory and resolution tasks has already represented some important steps in this direction as they helped overcome some longstanding fragilities of the European banking system, for example by reducing non-performing loans owned by financial institutions and increasing their recapitalisation level. Despite these important achievements, the European banking union is still an incomplete project. The following analysis will specifically take into consideration the deficit of effectiveness of the banking governance, meaning what the latter is still missing to better contribute to the cause of stability in the euro area.

Considering the existing tools, the bank restructuration regime requires some important improvements. While the SRB does not have a direct power in the application of resolution regime, national authorities have proved unable to effectively apply European rules. There is for example a strong reluctance to recur to the bail- in tool in order to ensure the participation of private actors in a banking restructuration. Over the last few years, the use of public resources is generally preferred also thanks to the indulgent application of state aid regime by the Commission.[181] At the same time, precautionary recapitalisations have still been adopted without a sufficient assessment of the bank's solidity. Another major deficit of the current banking union regards the lack of sufficient instruments to avoid high concentration of specific sovereigns in the banking sheets, which is the main reason why the toxic loop between banks and sovereign is still alive.[182]

Aside from the fragilities of the existing tools, the banking union still requires two important instruments to ensure the resilience of the European financial system towards adverse economic shocks.

The first outstanding deficit of the banking union regards the lack of a common deposit guarantee scheme. Notably, the existence of different protection regimes for savers within the Eurozone may represent a source of instability: if one or more Member States were to meet financial difficulties, capitals would flow to other countries, where deposit guarantees are stronger. At the same time, the competition between national deposit guarantee schemes (DGSs) in order to attract savings might drain liquidity from credit institutions in several Member States and jeopardise the financial stability of the Eurozone.[183] In the light of these risks, Directive 2014/49/

[181]Cf. Bénassy-Quéré et al. (2018), p. 6.

[182]Ibid. p. 4.

[183]'In times of stability it is possible that different coverage leads to depositors choosing the highest deposit protection rather than the deposit product best suited to them. It is possible that such different coverage results in competitive distortions in the internal market'. See Whereas

EU tried to harmonise national DGSs by setting a uniform level of protection for depositors throughout the Union. At the same time, DGSs remain independent and are therefore exposed to the weaknesses of Member States in regard to the tenure of both their sovereign debt and banking system. Even if Directive 2014/49/EU foresees the possibility for DGSs to borrow resources from each other, this can happen only through *ad hoc* agreement to be stipulated on a voluntary basis. There is therefore no real mechanism, which may ensure the sustainability of national deposit guarantees.

Another important vulnerability of the banking union regards the lack of a common backstop, which may intervene in case the Single Resolution Fund (SRF) is unable to manage systemic economic shocks. First of all, the SRF is still under construction and will be completed only in 2024 after the contribution of banks in the Member States have been fully collected and gradually mutualised.[184] Second, once completed, the SRF will be able to count only on around €55 billion (1% of the amount of covered deposits). This sum is clearly too low when considering the costs Member States had to incur during the global financial crisis to bailout their banks. Regulation (EU) No 806/2014 foresees the possibility to integrate the fund with *ex post* contributions or ask for loans and other forms of support from financial institutions or national resolution funds. These procedures are, however, long and complex, meaning that in the event of a crisis it may be difficult to collect sufficient resources to stabilise financial institutions. Last, the SRF has a limited range of intervention, in the sense that it can offer guarantees and make loans, but it can't absorb losses or provide direct recapitalisation. Accordingly, the SRF shall not be qualified as a bailout fund.[185] In the current legal framework, only the ESM could intervene to provide fresh resources to banks on the edge of bankruptcy, even if several conditions shall be fulfilled and only €60 billion can be spent for direct bank recapitalisations.

Due to these structural limits, it is unlikely that the SRF will be able to provide sufficient support to banks in distress in the event of a pandemic crisis. In this situation, the function of last resort guarantor could realistically be played only by the Member States,[186] who can collect unlimited resources through their power of taxation. The problem is that bailouts financed by tax payers may reinforce the toxic loop between banking crisis and debt crisis, which is exactly the result, the project of banking union aimed to defuse. At the same time, Regulation (EU) No 806/2014 did

---

(19) Directive 2014/49/EU of the European Parliament and of the Council of 16 April 2014 on deposit guarantee schemes Text with EEA relevance, (2014) OJ L 173/149.

[184]In the transitional phase, until the Fund reaches the target level of resources, the SRB shall use the SRF in accordance with principles founded on a decision of the SRF into national compartments corresponding to each participating Member State, as well as on a progressive merger of the different funds raised at national level to be allocated to national compartments of the Fund. Cf. art. 77 of Regulation (EU) No 806/2014.

[185]In some exceptional circumstances, the Fund may still be able to absorb losses (up to 5% of the total liabilities). Busch (2017), p. 463.

[186]See Moloney (2014), p. 1628.

not mention the obligation for the Member States to grant access to public funds, because this provision would interfere with national fiscal competence.[187]

In conclusion, the full effectiveness of the banking union remains conditional to the implementation of further reforms in the field of the economic governance. Evidently, as long as the Member States continue to hesitate over the completion of the banking union and refuse to accept the implicit sharing of risks that this project demands, the European financial system will remain substantially fragile and the objective of the stability of the euro area as a whole will be at stake.

4.3.8 Deficit of Effectiveness: Conclusive Remarks

The analysis developed in the previous paragraph explained why the economic union, despite the implementation of several reforms, still presents some structural inability to pursue those stabilisation and consolidation policies, which are meant to ensure the existence of the monetary union. The outstanding fragilities of the governance are rooted in the decentralised model of economic union. Notably, consolidation policies lack sufficient instruments to encourage compliance with fiscal rules and stop moral hazard behaviours. The economic governance is still based on intergovernmental mechanisms based on the logic of political consensus, while the European Commission is still struggling to impose its leadership. Also financial markets proved unable to play an efficient regulatory role on public finances, while there is no effective debt restructuration regime yet. At the same time, the governance is still missing effective tools to encourage economic recovery and pursue stabilisation policies in the event of an emergency. In particular, both the ESM and the banking union still present major weaknesses, which may undermine their ability to deal with heavy economic shocks. Even EFSI, despite the significant results achieved so far, is unable to make a real difference in the absorbing economic shocks and encouraging convergence within the euro area.

In conclusion, the ineffectiveness of the governance represents a risk for the stability of the euro area. The disappointing results of consolidation and stabilisation policies have undermined economic recovery and convergence between the Member States, thus feeding social distress and citizens' mistrust in EU institutions.[188] These weaknesses can be better understood by considering the democratic deficit of the governance.

---

[187]Busch (2017), p. 474. Art. 74 of Regulation (EU) No 806/2014 only foresees that the SRB shall contract for the SRF financial arrangements, including, where possible, public financial arrangements, regarding the immediate availability of additional financial means.

[188]On the impact of the economic governance on the European social dimension see Costamagna (2014).

4.4 The Deficit of Democracy

4.4.1 Preliminary Remarks: An Undemocratic Governance

The efforts made to pursue the stability in the euro area as a whole have been characterised by another important limit, which is strictly related to the scarce effectiveness of the governance and the lack of competence of the Union: the deficit of democratic control. As the following analysis will explain in more detail, democratic accountability provides an important contribution to the stability of the euro area. The economic governance needs indeed a strong relationship with the people not only to orient its policies, but also to foster the effectiveness of its action.

Several scholars have tried to explain whether the EU could develop genuine democratic institutions and how. In order to analyse the democratic deficit of the Union, the legal analysis has often recurred to the concept of 'accountability', meaning the relationship between an actor and a forum, according to which the actor shall explain and justify his or her behaviour, the forum can pose questions and pass judgment, and the actor may face consequences.[189] Accordingly, accountability demands the fulfilment of at least three actions: the actor shall inform the forum about his or her conduct; the forum shall be able to interrogate the actor and pose questions on the adequacy of the information or the legitimacy of the conduct; the forum may impose consequences on the actor in case it disagrees or gives a negative judgment of its conduct.[190] Accountability to the people is mainly granted through political representation: citizens choose their representatives through periodical elections, which shall be general, equal and free. The elected government exercises the public power in accordance with the rule of law and it shall guarantee the possibility of a change in power.[191] In the current functioning of the European Union, there are two main sources of democratic legitimation: European citizens and national communities. The European citizens are directly represented in the European Parliament, which is renewed every 5 years, while national communities are indirectly represented in the intergovernmental institutions, namely the Council and the European Council, as their members are accountable to domestic parliaments. According to this dual source of democratic legitimation,[192] the management of public power is accountable to the European citizens through the involvement of the European Parliament in the decision-making process, and to the national people

[189]Bovens (2007), p. 450. On the issue of European democracy and accountability see Harlow (2002), Papadopoulos (2007), Bredt (2011) and Von Bogdandy (2012).

[190]See Curtin (2016), pp. 183, 186, 190.

[191]See Von Bogdandy (2012), p. 321.

[192]According to Habermas citizens and peoples are the two constituent subjects of the European Union. Habermas (2012), p. 343. Accordingly, the Union is based on a dual structure of democratic legitimation: the EU citizens and the national peoples. Von Bogdandy (2012), p. 322. The community method complies with this 'dual legitimacy concept' as the legal acts shall be adopted by both the European Parliament and the Council. See Calliess (2016), p. 40.

through the participation of intergovernmental bodies. Aside from representation, it is important to recall that democratic accountability can also be pursued in other ways: the principle of transparency allows public scrutiny over the activities performed by the public authorities; the consultation and participation of stakeholders can help the rulers to take into account their opinion on a specific matter; the principle of deliberation provides that the decision-making process shall be accompanied by a dialogue with the other institutions in order to take into consideration their point of view.[193]

Another way to measure the democratic deficit in the economic union is by applying the concept of 'legitimacy', which in public law explains why a certain authority or the management of a specific power is justified. Notably in a democratic system, legitimacy is not something static, but must be constantly earned.[194] Accordingly, legitimacy crisis happens when the public authority is contested by the citizens either because of the scarce results of its policies or for the malfunctioning of the accountability procedures. In this sense, Scharpf has introduced two different applications of the concept, namely input and output legitimacy. 'Under modern (Western) conditions, [. . .] legitimacy has come to rest almost exclusively on trust in institutional arrangements that are thought to ensure that governing processes are generally responsive to the manifest preferences of the governed (input legitimacy, "government by the people") and/or that the policies adopted will generally represent effective solutions to common problems of the governed (output legitimacy, "government for the people")'.[195] Accordingly, effective accountability mechanisms help to fulfil a sufficient degree of input legitimacy in the governance, because the citizens can choose who will take part in the decision making power and replace them, in the event they are doing a bad job. At the same time output legitimacy should be measured considering the ability of the economic union to perform well and take care of the interests of the people subject to its authority.[196]

Evidently, the analysis of the democratic deficit of the European Union goes far beyond the object of this work. For the purpose of the current research, it is enough to say that, while strengthening democratic accountability and legitimacy is a challenge for the process of European integration as a whole, the reform of the economic governance did pose some new issues, which specifically regard the Eurozone Member States. More precisely, the limitation of national sovereignty following the consolidation of European surveillance on budgetary policies and the setup of the intergovernmental mechanism of conditional financial support has significantly sharpened the democratic deficit of the governance. This occurred in two ways. On the one hand, domestic parliaments lost some of their sovereign prerogatives, as they are *de facto* subject to the decisions taken collectively by all

---

[193]See Starita (2017), pp. 19–24.

[194]Lenaerts and Desomer (2002), p. 1222.

[195]Scharpf (2003).

[196]Schwarz (2014), pp. 403–404.

the executives of the euro area. At the same time, the weakening of national democracies has not been balanced by the strengthening of EU democratic institutions.[197] This has produced some negative consequences as the application of the governance has not always been able to preserve the common European interest and protect the weaker parts of the society exposed to the crisis.

The following analysis will better focus on the deepening of democratic deficit in the economic union following the recent reforms of the governance. First, it will be analysed the marginalisation of domestic parliaments in the definition of fiscal policies due to both the enhanced supervision from EU institutions on the budgetary cycle and the compliance with conditionality policies, for those countries, which have requested the support of the ESM. Second, the research will focus on the European parliament and the limited role it plays in the management of the economic governance. The weak democratic control at European and national levels will be considered in relation to the rise of intergovernmental bodies. Finally, the last paragraphs will consider the impact, the pursuit of stability policy in the euro area may have on social cohesion and political consensus.

4.4.2 *Decline of National Democracy*

Fiscal competence is a fundamental parliamentary prerogative. Indeed, modern democracies were born when people's representatives gained the authority to decide on the collection and spending of public resources.[198] In this perspective, the adherence to the decentralised model of economic union had the dual purpose to protect national fiscal sovereignty and to preserve domestic democracy from external control. Evidently, as long as the fundamental decisions on taxation and public spending stay in the hands of home parliaments, national democracy shall remain intact. In this sense, the principle of no bailout aimed not only to avoid the establishment of a transfer union between Member States, but also to protect the self-determination of national parliaments, which shall not assume obligations and risks against their will.[199] The reforms of the economic governance notably had an impact on the original Maastricht model, by undermining the guarantees given by the EU Treaties to the sovereign rights of domestic parliaments.

A first formal challenge comes from the strengthening of European surveillance on national economic policies. Notably the hardening of soft law procedures, namely the MSP, the MIP and the EDP, and the creation of a European monitoring cycle on

[197] Starita (2017), p. 16.

[198] For this reason, the German Federal Constitutional Court considered the fiscal autonomy of the *Bundestag* as a necessary element to protect the constitutional identity of the country. See German Federal Constitutional Court, Judgement, 30 June 2009, [2 BvE 2/08], para. 252; German Constitutional Court, Judgement, 7 September 2011, [2 BvR 987/10], paras. 38, 121–124. On the judgment of the *Bundesverfassungsgericht* see Rüffert (2011), pp. 847–849.

[199] Cf. Ketterer (2016), pp. 263–264.

the adoption of national budgetary policies (European semester) have formally tightened the autonomy of domestic parliaments.[200] The Member States shall account for their fundamental decisions on budgetary policy, structural reforms and the correction of macroeconomic imbalances to European institutions. The reform adopted in recent years evidently aimed to create some form of co-responsibility (*Mitverantwortlichkeit*) for the management of national economic polices between the Member States and the Union. The previous analysis has already explained that this process succeeded only in part due to limited effectiveness of economic coordination.

A second more substantial challenge to national democracies comes from the financial assistance programmes adopted in the framework of the ESM. Notably, the latter can intervene only when two conditions are fulfilled at the same time: a Member State is risking a sovereign default, which may undermine the stability of the euro area as a whole (indispensability criterion); the concerned government has accepted to implement the reforms negotiated in a MoU by the Commission with the support of the ECB and the IMF (conditionality criterion). The application of these criteria poses different constraints to the fiscal autonomy of national parliaments. On the one hand, the state of necessity pushes the debtor countries to accept and enforce the conditions set out in the MoU. The possibility to reject conditionality is rather fictitious.[201] As proven by the Greek crisis of July 2015,[202] neither national parliaments, nor popular referendum have the power to reject a MoU. In this perspective, the only hypothetical alternative, national parliaments can take is to move towards the exit from the monetary union either through a formal decision or as a consequence of budgetary policies leading to a sovereign default.[203] On the other hand, the constraints on fiscal autonomy regards also the parliaments of creditor countries. Due to the level of interdependence within the Union, the refusal to concede financial assistance to a Member State in financial difficulties may have a negative impact on the rest of the Eurozone. In this way, the TINA ('there is no alternative') principle limits the margin of discretion also of those parliaments called to authorise the concession of the ESM financial support. Regardless of the efforts of the *Bundesverfassungsgericht* to protect the sovereign prerogatives and the autonomy of the German parliament, the authorisation of the *Bundestag* to the activation of the

---

[200]On the marginalisation of national parliaments see Chalmers (2012), pp. 685–687; Crum (2012), p. 622; Fasone (2014), Majone (2014), p. 1221; Martucci (2017), pp. 35–37. According to Jancic not all national parliaments have been 'passive receivers' of EU policies. On the contrary, some developed legal and political ways to mitigate the effects of such centralization. Furthermore, domestic parliament maintains some relevant soft powers: voting, scrutiny, information access and public debate. See Jančić (2016), pp. 242–245.

[201]See Dawson and de Witte (2013), p. 834; Ioannidis (2014), p. 42.

[202]In July 2015, the Greek government called a referendum to decide whether the country should have accepted the bailout conditions proposed by the *Troika*. Despite the majority rejected it, the governments decided after few days to sign a new MoU setting even harsher conditions for the bailout in order to avoid the exit from the monetary union.

[203]On the possible exit from the monetary union cf. *supra* Sect. 2.4.7.3.

ESM is more formal than substantial. Indeed, in no case the German parliament may refuse to grant financial support to Greece and another country in difficulty, except if it accepts to allow a general destabilisation of the euro area occur.

Considering the decision-making process at European level, the interinstitutional dialogue offers a little space for intervention for national parliaments. Notably, like the European Parliament, also domestic assemblies have the right to be informed and to interrogate the Presidents of the Council, the European Council, the Commission, the Eurogroup and the ESM. This is clearly not enough. Despite having the merit to improve transparency and the deliberative process, the dialogue does not represent an effective mechanism of democratic control, because it does not give national parliaments any power to censor decisions taken at European level.[204] Evidently, the only way, they have to directly intervene in the outcome of the decision-making process, is to request the national government to use a veto power in the Council, when it is allowed.[205]

In conclusion on this point, the weakening of national parliamentary democracy is a natural consequence of the strengthening of the surveillance model that Member States and EU institutions have implemented in order to pursue the stability of the euro area as a whole. As the fiscal position of one country has an influence on the others, fundamental decisions on national budgetary policies can't be decided autonomously by domestic parliaments, but they must be agreed with the other governments, in the framework of the Council or the European Council. According to Majone, this process might be able to turn the democratic deficit of the EU into a democratic default.[206]

4.4.3 The Limited Role of the European Parliament in the Economic Governance

While fiscal rights are slowly slipping through the hands of national parliaments, the European parliament has not been able to consolidate its authority yet. Its marginal role essentially depends on the decentralised model of fiscal integration outlined in the Maastricht Treaty, according to which fundamental decisions on fiscal policy shall remain in the hands of national governments, making the creation of a strong mechanism of democratic accountability at European level less necessary. While the reforms adopted after the crisis have strongly modified the functioning of the economic governance, the role of the European Parliament has substantially remained unscathed.[207]

---

[204]See Ioannidis (2016), p. 1277; Curtin (2016), p. 190.

[205]Cf. Dawson and de Witte (2013), p. 834.

[206]Majone (2014), p. 1221.

[207]Daniele (2016), p. 270.

Considering first of all the adoption of reforms, the European Parliament has participated as co-ruler on some occasions. Following the procedures dictated in the enabling clauses ex art. 121(6) and 136(1) TFEU, it agreed on the adoption of the Six Pack and the Two Pack in accordance with either the ordinary or special legislative procedure. Similarly, it also participated in the setup of the regulations founding the banking union. In accordance with the procedure outlined in art. 48(6) TEU, the Parliament was consulted for the approval of Decision 2011/199/EU amending art. 136(3) TFEU. Looking instead at the stipulation of intergovernmental agreements beyond EU law, the participation of the European Parliament has been obviously quite marginal. More precisely, it did not participate at all in the stipulation of the TESM, while it managed to send only some observers to the intergovernmental conference, which negotiated the TSCG.[208]

Moving to the actual functioning of the governance, both EU law and the intergovernmental agreements relegate the European Parliament to the role of observer. Indeed, democratic accountability in the SGP, the TESM and the TSCG is essentially pursued through the interinstitutional dialogue, according to which the decisions taken in the framework of the economic governance are subject to the political review of the European Parliament.[209] The dialogue results from the obligation for the Presidents of the Council, the Commission, the Euro group and the European Council to report periodically to the Parliament on the state of European surveillance, as well as the right for the latter to invite the same Presidents before the competent parliamentary committee to discuss the adoption of specific decisions. At the same time, the European Parliament may offer the opportunity to the Member States, which is subject to a council recommendation to participate in an exchange of view. In this case, the economic dialogue may also work as a platform of mediation between European institutions and the national governments.[210] Evidently the interinstitutional dialogue complies with the principles of deliberative democracy, according to which political decisions are the results of a debate between several actors, which may put forward their own perspectives and interests on a specific issue.

The right to ask information and the duty to report is expressly foreseen in regards to the most important decisions of European surveillance, notably those about the existence of an excessive deficit, the violation of the MTO, the preparation of stability and national reform programmes in the framework of the European semester and the presence of a macro-economic excessive imbalance in the Member States.[211] Similar obligations are also foreseen by the TSCG, which involves the Euro Summit

[208] See Fasone (2014), p. 172.

[209] See Starita (2017), pp. 23–24.

[210] Art. 2ab(3) of Regulation (EC) No 1466/1997.

[211] In the event the Commission and the Council refused to participate in the dialogue, the ECJ could be activated through a procedure for failure to act ex art. 265 TFEU. Fasone (2014), p. 176.

in the economic dialogue with the EU parliament,[212] and recalls the possibility of inter-parliamentary cooperation between the European and the national parliaments.[213] Quite importantly, the TESM does not foresee a dialogue between the Board of Governors and the European Parliament, but only with domestic parliaments and audit institutions, as well as the European Court of Auditors. Regulation (EU) No 472/2013 has partially corrected this deficit, by extending to the European Parliament the rights of information and discussion in relation to the conditionality policy defined by the Council and implemented by the Commission.

Interinstitutional dialogue applies also to the banking union. Aside from the obligation to report and the right to ask for information, the SSM Regulation foresees that the European Parliament and the Council shall be involved in the appointment and removal of the chair and vice chair of the Supervisory Board. Considering instead the SRM, the Commission and the Council have a direct power of control on the Single Resolution Board, as they can prevent it from adopting a resolution scheme.[214] At the same time, the European Parliament does not have any role in this procedure, but it shall only approve the decision of the Council to appoint or remove the members of the Board.[215]

After having recalled the fundamental functioning of the economic dialogue, it is possible to identify some concerns on its effective ability to pursue democratic accountability. First, the European parliament is involved too late, in the sense that it discusses decisions, which have been substantially already taken by the Commission, the Council and the Member States individually or together.[216] The public giving of reasons, which is the purpose of the dialogue, doesn't upgrade the role of the European Parliament, which remains a simple spectator of a decision-making process in the hands of other actors. Second, the economic dialogue does not provide any mechanism to ensure that the authorities in charge of decisions face some form of consequences for their action.[217] Indeed, the European Parliament can neither censor intergovernmental bodies, which derive their legitimacy from national parliaments, nor exercise a veto power on what has been already decided. Technically the only instrument to impact the functioning of the economic governance would be

---

[212]The President of the European Parliament shall be invited to the summits, while the President of the Euro Summit shall present a report to the European Parliament after each meeting.

[213]The inter-parliamentary cooperation should work in accordance with the existing legal framework under EU primary law. See Protocol No 1 of the Lisbon Treaty on the role of national parliaments in the European Union. The role for the conference of national parliamentary committees (known in practice as 'COSAC'), however, is not specified. *De facto* neither the European Parliament, nor national parliaments play a substantial role in the Fiscal Compact.

[214]The SRB is in fact an EU agency. In particular the resolution scheme drafted by the Board enters into force only if, within 24 h after its adoption, there are no objections from the Commission or the Council. Cf. Art. 18 of Regulation (EU) No 806/2014.

[215]The procedures involve the Commission, which shall make a proposal, and requires the approval of the European Parliament.

[216]Cf. Fasone (2014), p. 184.

[217]See Ioannidis (2014), p. 42; Curtin (2016), p. 191.

passing a motion of censure on the Commission. In reality, even this procedure, regardless the several formal and political difficulties for its activation, would not be able to modify the orientation of the governance, as the Commission can only adopt recommendations and proposals, while fundamental decisions are taken by national governments in the Council. In this perspective, the European Parliament remains foreign to the management of the governance.[218] Last, the economic dialogue does not cover some important decisions taken in the framework of the ESM, notably the preparation of the macroeconomic adjustment programme and the monitoring of its implementation.[219] Even if Regulation (EU) No 472/2013 does oblige the Commission to publish decisions on enhanced surveillance, the macroeconomic adjustment programme and the results of the supervision, the disclosure of further information is limited. Evidently, the negotiation of the conditionality policy escapes the (weak) scrutiny of the economic dialogue because most negotiations between the *Troika* and the Member States are still based on informal decisions.[220] Furthermore, the ESM is not subject to the same transparency requirement of other EU institutions, because some of its decision comply with strict confidentiality needs.[221]

4.4.4 The Rise of Intergovernmentalism

The evaporation of national democratic control on fiscal policies in the Eurozone and the difficult consolidation of a European level of democracy follow the intergovernmental drift of the European economic governance.[222] In this regard, several authors identify a 'rise of intergovernamentalism' in the EMU in the sense that supranational institutions, like the Commission, are delegated a supervisory role, while political

[218]De la Parra identified other limits of the economic dialogue. First, many MEPs do not make optimal use of this new tools: either they don't ask questions, but just criticism or they leave short margin for reply or just use the time given to enhance their visibility. Second, the debate has been characterised over the last years by the dispersion of questions, a scarce knowledge of the topic, vagueness of the answer. Third, the Eurogroup President attends meetings with the Parliament when it is more convenient for him and shall refuse to answer certain questions regarding the MoUs. See De La Parra (2017), pp. 116–118.

[219]The chair and vice chair of the competent committee can be informed only in confidential way. See De La Parra (2017), p. 110.

[220]See Ioannidis (2014), p. 39.

[221]Art. 34 TESM provides for duties of professional secrecy for the Members or former Members of the Board of Governors and of the Board of Directors and any other persons who work or have worked for or in connection with the ESM. Furthermore, the minutes of the Board of Governors meetings are confidential in accordance with art. 17(6) of the ESM By-Laws. On the limited transparency of the ESM see Tuori and Tuori (2014), pp. 218–219; Hinarejos (2015), pp. 95–96; De Nes (2015), Ban and Seabrooke (2017), Simone (2017), pp. 205–208.

[222]See Hinarejos (2015), p. 95; Daniele (2016), pp. 262–266; Pace (2018), p. 145.

decisions are taken at intergovernmental level, by the Council, the European Council or new informal bodies set up by the Member States during the crisis.[223]

The rise of intergovernamentalism is proven by the new prominent role of the European Council, which in few years has become the real centre of political decision in the economic governance.[224] First of all, it has been directly involved in the process of budgetary surveillance, for example in the adoption of guidelines within the European semester.[225] Similarly, the European Council has become the primary body in charge of dealing with situation of emergency, which require prompt and flexible solutions at the highest political level.[226] Even if formal decisions are still adopted by the Ecofin Council, the latter has been relegated *de facto* to be the minor chamber of the economic governance, which implements the fundamental decisions taken by the Head of States or Governments.[227] At the same time, the European Council is using its political authority to consolidate its power of legislative initiative in the EMU. This happens not only in regard to the political and intergovernmental agreements, which shape the economic governance (i.e. conditional financial assistance), but also to the legislative process within the EU. Even if the Commission keeps the formal power of initiative, in reality it is not able to amend the draft proposals, which have already been developed by the leaders of the Member States within the European Council.[228]

The strengthening of intergovernamentalism has also favoured the setup of parallel decision-making processes aside from the official ones defined by the EU treaties.[229] More precisely, informal bodies of discussion composed only of Eurozone governments, namely the Eurogroup and the Euro summit, can exercise a huge influence on the management of the governance, despite lacking clear powers defined in EU law. More precisely, the Eurogroup is *de facto* in charge of the activation of the financial assistance, as it is composed of the same members of the Board of Governors of the ESM. In accordance with Regulation (EU) No 473/2013, it shall also receive a copy of the draft budgetary law of each government before its adoption at the end of the year and issue an opinion. At the same time, the TSCG gives the Euro Summit the responsibility of discussing questions relating to the specific responsibilities of the Member States, other issues concerning the

---

[223]Cf. Habermas (2015), pp. 550–551.

[224]This is also testified by the more and more frequent meetings of the European Council: between February 2010 and January 2016 it met 41 times, while the Euro council 14 times. See Allemand (2017), p. 83. On the role of the European Council cf. Puetter (2016), pp. 258–262.

[225]This is the reason why the European Council has become part of the economic dialogue with the European Parliament. See Allemand (2017), p. 84

[226]Cf. Puetter (2016), p. 259.

[227]See Allemand (2017), pp. 86–87.

[228]Cf. Starita (2017), pp. 13–14.

[229]Tuori and Tuori (2014), p. 217.

governance of the euro area and strategic orientations for the conduct of economic policies to increase convergence.[230]

The rise of intergovernamentalism has had a significant impact also on the Commission by reducing its role to secretarial tasks.[231] This is happens for example in the application of the conditionality policy under the ESM. As it was already explained, in this situation, the Commission does play an important and necessary role, as it leads negotiations with the beneficiary Member States and monitors the implementation of the MoUs, which require considerable expertise and technical knowledge. At the same time, the real margin of political action of the Commission is limited, as it cannot overcome the mandate received by the Council and the Board of Governors of the ESM. Considering the decision-making process within the EU legal framework, the introduction of semiautomatic sanctions did not completely upgrade the role of the Commission in the process of economic coordination. Indeed, the margin of action, the Commission can enjoy in concrete, is still conditioned by the creditor Member States, which can achieve a minority block in the Council to stop its proposals and recommendations.[232] Furthermore, the adoption of sanctions by RMV will normally be preceded by a decision by standard majority voting acknowledging a situation of non-compliance with EU law. More generally, it looks like the European Commission is not willing to fully exploit the instruments available under EU and international law to foster compliance with EU rules and gain some stronger role in the reform of the governance. Some cases are rather topical to understand the structural weakness of the Commission. First, the Commission adopted a rather soft approach in monitoring the enforcement of the Fiscal Compact in domestic law. As the previous analysis has already explained, governments could enjoy a wide margin of discretion in the implementation of the obligations outlined in the Treaty, thus undermining the effectiveness of fiscal discipline. Second, the Commission has not yet been able to ensure the full application of the EDP, regardless the use of RMV for the adoption of decisions. For example the violation of fiscal rules by Spain and Portugal in 2016 did not lead to the application of sanctions.[233] The case of Italy is even more significant. Even if in 2018 the Italian government significantly reduced its efforts to pursue budgetary consolidation, the Commission did not trigger any sanctioning procedure.[234] Third,

[230]Cf. Menendez (2014), p. 133.

[231]Other authors have a more positive interpretation of the role played by the European Commission in the governance. Cf. Bauer and Becker (2014). According to Daniele the strengthening of the intergovernmental method over the last few years has been balanced by the conferral of important advisory, preparatory and executive tasks to the Commission. See Daniele (2016), p. 271.

[232]See Menendez (2014), p. 135.

[233]Cf. Council Implementing Decision No 11554/16 on imposing a fine on Portugal for failure to take effective action to address an excessive deficit, OJ L 306/1; Council Implementing Decision No 11555/16 on imposing a fine on Spain for failure to take effective action to address an excessive deficit, OJ L 306/1.

[234]Regardless the violation of its previous budgetary commitments, the European Commission decided to launch an EDP against Italy on the 19 December 2018. Dombrovskis (2018).

while the Commission has still been able to advance several proposals on the reform of the governance, the latter must be still filtered by the European Council, which has become the real agenda setter of the EU.

In conclusion on this point, while fundamental decisions are taken by the executives of Member States, the Commission has become a sort of secretariat, which is used for its expertise and technical analysis.[235] The legal and political doctrine has clearly explained the dangers of 'intergovernamentalism' and the marginalisation of parliamentary representation.[236] Thanks to their ability to balance the preservation of national sovereignty and fulfil coordination with the other countries, executives have *de facto* imposed their prominence on domestic parliaments, while preventing the emergence of a genuine level of European democracy. Accordingly, the role of parliaments consists only of ratifying decisions taken by national governments in both formal and informal bodies. In a context, where parliaments are marginal and the EU Commission works as a technical institution, some major risks arise. First, decisions are taken in accordance with the rule of force, which regulates the relationship between governments: the stronger and financially more stable countries will be able to impose their leadership on the weaker ones by counting on formal and informal instruments. Second, the intergovernmental management of power is unable to effectively pursue common objectives, which go beyond national-wide perspectives and require a genuinely European approach. What national governments can do at their best is to achieve a precarious balance between the different particular interests. Finally, another specific danger resulting from the rise of intergovernamentalism and more specifically from the creation of informal decision-making bodies touches upon the possible violation of principles of institutional balance and conferral. If the purpose of these new fora is to coordinate *ex ante* the position of the Eurozone countries within the Council and European Council,[237] the latter institutions will behave only as the 'echo chamber' of resolutions agreed elsewhere.

4.4.5 Is the Economic Governance Acting in the Interest of the People?

The weakening of accountability mechanisms has caused a progressive estrangement of EU institutions from the European citizens. As the previous analysis has

---

[235]The surveillance model is based on a process of de-politicisation of fiscal and economic policy, which is considered a technical subject. In this perspective, national fiscal choices shall be taken within given objective parameters. Tuori and Tuori (2014), p. 211. In reality, the Commission can't be completely impartial in the management of the governance, as technical decisions are influenced by political considerations. Allemand (2017), pp. 92–93.

[236]See Crum (2012), pp. 622–623.

[237]See Calliess (2012), pp. 109–110; Tuori and Tuori (2014), p. 179; Menendez (2014), p. 133.

explained, the economic recipes adopted over the last few years have been decided by intergovernmental bodies, which are subject to weak accountability mechanisms. Furthermore, as governments are individually responsible only to their national community, it is difficult to put forward the common European interest, especially when this would require balancing the different priorities of the Member States. The instruments of deliberative democracy, namely the interinstitutional dialogue, are not sufficiently incisive to ensure the responsiveness of the governance to the people.[238] Due to the democratic deficit of the economic union, the Council, the European Council and the other intergovernmental bodies have been applying economic rules with no regard for the recipients of their decisions. Many citizens have therefore developed growing discontent regarding in particular the application of budgetary consolidation (i.e. higher taxes, cuts to the welfare state) and structural reforms (i.e. flexibilisation of the labour market and increase of the retirement age). While these measures have been necessary to ensure fiscal stability in the Member States, their implementation has been harsher in those countries presenting high level of public debt or requesting the financial support of the ESM. A significant part of the academic doctrine has highlighted the negative consequences of the reforms on the weaker part of the European society and the fundamental rights protected by EU law.[239] The case law previously analysed on the violation of the EUCFR after the application of the ESM conditionality policy does clearly explain how devastating austerity policy on the fundamental rights of the citizens can be.

As the same time, the efforts made under European supervision to regain economic competitiveness through structural reforms have not been sufficient to relaunch economic growth on a continental level. The Eurozone governance has developed the instrument to impose Member States some form of self-limitation of fiscal sovereignty without, however, creating efficient tools to pursue economic growth at European level. Indeed, the significant resources mobilised by EFSI in favour of projects in the field of infrastructures, education, research and innovation could not trigger real countercyclical effects on the whole European economy. A more important contribution in this regard has been given instead by the ECB through the adoption of non-conventional monetary policies, such as Quantitative Easing.

Evidently, the detachment between governors and governed has allowed the implementation of economic policies, which despite being necessary to ensure the stability of the euro area as a whole have also determined social distress in several Member States. This malcontent has slowly undermined the popular consensus around the process of European integration and made many citizens become more sceptical towards the EU and the single currency itself.[240] As a consequence, the output legitimacy of the governance has been strongly undermined.

---

[238] On the necessity to strengthen democratic accountability at European level cf. Ruffert (2011), pp. 1801–1802; Baratta (2013), pp. 59–60.

[239] Cf. Viterbo and Costamagna (2013) and Cafari Panico (2017), pp. 311–315.

[240] Cf. Allemand and Martucci (2012), p. 455.

4.4.6 *The Deficit of Democratic Accountability: Conclusive Remarks*

The ongoing reform of the economic union has deepened the democratic deficit of the European governance. Notably, domestic parliaments maintain only a formal grip on national macroeconomic policy. Fundamental decisions are taken instead at European level through a concertation of national governments. The weakening of parliamentary representation is even stronger in relation to those Member States demanding financial support from the ESM. In their case, economic reforms are *de facto* dictated by the creditor countries.

While national democracies are overshadowed by the rise of intergovernamentalism, the European parliament has not been able so far to gain any substantial role in the functioning of the governance. On the contrary, fundamental decisions stay with the national governments, either in the institutions (Council, European Council) and the informal meeting (Eurogroup, Euro summit) of the Union, or even in the ruling bodies of international organisations (Governing council of the ESM).

The weakening of democratic accountability is extremely dangerous for the pursuit of stability of the euro area as a whole. As citizens don't have a say in the decision-making process, European intergovernmental bodies can ignore the social and political impact of their policies. While diminishing its legitimacy, the governance also risks losing its grip on the political and social situation in the euro area. This is proven by the rise of Eurosceptic forces, which have recently gained significant electoral success in several Member State on the basis of anti-austerity political programme. Notably the economic union is based on the compliance with common rules, the prohibition of moral hazard behaviours and the mutual financial assistance in case of systemic risks. The electoral success of these parties and the policies they are willing to implement may lead to a breakup of the solidarity of fact and the mutual trust between the Member States, thus undermining the stability of the euro area as a whole.

References

Adamski D (2012) National power games and structural failures in the European macroeconomic governance. Common Mark Law Rev 49:1319–1364

Adamski D (2016) Economic policy coordination as a game involving economic stability and national sovereignty. Eur Law J 22:180–203

Adamski D (2018) Redefining European economic integration. Cambridge University Press, Cambridge

Allemand F (2017) More or less intergovernmental cooperation within the new EMU? In: Daniele L, Simone R, Cisotta P (eds) Democracy in the EMU in the aftermath of the crisis. Springer, Berlin, pp 73–99

Allemand F, Martucci F (2012) La nouvelle gouvernance économique européenne. Cahiers de droit européen 48:17–99, 409–457

Allemand F, Bion M, Sauron J (2016) Gouverner la zone euro après la crise: l'exigence d'intégration. Gualino, Paris
Amtenbirik A, De Haan J (2003) Economic governance in the European Union - fiscal policy discipline versus flexibility. Common Mark Law Rev 40:1057–1106
Antpöhler C (2012) Emergenz der europäischen Wirtschaftsregierung - Das Six Pack als Zeichen supranationaler Leistungsfähigkeit. Zeitschrift für ausländisches öffentliches Recht und Völkerrecht 72:354–391
Audit M (2014) A debt restructuration mechanism for European sovereigns: an emerging idea. In: Paulus CG (ed) A debt restructuring mechanism for sovereigns. Do we need a legal procedure? Beck-Hart-Nomos, Munich, pp 213–222
Avgouleas E, Eichengreen B, Panizza U, Maduro M P, Portes R, di Mauro B W, Wyplosz C, Zettelmeyere J (2018) Independent report on the Greek official debt. CEPR Policy Insight No 92
Ban C, Seabrooke L (2017) From crisis to stability. How to make the European stability mechanism transparent and accountable. Transparency International EU
Bandilla R (2017) Artikel 25 AEUV. In: Grabitz E, Hilf M, Nettesheim M (eds) Das Recht der Europäischen Union. Beck, München
Bantekas I, Vivien R (2016) The odiousness of Greek debt. Eur Law J 22:539–565
Baratta R (2013) Legal issues of the fiscal compact in the euro crisis. In: De Witte B, Heritier A, Trechsel A (eds) The euro crisis and the state of European democracy, 2013. European University Institute, Florence, pp 31–63
Bauer MW, Becker S (2014) The unexpected winner of the crisis: the European Commission's strengthened role in economic governance. J Eur Integr 39:213–229
Beck G (2014) The Court of Justice, the Bundesverfassungsgericht and legal reasoning during the euro crisis: the rule of law as a fair-weather phenomenon. Eur Public Law 20:539–566
Bénassy-Quéré A, Brunnermeier M, Enderlein H, Farhi E, Fratzscher M, Fuest C, Gourinchas P, Martin P, Pisani-Ferry J, Rey H, Schnabel I, Véron N, Weder di Mauro B, Zettelmeyer J (2018) Reconciling risk sharing with market discipline: a constructive approach to euro area reform. CEPR Policy Insight No. 91
Bernard C (2013) The carter in time of crisis: a case study of dismissal. In: Countouris N, Freedland M (eds) Resocialising Europe in a time of crisis. Cambridge University Press, Cambridge, pp 250–277
Beukers T (2013) The Eurozone crisis and the legitimacy of differentiated integration. In: De Witte B, Heritier A, Trechsel A (eds) The euro crisis and the state of European democracy, 2013. European University Institute, Florence, pp 7–30
Boggero G, Annicchino P (2014) 'Who will ever kick us out?': Italy, the balanced budget rule and the implementation of the fiscal compact. Eur Public Law 20(2):247–261
Borger V (2013a) The ESM and the European Court's predicament in pringle. Ger Law J 14:113–140
Borger V (2013b) How the debt crisis exposes the development of solidarity in the euro area. Eur Const Law Rev 9:7–36
Bovens M (2007) Analysing and assessing public accountability. A conceptual framework. Eur Law J 13:447–468
Bredt S (2011) Prospects and limits of democratic governance in the EU. Eur Law J 17:35–65
Busch D (2017) Governance of the European Banking Union's Single Resolution Mechanism. European Banking Institute Working Paper Series, No 9
Cafari Panico R (2017) L'affievolimento dei diritti nella crisi economica e politica dell'Unione Europea. Studi sull'integrazione europea 12:289–316
Calliess C (2011–2012) From fiscal compact to fiscal union? New rules for the Eurozone. Camb Yearb Eur Leg Stud 14:101–117
Calliess C (2016) The governance framework of the Eurozone and the need for a treaty reform. In: Fabbrini F, Ballin EH, Somsen H (eds) What form of government for the European Union and the Eurozone? Hart, Oxford, pp 37–56

Castaneda JE, Schwartz P (2017) How functional is the Eurozone? An index of European economic integration through the single currency. Econ Aff:365–369

Chalmers D (2012) The European redistributive state and a European law of struggle, the European redistributive state and a European law of struggle. Eur Law J 18:667–693

Chamon M (2018) Fining member states under the SGP, or how enforcement is different from implementation under Article 291 TFEU: Spain v. Council. Common Mark Law Rev 55:1495–1520

Chiti E, Teixeira PG (2013) The constitutional implication of the European responses to the financial and public debt crisis. Common Mark Law Rev 50:683–708

Cisotta R (2015) Financial stability and the reconstruction of the EU legal order in the aftermath of the crisis, in European Central Bank Legal Conference (2015), From Monetary Union to Banking Union, on the way to Capital Markets Union. New opportunities for European integration

Clayes G, Leandro A (2016) Assessing the Juncker Plan after one year. Bruegel Blog Post, 17th May 2016

Condinanzi M (2016) Unione economica e monetaria e politica sociale. In: Tizzano A (ed) Verso i 60 anni dai Trattati di Roma. Giappichelli, Torino, pp 241–252

Corti Varela J (2015) Direct recapitalization of banks and sovereign debt: the ESM direct recapitalization instrument and its impact on sovereign debt. In: Hinojosa-Martmez LM, Beneyto JM (eds) European Banking Union. The new regime. Wolters Kluwer, Alphen aan den Rijn, pp 121–136

Costamagna F (2014) The impact of stronger economic policy coordination on the European social dimension: issues of legitimacy. In: Adams M, Fabbrini F, Larouche P (eds) The constitutionalization of European budgetary constraints. Hart, Oxford, pp 359–378

Costamagna F (2015) Il coordinamento delle politiche economiche nell'ambito del Semestre europeo. In: Porchia O (ed) Governance economica europea. Strumenti dell'Unione, rapporti con l'ordinamento internazionale e ricadute nell'ordinamento interno. Editoriale Scientifica, Napoli, pp 127–140

Craig P (2012) The stability, coordination and governance treaty: principle, politics and pragmatism. Eur Law Rev 37:231–248

Craig P (2013) Pringle legal reasoning, text, purpose and teleology. Maastricht J Eur Comp Law 20:3–11

Craig P (2017) The euro group, power and accountability. Eur Law J 23:234–249

Crum B (2012) Saving Europe at the cost of democracy. J Common Mark Stud 51:614–630

Curtin D (2016) Democratic accountability of EU executive power: a reform agenda for parliament. In: Fabbrini F, Ballin EH, Somsen H (eds) What form of government for the European Union and the Eurozone. Hart, London, pp 171–194

Daniele L (2016) Misure anti-crisi, riforma della governance della zona euro e assetto istituzionale della UEM. In: Tizzano A (ed) Verso i 60 anni dai Trattati di Roma. Giappichelli, Torino, pp 253–272

Darvas Z, Leandro A (2016) Implementation of European Semester recommendations worsens further. Bruegel Blog Post, 15th June 2016

Dawson M, de Witte F (2013) Constitutional balance in the EU after the euro-crisis. Mod Law Rev 76:817–844

De Gregorio Merino A (2012) Legal developments in the economic and monetary union during the debt crisis. Common Mark Law Rev 49:1613–1645

De La Parra S (2017) The economic dialogue: an effective accountable mechanism. In: Daniele L, Simone R, Cisotta P (eds) Democracy in the EMU in the aftermath of the crisis. Springer, Berlin, pp 101–120

De Lhoneux E, Vassilopoulos C (2013) The European stability mechanism before the Court of Justice of the European Union. Comment to the Pringle case. Springer, London

De Nes M (2015) The ESM and the principle of transparency. Perspect Federalism 7(3):128–141

De Streel A, Etienne J (2012) Le Traité sur la stabilité, la coordination et la gouvernance au sein de l'Union économique et monétaire. Journal de droit européen 73:182–185

De Witte B, Beukers T (2013) The Court of Justice approves the creation of the European stability mechanism outside the EU legal order: Pringle. Common Mark Law Rev 50:805–848

Della Cananea G (2011) L'Unione Economica e monetaria vent'anni dopo: crisi e opportunità. Costituzionalismo.it. Issue No 3

Dimopoulos A (2014) The use of international law as a tool for enhancing governance in the Eurozone and its impact on EU institutional integrity. In: Adams M, Fabbrini F, Larouche P (eds) The constitutionalization of European budgetary constraints. Hart, Oxford, pp 41–63

Dombrovskis V (2018) Speech of Vice-President Valdis Dombrovskis: College read-out and remarks on the Italian budget, Brussels, 19th December 2018, SPEECH/18/6886

Efstathiou K, Wolff G (2018) Is the European Semester effective and useful. Bruegel Policy Contribution No 9

Estella A (2016) European Union bailouts and credibility: the constitutional dimension. Eur Public Law 22:507–540

Estella A (2018) Legal foundations of EU economic governance. Cambridge University Press, Cambridge

European Commission Analytical Grids (2015) on the application of State aid rules to the financing of infrastructure projects. 21st September 2015

European Commission Communication (2015) Making the best use of the flexibility within the existing rules of the Stability and Growth Pact, COM(2015) 12 final

European Commission Communication (2018a) On the review of the flexibility under the Stability and Growth Pact, SWD (2018) 270final

European Commission Communication (2018b) On 2018 European Semester - Country-specific recommendations, COM(2018) 400 final

European Commission Green Paper (2011) On the feasibility of introducing Stability Bonds, 23rd November 2011, COM(2011) 818 final

European Commission Press Release (2019) Spring Package: Commission issues recommendations for Member States to advance sustainable and inclusive economic growth, IP/19/2813, 5th June 2019

European Commission Proposal for a Council Regulation (2017) On the establishment of the European Monetary Fund, 6th December 2017, COM/2017/0827 final

European Commission Report (2017) Report from the commission presented under article 8 of the treaty on stability, coordination and governance in the economic and monetary union, C/2017/1201 final

European Parliament Briefing (2018) Country-specific recommendations, PE 624.404, 4th September 2018

Fabbrini F (2016) Economic governance in Europe. Comparative paradoxes and constitutional challenges. Oxford University Press, Oxford

Fasone A (2014) European economic governance and parliamentary representation. What place for the European Parliament? Eur Law J 20:164–185

Fernandes S (2017) Social Investment and the Juncker Plan, Notre Europe, Synthesis, 17th July 2017

Fischer-Lescano A, Oberndorfer L (2013) Fiskalvertrag und Unionsrecht. Neue Juristische Wochenschrift 65:9–14

Fromage D (2017) Creation and reform of independent fiscal institutions in EU member states: incomplete and insufficient work in Progress? In: Beukers T, de Witte B, Kilpatrick C (eds) Constitutional change through euro-crisis law. Cambridge University Press, Cambridge, pp 108–142

Fromage D, Dermine P (2017) The Commission's report on the Fiscal Compact and its expected (cautious) assessment, Eufinacco, 31st March 2017

Fuest C, Heinemann F, Schroeder C (2014) A Viable Insolvency Procedure for Sovereigns in the Euro area, ZEW Discussion Paper No. 14-053. Available at: http://ftp.zew.de/pub/zew-docs/dp/dp14053.pdf
Grimm H (2016) Zur Reform der Wirtschafts-und Wahrungsunion nach der Krise. Nomos, Baden-Baden
Gros D, Alcidi C (2014) The case of the disappearing Fiscal Compact, CEPS Commentary, 5th November 2014
Habermas J (2012) The crisis of the European Union: a response. Eur J Int Law 23:335–348
Habermas J (2015) Democracy in Europe: why the development of the EU into a transnational democracy is necessary and how it is possible. Eur Law J 21:546–557
Häde U (2010) Kommissionsentwürfe für offensichtliche Ultra-vires-Akte. Europäische Zeitschrift für Wirtschaftsrecht 12:921–922
Häde U (2012) Euro-Rettung zwischen Exekutivprimat und Parlamentsvorbehalt. Nomos, Badan-Baden
Häde U (2016) Artikel 125 AEUV. In: Calliess C, Ruffert M (eds) EUV, AEUV, Kommentar. Beck, München
Harlow C (2002) Accountability in the European Union. Oxford University Press, Oxford
Haroutunian S, Hauptmeier S, Leiner-Killinger N (2018) Country-specific recommendations for fiscal policies under the 2018 European Semester, ECB Economic Bulletin No 4
Hentschelmann K (2011) Finanzhilfen im Lichte der No-Bailout Klausel – Eigenverantwortung und Solidarität in der Währungsunion, Europarecht, 282–312
Herrmann C (2010) Griechische Tragödie – der währungsverfassungsrechtliche Rahmen für die Rettung, den Austritt oder den Ausschluss von überschuldeten Staaten aus der Eurozone. Europäische Zeitschrift für Wirtschaftsrecht 21:413–418
Hinarejos A (2013) Fiscal federalism in the European Union: evolution and future choices for EMU. Common Mark Law Rev 51:1621–1642
Hinarejos A (2015) The euro area crisis in constitutional perspective. Oxford University Press, Oxford
Hinarejos A (2016) Changes to economic and monetary union and their effects on social policy. Int J Comp Labour Law Ind Relat 32:231–250
Hoffmeister H (2010–2011) To bail out or not to bail out? – legal aspects of the Greek crisis. Camb Yearb Eur Leg Stud 13:113–134
Horvath M (2018) EU independent fiscal institutions: an assessment of potential effectiveness. J Common Mark Stud 56:504–519
Huguenot-Noël R, Zuleeg F (2016) Rethinking the EU's investment strategy: EFSI 2.0 needs a Social Pillar to address economic insecurity. EPC Publications, 15 November 2016
Inderst G (2013) Private Infrastructure Finance and Investment in Europe. EIB Working Papers No 2
Ioannidis M (2014) EU financial assistance conditionality after "two pack". Zeitschrift für ausländisches öffentliches Recht und Völkerrecht 74:1–44
Ioannidis M (2016) Europe's new transformations: how the EU economic constitution changed during the Eurozone crisis. Common Mark Law Rev 53:1237–1282
Jančić D (2016) National parliaments and EU fiscal integration. Eur Law J 22:225–249
Kegels C, Verlinden J (2013) La détection et la correction des déséquilibres macroéconomiques. Reflets et perspectives de la vie économique 52:51–66
Kerber M (2013) Une apologie téléologique sans limites. Les Petites affiches, 7–11
Ketterer L (2016) Zustimmungserfordernis beim Europaischen Stabilitaetsmechanismus. Mohr Siebeck, Tübingen
Leino-Sandberg P, Salminen J (2017) A multi-level playing field for economic policy-making: does EU economic governance have impact? In: Beukers T, de Witte B, Kilpatrick C (eds) Constitutional change through euro-crisis. Cambridge University Press, Cambridge
Lenaerts K, Desomer M (2002) New models of constitution-making in Europe: the quest for legitimacy. Common Mark Law Rev 39:1217–1253

Lo Schiavo G (2017) The role of financial stability in EU law and policy. Wolters Kluwer, Alphen aan den Rijn
Louis J (2004) The economic and monetary union: law and institutions. Common Mark Law Rev 41:575–608
Louis J (2010) Guest editorial: the no-bailout clause and rescue packages. Common Mark Law Rev 47:971–986
Majone G (2014) From regulatory state to a democratic default. J Common Mark Stud 52:1216–1223
Manzini P (2013) La riforma delle regole UE sulla sorveglianza dei bilanci pubblici nazionali. In: Adinolfi G, Vellano M (eds) La crisi del debito sovrano degli stati dell'area Euro. Giappichelli, Torino, pp 29–48
Markakis M, Dermine P (2018) Bailout, the legal status of memoranda of understanding and the scope of application of the EU charter: Florescu. Common Mark Law Rev 55:643–671
Martucci F (2017) The democratic foundations of the EMU. In: Daniele L, Simone R, Cisotta P (eds) Democracy in the EMU in the aftermath of the crisis. Springer, Berlin, pp 27–50
Menendez AJ (2014) Editorial: a European Union in constitutional mutation? Eur Law J 20:127–141
Miglio A (2015) L'Assegnazione di Compiti alle Istituzioni Europee nell'ambito di accordi internazionali tra Stati Membri. In: Porchia O (ed) Governance economica europea. Strumenti dell'Unione, rapporti con l'ordinamento internazionale e ricadute nell'ordinamento interno. Editoriale Scientifica, Napoli, pp 143–169
Moloney N (2014) European banking union: assessing its risks and resilience. Common Mark Law Rev 51(6):1609–1670
Munari F (2015) Da Pringle a Gauweiler: i tormentati anni dell'Unione monetaria e i loro effetti sull'ordinamento giuridico europeo. Il Diritto dell'Unione Europea, 723–755
Munari F (2018) The European Monetary Union: a hard test for the rule of law within the EU legal system. Am Univ Int Law Rev 33:345–390
Murswiek D (2016) Die Eurokrise vor dem Bundesverfassungsgericht. Nomos, Baden-Baden
Nettesheim M (2012) Staatshilfen aus der Sicht des Europarechts und der Verfassung. In: Kadelbach S (ed) Nach der Finanzkrise. Nomos, Baden-Baden, pp 31–78
O'Gorman R (2017) The failure of the troika to measure the impact of the economic adjustment programmes on the vulnerable. Leg Issues Econ Integr 44:265–291
Ohler C (2011) The European stability mechanism: the long road to financial stability in the euro area. Ger Yearb Int Law 54:47–74
Ohler C (2014) A governance crisis? Treaty change, fiscal union and the ECB. In: Ringe W, Huber PM (eds) Legal challenges in the global financial crisis: bail-outs, the euro and regulation. Hart, London, pp 121–130
Pace LF (2018) Il regime giuridico dell'euro. La nascita dell'Unione economica e monetaria, la sua crisi e la risposta dell'Unione europea. Cacucci, Bari
Palm U (2017) Artikel 136 AEUV. In: Grabitz E, Hilf M, Nettesheim M (eds) Das Recht der Europäischen Union. Beck, München
Palmstorfer R (2014) The reverse majority voting under the 'six pack': a bad turn for the union? Eur Law J 20:186–203
Panizza U (2014) Do we need a mechanism for solving sovereign debt crises? A rule-based discussion. In: Paulus CG (ed) A debt restructuring mechanism for sovereigns. Do we need a legal procedure? Beck-Hart-Nomos, Munich, pp 223–240
Papadopoulos Y (2007) Problems of democratic accountability in network and multilevel governance. Eur Law J 13:469–486
Peroni G (2012) La crisi dell'euro: limiti e rimedi dell'unione economica e monetaria. Giuffré, Milano
Pistoia E (2018) Limiti all'integrazione differenziata dell'Unione europea. Cacucci, Bari
Poulou A (2017) Financial assistance conditionality and human rights protection: what is the role of the EU charter of fundamental rights? Common Mark Law Rev 54:991–1025

Puetter U (2016) New intergovernmentalism: the European council and its president. In: Fabbrini F, Ballin EH, Somsen H (eds) What form of government for the European Union and the Eurozone? Hart, Oxford, pp 253–270
Richter C (2013) Article 125 TFEU. In: Geiger R, Khan D, Kotzur M (eds) European Union treaties: a commentary. Beck-Hart, Munich
Rinaldi D, Nuñez Ferrer J (2017) The European Fund for Strategic Investments as a New Type of Budgetary Instrument, CEPS Research Report, No 07, April 2017
Rossolillo G (2018) Fiscalità e sovranità: riflessioni sulla ripartizione delle competenze tra Stati membri e Union Europea. Il Diritto dell'Unione Europea, 123–152
Rubio E, Rinaldi D, Pellerin-Carlin T (2016) Investment in Europe: making the best of the Juncker Plan with case Studies on digital infrastructure and energy efficiency. Jacques Delors Institute, Paris, April
Ruffert M (2011) The European debt crisis and European Union law. Common Mark Law Rev 48:1777–1806
Rüffert M (2011) Die Europäische Schuldenkrise vor dem Bundesverfassungsgericht – Anmerkung zum Urteil von 7 September 2011, Europarecht, 842–856
Ruffert M (2013) Anmerkung Pringle-Urteil. JuristenZeitung 68:257–259
Salomon ME (2015) Of austerity, human rights and international institutions. Eur Law J 21:521–545
Scharpf FW (2003) Problem-Solving Effectiveness and Democratic Accountability in the EU. MPIfG Working Paper 03/1
Schepel H (2017) The bank, the bond, and the bail-out: on the legal construction of market discipline in the Eurozone. J Law Soc 44:79–98
Schwarz M (2014) A memorandum of misunderstanding – the doomed road of the European stability mechanism and a possible way out: enhanced cooperation. Common Mark Law Rev 51:389–424
Seikel D (2016) Flexible austerity and supranational autonomy. The reformed excessive deficit procedure and the asymmetry between liberalization and social regulation in the EU. J Common Mark Stud 54:1398–1416
Simone P (2017) Respecting the democratic principle in ESM activities related to the context of the economic and financial crisis. In: Daniele L, Simone R, Cisotta P (eds) Democracy in the EMU in the aftermath of the crisis. Springer, Berlin, pp 195–214
Smits R (2012) Correspondence: the European debt crisis and European Union law: comments and a call for action. Common Mark Law Rev 49:827–831
Solomos D, Koumparoulis D (2012) The recent reform of European governance. Intereconomics 47:298–303
Starita M (2017) Democratic principles and the economic branch of the EMU. In: Daniele L, Simone R, Cisotta P (eds) Democracy in the EMU in the aftermath of the crisis. Springer, Berlin, pp 3–26
Thymes D, Wendel M (2012) Preserver le Respect du Droit dans la Crise: La Cour de Justice, le MES and le Mythe du declin de la comunaute de droit. Cahiers de droit européen 48:733–757
Tomkin J (2013) Contradiction, circumvention and conceptual gymnastics: the impact of the adoption of the TESM on the state of European democracy. In: De Witte B, Heritier A, Trechsel A (eds) The euro crisis and the state of European democracy, 2013. European University Institute, Florence, pp 64–82
Tosato GL (2010) Il salvataggio della Grecia rispetta i Trattati? Affari internazionali, 21st May 2010
Tosato GL (2012) L'integrazione Europea ai tempi della crisi dell'euro. Rivista di Diritto Internazionale, 681–703
Tovo C (2016) Il Fondo europeo per gli investimenti strategici: statuto giuridico, profili istituzionali e funzionamento. Il Diritto dell'Unione Europea, 357–400
Tufano ML (2002) Il principio di bail-out nel diritto comunitario. Il Diritto dell'Unione Europea, 505–517

Tuori K (2012) The European financial crisis – Constitutional Aspects and implications. EUI Law Working Papers No 28
Tuori K, Tuori K (2014) The Eurozone crisis. A constitutional analysis. Cambridge University Press, Cambridge
Vellano M (2013) Il caso di Cipro come epilogo, ovvero prologo dell'ultima fase della crisi dell'area euro. In: Adinolfi G, Vellano M (eds) La crisi del debito sovrano degli stati dell'area Euro. Giappichelli, Torino, pp 227–238
Viterbo A, Costamagna F (2013) L'impatto sociale della politica di condizionalità nel contesto della crisi dell'euro: profili giuridici. In: Napoletano N, Saccucci A (eds) Gestione internazionale delle emergenze globali. Scientica, Napoli, pp 167–194
Vogel M (2012) Die europarechtliche Bewertung der Euro-Rettung. Zeitschrift für Staats- und Europawissenschaften 5:459–491
Von Bogdandy A (2012) The European lesson for international democracy:the significance of articles 9-12 EU treaty for international organisations. Eur J Int Law 23:315–334
Wilkinson M (2015) The euro is irreversible! ... or is it? on OMT, austerity and the threat of "Grexit". Ger Law J 16:1049–1072
Zettelmeyer J (2018) Managing deep debt crises in the euro area: towards a feasible regime. Global Pol 9:70–79
Ziller J (2015) Il Quadro Costituzionale della Governance Economica Europea. In: Porchia O (ed) Governance Economica Europea. Editoriale Scientifica, Napoli, pp 13–31

Chapter 5
Completing the Economic Union: The Different Paths Towards Stability

5.1 Introduction

The outbreak of the sovereign debt crisis in 2009 marked the end of the political and legal balance, which was overseeing the functioning of the EMU since its setup in the Maastricht Treaty. Since then, Member States and European institutions have been looking for a new equilibrium, which could ensure the stability of the euro area as a whole in the long term. The previous analysis explained how the reforms adopted so far tried to correct the main fragilities of the economic governance: surveillance on national economic policies has become tighter, emergency mechanisms have provided financial assistance in case of systemic crisis and the setup of the banking union has started weakening the toxic loop between sovereigns and banks. At the same time, the reforming process had to deal with the structural limits of an economic union based on the preservation of the national exclusive right on fiscal sovereignty. The pursuit of the stability of the euro area as a whole in the context of a decentralised model of economic union has caused the rise of three main deficits, the previous chapter has analysed in detail: legal incoherence of the reforms, as the latter either don't have a suitable legal basis or might be in contrast with EU primary law; limited effectiveness of consolidation and stabilisation tools; lack of sufficient democratic accountability of the governance.

As the flaws of the economic union are undermining the process of budgetary consolidation and economic convergence among the Member States, as well as its ability to react to new crisis, a debate has started between EU institutions, national governments, academics and the public opinion on the further reforms, the euro area still requires in order to finally achieve stability. Numerous papers, blueprints and reports have been issued over the last few years for this purpose. At the same time, EU institutions and national governments have also come forward with some official proposals on the reform of the economic union.

L. Lionello, *The Pursuit of Stability of the Euro Area as a Whole*, Studies in European Economic Law and Regulation 18,
https://doi.org/10.1007/978-3-030-28045-1_5

This chapter analyses the main proposals of reform of the economic union: finalisation of the banking union, creation of a capital market union, amendments to the Treaty on the European Stability Mechanism, establishment of an additional budgetary capacity for the euro area, creation a debt restructuration mechanism, incorporation of intergovernmental instruments in EU law and the setup of a European Minister of Economy and Finance. After having described the main features of these proposals, the chapter will study the most relevant legal challenges, the process of completion of the economic union will present considering both the process of fiscal centralisation and the restoration of the decentralised model of economic union.

5.2 The Possible Ways Forward for a More Perfect Pursuit of the Stability of the Euro Area as a Whole

In the second chapter, the stability of the euro area as a whole has been defined as the 'preservation of both the existence and the integrity of the monetary union'. This definition has been deduced by considering the aims of the instruments, the economic governance has been provided with after the outbreak of the sovereign debt crisis: resolving emergencies of systemic relevance, which may cause a full or partial dissolution of the euro area, and avoiding their incurrence in the first place. A more careful analysis of the functioning of the economic union, however, explained how the governance has not yet been able to succeed in this ambitious objective. The refusal to amend primary law, the rise of intergovernamentalism, the reluctance of sharing resources and risks, the difficulty to comply with fiscal rules and implementing structural reforms, as well as the weakening of democratic control on the decisions-making process are some of the reasons why the economic union is still looking for stability. Evidently, the measures adopted since 2010 to improve the resilience of the euro area aimed more at adapting the Maastricht model of economic union to the new contingencies that emerged during the crisis, rather than addressing the structural deficits coming from the asymmetry between the economic and the monetary union. As a consequence, several sources of instability have remained unresolved.

In the light of the critical assessment of the governance developed in the previous chapter, it is possible to identify at least three priorities, the future reforms of the economic union should take into consideration.[1] First, economic convergence within the euro area is not sufficient: in this regard, the governance should provide Member States with stronger and more effective incentives to respect fiscal rules and implement structural reforms. Second, the monetary union still remains vulnerable to major economic crisis because of the fragilities of both public finances and the

[1] Bénassy-Quéré et al. (2018), pp. 2–3.

banking system in several Member States.[2] Finally, there is a growing dissatisfaction with EU institutions, depending mainly on the lack of sufficient instruments of democratic control, but aggravated also by the complexity of the legal system.

In order to face these challenges, a number of projects have been put forward over the last few years proposing further reforms of the economic union. The latter aim to correct the deficits of the governance in different ways: reforming the institutional framework in charge of the decision-making process, strengthening the consolidation and stabilisation tools already available at European level and creating new instruments to foster convergence and budgetary discipline.

5.3 Proposals for the Completion of the Economic Union

5.3.1 The Ongoing Debate

The institutional debate on the overall reform of the economic union started during the most dramatic moments of the sovereign debt crisis. In June 2012, while it was still unclear whether Spain and Italy would have survived the storm on the financial markets or would go down taking with them the rest of the euro area, the President of the European Council, Hermann Van Rompuy, issued a 'Road Map on deepening the EMU'.[3] The latter document, which has been finalized in December, substantially argued that, in order to survive, the monetary union should be backed up by a stronger architecture, based on integrated frameworks for the financial sector, for budgetary matters and for economic policy, as well as stronger democratic legitimacy and accountability. The European Commission also came out with a project to reform the EMU: the 'Blueprint on a genuine and deep Economic and Monetary Union'[4] of November 2012 recalled and detailed most of the reforms suggested by Van Rompuy. While some of these proposals were immediately picked up by the Council and the Parliament, which between 2013 and 2014, adopted the founding regulations of the banking union, the debate on the completion of the EMU continued only after the entry into force of the new European Commission chaired by Jean Claude Juncker. In June 2015, the 'Five Presidents Report'[5] reaffirmed the necessity to finalize the project of a banking union, create some form of fiscal union in the euro area, set up a capital market union and eventually reform the institutional framework of the governance by granting a stronger role to the European Parliament and the Commission. Other important contributions to the institutional debate on the

[2]On the limited ability to absorb large macroeconomic shocks in the euro area cf. European Commission Staff Working Document (2018), pp. 6–13.

[3]The final version of the document was released on 5 December 2012. President of the European Council, Final Report (2012).

[4]European Commission Communication (2012).

[5]President of the European Commission, Report (2015).

completion of the EMU have been the Monti Report on the reform of the EU budget and the own resources system of December 2016,[6] the Berès-Böge Resolution of the European Parliament advocating in February 2017 the creation of a budgetary capacity of the euro area,[7] as well as several Communications and Reports of the European Commission on some important related topics, such as Eurobonds and the finalisation of the banking union.[8] The debate on the reform of the economic union did not see only the participation of European actors. National institutions also expressed their position. Proposals have been advanced by both national executives, the Governors of the Central Banks, as well as domestic parliaments. At the same time, the academic doctrine also contributed to the analysis of the different proposals from a technical point of view.

An important acceleration in the debate on the reform of the economic union was triggered after the Brexit referendum and the election of Emmanuel Macron to the Presidency of the French Republic. In the 'Discours de La Sorbonne' in September 2017 President Macron argued for the creation of a separate budget for the euro area as one of the keys for the creation of a genuine European sovereignty.[9] Few months later, the European Commission issued in December 2017 a number of formal proposals for the reform of the EMU, more precisely the creation of a European Monetary Fund,[10] the setup of a budgetary line for the euro area within the EU Budget,[11] the incorporation of the TSCG in EU law[12] and the creation of a European Minister of Economy and Finance.[13] In June 2018, the Meseberg Declaration of the French and German governments endorsed the idea of a separate budget for the euro area, the completion of the banking union and the reform of the European Stability Mechanism.[14] Finally, in May 2019, the European elections saw the success of pro-European parties, which are in favour of a reform of the eurozone governance.

The following analysis will focus more in detail on the main proposals advanced so far for the reform of the economic union. It is possible to identify in particular two main approaches to the completion of the EMU[15]: decentralisation (or market model) and centralisation (or fiscal federalism).

---

[6]High-Level Group on Own Resources (2016).

[7]European Parliament Resolution (2017).

[8]European Commission Green Paper (2011) and European Commission Communication (2017a).

[9]President of the French Republic, 'Initiative pour l'Europe - Discours d'Emmanuel Macron pour une Europe souveraine, unie, démocratique', (2017).

[10]European Commission Proposal for a Regulation (2017).

[11]European Commission Communication (2017b).

[12]European Commission Proposal for a Directive (2017).

[13]European Commission Communication (2017c).

[14]President of the French Republic, Chancellor of the German Federal Republic 'Meseberg Declaration', (2018).

[15]Hinarejos (2013), pp. 1634–1636.

5.3.2 *Regulating Decentralisation and Restoring Market Discipline*

5.3.2.1 Preliminary Remarks: Making Decentralisation More Efficient

The first approach is based on the preservation of the decentralised model of economic union. This choice is motivated on the assumption that budgetary stability shall essentially come from market regulation and surveillance. On the one hand, reforms should go in the direction of restoring and improving market discipline, by introducing mechanisms and procedures able to manage and contain individual crisis, such as debt restructuration and sovereign default. Capital markets should also develop a stabilisation role by complementing banks as a source of financing for families, companies and public authorities across the EU. On the other hand, the Union should improve its role of discipline enforcer by adopting rules, which are more and more detailed and enforceable. Eventually, the EU should gain the legal power to oblige Member States to adopt certain policies and pass certain measures.[16] This approach requires a less intense application of the principle of solidarity between countries, and aims to fully restore and improve the original model of economic union based on the preservation of national fiscal competences.

5.3.2.2 Debt Restructuration

5.3.2.2.1 Rationales of the Proposal

According to several economists, the decentralised model of fiscal union does still have some chance to provide a substantial contribution to the stability of the euro area as a whole. Learning from the mistakes of the past,[17] it should be possible to restore the regulatory role of financial markets and overcome the ‘too big to fail’ mentality, which has eventually convinced Member States to adopt a wide bailout policy after the outbreak of the crisis. This should be done first of all by reducing the interdependence between sovereign debt and banking system, for example by introducing stricter capital requirements for banks, improving the risk rating regulations and diversifying banks’ portfolios in state bonds, which should be backed anyway by sufficient equity.[18] More importantly, a debt restructuration mechanism should be introduced in order to shift the burden of a fiscal crisis from taxpayers onto the shoulders of private creditors. Accordingly, in the event a country was not able to finance itself anymore, aside from requiring the support from the ESM, it should also be possible to restructure its sovereign debt by imposing some losses to those who

[16] Hinarejos (2013), pp. 1634–1635.

[17] According to this vision, the no bailout clause has not been effective because of the weaknesses of the financial sector and its excessive exposure to sovereign debt. See Fuest and Peichl (2012), p. 9.

[18] Ibid. pp. 9–10.

invested in it. In this way, sovereign default wouldn't' represent a catastrophic event, which could lead to the destabilisation of the country and the breakup of the single currency, but a manageable situation, which complies with predicable and reliable procedures. Evidently, the project aims to replicate for the fiscal union the existing bail-in facility for the banking union: in the event of a crisis, investors shall participate in the rescue of the country, as they do with financial institutions.

The reasons for the establishment of such mechanisms are multiple.[19] First of all, a debt restructuration regime would help to restore the credibility of the no bailout clause and ensure the correct functioning of market discipline: investors would be obliged to pay more attention to the effective liability of each borrower because they might effectively lose their capitals. Furthermore, Member States would be more cautious about managing their public finances, being aware that they won't be bailed out by their partners. Second, the ESM has limited resources (€700 billion) to intervene in case of fiscal crisis in bigger European economies. Even if new capital calls are possible, it is unlikely Member States would agree to rescue big countries like Spain and Italy.[20] In order to reduce the weight of the bailout then, it would be necessary to impose part of the losses to the private investors. In this way, the burden of a crisis management would not fall entirely on the shoulders of taxpayers. Third, the conditionality policy of the ESM would become more credible, if sovereign default became a realistic option. In the event a government refuses to comply with the conditions of creditor countries, the perspective of an orderly default may be politically and economically acceptable.[21] In this way, the introduction of a debt restructuration procedure would be able to neutralise the already mentioned TINA ('There is no alternative') principle. The Board of Governors of the ESM would be able to reject a request from a Member State whose public debt is unsustainable or which is refusing to comply with conditionality policy. While limiting the blackmailing power of countries 'too big to fail', debt restructuration would also reduce the risks for moral hazard.

5.3.2.2.2 Different Options for a Debt Restructuration Mechanism in the Euro Area

As it was explained in the previous chapters,[22] debt restructuration has not been foreign to the management of the sovereign debt crisis. In March 2012, bondholders agreed with the Greek government for a haircut on their debt. More precisely, bonds were exchanged for new bonds with lower principal and interest rate and longer

[19]Cf. Panizza (2013), pp. 3–9; Nunner-Krautgasser (2014), pp. 244–247; Fuest et al. (2016), p. 302; Andritzky et al. (2016), pp. 2–5.

[20]Countries like Italy are indeed 'too big to save'. Buchheit and Gulati (2018), p. 66.

[21]Nunner-Krautgasser (2014), p. 246; Fuest et al. (2016), p. 302.

[22]In particular see *supra* Sect. 3.4.3.

maturity.[23] In the light of this experience, the TESM has obliged the Member States of the euro area to issue, since 2013, sovereign bonds with more than 1 year of maturity provided with common 'collective action clauses' (CACs). These standardised euro-CACs allow reform of the contractual terms of the loan by qualified majority of the bondholders, thus making debt restructuration easier. At the same time, despite representing an important step forward in the process of risk sharing with the private sector, the effectiveness of CACs has been questioned for several good reasons, in particular, the different application of the clauses in accordance with the competent national legislation, the possibility to apply them only to a single bond issuance, as well as the lack of coordination mechanisms, which may discourage holdout behaviours.[24] Evidently, the creation of a debt restructuring mechanism for the euro area aims to address, as least, some of these issues.

The economic doctrine has advanced so far different proposals regarding the possible functioning of a euro area debt restructuration regime.[25]

The first option consists of creating an *ad hoc* legal procedure for sovereign default resembling corporate bankruptcy. A European restructuration regime should be managed by a sovereign bankruptcy authority or court, possibly a new specialised Tribunal of the European Court of Justice. The latter should be able to impose binding decisions to all creditors.[26] According to this proposal, taking debt restructuration away from politics and giving it to courts would make the procedure more impartial and transparent.[27]

The second option is to introduce debt restructuration as a possible tool of the ESM.[28] In the event sovereign debt was not considered sustainable anymore, debt restructuration should be negotiated in the framework of an ESM assistance program and/or agreed by a (super) majority of bondholders. Accordingly, bonds covered by the agreement should be granted immunity from judicial claims.[29]

---

[23]See Hofmann (2013), p. 552. Furthermore, the Greek Republic could enjoy several grace periods for the repayment of loans received in the framework of the EFSF and ESM. Cf. Buchheit and Gulati (2018), p. 66.

[24]Panizza (2013), p. 5; Audit (2014), pp. 218–220; Fuest et al. (2016), pp. 311–312.

[25]The following tri-partition and analysis of the proposals were developed by Zettelmeyer. See Zettelmeyer (2018), p. 72. For a review of literature on debt restructuration regime see also Andritzky et al. (2018), pp. 3–5.

[26]Gianviti et al. (2010) and Paulus and Tirado (2013).

[27]The creation of a court for sovereign default, regardless the mandate and tasks it would be provided with, may have jurisdiction only on the bonds issued under the governing law of a euro area countries. Zettelmeyer (2018), p. 73.

[28]This proposal was advanced by Buchheit et al. (2013), Fuest et al. (2016) and Corsetti et al. (2016).

[29]At the same time the possibility for a debt restructuration within the ESM financial assistance would allow for an immunity from judicial claims only in the euro area. Zettelmeyer (2018), p. 73.

The third proposal regards the reform of CACs by introducing so called 'single-limb aggregation' of bondholders.[30] The latter rule should replace the qualified majority of each bond, which must be restructured, with the qualified majority of all bondholders. This would make debt restructuration easier, by reducing the margin of holdouts.

Aside from these projects, debt restructuration may be encouraged also by preventing the ESM to bailout countries with unsustainable debts. This may be granted for example by limiting the time or size of the ESM support,[31] or making it conditional to *ex ante* compliance with certain macroeconomic parameters,[32] or providing for an automatic bonds maturity extension once the country has applied for the ESM assistance.[33]

The support of the economic doctrine in favour of introducing a debt restructuration regime has found some endorsement also in the political debate. In October 2017, the German Minister of Finance Wolfang Schäuble issued a 'Non-paper for paving the way towards a Stability Union',[34] where he suggested incorporating into the legal text of the ESM Treaty: (a) the automatic extension of the maturities of sovereign bonds in the event that an ESM programme is granted, (b) the obligation to carry out comprehensive debt restructuring if this is necessary to ensure debt sustainability, and (c) an amendment of the CACs, moving to 'single limb aggregation'. At the same time, the Meseberg Declaration between France and Germany of June 2018 re-affirmed the necessity to perform a debt sustainability analysis before allowing for an ESM intervention and introducing new Euro CACs with single-limb aggregation.

Finally, governments of the euro area agreed in December 2018 to amend the TESM by providing an expressed reference to the introduction of single limb CACs by 2022.[35] Furthermore, Member States also decided to reaffirm in the TESM that financial assistance shall be granted only to those countries whose debt is sustainable and whose repayment capacity is confirmed.[36] Quite significantly, the new draft of the TESM does also affirm that 'in exceptional cases an adequate and proportionate form of private sector involvement, in accordance with IMF practice, shall be considered in cases where stability support is provided accompanied by conditionality in the form of a macro-economic adjustment programme',[37] thus hinting at the

---

[30] According to this clause, it would be only required one vote on the debt restructuring of all the bonds involved without additional votes on the individual bond series. In favour: Gelpern (2014a), IMF (2014), pp. 20–22.

[31] See Gros and Mayer (2010), p. 4; Fuest et al. (2016), pp. 308–309.

[32] Corsetti et al. (2016), p. 2; Weder di Mauro and Zettelmeyer (2017), p. 14.

[33] Corsetti et al. (2015), p. 36; Andritzky et al. (2016) p. 3. An extension of bonds maturity was organised in Cyprus in June 2016. Cf. Andritzky et al. (2016), p. 4.

[34] Schäuble (2017).

[35] Eurogroup (2018a). See Whereas (11) Draft revised text of the treaty establishing the European Stability Mechanism as agreed by the Eurogroup on 14 June 2019.

[36] Whereas (12A) Ibid.

[37] Whereas (12B) Ibid.

possibility of debt restructuring.[38] It should be noted that in principle debt restructuring in the euro area would be favoured by the fact that most debt stock issued by the Member States are regulated by the law of the debtor country. This should give domestic parliaments the possibility to reform the law in a way to facilitate the restructuring of bonds.[39]

5.3.2.3 Stronger Control on National Budgets

Another way to restore the decentralized model of economic union may be strengthening even further European surveillance on the budgetary policies of the Member States. Accordingly, the EU should improve its role of discipline enforcer, by adopting more detailed resolutions and reacting in a more effective way in case of non-compliance. Eventually, the EU may also gain the legal power to oblige Member States to adopt certain policies and pass certain measures.[40]

Looking at the proposals advanced so far, there are two man options to further strengthening surveillance on national budgets. First, the European Commission might be deprived of its role in the economic governance, and surveillance should be managed by a purely independent institution, which is completely detached from political considerations. A European Fiscal Council or a new body of experts within the ESM should be able to provide a more technical and neutral assessment of compliance with European rules and take binding decisions.[41] The latter should represent an evolution of the existing European Fiscal Board set up in 2015 in order to evaluate the implementation of EU fiscal rules, cooperate with national IFIs and advise the Commission on economic surveillance.[42] In perspective, sanctions against Member States, which are not complying with European rules might become heavier and fully automatic. Alternatively, an even more extreme solution, may consist of providing the EU with some form of veto power on the adoption of

---

[38]In the event of a debt restricting the ESM should facilitate the dialogue between the country and private investors.

[39]Buchheit and Gulati (2018), p. 67. This is what happened in the case of the Greek debt restructuration in March 2012. On the legitimacy of the parliamentary decision to impose a class voting mechanism on all bond holders see Mamatas and Others v Hellenic Republic, Greece App. No. 63066/1464297/14 66106/14 (ECHR, 21 July 2016).

[40]Hinarejos (2013), pp. 1634–1635.

[41]This is part of the vision of the former German Minister of Finance, Wolfgang Schäuble, on the reform of the ESM. The new ESM (recalled European Monetary Fund) should be able to exercise a wide control on public finances and gradually replace the Commission in the application of the SGP. See Schäuble (2017). According to the proposal of Schäuble, the new ESM should remain an intergovernmental body: the decisions would be taken by the stronger Member States, making it difficult to pursue the interest of the euro are as a whole. See Wolff (2017), pp. 2–3.

[42]Commission Decision (EU) 2015/1937 of 21 October 2015 establishing an independent advisory European Fiscal Board. See *supra* Sect. 3.5.2.

national budgets.[43] Clearly, the development of a similar authority does not appear to be consistent with the current distribution of competences outlined in the EU Treaties. Nevertheless, a possible step in this direction may be centralising at European level the supervision on the compliance with numerical fiscal rules introduced in national law according to the Six Pack and the TSCG. While their application is currently a task for national Independent Fiscal Institutions (IFIs) and, in certain situations, national constitutional court, the CJEU or the European Fiscal Board might assume this function.

For the moment, there is no political consensus among all the Member States about a possible tightening of European fiscal rules.

5.3.2.4 The Project of Capital Market Union

Among the different proposals to complete the EMU, the European Commission has strongly supported the creation of a capital market union (CMU). The latter aims to 'complement banks as a source of financing, [. . .] unlock more investment for all companies, especially [small and medium-sized enterprises], and for infrastructure projects; attract more investment into the EU from the rest of the world; and make the financial system more stable by opening up a wider range of funding sources'.[44] Notably capital markets, which are composed of equity and bonds, securitizations, lending from insurance companies and asset managers or venture capital,[45] do represent important sources of financing, which may be complementary to the traditional funding from banks. The creation of the CMU has the purpose to make these resources available for families, companies and public authorities across the EU.

The establishment of a CMU is part of the process of completion of the single market and is meant to involve all the Member States of the European Union. The creation of a European capital market for investments is currently prevented by a number of factors: the dependence of credit on the national banks,[46] the different financing conditions, rules and market practices among the Member States, as well as the difficulty for shareholders and buyers of corporate debt to invest in other EU countries. The construction of a European CMU would remove these obstacles. Clearly, the use of the term 'union' in regard to the project is rather misleading, as the CMU aims more at improving the regulatory framework and surveillance, rather than centralising competences or creating common mechanisms.[47] At the same time, the setup of a CMU may also contribute to pursue stability of the euro area, because

---

[43]This was for example the proposal put forward by the former German Minister of Finance, Wolfang Schäuble. See. Reuters (2014).

[44]European Commission Green Paper (2015), p. 2.

[45]Sapir et al. (2018), p. 2.

[46]In 2015, 80% of European financial assets consisted of bank credit, while in the US only 20%. See Quaglia et al. (2016), p. 186.

[47]Quaglia et al. (2016), p. 197.

it would weaken the loop between banks, public finances and real economy, by creating a more diversified funding system in which financial institutions are not the only actors.

In September 2015, the European Commission issued an action plan explaining the most important legislative and non-legislative initiatives to create the capital market union in Europe.[48] Accordingly, the Commission managed to make the Parliament and the Council approve several important pieces of legislation, including a new regime for securitisation and a new regime for European venture capital funds and European social entrepreneurship funds.[49] More recently, the Union adopted a regulation creating a 'pan-European pension product', whose features will be the same throughout the EU, as well as a package of measures aimed at removing existing barriers to the cross-border distribution of investment funds.[50] Other Commission proposals, however, are still under discussion, including the introduction of a Common Consolidated Corporate Tax Base (CCCTB) for companies, and, more importantly, the reform of the European Securities and Markets Authority (ESMA).[51]

The strengthening of the supervisory role of the ESMA is an absolute priority to the success of the integration of capital markets in Europe.[52] Indeed, despite regulations having been widely harmonised, the presence of different national authorities in charge of supervision and enforcement does prevent the convergence of practices and outcomes among the Member States.[53] While ESMA is at the moment only an agency in charge of coordination and preparation of technical standards, the reform should provide it with real powers of supervision and a stronger independence.[54] Accordingly, ESMA should develop a direct authority on increasing range of market segments and promote the definition of a single rulebook for the capital market.[55]

---

[48]European Commission Communication (2015). The action plan covers six areas: (1) financing for innovation, start-ups and non-listed companies; (2) entering and raising capital on public markets; (3) facilitating long-term investment; (4) fostering retail and institutional investment; (5) facilitating securitisation; and (6) facilitating cross-border investment.

[49]Regulation (EU) No 2402/2017 of the European Parliament and of the Council of 12 December 2017 laying down a general framework for securitisation and creating a specific framework for simple, transparent and standardised securitisation, and amending Directives 2009/65/EC, 2009/138/EC and 2011/61/EU and Regulations (EC) No 1060/2009 and (EU) No 648/2012, (2017) OJ L 347/35; Regulation (EU) No 2017/1991 of the European Parliament and of the Council of 25 October 2017 amending Regulation (EU) No 345/2013 on European venture capital funds and Regulation (EU) No 346/2013 on European social entrepreneurship funds, (2017) OJ L 293/1.

[50]Council (2019).

[51]For a survey of the legislation proposed and adopted see Sapir et al. (2018), pp. 4–5.

[52]Sapir et al. (2018), pp. 7–8.

[53]Ibid. p. 9.

[54]Ibid.

[55]Bénassy-Quéré et al. (2018), p. 9. On the reform of ESMA and the other European Supervisory Authorities see Ortino (2018).

In conclusion, the setup of a CMU is a long-term project, which will require time in order to be fully effective. While the action Plan outlined by the European Commission has not been fully achieved yet,[56] it should be noted that the process of convergence and harmonization among the Member States may involve also other strategical policy areas, such as insolvency, taxation of investments and savings, housing finance and pensions.[57]

5.3.3 *Centralisation of Powers and Resources*

5.3.3.1 Preliminary Remarks: Towards a Genuine Economic Union?

Aside from the proposal to improve the functioning of the decentralisaed model of economic union, a different approach goes in the direction of centralising more resources and powers at European level in order to accelerate the process of risk sharing among the Member States. This should be done by completing the banking union, strengthening the role of the ESM and, more importantly, creating some form of fiscal capacity at European level.[58] The latter consists of a mechanism able to collect, mutualise and spend resources across the euro area. The setup of a fiscal instrument would definitely require stronger solidarity and political integration between the participating Member States. The institutional framework of the governance should also be updated by incorporating intergovernmental mechanisms in EU law and strengthening democratic accountability and effective governability.

5.3.3.2 Finalising the Banking Union

As the previous analysis has already explained,[59] the creation of the banking union had the purpose to break the toxic loop between sovereigns and banks and avoid that the costs of bank bailouts were carried by taxpayers. The establishment of the Single Supervisory Mechanism, the Single Resolution Mechanism and Single Rulebook has already helped to achieve this result. Over the last few years, the European

[56] According to the Action Plan, the CMU should have been completed by the end of 2019. In order to accelerate the completion of the project, the 16 May 2019 the French, German and Dutch Finance Ministers proposed to create a high-level working group on the Capital Markets Union (CMU), in a letter signed in the margins of the Eurogroup.

[57] Sapir et al. (2018), p. 10; Adamski (2018), pp. 182–183.

[58] The concept of fiscal federalism was invented in the United States to analyse the fiscal relationship between the federal level and the Member States. Today, it is used to define the fiscal relationship within a state between the different levels of government. The public finances of each level can potentially take care of three functions: efficient allocation of resources, income distribution and macroeconomic stabilisation. Fiscal federalism analyses what function should be better exercised at different level. Cf. Carboni (2014), pp. 4–5.

[59] See *supra* Sect. 3.8.

banking system has become more resilient, risks have been reduced, financial institutions have become more solid and the EU has developed some effective instruments of supervision and intervention.[60] Despite these important achievements, some relevant sources of instability remain.[61] Several banks still present weak balance sheets due to the still high level of non-preforming loans (NPLs), which is undermining their competitiveness and lending capacity.[62] Furthermore, banks are struggling to differentiate their investment in sovereign bonds, as many are still excessively exposed to the public debt of their 'home country', thus keeping the toxic loop between sovereigns and banks alive.[63] More importantly, the banking union does not seem sufficiently equipped to deal with new crisis. In fact, deposit guarantees are still fragmented along national borders, while the Single Resolution Mechanism cannot count on a sufficient backstop to rescue financial institutions when crisis of significant magnitude occur.[64]

In order to overcome these deficits, several proposals have been advanced to complete the banking union in a way to share the risks and the responsibility for the stabilisation of the banking system, and consequently pursue the stability of the euro area as a whole.

The first missing element of the banking union is notably a *common backstop* in charge of intervening as a last resort mechanism in the event of systemic crisis, when the stability of the euro area as a whole is at stake.[65] Such an instrument should be able to back the Single Resolution Fund, when its immediately available resources prove to be insufficient for capital or liquidity purposes.[66] The proposal of a common backstop was formally put forward in 2017 by the European Commission.[67] After long resistances the governments of the euro area finally accepted in December 2018 that the ESM shall assume the responsibility of providing an effective backstop to the Single Resolution Fund.[68] More specifically, on the basis of a request by the SRB and of a proposal by the Managing Director, the Board of Governors of the ESM will

---

[60] Since 2014, banks in the euro area have been subject to a comprehensive asset quality review, stress test and recapitalisation. See European Commission Communication (2017a), p. 4.

[61] See *supra* Sect. 4.3.7.

[62] See European Commission Communication (2017a), p. 6.

[63] The diversification of banks' sovereign portfolios should reduce risks to financial stability. Ibid. p. 18.

[64] The problem is that the actions of the SRB would not be credible if there wasn't a sufficient guarantee that all Member States are actually willing to stabilise the euro area banking system.

[65] This situation may happen when the SRF is depleted and the SRB is not able to raise sufficient *ex-post* contributions or borrow funds from other sources at acceptable rates.

[66] Explanatory Memorandum to the European Commission Proposal for a Regulation (2017), p. 6.

[67] European Commission Communication (2017a), p. 14.

[68] Euro Summit (2018). The Euro Summit has endorsed the package of proposal agreed by the Eurogroup on 4 December 2018. See Eurogroup (2018c). The new backstop function should be introduced in the TESM by December 2019.

create a backstop facility to the SRB covering all possible uses of the SRF as enshrined in European Union law, subject to adequate safeguards.[69]

The backstop facility shall take the form of a revolving credit line under which loans can be provided. It will be able to count on around € 55 billion with a nominal cap above the initial size determined by the Board of Governors.[70] In order to ensure the fiscal neutrality of the mechanism in the medium-term, the SRF shall pay back the loan to the ESM through bank contributions to be collected normally within 3 years. The activation procedure of the mechanism should be able to ensure swift and efficient decisions,[71] in compliance with both the constitutional requirements of the Member States and the need of confidentiality because of the sensitive data involved.[72] On the basis of a request by the SRB,[73] the Board of Directors[74] shall decide by mutual agreement, guided by the criteria provided for Board of Governors, on loans and respective disbursements under the backstop facility. An emergency voting procedure shall be used where the European Commission and the ECB conclude that a failure to urgently activate the backstop facility would threaten the stability of the euro area. In this case decisions will be taken by qualified majority of 85% of the votes cast.[75]

The common backstop should be in place by 2024. Only in the event of sufficient progresses in reducing banks' exposure to risks, might it be introduced earlier. Assessments in this regard are scheduled for 2020 with respect to the build-up of 'minimum requirement for own funds and eligible liabilities' (MREL) and the trend in non-performing loans (NPLs) reduction.[76] It should be noted that, once

---

[69]See Art. 18A(1) Draft revised text of the treaty establishing the European Stability Mechanism as agreed by the Eurogroup on 14 June 2019.

[70]The size of the credit line will be aligned with the SRF funds.

[71]As a rule, disbursement should be approved maximum 12 h as from the SRB's request. In exceptional cases, especially in the case of a particularly complex resolution operation, the ESM Managing Director might agree to lengthen the deadline up to 24 h. See Eurogroup (2018b); Whereas (15B) Draft revised text of the treaty establishing the European Stability Mechanism as agreed by the Eurogroup on 14 June 2019.

[72]Some Member State may indeed require an authorisation from the national parliaments in order to vote in favour of the activation of the ESM.

[73]The request shall be accompanied by a proposal from the Managing Director and an assessment of the SRB's repayment capacity and, where relevant, the assessments by the European Commission and the ECB.

[74]These are high-level officials from the finance ministries of the Member States of the euro area.

[75]See art. 18A(5) and (6) Draft revised text of the treaty establishing the European Stability Mechanism as agreed by the Eurogroup on 14 June 2019. After two instances of the use of the emergency voting procedure, it application shall be suspended until the Board of Governors decides to cancel such suspension.

[76]Eurogroup (2018b). In this regard, it is important the adoption of Regulation (EU) 2019/630 amending Regulation (EU) No 575/2013 as regards minimum loss coverage for non-performing exposures, (2019) OJ L 111/4.

introduced, the common backstop will replace the Direct Recapitalisation Instrument of the ESM set up in 2014.[77]

The conferral of the common backstop function to the ESM may create some practical challenges. First, while the banking union is open to all Member States of the European Union, the ESM is a mechanism in charge only of the stability of the euro area and for this reason it foresees only the participation of countries whose currency is the euro.[78] In this regard, the countries, which are not part of the euro area, can still participate in the common backstop by providing credit lines to the SRF.[79] Second, under the current proposal the ESM shall only be able to contribute around €55 billion to the backstop function, which may not be sufficient to contain a systemic crisis, like the one which started in Europe in 2008.[80] In order to deal with this possible difficulty, the Board of Governors, has anyway the power to increase the ceiling (by unanimity).[81]

While the establishment of a common backstop does represent an important step forward in the consolidation of the banking union, the Member States of the euro area did not agreed on the setup of the last missing element, namely the *European Deposit Insurance Scheme* (EDIS). In 2015, the Commission officially proposed a Regulation on the setup of EDIS based on art. 114 TFEU on the approximation of national provisions in order to ensure the correct functioning of the single market.[82] EDIS should be financed by administrative contribution from credit institutions affiliated with participating Domestic Guarantee Systems (DGSs), thus being independent from the European budget,[83] and it would be administered by the Single Resolution Board. According to the Commission's proposal, EDIS should be set up in three successive stages: in the reinsurance phase, EDIS may provide limited funding, and cover a limited share of the loss of a participating DGS that encounters a payout event or has been requested to contribute to the resolution; in the co-insurance phase, participating DGS may immediately requests both funding and loss cover from the EDIS, whose exposure would increase over time; in the last phase, participating DGSs should be fully insured by EDIS, which will take care

[77]Eurogroup (2018b). The risks for the stability of the euro area as a whole posed by a banking crisis of systemic relevance will be neutralised by the SRF with the support of the ESM, rather than by the ESM directly.

[78]Moloney (2014), p. 1628.

[79]Whereas (9A) Draft revised text of the treaty establishing the European Stability Mechanism as agreed by the Eurogroup on 14 June 2019.

[80]Looking at the US experience the total losses of deposits during the crisis in 2008–2009 was 0.5% of the American GDP. A fund of €90 billions would amount to almost 1% of the GDP in the euro area. See Gros and Schoenmaker (2014), p. 542.

[81]Eurogroup (2018b).

[82]European Commission Proposal for a Regulation (2015).

[83]Considering the size of the deposit insurance, Gros and Shoenmaker, suggest it should consist of 1.5% of covered deposit over a period of 10 years. A total of 1.5% of €5980 billions would amount to around €90 billions. Then it should be added 0.5% of cover deposits that the fund could call up *ex post*. See Gros and Schoenmaker (2014), pp. 540–541.

of the liquidity needs and cover all losses arising from a payout event or a request to contribute to the resolution. This gradual setup should offer the opportunity to check that the process of risk sharing is conditional to the effective consolidation of the national banking system and prevention of moral hazard behaviours.

The opposition of Member States to create EDIS, as well as the many conditions they posed for the setup of the common backstop depend on the reluctance of mutualising risks for the stability of the banking sector. Notably, the creation of a common backstop would already make national budgets play a major role in the stabilisation of the banking system as they would *de facto* finance the credit line to the SRF through the ESM. The setup of EDIS may represent an even wider assumption of risks for the stronger countries, whose banks (and thus depositors) may be called to grant resources to ensure the stability of credit institutions in the weaker Member States. Furthermore, as banks are still excessively exposed to national sovereigns, the completion of the banking union may not only determine a significant mutualisation of risks, but even turn into some form of hidden transfer union. In conclusion, the establishment of EDIS does require that Member States first limit the burden of risk to share, for example by accelerating the reduction of NPLs, and strictly limiting the presence of national bonds in the banks' portfolio.[84]

5.3.3.3 The Reform of the ESM

The establishment of the European Stability Mechanism (ESM) has represented a significant step forward in the process of fiscal integration of the euro area. Indeed, for the first time Member States decided to mobilise a significant amount of resources across national borders in a way to share the risks for the fiscal solidity of each country and preserve the existence and the integrity of the monetary union.

The previous chapter has highlighted some limits of the current functioning of the ESM: it is an intergovernmental mechanism created through a lateral agreement beyond EU law, the EUCFRs does not apply to it, the available resources and crisis management tools might be unable to efficiently address fiscal crisis in bigger countries, conditionality is excessively intrusive in national economic policies, the activation of the mechanism is inefficient as it normally requires the agreement of all participating Member States. In the light of these considerations, the European Commission has advanced in December 2017 some important proposals of reform

[84]This will be possible only if there is also a reduction of risks. In this sense, measures shall be taken to reduce the non-performing loans owned by the banks of several Member States. See European Commission Communication (2017a), pp. 15–16. Aside from these major reforms, the European Commission proposed other important measures to reduces risks in the banking sector, for example requiring banks to build up buffers of liabilities that can, if necessary, be bailed in, introducing a common approach to the bank creditor hierarchy in a way to enhance legal certainty in case of resolution, as well as harmonising the insolvency law in order to support efforts to reduce NPLs. European Commission Communication (2017a), p. 15.

of the ESM.[85] Finally in December 2018 the Eurogroup and the Euro Summit have finally agreed to amend the TESM.[86] The following analysis will recall the most important amendments of the ESM Treaty, which should be implemented in the near future.[87]

Considering the mandate of the ESM, the Member States have agreed some important extensions. *First* of all, the previous paragraph has already explained that it should provide a common backstop to the banking system to be granted through either a credit lines to the Single Resolution Fund.[88] *Second*, the effectiveness of the existent precautionary instruments of the ESM will be enhanced. More precisely, the access to the Precautionary Conditioned Credit Line (PCCL) and Enhanced Conditions Credit Line (ECCL) will be eased by making the eligibility process more transparent and predictable. Notably the latter are instruments meant to support countries whose financial situation is sound, but they are affected by an adverse economic shock beyond their control.[89] The provision of this credit line should calm markets concerns without the need of effective disbursement. The activation of PCCL on request of the concerned government will not be conditional to the agreement of a MoU, but to the full respect of the existing European fiscal rules under the SGP and the TSCG.[90] The beneficiary Member States shall commit to the continuous compliance with these *ex-ante* eligibility criteria in a Letter of Intent to be approved by the Board of Governors of the ESM.[91] Adherence to the eligibility criteria will be then assessed every six month by the competent EU institutions, which will issue a report.[92] In case of compliance, the PCCL will continue unless the Board of Directors decides otherwise. In the event the eligibility criteria are not respected anymore, this precautionary financial assistance will instead end, expect if the Board of Directors accepts to maintain the credit line. If the financial situation gets worse and the conditions to grant PCCL are lacking, a

[85]European Commission Proposal for a Regulation (2017).

[86]Eurogroup (2018c), Euro Summit (2018). A first draft was published by the Eurogroup in June 2014. See Draft revised text of the treaty establishing the European Stability Mechanism as agreed by the Eurogroup on 14 June 2019.

[87]Amendments should be adopted by December 2019.

[88]Cf. *supra* Sect. 5.3.3.1.

[89]Cf. *supra* Sect. 3.6.2 note 76. See art. 14(1) of the Draft revised text of the treaty establishing the European Stability Mechanism as agreed by the Eurogroup on 14th June 2019.

[90]Eurogroup (2018c); 'Eligibility criteria for ESM precautionary financial assistance' Annex III of the Draft revised text of the treaty establishing the European Stability Mechanism as agreed by the Eurogroup on 14 June 2019. The eligibility criteria include a track record of 2 years preceding the request for a PCCL with a general government deficit not exceeding 3% of GDP, a general government structural budget balance at or above the country specific minimum benchmark, a debt/GDP ratio below 60% or a reduction in the differential with respect to 60% over the previous two years at an average rate of 1/20 per year.

[91]See art. 14 (2) Draft revised text of the treaty establishing the European Stability Mechanism as agreed by the Eurogroup on 14 June 2019.

[92]The Managing Director of the ESM and Commission in cooperation with the ECB will be responsible for the report ex art. 13(7) TESM 2019. See art. 14(6) ibid.

country can apply for an 'enhanced conditions credit line' (ECCL) or a full macro-economic adjustment programme.[93] In this case, a MoU will be signed in accordance with the rules of the TESM. It should be also remembered that when an ECCL is granted or a PCCL drawn, the beneficiary Member States will be subject to enhanced surveillance by the Commission. Considering the financing terms of precautionary instruments, the margin will increase in the event of non-compliance with the eligibility criteria and the MoU.[94]

Evidently, the strengthening of precautionary financial assistance tools has the purpose to shift the margin of action of the ESM from stabilisation (or crisis management) to consolidation (or crisis prevention).[95] While this reform may help anticipating the outbreak of new crisis, it might also jeopardise the compliance with the competences of EU institutions in the domain of economic coordination.[96] Even if the *ex-ante* eligibility criteria mainly consists of compliance with the existing rules under the SGP and TSCG, the Board of Directors remains independent from the assessment of the EU institutions.[97] Accordingly, the lead on surveillance may shift even more from the European Commission to a purely intergovernmental body. Furthermore, it should be noted that the application of the indispensability principle (on which the TESM is based) may be difficult to assess in the field of precautionary financial assistance. While the compliance with this criterion is perfectly reasonable in a situation of clear emergency, when a country is on the verge of default, it make much less sense when the latter is still relatively stable and financially self-sufficient. The risk then is that the concession of precautionary financial support may become essentially discretional.

[93]See art. 14(7) ibid.

[94]'As regards the financing terms of precautionary instruments, the margin will be set at 35 bp In case of an extension of maturities, a step-up margin of 50 bp will be applied. Once the credit line is drawn, in case of non-compliance with the Letter of Intent for the PCCL or with the MoU for the ECCL, which is not due to events outside the control of the government as assessed by the ESM BoD, an additional margin of 50 bps will be applied, which increases by 65 bp after six months, and access to the funds would be discontinued'. Eurogroup (2018c).

[95]It might by surprising that the ESM was missing an efficient mechanism to provide precautionary assistance. This can be explained for two reasons. Whereas (4) TESM envisages that the main precaution for stability in the euro area should be the compliance with economic coordination rules. Furthermore, the ESM was set up in a situation of extreme emergency, when it was too late to use precautionary instruments. It should be noted that art. 13(6) TESM provides for the establishment of an appropriate warning system to ensure that the ESM receives any repayments due by a Member State under the stability support in a timely manner. Cf. Forsthoff (2018), p. 114.

[96]This is a risk identified also by the Eurogroup. Whereas (15A) of Draft revised text of the treaty establishing the European Stability Mechanism as agreed by the Eurogroup on 14 June 2019 states that: 'the ESM should not serve the purpose of economic policies coordination among ESM Members for which European Union law provide the necessary arrangements'.

[97]As it was already explained the Board of Directors can dismiss the report issued by the Commission and the Managing Director on the compliance with the eligibility criteria. See art. 14(6) Draft revised text of the treaty establishing the European Stability Mechanism as agreed by the Eurogroup on 14 June 2019.

Looking at the functioning of the ESM, the governments of the euro area have supported the agreement between the European Commission and the ESM regarding their future cooperation for the preparation and monitoring of future adjustment programmes.[98] As every future MoU will be signed by both, the ESM will step in the design of policy conditionality. More precisely, the Commission and the ESM will assess together the financial stability, financing needs and debt sustainability of the country, which has requested assistance. Only in case the collaboration does not yield a common view, the Commission will be in charge for the debt sustainability analysis, while the ESM will verify the beneficiary country is actually able to repay the loan. The negotiation of conditionality as well as the monitoring of compliance during the programme will be managed by the Commission in strict cooperation with the ESM and the ECB. This new arrangement seems excluding the IMF from the future financial assistance to the Member States of the euro area. Accordingly, the new *Troika* in charge of negotiation and execution will be composed then of the Commission, the ECB and the ESM. This emancipation depends on the fact that, after several years of partnership, the Commission has gained the technical expertise to manage conditional financial assistance and consequently the participation of the IMF is no longer necessary.[99] Furthermore, the IMF approach to the management of the crisis has proven to be excessively focused on the financial stabilisation of single Member States, rather than on the objective of the stability of the euro area as a whole.[100] Finally, the ESM and the IMF have experienced divergences regarding necessary measures to restore economic stability in the Member States: for example during the Greek crisis the IMF suggested a partial restructuration and monetisation of the Greek debt.[101] Probably, replacing the IMF with the ESM will make the management of conditional financial assistance easier to negotiate and implement.[102]

The reforms agreed by the Euro Summit do clearly aim to innovate the ESM under several profiles. At the same time, it should be noted that they do not question its fundamental features, namely the compliance with the conditionality and indispensability criterion, the national ownership of resources, the intergovernmental functioning of the mechanism and the provision of loans rather than transfers.

Quite importantly, the Euro Summit decided not to support for the moment other important proposals put forward by the Commission in regard to the transformation of the ESM. First of all there was not consensus to rename it European Monetary Fund (EMF) and absorb it in EU secondary legislation on the basis of the flexibility

[98]Eurorogrup (2018c). These agreements are: Memorandum of Understanding on the working relations between the European Commission and the European Stability Mechanism, 27 April 2018; Joint Position on the 'Future cooperation between the European Commission and the European Stability Mechanism', 14 November 2018.

[99]Forsthoff (2018), p. 115.

[100]Ibid. p. 115.

[101]'Greece needs debt restructuring, interest rate cuts: IMF's Lagarde'. Reuters, 22 February 2017.

[102]Forsthoff (2018), p. 115.

clause ex art. 352 TFEU.[103] Also the idea to let the ESM contribute to the stabilisation function of the budgetary instrument for the euro area with the purpose to attenuate the effects of large asymmetric shocks was discarded.[104]

5.3.3.4 The Creation of a Budgetary Instrument for the Euro Area

5.3.3.4.1 Why Does the Euro Area Need a Budgetary Instrument?

The idea of introducing a common budgetary instrument or capacity between the Member States of the monetary union was not something completely foreign to the European political debate before the outbreak of the sovereign debt crisis. In 1970, the Werner report on the creation of the Economic and Monetary Union already envisaged increasing the Community budget after the Member States would have introduced a common currency.[105] In 1977, the MacDougall report explained that the establishment of a monetary union would require a European budget of 2–2.5% of GDP in a pre-federal stage, 5–7% at a middle stage and 20–25% if the Union were ever to become a federation.[106] However, once the Maastricht Treaty created the EMU on the basis a decentralized model of economic integration, the idea of establishing an additional budgetary capacity was completely shelved. Notably, the current EU budget is much smaller than national budgets as it can count only on 1% of the total EU GDP. The budget is financed through a system of 'own resources' consisting of traditional own resources (custom duties and sugar levies), VAT and the GNI-based own resources. The main destination of the EU budget is the common agriculture policy and the cohesion policy.[107] The balanced budget rule and the prohibition to recur to borrowing would normally prevent the budget from collecting more resources. In reality, these principles have been interpreted with flexibility over the last few years, as the budget was used either to backup investment schemes (i.e. EFSI) or to guarantee lending mechanism to the Member States (i.e. ESFM ex art. 122(2) TFEU).[108]

The economic doctrine has strongly advocated for the creation of a budgetary instrument of the euro area. There are several reasons why an additional budget would be beneficial for the monetary union: it would help foster economic convergence between Member States by providing support and incentives for structural

---

[103]The ESM should be incorporated in EU law and assume wide autonomy on the model of the EIB. Pilz (2017), p. 642.

[104]See *infra* note 133.

[105]On 6 March 1970, the Council of Ministers appointed Pierre Werner, Prime Minister of Luxembourg, as the chair of the Committee in charge of developing a project of Economic and Monetary Union. The final report was presented to the Commission on 8 October 1970.

[106]Commission of the European Communities (1977).

[107]For a general analysis of the EU budget cf. Santini (2015).

[108]The latter instruments did not cause an impact on the EU budget as they finance themselves on the markets and they are only backed by the EU budget.

reforms; it would also help national governments to pursue fiscal discipline, as the centralisation of fiscal policy decisions would reduce the risks that Member States take unsustainable fiscal policy decisions; a budget that centralises spending and revenues will be able do deficit at better conditions than smaller Member States and develop more effective countercyclical policies; it would underpin countries' capacities to absorb both specific and area-wide shocks.[109] As a whole, a Eurozone provided with a sufficient budget would become more resistant to economic shocks and cohesive. Furthermore, the proposal of establishing an additional budgetary capacity gained more and more consensus in the light of two subsequent failures of the economic governance: the ante-crisis system based on the regulatory role of the financial markets proved to be ineffective due to the lack of credibility of the no bailout clause and the lack of crisis management tools and convergence drivers; the post-crisis system based on enhanced surveillance also failed due to the struggles, several governments experienced, when they tried to consolidate public finances and restore competitiveness through austerity measures and structural reforms, while maintaining, at the same time, the necessary political consensus.[110]

The political debate on the project of introducing a budgetary instrument for the euro area is rather advanced. In December 2017, the Commission has officially proposed the creation of a budgetary line for the euro area within the EU budget.[111] Also France and Germany have proposed the creation of an *ad hoc* budget for the euro area to promote competitiveness, convergence and stabilisation to be introduced from 2021.[112] In December 2018, the Euro Summit gave mandate to the Eurogroup to draft a project of *ad hoc* budget for the euro area.[113] After long and difficult negotiations, the project has started to emerge in June 2019.[114]

5.3.3.4.2 The Possible Features of the Mechanism According to the Political and Academic Debate

Before considering the most recent decisions regarding the establishment of a separate budget for the euro area, the following analysis will recall the fundamental features this instrument should be provided with. Notably, the creation of a eurozone

---

[109] On the reasons, why the euro area should be provided with a stabilisation function: Cottarelli (2016), pp. 5–6; Thirion (2017), pp. 10–11; Arnold et al. (2018), pp. 7–9. In favour of a stabilization instrument for the euro area also: Pisani-Ferry et al. (2013), Delbecque (2013), Lellouch and Sode (2014), Beblavý and Maselli (2015), Dullien et al. (2017), Carnot et al. (2017), Bénassy-Quéré et al. (2018), pp. 14–16, Adamski (2018), pp. 153–155.

[110] Scott (2012), pp. 51–52; Pilz (2017), p. 644.

[111] See European Commission Communication (2017b), European Commission Communication (2018), pp. 10–11.

[112] See 'President of the French Republic, Chancellor of the German Federal Republic 'Meseberg Declaration', (2018).

[113] Euro Summit (2018).

[114] Eurogroup (2019), Euro Summit (2019).

budget represents an ambitious and complex project, which is meant to be implemented gradually. Even if its initial setup may be minimal, the instrument may develop its features, mandate and size over time according to the changing political needs.

Most of the proposals presented over the last few years essentially describe the Eurozone budget as an instrument aimed at collecting and spending resources across Member States through a centralised mechanism at European level in order to pursue the stability of the euro area as a whole. In the light of the academic debate put forward so far, it is possible to highlight some defining features of the instrument, which should distinguish it from other tools of economic policy already available.

First, unlike the ESM the Eurozone budgetary instrument shouldn't be an emergency tool, but it would operate in ordinary times to foster the macroeconomic consolidation and convergence of participating Member State. Accordingly, it would work on the preventive side of the governance, thus helping to avoid those critical situations, which may demand the last resort intervention of the ESM or a debt restructuration.[115]

Second, contrary to the ESM and like the current EU budget, the Eurozone budgetary instrument should not provide loans, but transfers.[116] Even if the purpose of the budgetary instrument is not redistribution, but stability, grants are meant to help countries to better shoulder the impact of economic shocks and facilitate the implementation of reforms. On the contrary, loans may aggravate the budgetary position of the recipient Member States.[117]

Third, the Eurozone budgetary instrument should be able to count on an adequate amount of resources to fulfil the functions, it has been conferred. Assuming that the main objectives for a euro area budget were promoting investments and absorbing economic shocks, most of the studies on the matter suggest that in an initial stage a transfer mechanism should dispose of between 1 and 3% of European GDP, depending on the stabilisation tasks that it will manage in concrete.[118]

---

[115]European Commission Staff Working Document (2018), p. 25.

[116]Several proposals alluded to the fact that the budgetary mechanism would entail a certain degree of transfers, even if the latter should not be permanent or unidirectional. Cf. President of the European Commission, Report (2015), p. 15; Explanatory Statement of the European Parliament Resolution (2017), p. 15; European Commission Staff Working Document (2018), pp. 24–25.

[117]It should be noted that not all proposals agree on this feature. Some for example suggest, the budgetary instrument may provide loans to the Member States, and only the cost of the interest rate on the latter should be covered by a grant. European Commission Communication (2018), p. 11. On the concession of favorable loans cf. European Commission Staff Working Document (2018), pp. 28–31.

[118]Marzinotto et al. (2011), p. 7; Allard et al. (2013), p. 19; Vallée (2014), pp. 59–60; De Grauwe (2016), pp. 217–218; Bénassy-Quéré et al. (2016), p. 14. Explanatory Statement of the European Parliament Resolution (2017), p. 22. The Commission argued that in order be effective in the euro area, the stabilization function for overall net payments should count on at least 1% of GDP. Cf. European Commission Communication (2017b), p. 14.

Fourth, in order to avoid moral hazard, the mechanism should not lead to Member States permanently depending on each other.[119] For the same reason, only governments complying with pre-defined eligibility criteria based on sound macroeconomic policies will be able to access the budgetary mechanism.[120] This would represent a significant incentive to comply with European rules.

Finally, the budgetary instrument should be able to intervene in a timely and effective manner, for example providing some form of automatism for those Member States fulfilling pre-defined parameters.[121]

When it comes to the *financing of the budgetary instrument* for the euro area, it is possible to identify in abstract four main possible sources. The easiest option may consist of *national conferrals*. The latter are periodic fees or contributions that Member States should transfer from their national budgets to the Eurozone budgetary instrument on the model of the GNI-based resources of the EU budget. In order to ensure the solidity of the mechanism, contributions should be proportional to national GDP and compulsory for all countries. An alternative may be the introduction of *new genuine own resources*, which have recently gained more attention thanks to the aforementioned report on the 'Future Financing of the EU' of the High-Level Group chaired by Mario Monti. Own resources do not consist of European taxes, but are revenues allocated irrevocably to the Union to finance its budget and accruing to it automatically without the need for any other decision by the Member States.[122] The advantage of this source of financing would be to emancipate the functioning of the Eurozone budgetary capacity instrument from the 'juste retour' discourse, which usually dominates every direct transfer from domestic budgets, and rediscover the added value of genuine European resources.[123] Evidently the budgetary instrument should be financed by some of the new own resources identified in the report, such as ECB seignorage, corporate taxes, carbon levies, taxes on fossil fuels, electricity tax-based resources, as well as a financial transaction tax.[124] Another source of financing to be introduced in the long term are

[119]According to the Commission, the stabilisation function shall be neutral over the medium-term and not lead to permanent transfers between Member States. European Commission Communication (2017b), p. 14.

[120]Ibid., pp. 14–15.

[121]Ibid. The Monti Report identifies some other principles which should regulate a separate budget for the euro area: unity (as the euro area budget should show in a single document all revenue and all expenditure); universality or non-assignment (all revenue should finance all expenditure and not be specifically assigned); accuracy (the euro area must not spend more than necessary); specification (the euro area budget needs to be detailed so that there is no ambiguity of purpose for all appropriations); annuality; equilibrium (this principle should be problematic if the euro area budget had a borrowing capacity). See High-Level Group on Own Resources (2016), p. 69.

[122]High-Level Group on Own Resources (2016), p. 22.

[123]On the added value of 'own resources' see Fabbrini (2016), pp. 164, 165; High-Level Group on Own Resources (2016), pp. 27–29.

[124]According to the Monti Report some of the envisaged 'new own resources' may be more adapt due to their connection to the existence of the single currency. This would be the case of revenue from seigniorage (approximately €4–5 billions per year) or the financial transaction tax (estimated

European taxes. The latter would represent a more advanced way to finance the budgetary capacity as they would be directly levied by the European authority. Evidently, the setup of such a source of revenue would require a partial shift of fiscal sovereignty from national to European level. While most governments are currently opposing such an option, the creation of a genuine European power of taxation would definitely pose some serious challenges to national constitutional law and require a deep reform of the EU Treaties. Finally, *European common debt* has been highlighted as a possible instrument of common self-financing since the outbreak of the sovereign debt crisis. A number of economists and think-tanks have already developed some detailed analysis of the project, highlighting the technical options for the setup of the so called 'Eurobonds'.[125] The European Commission itself endorsed the idea of a Eurozone-joint stability bond in a Green Paper published in 2011.[126] Evidently the mutualisation of sovereign debts would require an even higher level of political integration among the Member States and should be prepared through an adequate process of economic convergence and institutional reforms. In particular, introducing Eurobonds before creating an effective European government provided with fiscal authority and democratically legitimised would not be realistic, due to the lack of credibility of the instrument.

Whatever sources of financing will be adopted, it is important that the euro area budgetary instrument would not rely only on loans from the markets backed by national budgets, but it may count also on a system of sufficient grants.[127]

Considering the *destination of resources and the mandate of the budgetary instrument*, the latter should foster the stability of the euro area as a whole by facilitating convergence between the Member States and making the Eurozone more resilient against economic shocks. Even if the existing weakness of European solidarity prevents for the moment the development of other tasks, such as income redistribution and social protection, the concept of convergence should be interpreted not only as fiscal consolidation according to common parameters, put also as the promotion of similar levels of economic development across the euro area. Accordingly, the additional budgetary capacity for the euro area may have at least one of the following functions. First of all, it may support *reforms and public goods* in the Member States under distress. By financing the implementation of structural reforms or strategic projects, the mechanism would help increase the

---

at €10–15 billions per year). In order to collect more resources, the Report suggest considering revenue from a share of national indirect or direct taxation, as well as cash contributions.

[125]On a deeper economic analysis of the different proposals see Brunnermeier et al. (2016a), pp. 111–114.

[126]European Commission Green Paper (2011).

[127]'Relying only on a system of loans could have a limited impact, since the Member State could simply borrow in the markets or access one of the existing precautionary credit lines. On the other hand, a loan component has the merit of addressing some possible liquidity concerns without creating risks of permanent transfers. A stabilisation instrument via a system of grants could have stronger and more immediate macroeconomic effects'. European Commission Communication (2017b), p. 14.

economic resilience of individual Member States and of the euro area, by reducing the risks of both country-specific shocks and subsequent systemic crisis. At the same time, it may pursue also convergence between the Member States. Second, the additional budgetary instrument may be able to *stabilise country specific (asymmetric) shocks*. In accordance with the principle of subsidiarity, only shocks of a sufficient magnitude should be managed centrally, while the stabilisation of minor externalities would fall on the shoulders of national governments. The mechanism might be implemented in different ways.[128] Following a macroeconomic approach, the additional budgetary instrument might work either as a rainy-day fund, meaning that resources will be collected in times of economic prosperity and transferred back to Member States, when they experience an economic shock, or as an Investment Protection Scheme, which shall protect investment in the event of a downturn.[129] Following instead a microeconomic approach, the budgetary capacity might finance a common European unemployment insurance for all citizens or residents living in the Eurozone. The insurance can be conceived either as an EMU-wide basic unemployment benefit scheme or as a re-insurance system for national unemployment schemes.[130] Third, the additional budgetary instrument may provide a common response to *(symmetric) shocks* hitting the Eurozone as a whole. This could be necessary in the event of a systemic crisis, like that which occurred in 2007 after the collapse of Lehman Brothers. In a similar situation, Member States may require a common fiscal stimulus to recover their economy. Financing pan European projects and strategic investments might serve this purpose.

5.3.3.4.3 Possible Concretisation of the Euro Area Budgetary Capacity

After considering the debate on the establishment of a budgetary capacity for the Eurozone, it is possible to analyse the most recent decisions on the matter and verify how much of the proposals advanced so far will be effectively implemented into legal acts. Following the meeting of December 2018, the Eurogroup has outlined the main features of a 'Budgetary Instrument for Convergence and Competitiveness' (BICC), the leaders of the euro area finally endorsed in June 2019.[131]

This decision has come at the end of a long and difficult negotiation between the EU governments and EU institutions. BICC shall replace two other proposals put forward over the last few years to provide the euro area with its own budgetary instrument. On the one hand, the European Commission had championed the

[128] Cf. European Commission Communication (2012), pp. 32–33; European Commission Communication (2017b), p. 14; Explanatory Statement of the European Parliament Resolution (2017), pp. 20–22. On the pros and contra of the microeconomic and macroeconomic approaches see Berger et al. (2018), pp. 32–33.

[129] See Adamski (2018), pp. 159–161.

[130] Ibid. pp. 161–165.

[131] Eurogroup (2019) and Euro Summit (2019).

creation of a budgetary line for the euro area within the euro budget. After presenting a Communication on this topic in December 2017,[132] the Commission proposed in May 2018 two draft Regulations, one on the creation of a Reform Support Programme and the other on the setup of a European Investment Stabilisation Function in the framework of the MFF 2020–2027.[133] At the same time, France and Germany proposed the creation of a separate budget for the euro area in the joint Meseberg Declaration of June 2018.[134] The agreement reached by the leaders of the euro area takes into consideration some of the most important contents of these two proposals,[135] while dropping at the same time those elements, on which it was impossible to find enough consensus.

According to the political compromise achieved so far, BICC should be a budgetary instrument created within the EU budget and essentially designed for

---

[132]European Commission Communication (2017b).

[133]European Commission Communication (2018), pp. 10–11; European Commission Proposal for a Regulation (2018a) on the establishment of the Reform Support Programme; European Commission Proposal for a Regulation (2018b). The Reform Support Programme should be an instrument meant to encourage the implementation of structural reforms in the Union with the purpose of improving the convergence and the resilience of national economies. It should be composed of three elements: a reform delivery tool in charge of providing financial incentives for the implementation of reforms in Member States; a technical support instrument to help Member States in their effort to design and implement reforms; a convergence facility for the countries which are preparing their membership for the euro area. The resources identified by the European Commission for the kick-off of the project are €25 billion. The European Investment Stabilisation Function (EISF) should be a mechanism in charge of absorbing economic shocks that Member States are unable to manage on their own by stabilising investment levels. EISF should have fulfilled a stabilisation function through the provision of 'back-to-back loans under the EU budget of up to €30 billion, coupled with a grant component to cover the costs of the interest'. In order to collect more resources, the Commission proposed that the stabilisation function may be complemented by additional financing resources outside the EU budget, such as precautionary loans by the ESM, and a possible voluntary insurance mechanism to be set up by the Member States. The intervention of the mechanism should be conditional to the respect of both eligibility criteria based on the compliance of Member States with fiscal rules under the SGP, and activation criteria proving the existence of a relevant economic shock.

[134]Meseberg Declaration (2018); Proposal on the architecture of a Eurozone Budget within the framework of the European Union, 16 November 2018. According to the Franco-German proposal, the separate budget for the euro area was supposed to be part of the EU budget, even if it would operate under the strategic guidance of the Euro summit. The Eurozone budget should have been primarily financed by external assigned revenues, including the allocation of tax revenues and European resources. The latter revenues would consist of regular contributions by Eurozone Member States, collected and transferred to the EU budget on the basis of an intergovernmental agreement. The aim of the Eurozone budget was to strengthen competitiveness and convergence, which would have been delivered through investments in innovation and human capital, thus pursuing the objective of the stability of the euro area as a whole. Finally, the proposal also mentioned that the Eurozone budget might finance a stabilisation tool in the form of a European Unemployment Stabilization Fund, in the case of severe economic crises, without transfers.

[135]For a comparison of the two proposals see Santini and Lionello (2018).

the Member States of the euro area.[136] The purpose of the instrument is to support structural reforms and public investments in the Member States through the conferral of grants, thus increasing the degree of convergence and competitiveness within the euro area. There was no consensus instead on providing the instrument also with a stabilisation function. This should remain for the moment a responsibility of the Member States, even if the mechanism may help to strengthen the adjustment capacities of Eurozone economies by fostering structural reforms and budgetary consolidation.

BICC shall be adopted in accordance with the legislative procedure, as foreseen by the Treaties, on the basis of the relevant Commission proposal to be amended.[137] At the same time, its functioning shall require other relevant legislative acts. First of all, the MFF Regulation, which will be adopted in accordance with art. 312 TFEU, shall define the total size,[138] revenue sources and spending targets of BICC in the framework of the wider EU budget. At the same time, participating Member States shall also stipulate an intergovernmental agreement where they define the governance framework of the mechanism, as well as any additional source of revenues, which is not going to be provided in EU law.

Considering the functioning of BICC, the Eurogroup and the Euro Summit will define the strategic guidance on the key reform and investment priorities for the convergence and competitiveness of the euro area.[139] Accordingly, they will adopt every year a 'strengthened recommendation for the euro area as a whole' in order to provide guidelines for the Member States, which are willing to access BICC.[140] On this basis, each government shall submit to the Eurogroup a 'reform and investment proposal' for which they are demanding the concession of a grant.[141] The size of the grant will be determined based on the cost estimate of the project. At the same time, a

[136]Having linked their currency to the Euro, the ERM II countries, however, may also join on a voluntary basis. The Eurogroup will take into account the participating ERM II Member States in the management of the instrument.

[137]It is not clear what legal basis will be chosen for the creation of the instrument. Both the Commission proposals and the Franco-German agreement identified a number of legal provisions, such art. 136 TFEU on the enhanced economic coordination within the euro area, art. 175(3) TFEU on specific actions outside the structural fund, art. 173 TFEU on the competitiveness of the industry and art. 182 TFEU on research and technological development. In July 2019 the European Commission proposed a regulation establishing a governance framework to enable the Council to provide strategic orientations on reform and investment priorities to be undertaken within the euro area by the Member States. The regulation should be adopted on the basis of art. 136(1) (b) and art. 121 (6) TFEU. See European Commission Proposal for a Regulation (2019).

[138]The future size of BICC is the main source of disagreement between the Member States. While France, supported by countries like Spain, imagined a mechanism able to mobilise significant resources, the Netherlands and other northers countries, including Germany, insist that the instrument shall maintain a modest size.

[139]These priorities shall also be set out in the European Semester.

[140]Structural reforms and public investment projects should reflect the strategic guidance on the use of the instrument provided by euro area Member States, through the Euro Summit and the Eurogroup, and set out in the European Semester. Eurogroup (2019).

[141]More precisely, 'the proposals shall include the estimation of the costs of investments and, where appropriate, of structural reforms, the justifications for the estimated costs, as well as the timeline for implementation of the structural reforms and investments, with the relevant milestones and targets'. Ibid.

minimum national co-financing rate will be requested to finance the investment and reforms.[142] This should ensure the ownership of the project at the national level.

The activation of BICC shall be subject to the compliance with some *ex ante* conditionality, meaning the implementation of structural reforms and investments, respecting the applicable macro-economic conditionality foreseen in the Common Provisions Regulation[143] and the compliance with horizontal rules applying to the implementation of the EU budget.[144] For this reason, governments will receive the financial support in instalments and report on the implementation of reform and investment commitments in the context of the European Semester.

The Commission will assess the Member States' proposals on the basis of transparent criteria and evaluate their effective implementation.[145] The relevant preparatory committees of the Eurogroup will also be involved in the discussion of the assessment of Member States' proposals and monitoring of progress. The Eurogroup will then discuss the assessments and the progress reports. In case of unsatisfactory implementation of the reforms and investments, payments will be first suspended, and eventually cancelled.[146]

5.3.3.5 European Minister of Economy and Finance

Another recurrent proposal for the reform of the EMU is the creation of a European Minister of Economic Affairs. The purpose of having an office of this kind is to simplify the functioning of the governance and make it more transparent and responsible. Notably, the economic union is composed of several bodies regulated

[142]'The national co-financing rate could vary based on a predictable and transparent commonly agreed procedure defined ex-ante involving euro area Member States'. At the same time, 'the allocation of funds per country will be determined on the basis of a transparent methodology, taking into account parameters reflecting the overarching aim of the instrument and legal basis. The available funds per country should be within an acceptable range of the contributions of that country'. Ibid.

[143]Regulation (EU) No 1303/2013 of the European Parliament and of the Council of 17 December 2013 laying down common provisions on the European Regional Development Fund, the European Social Fund, the Cohesion Fund, the European Agricultural Fund for Rural Development and the European Maritime and Fisheries Fund and laying down general provisions on the European Regional Development Fund, the European Social Fund, the Cohesion Fund and the European Maritime and Fisheries Fund and repealing Council Regulation (EC) No 1083/2006, (2013) OJ L 347/320.

[144]Regulation (EU, Euratom) 2018/1046 of the European Parliament and of the Council of 18 July 2018 on the financial rules applicable to the general budget of the Union, amending Regulations (EU) No 1296/2013, (EU) No 1301/2013, (EU) No 1303/2013, (EU) No 1304/2013, (EU) No 1309/2013, (EU) No 1316/2013, (EU) No 223/2014, (EU) No 283/2014, and Decision No 541/2014/EU and repealing Regulation (EU, Euratom) No 966/2012(1), (2018) OJ L 193/1.

[145]'The Commission will be responsible for budgetary implementation and the European Parliament for giving the discharge, after the Council has given its recommendation. Implementation will be subject to the scrutiny of the European Court of Auditors.' Eurogroup (2019).

[146]Ibid.

by both EU law and international agreements, each of which has its own president, accountability rules and mandate. The result is a governance suffering from chronic inefficiency and scarce democratic control. In order to contain this trend, since 2011 the Commissioner for Economic and Monetary Affairs has become a Vice President of the Commission and started taking care of all the issues regarding the economic governance. He assists the President of the European Commission in all works of the European Council, Euro summits, Board of Governors of the ESM and the other relevant meetings.[147] Despite these important tasks, this figure cannot be assimilated to a real Minister of Economic affairs: as the Commission plays only an assisting role in the management of the governance, the Vice President in charge of Economic and Monetary Affairs does not have any power or responsibility on the real decision-making process, which notably belongs to intergovernmental bodies.

In the light of these longstanding problems, the Commission issued in December 2017 a Communication proposing the creation of a European Minister of Economy and Finance within the existing EU legal framework.[148] Despite not involving any additional conferral of competences to the Union,[149] this new 'Minister' should be provided with several important tasks.[150] First of all, the Minister should represent the EU and the euro area at global level, especially in international financial institutions, where every country has its own representation (i.e. IMF). In this way, the Minister should be a privileged interlocutor in regard to the economic, fiscal and financial policy of the euro area. Second, the Minister should encourage and facilitate policy coordination and ensure compliance with economic, fiscal and financial rules in the euro area, by ensuring consistency across policy areas. In this way, he or she would help the coordination and implementation of reforms in the Member States. In connection to this function, the Minister should also pronounce on the adequate fiscal policy for the euro area in support of the monetary policy of the ECB. In this sense, the Minister would ensure the application of the SGP by finding a balance between national priorities and the interest of the euro area as a whole. Last, the Minister should oversee the use of the EU and euro area budgetary instruments in support of reforms, macroeconomic stabilisation and convergence (i.e. the EFSI, the ESIF, the EIB, the ESM and in perspective the budgetary instrument for the euro area). Despite the limited resources available, the Minister should coordinate the use of these budgetary instruments and maximise their impact in support of shared priorities.

Moving to the institutional setting, the proposal suggests the Minister should be provided with a double hatting as Vice President of the Commission and President of the Eurogroup. While the Commission can easily reform itself to create this new office, the Eurogroup shall decide to elect the Minister as its President for the duration of the Commission's mandate. Accordingly, the Minister will also chair

[147]Allemand (2017), p. 92.

[148]European Commission Communication (2017c).

[149]The transfer of competence to the EU level would require a treaty change. Pilz (2017), p. 642.

[150]European Commission Communication (2017c), pp. 3–5.

the Board of governors of the ESM, by assuming the role previously exercised by the President of the Eurogroup.[151] In this way, the creation of a Minister of Economy and Finance would ensure a stronger democratic accountability of the governance, as intergovernmental bodies, such as the Eurogroup and the Board of Governors of the ESM, would be subject through their new President to the checks and balances controls, which apply to the Commission.

Coming to an assessment, the idea of a European Minister of Economy and Finance may make sense, but its impact on the functioning of the economic union will depend on the effective autonomy, it will have in the management of the governance tools. For this reason, it is important to define what role, the Minister will have in regard to the budgetary instrument for the euro area, the activation of the ESM and the surveillance of national budgets, these being the three main ways, the EU aims to shape the economic policy of the euro area in the future. If the Minister will work only as a coordinator or a secretary of intergovernmental bodies, like the 'High Representative of the Union for Foreign Affairs and Security Policy', its contribution to the effectiveness and the accountability of the governance will be limited. If instead it will have some form of decisional autonomy, the introduction of the Minister of Economy and Finance may represent a qualitative leap in the process of democratisation, simplification and strengthening of the economic union.[152]

Regardless of the objective advantages and challenges, the establishment of a European Minister of Economy may create, it looks like the project doesn't have, at least for the moment, enough support from the Member States.

5.3.3.6 Incorporation of Intergovernmental Instruments in the EU Legal Framework

Another important proposal for the completion of the EMU regards the incorporation in EU law of all those components of the governance, which during the crisis have been implemented through intergovernmental agreements. The two most important cases are notably the TESM, which is an intergovernmental agreement between the countries of the euro area, and the TSCG, which has been stipulated between 25 Member States of the EU. The incorporation of the ESM and the TSCG in EU

[151] From the practical point of view, it may be problematic as the role of President of the Eurogroup should be a full-time position and avoid accumulation of roles (i.e. national minister of finance or member of the Commission). Cf. Wolff (2017), p. 4. Furthermore, art. 16(9) TEU may prevent a Commissioner from becoming President of the Ecofin Council. Cf. Pilz (2017), p. 641.

[152] In order to make sense, a Minister of Finance should have several responsibilities including oversee the coordination of fiscal and economic policies; oversee and politically defend the enforcement of the rules; lead negotiation in the framework of the ESM about the adjustment programme; help buffer regional shocks by using a small EU budget for investments; represent the euro area externally. The implementation of these important tasks requires that the Minister may count on some fiscal instruments: a European investment budget in charge of counterbalancing asymmetric shocks and supporting reforms, as well as a European Monetary Fund to intervene in the event of systemic crisis. See Enderlein and Haas (2015), pp. 4–6.

law should provide a number of benefits. First, it would increase the transparency, clarity and efficiency of the decision-making process, by diminishing the possible risks of duplications and conflicting actions inherent in the co-existence of intergovernmental arrangements alongside the mechanisms of EU law.[153] Furthermore, incorporation would improve accountability towards the European Parliament and widen the jurisdiction of the CJEU on the single actions taken in the process of economic coordination, thus making it less political. More in general, the economic governance would experience a more consistent and coordinated evolution. In the light of these observations, the European Commission has advanced so far two proposals.

In December 2017, the Commission drafted a Regulation for the transformation of the ESM into a body of EU law on the basis of the flexibility clause ex art. 352 TFEU. According to the proposal, the ESM should be renamed European Monetary Fund (EMF)[154] and should be provided with its own legal personality. The peculiarity of the mechanism is that, even if it will become part of the EU legal framework, its members shall only be the countries of the euro area and it shall maintain a significant autonomy. Furthermore, according to the proposal, the financial and institutional structure of the ESM shall remain essentially untouched, with few adjustments regarding the decision-making process and the voting rules.[155] For example, in order to ensure the compliance with the Meroni doctrine developed by the CJEU,[156] every discretional decision taken by the Board of Governors and Directors shall be approved by EU institutions, and more precisely by the Council.[157] In this regard the same proposal says that ‘the votes of member of the Council representing Member States whose currency is not the euro shall be suspended’. This means that the Council and the Board of governors of the EMF will essentially

---

[153]Whereas (8) European Commission Proposal for a Regulation (2017), European Commission Proposal for a Directive (2017), p. 3.

[154]The new name may create confusion with the tasks conferred to the ECB.

[155]According to the proposal, the most important decisions (i.e. capital calls; modify minimum lending capacity, change in capital distribution) are taken by unanimity. Decisions on the activation of the EMF (i.e. provision of stability support, adoption of conditionality policy as stated in the MoU) are taken by a reinforced qualified majority (85% of the votes cast). Decision on the statutory roles and the internal functioning are instead taken by qualified majority (80% of the votes cast). The qualified majority gives a veto power only to bigger States (Germany, France and partially Italy). It is important that also the EMF Regulation foresees that if any Member fails to pay any part of the amount due in respect of its obligations in relation to paid-in shares or calls of capital its voting rights shall be suspended for so long as such failure continues. See art. 4(8) of Annex to the European Commission Proposal for a Regulation (2017) (Statute of the EMF).

[156]In the Meroni case, the Court recalled the principle of institutional balance to introduce a general ban on the delegation of discretionary powers to EU agencies. According with this case law, powers can be conferred to agencies only if they are clearly defined and have an executive nature. See Judgment of the Court of 13 June 1958, Case C-9/56 Meroni & Co., Industrie Metallurgiche, SpA v High Authority of the European Coal and Steel Community, ECLI:EU:C:1958:7.

[157]See Whereas (34) European Commission Proposal for a Regulation (2017).

consist of the same people, but just wearing different hats.[158] Unfortunately, the proposal of the Commission does not introduce any significant innovation in regard to the instruments of democratic control. Accountability to the European parliament and the national parliaments shall be ensured through the classical instruments of interinstitutional dialogue.[159] Also the improvement of transparency is only partial: even if the EMF should be subject to the Union rules on public access to documents,[160] the Parliament can only organise confidential oral discussions with the EMF's Managing Director, given the sensitive nature of the activities of the EMF and their impact on financial markets. It is appreciable instead the reference to art. 152 TFEU on the dialogue between the social partners and art. 28 EUCFRs on the right of collective bargaining and action. These legal provisions should strengthen cooperation between EU institutions, citizens and group of interests in regard to the implementation of conditional financial support. Another important aspect of the Commission proposal regards the fact that the incorporation of the ESM in the EU legal framework would have no budgetary implications. As for the ESM, the liability of each Member State shall be limited, in all circumstances, to its portion of the authorised capital stock at its issue price. At the same time, also the Union budget shall not be held liable for the expenses or losses of the EMF.

In December 2017, the Commission also put forward a proposal regarding the incorporation of some provisions of the Fiscal Compact in the EU legal framework.[161] This result should be pursued through the adoption of a Directive based on art. 126(14) TFEU and applicable only to the Member States whose currency is the euro. The proposal of the Commission is consistent with the incorporation clause outlined in art. 16 TSCG.[162] The purpose of the directive is to introduce numerical fiscal rules in the national legal order in a way to ensure the national ownership of the latter. In this sense, the Directive mirrors the Fiscal Compact in three ways. First, it obliges Member States to set in national law a medium-term objective in terms of structural balance that is binding in the budgetary cycle.[163] Second, the Directive prescribes the creation of a correction mechanism, to be activated automatically in

[158]Editorial Comment (2018), p. 712.

[159]According to the proposal, the EFM has the obligation to submit annual report and the European Parliament, the Council, the Commission and the national parliaments on the execution of its tasks. The European and national parliaments may pose oral and written questions and clarification to the EMF in the person of the Managing Director, by taking in due account the confidentiality need. See art. 5 and art. 6 of European Commission Proposal for a Regulation (2017).

[160]See Regulation (EC) No 1049/2001 of the European Parliament and of the Council of 30 May 2001 regarding public access to European Parliament, Council and Commission documents, (2001) OJ L 145/43.

[161]European Commission Proposal for a Directive (2017).

[162]Art. 16 TSCG prescribes the incorporation of the Fiscal Compact in EU law within 5 years since its entry into force.

[163]The preference for fiscal rules of 'constitutional nature' is not mentioned in the text of the Directive, but only in Whereas (13). This might represent *de facto* a downgrading of the duty of constitutionalization of numerical fiscal rules introduced by the TSCG.

the event of a significant deviation from the adjustment path towards the MTO. Third, the mechanism should be in the hands of independent fiscal institutions. In order to fulfil their mandate, Independent fiscal institutions (IFIs) shall address recommendation to the national fiscal authority demanding to comply with it or justify their decision not to (comply or explain principle). The other provisions of the Fiscal Compact are not mentioned in the Draft Directive. According to the Commission this is due to the fact that some norms have been already integrated in EU law (i.e. Two Pack), while the incorporation of the others would have required a Treaty Change.[164] Consequently, the obligations assumed under the TSCG, which are not affected by the process of incorporation, are still valid under international law.[165] This should regard art. 7 TSCG on the extension of RMV to all the stages of the EDP, art. 12 TSCG on the Euro summit and art. 13 TSCG on inter-parliamentary meeting between the European and national parliaments of the contractive parties.

Unfortunately, as with the proposal of a European Minister of Finance, the incorporation of intergovernmental mechanisms in EU law also seems to be more of a priority for the EU Commission, than the Member States. In fact, the ongoing discussion within the Eurogroup and Euro summit on the possible reform of the EMU has completely ignored the proposals of the European Commission, regardless the fact that the deadline foreseen by the incorporation clause ex art. 16 TSCG has already passed.

5.4 Legal Challenges to the Completion of the EMU

The analysis developed above has shown the complexity and the importance of the debate on the future reform of the EMU. The different projects put forward so far by European institutions, Member States and the academia aim to complete the governance and make it able to manage the existing challenges to the stability of the euro area as a whole.

The review of the reform proposals has already highlighted the existence of two different approaches to the completion of the EMU: preserving and updating the decentralised model of economic union or centralising competences and resources at European level. Each approach does clearly present a number of advantages and disadvantages. As a premise, it is opportune to remember that the future reform of the economic union will not necessarily implement measures belonging only to one model, meaning either decentralisation or centralisation. On the contrary, some balance can be found in concrete. Indeed, endorsing the centralised model of economic union does not mean to renegade market discipline, the project of CMU or the opportunity of debt restructuration in some exceptional situation, but

---

[164] European Commission Proposal for a Directive (2017), p. 3. Cfr. Croci (2018), p. 5.

[165] See Whereas (15), Whereas (16), Whereas (17) European Commission Proposal for a Directive (2017).

accepting that stability will be pursued also through the development of a genuine European economic policy based on its own resources. At the same time, adopting the decentralised model of economic union will keep the responsibility for budgetary stability on the shoulders of national governments and exclude the consolidation of fiscal solidarity between the Member States. Financial assistance in favour of a country experiencing economic difficulties, however, will still be possible in the event the stability of the entire monetary union is at stake. Evidently, rather than choosing only one of the two approaches to the completion of the economic union, it will be necessary to understand which model should be prioritised and what balance they should find in concrete in order to overcome the existing deficits of the governance.[166]

The following analysis will explain the main challenges the implementation of each model will have to face in concrete, by taking into consideration the three fundamental fragilities, which notably characterise the existing economic governance and undermine the pursuit of stability of the euro area as a whole: deficit of legality, deficit of effectiveness and deficit of democracy.

5.5 The Limits of the Decentralised Model

5.5.1 The Decentralised Model of Economic Union: An Eternal Recurrence?

Despite its constant failures, the decentralised model of economic union has maintained a relevant consensus in the political and academic debate. The reasons of this persistent popularity are many. The first and most obvious one is that Member States do not want to lose their exclusive competence on fiscal policy. As the latter represents the main source of consensus and political power, it is understandable they don't want to share it with the EU institutions. The preservation of fiscal rights is also motivated by the supposed need to protect national democracy. As decisions on revenues and public spending are normally parliamentary prerogatives, the decentralised model of fiscal union seems to guarantee that decisions are effectively taken by the representatives of the (national) people. Another important argument in favour of the decentralised model of fiscal union regards the relative facility of its implementation. Indeed, by representing a natural continuation of the *status quo*, the adjustment of the surveillance mechanisms would not require a significant reform of the EU Treaties, but simply an amendment of the SGP or the intergovernmental agreements, which regulate the governance, such as the TSCG or the TESM. In this regard, it should be noted that, unlike fiscal integration, the perpetration of the decentralised model of economic union would not require the incorporation of intergovernmental instruments in EU law. On the contrary, national fiscal rights

[166]On the balance between centralisation and decentralisation see Van den Bergh (2016).

would be better protected in a hybrid model where some mechanisms are going to be regulated by international law. Finally, the advocates of the surveillance model doubt that Member States and their citizens feel sufficient solidarity and mutual trust to adopt a different approach based on the further sharing of sovereignty and resources.

Unfortunately, the reasonability of some of these arguments clashes with the analysis developed in the previous Chapter. The structural deficits of the existing decentralised model of governance regarding both legality, effectiveness and democratic accountability are notably the reasons why the euro area risked collapse during the sovereign debt crisis. The point is now to understand whether the proposals advanced so far to restore the decentralised model of economic union may be able to fix these vulnerabilities.

5.5.2 Decentralisation and the Deficit of Legality. Is It Possible to Make Surveillance Even Tighter?

As it was already explained, a fundamental proposal to restore the decentralised model of the economic union consists of tightening coordination on national economic policies. Dealing with the disappointing results of the process of fiscal consolidation and correction of macroeconomic imbalances,[167] a natural development of the governance may be increasing the amount of sanctions in case of non-compliance with European rules, making their approval fully automatic, and possibly creating some form of European veto on national budgets. The problem is now to understand whether the current legal framework provides some margin to implement this strategy.

The analysis developed in the previous Chapter on the deficits of legality of the governance may help to dispel some doubts. Notably, the existing EU primary law poses some important limits to the strengthening of surveillance. The principle of conferral does not allow the EU to annul the fiscal sovereignty of Member States and prevents economic coordination from being excessively intrusive on the choices of national authorities. Accordingly, the reforms of the governance adopted over the last few years, i.e. semi-automatic sanctions and enhanced surveillance in the framework of the SGP, have been strongly criticised for having overcome the limits of the available legal basis and forced some eclectic interpretation of EU primary law in order to avoid inconsistencies.[168] The use of intergovernmental instruments may offer some room to bypass the limits of the EU legal order, for example extending the application of RMV on the model of art. 7 TSCG or strengthening the role of technical authorities in charge of monitoring compliance with fiscal rules. At the same time, the use of international agreements between the Member States cannot

[167]Cf. *supra* Sect. 4.3.2.

[168]See *supra* Sect. 4.2.3.

challenge the consistency with EU primary law and the institutional balance within the Union.[169] In the light of these observations there is no doubt that continuing strengthening European surveillance may undermine the legality of the reforms even further. Regardless the formal ownership of fiscal sovereignty, if the EU or a parallel intergovernmental mechanism became *de facto* able to decide how resources are collected and spent at national level for each policy, the division of competences sanctioned in the EU Treaties would be definitely undermined.[170] Unlike the fiscal federalism model, where both the Member States and the supranational level have an autonomous margin of public spending, governments subject to European surveillance would have a little margin of discretion on determining the content of their budgetary law. This situation shows once again that the preservation of national sovereignty in the surveillance model risks becoming a legal *fictio* in the sense that even if national budgets are formally adopted by domestic parliaments, their content may be *de facto* etero-determined by the intergovernmental institutions of the European Union.

As the following analysis will explain, strengthening surveillance on national budgetary sovereignty (*Budgethoheit*) may also cause a reaction from domestic constitutional courts. The German Constitutional Court has been very clear to stress that fundamental fiscal decisions must remain with the national parliaments, meaning that no external authority can have a legal power to determine the amount of revenues and public spending defined by the national budgetary law.[171] According to the judges of Karlsruhe, the principle of national budgetary autonomy represents a *sine qua non* condition to protect the principle democratic self-government through representative institutions as provided in the German Constitution.[172]

5.5.3 *Decentralisation and the Deficit of Effectiveness*

5.5.3.1 Strengthening Surveillance. It Is Effective?

Aside from the consistency with the EU Treaties, the restoration of the decentralised model should be done in a way to overcome the longstanding deficit of effectiveness, which has prevented in the past the successful pursuit of the stability of the euro area as a whole. Particular attention should be paid to the application of European surveillance on national macro-economic policies.

Notably, the advocates of the decentralised model of economic union believe that surveillance may be improved through the imposition of heavier fines, the

[169]See *supra* Sect. 4.2.8.

[170]Hinarejos (2013), pp. 1639–1640.

[171]See German Federal Constitutional Court, Judgment of 30 June 2009, [2 BvE 2/08] paras 252, 256.

[172]Cf. Beck (2014), p. 553.

automatisation of the decision-making process up to the development of a genuine veto power on national budgets. In reality, introducing more and stricter constraints on national fiscal policies may be difficult to accept. The fiscal rules posed by EU law are already perceived as an excessive limitation of national sovereignty.[173] Continuing on the same path by containing national economic autonomy even further may increase the frustration of several Member States and in large part of the public opinion. As explained in the previous chapter,[174] surveillance works on the basis of a cooperation between the supervisor and the supervised. In the event economic coordination became too rigid, it may trigger a negative reaction from the concerned Member States. More precisely, the result of stiffening surveillance may be either a general disapplication of fiscal rules, as national governments may be politically unable to implement them, or some form of open opposition between European and national authorities in the event they clearly refused to accept EU requests. In both scenarios, fiscal rules would remain unattended.

5.5.3.2 Risks and Conditions for Debt Restructuration

The effectiveness of the decentralised model of economic union should be considered also in regard to the introduction of a genuine debt restructuration regime in the euro area. As the previous analysis has already explained this may happen essentially in two ways: creating an *ad hoc* procedure for state bankruptcy (for example through a reform of the TESM) or amending the standardised euro-CACs included in long-term bonds in a way to overcome possible holdout behaviours of creditors.

From an abstract point of view, the logic of debt restructuration is flawless. Alleviating the weight of unsustainable public debt would make it easier for a Member State to restore its fiscal stability and for the ESM to stand the cost of a financial assistance programme. At the same time, a debt restructuration regime would help restore the regulatory role of financial markets: the latter would request an interest rate effectively proportional to the risk of investment, if they realise that sovereign bonds are no longer safe assets. Regardless of the strength of these arguments, EU institutions and Member States have so far been reluctant to set up a formal debt restructuration regime. This is probably due to the outstanding risks coming from the application of debt restructuration in concrete.

First of all, the creation of an official mechanism of debt restructuration may trigger destabilising effect in the euro area and produce self-fulfilling prophecies. Indeed, the introduction of some form of insolvency mechanism may be considered by investors as the signal for an imminent debt restructuring, thus increasing the flight of capital from weaker Member States. In other words, making it possible to restructure unsustainable debts may cause a negative reaction from the financial markets, which may result in making the debt of weaker Member States

[173] See *supra* Sect. 4.4.5.

[174] See *supra* Sect. 4.3.5.2.

unsustainable.[175] This is exactly what happened after the 'Deauville beach walk' in October 2010, when the German Chancellor Angela Merkel and French President Nicolas Sarkozy agreed to the creation of the ESM and the general principle of private sector involvement. This immediately caused a new crisis on the bond markets, which contributed to the spread of contagion in the Eurozone. In order to obviate the risks of panic contagion on the financial market, several authors suggest introducing a 'phasing-in stage' before the introduction of the debt restructuration regime. The latter would consist of a transitional period of several years, which should dispel doubts on the immediate solvency of debtors and avoid excessive turbulences on the financial markets.[176]

Second, it may be difficult to decide precisely if the sovereign debt of a country is not sustainable. Solvency is notably a complex issue, which can't be identified on the basis of only one indicator, such as deficit or public debt. Aside from the level of indebtedness, other factors should also be taken into consideration, for example the country's net international investment position, private sector wealth and indebtedness interest cost as a share of government revenue.[177] Consequently, the application of a debt restructuration may result in an arbitrary decision dictated more by political interests than effective economic needs.

Third, the consequences of a sovereign default (even if partial) may be unbearable for both the concerned Member State and the rest of the euro area. In this regard, it is possible to identify two possible situations triggered by the implementation of a debt restructuration in the monetary union. In a Greece-like scenario, where the public debt is mostly owned by foreign (European) investors, a default may destabilise the other countries and the financial institutions, which have purchased sovereign bonds of the concerned Member State.[178] In an Italy-like scenario instead, a debt restructuration would mainly hurt domestic bond holders, in particular banks.[179] Both situations would be clearly destabilising for the euro area triggering either a new sovereign debt crisis and forcing the most exposed countries to exit the monetary union. The objective of the stability of the euro area as whole, would then be undermined.

Finally, considering specifically the introduction of the new 'Euro-CACs' with single-limb clause, their effectiveness may be limited for three reasons: they would only apply in respect to the new bondholders and not the previous stock; they will probably meet the opposition of investors, which were already obliged to accept

---

[175]See Mody (2013), pp. 28–29; Fuest et al. (2016), p. 302; Zettelmeyer (2018), p. 73.

[176]According to Gelpern there are other possible risks coming from the introduction of a debt restructuration regime: sovereign debt is mostly not enforceable and not dischargeable; sovereign debtor has different creditor groups: official and private, domestic and foreign, bilateral and multilateral. Gelpern (2014b), pp. 273–277.

[177]Barbieri Hermitte (2017), p. 114.

[178]Ibid. p. 116.

[179]Ibid. p. 116.

reform of the clauses in 2013[180]; furthermore, lacking a real insolvency procedure the outcome of debt restructuration may be unpredictable and some creditors may be discriminated.[181]

According with the previous analysis, as debt restructuration in one or more Member States may turn into a full destabilisation of the euro area, it is necessary to take some precautions. First, it would be necessary to reduce the exposure of banks to domestic state bonds, thus containing the toxic loop between banks and sovereigns. An important incentive in this regard may be represented by replacing national bonds, with some form of European safe assets, such as Eurobonds or European Safe Bonds.[182] Second, as it has been already explained in the previous paragraphs, it would be necessary to set up a European deposit insurance system (EDIS) to protect savers and avoid capital flight in the event of a debt restructuration in a Member State. Third, it will be necessary to create some form of insurance mechanism to ensure the stability of the euro area as a whole through the restructuration process. The defaulting country will be clearly the first one to need access to external funds to exercise basic governmental functions.[183] At the same time, also the other Member States of the euro area may suffer some form of contagion, thus making necessary external financial assistance. Evidently, the problem is to find a balance between restructuration and financial support. The risk is that a piloted sovereign default may still cause economic harm, social distress and increase divergence within the euro area. In this regard, financial support to the countries suffering from the negative spill-overs of a debt restructuration may be fulfilled by the ESM[184] or a new budgetary capacity of the euro area.

In the light of this analysis it is possible to draft two considerations. First, as debt restructuration can always turn into a traumatic event, it should be accepted only as an exceptional circumstance.[185] Even if it was possible to organise and pilot a partial sovereign default of a Member State, it would still be difficult to predict all possible outcomes of the procedure, especially considering that the euro area, is a less compact and solid monetary union than the other sovereign states. Rather than institutionalising restructuration regimes then, partial sovereign default should be managed by using *ad hoc* instruments designed on the specific case. Second, in order to contain the possible negative consequences of a sovereign default the monetary union should be equipped with some instruments, i.e. full banking union, a common budgetary instruments and stronger ESM, which would contain the possible

[180]Zettelmeyer (2018), pp. 72–73.

[181]Fuest et al. (2016), p. 303.

[182]'European Safe Bonds' (ESBies) were proposed by Brunnermeier. The aim of this project is to replace the sovereign bonds of Eurozone governments that are currently in use as safe assets with new Eurozone safe assets. On the technical feature of the proposal See Brunnermeier et al. (2016b).

[183]Panizza (2013), p. 6.

[184]Zettelmeyer (2018), pp. 75–76.

[185]For this reason, the restructuration of Greek debt in March 2012 was presented an as 'unique and exceptional' event. Wyplosz (2014), p. 2.

destabilisation of the rest of the euro area, as well as excessive economic and social distress in the concerned Member States. The development of these instruments, however, would require some form of fiscal centralisation in the euro area.

5.5.4 Decentralisation and the Deficit of Democracy

Faced with the need to provide the economic governance with stronger democratic accountability and re-establish a relationship of trust between European citizens and European authority, the surveillance model does not offer a solution, but poses on the contrary some unresolved challenges. In fact, the recent experience analysed in the previous chapter has substantially proven that the surveillance on national fiscal sovereignty does necessarily imply a surveillance of national democracy. The stricter the supervision on national economic policy, the tighter external control on national parliamentary autonomy. It is not a coincidence that the loss of trust in the process of European integration, and in particular in the project of single currency started only after the sovereign debt crisis broke out and EU decisions have been implemented at national level to deal with it. More precisely, until the constrictions of European economic coordination were loosened, nobody imagined that the process of economic and monetary integration could have undermined national democracy. Today, instead, many people living in the Eurozone, realise that they don't have a say on those European rules, which influence the tax they pay, the labour law they shall comply with, and the social services they receive in their country.[186] The perception is that decisions are taken by bureaucrats in Brussels, who are not accountable to the citizens. This has also been facilitated by national political forces, who have turned the European Union into a scapegoat for all the austerity measures, citizens had to accept over the last few years in order to implement structural reforms and consolidate public finances in their country.

In this regard, some authors suggested that the weakening of national democracy can be balanced by involving domestic parliaments in the decision-making process at European level, which regulates surveillance. This approach would represent the logical upgrade of the interinstitutional dialogue. National parliaments do already have the right to ask information and interrogation to the bodies in charge of the economic governance, even if they don't take part in the decision-making process. A possible step forward to preserve national democracy in the reformed surveillance model may be passing from inter-institutional dialogue to some form of co-decision. In reality, despite the good faith of these proposals, it should be doubted, domestic assemblies may be in a better position than national governments to take care of the European interdependence and common interest.[187] This is particularly true in

[186]On the impact of MoUs on domestic policies cf. Ioannidis (2016), p. 1266.

[187]On the inability of national politics to consider and incorporate existing European interdependence cf. Maduro (2012), pp. 5–6.

regard to the pursuit of the stability of the euro area as a whole, which is an objective transcending the narrow perspective of national authorities. As long as their legitimation comes from national community, domestic parliaments will not be able to acknowledge and put forward stability in an effective way, at least not better than what national governments are already doing.[188] Evidently, the problem is that the governance will remain 'inter-state' regardless of the fact that the national representation in the EU is expressed by the executive or the legislative of the country.[189] In both situations, national authorities, either parliaments or governments, will act *uti singuli*, thus making difficult to acknowledge and efficiently pursue a common good, such as stability. In other words, the rise of intergovernamentalism can't be corrected simply through a democratisation of national representations in the governance.[190] The solution should instead be giving more responsibility to supranational bodies acting *uti universi*, in particular the European Parliament, which may enjoy a better perspective to balance the different national interests and identify some possible compromise. The empowerment of supranational bodies on policies falling in the exclusive competence of Member States remains nevertheless difficult. Once again, the existing functioning of governance is based on a fundamental paradox, according to which the perpetration of national fiscal competence in the hands of Member States is essentially a *fictio*, as domestic parliament cannot act independently anymore, while European democratic institutions are not allowed to make any decision.

5.6 Challenges of Fiscal Centralisation

5.6.1 What Does It Mean Building a Fiscal Union?

In the light of the structural limits of the decentralised model of economic union, most proposals of reform of the EMU have endorsed a different approach based on the centralisation of powers and resources at European level in a way to create some form of fiscal union.[191] As the previous analysis has already explained, the latter

[188] A stronger role of national parliament in the governance makes sense in a surveillance model, while in the case of a stronger fiscal integration, democratic accountability should be ensured at European level. Hinarejos (2015), p. 164.

[189] Cf. Daniele (2009), p. 54; Triggiani (2010), p. 29.

[190] During the sovereign debt crisis, for example, both the German parliament and the Greek parliament demanded to be the 'sole responsible' for the management of the crisis. Ioannidis (2016), p. 1278. Democratic constituencies during the crisis proved being 'parochial', Ibid. p. 1279.

[191] Weber considers it as a budgetary union provided with wide powers of intervention, which *de facto* reduce the importance of national budgets; the latter would be, at least partially, replaced by a common budget. Weber (2013), p. 376. De Streel identified different options to centralise fiscal policies at European level: a budget set up between the Member States with insurance characteristics and stabilisation functions, a common employment benefit scheme for the labour market or the common issuance of sovereign bonds. De Streel (2014), p. 103. Fuest and Peichl noticed that different forms of fiscal union are possible depending on the level of integration desired by the

project is based on the establishment of a common authority in charge of stabilisation or consolidation policies thank to the mobilisation of resources across the Eurozone. This result should be pursued not only by strengthening the existing mechanisms of stabilisation (i.e. ESM), but also creating new common instruments to foster convergence between the Member States (i.e. budgetary capacity of the euro area) and reversing the intergovernmental drift of the governance through a (partial) incorporation of separate agreements, such as the TESM and the TSCG, in EU law. Evidently, in order to succeed, the project of fiscal union must be built on a solid trust between the Members States and ensure an efficient balance between financial solidarity and fiscal responsibility. Indeed, while governments are called to share the risks of the stability of the union, they should not take advantage of their partners and perform moral hazard behaviours. At the same time the (partial) shift of fiscal powers from national to European level would require setting up stronger accountability mechanisms.

The process of fiscal centralisation would profoundly innovate the economic union by emancipating it from the original model outlined in the Maastricht Treaty. While this may help solve the longstanding deficits of the governance identified in the previous chapter, the implementation of the project of fiscal union shall also take into consideration a number of legal challenges.

5.6.2 Centralisation and the Deficit of Legality

5.6.2.1 Is It Possible to Develop a Genuine European Fiscal Instrument?

5.6.2.1.1 EU Law and Fiscal Sovereignty

As it has been already mentioned a number of occasions, the current formulation of the EU Treaties does not allow the Union to develop any form of fiscal rights. The EU does not have the power of revenue and spending and art. 2(3) TFEU conceive economic policy only in terms of coordination.[192] Even interpreting art. 113 TFEU on the harmonisation of national tax law in the widest sense possible,[193] perhaps in

---

participating Member States. Accordingly, a fiscal union may consist of coordination and supervision on national budgetary polices (Maastricht model), the setup of a crisis resolution mechanism to avoid sovereign default (ESM model) or organise an orderly debt restructuration, the creation of joint guarantees for government debt, the setup of a transfer mechanism between countries or even the establishment of a larger budget and common taxes. Fuest and Peichl (2012), pp. 2–7.

[192]Hinarejos (2012), pp. 259–260.

[193]Art. 113 TFEU applies only to the harmonisation of indirect taxation. The provision has been used for the adoption of several directives on the collection of VAT and excise duties. Cf. Council Directive 92/84/EEC of 19 October 1992 on the approximation of the rates of excise duty on alcohol and alcoholic beverages (1992) OJ L 316/29; Council Directive 2003/96/EC of 27 October 2003 restructuring the Community framework for the taxation of energy products and electricity, (2003) OJ L 283/51; Council Directive 2008/118/EC of 16 December 2008 concerning the general

conjunction with art. 136 TFEU or the flexibility clause as per art. 352 TFEU,[194] the setup of genuine European taxes would clash with the principle of conferral. Things may change only through a Treaty amendment.[195]

The lack of a genuine European power of taxation can be better understood looking at the meaning of 'own resources' on which the EU budget is based. Correctly the Monti report considers them as 'revenue allocated irrevocably to the Union to finance its budget and accruing to it automatically without the need for any subsequent decision by the national authorities'.[196] Within the current system, it should be distinguished between traditional own resources, such as sugar levies and external tariffs, and the VAT- and the GNI-based own resources. Traditional own resources are related to policies regulated by EU law, their financial incidence can't be attributed to one country, and they are almost entirely versed in the EU budget. Even if Member States are in charge of their collection and for this reason retain a share of 20%, traditional own resources are not accounted for as an expenditure item in national budgets, but only as a receipt attributed to the EU.[197] Different considerations should be given instead to the VAT- and the GNI-based own resources. The latter do not depend on a common European policy, but consist of statistical aggregates. Consequently, these resources are taken from the body of general income in national budgets, which makes them qualify as an expenditure item.[198] Beyond these important distinctions, whatever kind they are, own resources are not an expression of a European tax competence. Indeed, the power to collect them and decide their allocation belongs with the Member States. For this reason, EU institutions would not be able to receive 'own resources' without the collaboration of national authorities. Technically, before being owned by the EU, the resources have been owned by the Member States. It is possible then to identify some form of transfer between the Member States and the Union, especially in regard to the VAT- and the GNI-based own resources, which at the moment represent most of the revenues of the EU budget.

---

arrangements for excise duty and repealing Directive 92/12/EEC, (2008) OJ L 9/12. According to Fabbrini, art. 113 TFEU may provide a sufficient legal basis for the setup of a taxing power together with art. 311 TFEU on the 'own resources'. See Fabbrini (2016), pp. 166–167.

[194]See Tosato (2016), p. 236. The use of the flexibility clause is doubtful as it may be used for *ad hoc* measures, not the transfer of fiscal sovereignty to the Member States. See Hinarejos (2012), p. 261. The German Constitutional Court expressly said that the flexibility clause cannot be interpreted as an unrestricted competence to extend competences and that art. 311 TFEU does not go beyond the current provision on the procurement of own resources. German Federal Constitutional Court, Judgment, 30 June 2009, [2 BvE 2/08], para. 142.

[195]See Hinarejos (2015), pp. 187–188; Brauneck (2018), p. 86.

[196]High-Level Group on Own Resources (2016), p. 22. For this reason, the own resources are similar to the fiscal revenues Member States allocate to decentralized regions or smaller geographical entities so that they can take care of certain functions. Ibid. p. 20.

[197]Ibid. p. 22.

[198]Ibid. p. 23.

The lack of a European power of taxation does not mean that the EU cannot influence the management of national fiscal policies in order to achieve the objectives outlined in the Treaties. This happens, more precisely, in three ways. The first source of influence is represented by the construction of the single market. Art. 113 TFEU allows the Council to harmonise domestic indirect taxation in order to ensure the correct functioning of the internal market and avoid distortions on competition.[199] For the same purpose, the CJEU has introduced some limits to the national management of tax law, when the latter is used in a way to violate EU law on free circulation or antitrust.[200] The second source of influence consists of the protection of fundamental rights, as protection in the EU Treaties and the EUCFRs. National tax law shall be consistent with the fundamental rights and principles protected in EU law, including equality, right of property, right to a fair trial, right to a good administration, prohibition of the abuse of law.[201] The last important source of influence on national tax law is clearly the economic governance. Art. 2 (3), art. 5 and art. 119 TFEU foresee the Union can coordinate national budgetary policies, this being functional, as explained by the CJEU in Pringle, to the pursuit of the stability of the euro area as a whole.

5.6.2.1.2 Limits of the Legal Basis

In the light of the analysis developed so far, the setup of a budgetary capacity counting on its own revenues and having its own spending targets must necessarily exclude the creation of European fiscal rights. A similar ambition may be satisfied only through an overall reform of the EU Treaties. Once excluded this option for political reasons, the establishment of a budgetary capacity for the euro area must comply with the current EU legal framework, which acknowledges the exclusive fiscal competence of the Member States. Evidently, as it was explained in the previous chapters, the margins of manoeuvre offered by the EU Treaties for the reform of the economic union are extremely tight. Significant projects can be implemented only in two ways: either stretching the available legal basis as much as possible or recurring to separate agreements beyond EU law.

---

[199] A common corporate tax base could be introduced on the basis of the test for the correct use of art. 113 TFEU defined by the ECJ in the Tobacco Advertising case. Judgment of the ECJ of 5 October 2000, Case C-376/98 Germany v EP and Council (Tobacco Advertising), ECLI:EU:C:2000:544. See Hinarejos (2012), p. 261.

[200] For example, in the Halifax and Cardbury Schweppes the ECJ said that a company can't move to a Member State to another for tax reasons if the economic activity is not also moving (fictitious transfer). See Judgment of the Court of 21 February 2006, Case C-255/02, *Halifax plc, Leeds Permanent Development Services Ltd and County Wide Property Investments Ltd v Commissioners of Customs & Excise,* ECLI:EU:C:2006:121; Judgment of the Court of 12th September 2006, Case C-196/04, Cadbury Schweppes plc and Cadbury Schweppes Overseas Ltd v Commissioners of Inland Revenue, ECLI:EU:C:2006:544. For a wider analysis of the relevant case law on the matter cf. Rossolillo (2018), pp. 127–138.

[201] Bizioli and Sacchetto (2016), p. 18.

The most reasonable option is clearly to establish the budgetary instrument for the euro area within the EU budget.[202] This is notably what the governments of the euro area have agreed on, when they recently decided to create the budgetary instrument for convergence and competitiveness (BICC).[203] The legal basis for this reform is art. 312 TFEU on the Multiannual Financial Framework (MFF). The latter will determine the size of the instrument, as well as the exact expenditures it will be in charge of. The introduction of new own resources to finance the budgetary instrument may require the use of art. 311 TFEU. If the budgetary instrument was financed also with a common financial transaction tax or a consolidated corporate tax base, another available legal basis could be art. 113 TFEU regarding the harmonisation of national tax legislation.[204] The main obstacle of creating a budgetary instrument within the euro area is the fulfilment of the unanimity rule requested by the relevant legal basis. Indeed, both reforms of the own resources systems and the MFF require the consensus of all the EU governments.[205]

In the event that reforming the EU budget was politically impossible, the Eurozone countries might create a separate fund within the EU legal framework as a derogation to the principle of unity of the EU budget as per art. 310(1) TFEU.[206] Some scholars identified a possible legal basis in art. 136(1) TFEU on the enhanced economic coordination within the Eurozone, possibly in connection with art. 122(2) TFEU on the solidarity clause and the flexibility clause ex art. 352 TFEU.[207] Technically, another possible way to create a budgetary

---

[202] In the Commission proposal, the stabilisation function shall be granted in three complementary ways: (i) the ESM/EMF could play a role of back-office to the stabilisation function by providing precautionary loans to deliver short-term liquidity support; (ii) the EU budget could provide some limited annually budget grant support to the Member States concerned. This would be a limited budget line as part of ESIF; this budgetary line would feed every year into the stabilization function to help build up its capital; (iii) an insurance mechanism based on voluntary Member States' contributions could complement the grant support of the stabilisation function over time. Cf. - European Commission Communication (2017b).

[203] See *supra* Sect. 5.3.3.4.3.

[204] Other useful legal basis may be art. 173 TFEU on the competitiveness of the industry and art. 182 TFEU on research and technological development and art. 175(3) TFEU on specific actions outside the structural funds.. For the possible use of art. 175(3) TFEU cf. European Commission Staff Working Document (2018), p. 23.

[205] Cafaro (2017), p. 79.

[206] Considering the possible setup of a euro area budget within the EU legal system, it is important to add the premise that there are no provisions in the existing treaties that expressly forbid this option. Article 310 (1) TFEU on the unity of the budget is not an absolute principle, as there are several EU bodies counting on their own separate resources, notably the European Investment Bank, the European Central Bank and the European Development Fund. These bodies, however, either have an independent legal personality (ECB, EIB) or their expenditure is referred to the Member States (EDF). See Repasi (2013), pp. 12–17.

[207] Allard et al. (2013), p. 24; Tosato suggests either the use of art. 352 TFEU or a simplified treaty amendment ex art. 48 (6) TEU. Tosato (2016), p. 236.

instrument bypassing the unanimity rule might be to use art. 20 TEU on enhanced cooperation.[208] The creation of a separate budgetary capacity through this procedure might be eased by the fact that art. 332 TFEU acknowledges that an enhanced cooperation may require its own expenditures and these shall be normally borne by the participating Member States. In this regard, it should be noted that art. 20 TEU has already been used to try and introduce a Financial Transaction Tax (FTT) directive.[209]

Looking at other possible legal basis, the EU Treaties do not offer much room for manoeuvre. As it was anticipated, an alternative option remains the conclusion of a separate agreement, similar to the Fiscal Compact model or the TESM. Such a solution would have a number of practical advantages, but it would also bring some lingering legal problems. On the one hand, it would be possible to create some form of budgetary instruments bypassing the unanimity rule in the Council and the European Council. Furthermore, national parliaments may have a stronger and clearer control on the allocation of resources and the definition of the spending mechanism, as they would be called to ratify the agreement. At the same time, such an option would also strengthen the 'intergovernmental drift' of the governance and present the well-known problems regarding transparency, consistency with EU law and EU-wide democratic control.

5.6.2.1.3 Compliance with the Principle of No Bailout

Due to the limits of the legal basis, the creation of a budgetary instrument for the euro area does naturally raise some questions regarding the consistency with the existing EU legal framework. The first provision it could clash with is the no bailout clause ex art. 125 TFEU, according to which the Union and the Member States shall not be liable for or assume the commitments of any other EU country.[210]

Notably, the no bailout clause does represent a major obstacle to the process of fiscal centralisation. This has already emerged in regard to the setup of the ESM, due to the implicit 'bailing out function' of the mechanism.[211] In the Pringle case, the Court managed to excogitate a reconciliation between the ESM and the no bailout clause through an eclectic legal reasoning built in three steps: (i) the ESM does not assume the existing obligations of the Member States, but only provides loans; (ii) the ESM financial assistance based on the principle of conditionality fosters budgetary discipline in the Member States, thus pursuing the same immediate

[208]European Commission Communication (2012), p. 22. On the issue see also Fabbrini (2016), p. 169; Cafaro (2017), p. 80.

[209]On 14 February 2013, the European Commission made a proposal for a Council Directive implementing enhanced cooperation on a Financial Transaction Tax (FTT) following the request by 11 Member States. The directive is based on art. 113 TFEU. The tax would apply to financial transactions between two parties, one of which is a financial institution established in a participating Member State. See Hinarejos (2015), pp. 107–108.

[210]Pilz (2017), p. 641.

[211]See *supra* Sect. 4.2.4.2.

objective of the no bailout clause; (iii) both the ESM and the no bailout clause aim to ensure the stability of the euro area as a whole. Evidently, the legal reasoning of the Pringle judgment cannot fully apply to the setup of budgetary instrument of the euro area, as the latter presents different features from the ESM: it may not provide loans, but transfers; it does not work as a last resort mechanism, but as an ordinary tool in charge of fostering convergence; the application of conditionality may be less stringent, as it would require compliance only with some eligibility criteria defined *ex ante*.[212] In the light of these differences, the consistency of the creation of a Eurozone budget with the no bailout clause can be justified on the basis of two arguments.

First of all, the EU legal framework does not forbid transfers *ex se*. The latter are already present within the framework of the European cohesion policy (European Regional Development Fund, the European Social Fund and the Cohesion Fund). Indeed, as it was already explained, with the exception of traditional own resources, most of the capitals, which accrue in the EU budget come from national budgets. This fact has never caused any problem of consistency with the no bailout clause, nor any other provisions of EU law.[213] Indeed, the transfers provided by the EU budget are limited in size,[214] as resources dedicated to the cohesion policy are almost €50 billion annually.[215] More importantly, the EU budget does not imply the assumption of previous liabilities or the sharing of existing obligations, but it aims to mutualise resources for the investment in common objectives. Accordingly, every country is exposed only for its share of contributions to the budget and is not taking risks for or together with other countries. In accordance with this analysis, as long as the euro area budget has a quantified size and does not imply any mutualisation of previous obligations, it should be consistent with the no bailout clause.[216]

Second, the consistency with the no bailout clause can be justified by considering that the budgetary instrument for the euro area would pursue the objective of the stability of the euro area as a whole. Evidently, this goal is not going to be achieved through emergency financial assistance, as the ESM does, but by fostering economic convergence in ordinary times. This will happen not only through the disbursement of resources for the financing of structural reforms and public investments, but also by requesting compliance with the eligibility criteria in order to benefit from the budgetary instrument.[217] Following the legal reasoning of the CJEU in the Pringle Judgment, as both the budgetary capacity and art. 125 TFEU have the same ultimate objective, there should be no substantial incompatibility.

---

[212]See *supra* Sect. 5.3.3.4.1.

[213]The European Cohesion Policy already provides for the transfer of resources between Member States through a central authority. See Tuori and Tuori (2014), p. 255.

[214]Brauneck (2018), p. 82.

[215]€351.8 billions were set aside for cohesion policy measures in the 28 EU Member States within the MFF 2014–2020.

[216]See *supra* Sect. 4.2.4.4.

[217]Pilz (2017), p. 641.

In the light of these considerations, the creation of an additional budgetary capacity would reduce the scope of art. 125 TFEU even further. The only lasting prohibition coming from the no bailout clause may regard the mutualisation of existing debts or the creation of a new common debt. Accordingly, it is unlikely the euro area budget may be financed on the market through the issue of common bonds.[218]

5.6.2.1.4 The Limits of the Principle of Conferral

The establishment of a budgetary capacity for the Eurozone may also clash with the principle of conferral, according to which competences that are not conferred upon the Union by the EU Treaties must remain with the Member States and the Union cannot directly or indirectly decide in their regard. Even if the EU Treaties could offer a sufficient legal basis for the setup of the euro area budget, the latter could still undermine the principle of conferral by influencing the development of several other policies that Member States did not intend to share with the EU.

Tax policy will be obviously the first one to be impacted. Indeed, independently from its concrete implementation, the Eurozone budgetary instrument will have the capacity to collect resources and spend them, thus making countries and their citizens, either net contributors or recipients. Considering for example the revenue side, this would happen both if the mechanism was fuelled by national contributions or through new genuine own resources: in the first case, national budgets would have to bear a cost; in the second scenario Member States would be deprived of resources, which could have been collected nationally. The development of the budgetary capacity for the euro area would have an impact more in general on the *macro-economic development* of the participating countries. For example, the creation of a common fund for investments would be able to support structural reforms and/or public goods in the Member States as to make national economic policies converge. In this way, the budgetary capacity would influence all the policies, it will be able to finance. Evidently, this phenomenon will be more relevant for those countries presenting economic difficulties, which might be more dependent on European investments. In the event the budgetary instrument for the euro area assumed the form of an unemployment insurance scheme, *labour policies* of Member States would be considerably conditioned. This would happen not only for the standardisation of social protection, but also for the necessary harmonisation of national labour law that the creation of a common unemployment benefit would require.[219]

---

[218]See Tuori and Tuori (2014), p. 255. This is something that has already happened in regard to the EFSM, which was backed by the EU budget, as well as the EFSF and the ESM. This mutualisation of risks for the financing of common mechanism may represent a violation of the no bailout clause.

[219]In regard to labour law and working conditions, art. 156 TFEU states that the Commission shall only encourage cooperation between the Member States and facilitate the coordination of their

These examples prove how fiscal centralisation, whatever form it may assume, will have an impact on the principle of conferral according to the implicit axiom by which whomever has the resources, holds the power. As correctly noticed by Hinarejos, a mechanism deciding on the transfer of resources between European countries would in fact modify the division of competences between the Member States and the Union. Among all powers, fiscal authority is indeed the closest to the *Kompetenz-Kompetenz*, because it determines, how many resources are available for the management of the other competences. If the EU was able to autonomously allocate resources, the distinction between EU and Member States' competences would be blurred.[220] In this way, the development of some form of fiscal federalism in the EMU would undermine the conferral principle, thus producing similar effects to the strengthening of the surveillance model, according to which the EU has full control on how Member States manage their budgetary policy.[221]

In the light of this analysis, it is not surprising that the process of fiscal integration in the euro area has raised the concerns of national constitutional courts. A particular role was played in this regard by the German Federal Constitutional Court (GFCC). As tax competence represents the core of national statehood, the *Bundesverfassungsgericht* tried to build a barrier to avoid any indirect erosion from European and international law. An effective instrument in this regard has been the concept of *Identitätskontrolle*. More precisely, the GFCC clarified in several judgments that the revenue and expenditure competence is part of the German constitutional identity and its national allocation is unmodifiable due to the eternity clause found in art. 79(3) of the *Grundgesetz*. According to the GFCC, the German parliament must maintain full control over budgetary policies, which cannot, under any circumstances, be transferred to the European level.[222] Consequently, the development of a European fiscal sovereignty must be ruled out. This interpretation of the German constitution clearly made difficult for the GFCC to authorise the setup of rescue mechanisms, such as the ESM, which seemed

action in all social policy fields. On the possible harmonization of social security systems see Adamski (2018), pp. 167–170.

[220]On the issue see Hinarejos (2012), p. 262; Rossolillo (2018), p. 147.

[221]Cf. *supra* Sect. 5.5.2.

[222]'Fundamental fiscal decisions on public revenue and public expenditure is part of the ability of a constitutional state to democratically shape itself', German Federal Constitutional Court, Judgment, 30 June 2009, [2 BvE 2/08], para. 252: 'A transfer of the right of the Bundestag to adopt the budget and control its implementation by the government which would violate the principle of democracy and the right to elect the German Bundestag in its essential content would occur if the determination of the type and amount of the levies imposed on the citizen were supranationalised to a considerable extent. The German Bundestag must decide, in an accountable manner vis-à-vis the people, on the total amount of the burdens placed on citizens. The same applies correspondingly to essential state expenditure.' (para 256)'. The same principle was reaffirmed in German Federal Constitutional Court, Judgment of 7 September 2011 [2 BvR 987/10], para. 101, 104; German Federal Constitutional Court, Judgment of 12 September 2012, [2 BvR 1390/12], para. 106–107. The transfer of fiscal competences to the EU would constitute an *ultra vires* act and a violation of Germany's constitutional identity.

triggering a process of fiscal centralisation in the euro area. The Court has eventually acknowledged their consistency with the *Grundgesetz* (GG), but it made the participation of Germany conditional to a number of criteria.[223] First, the Parliament must individually authorise every large-scale aid measure provided by the ESM. The government has to receive in particular the approval of the *Bundestag* before authorising financial support in the Council.[224] Second, the financial exposure of Germany to the mechanism must be limited *ex ante* and be proportional to the size of the national budget.[225] The liability of Germany to the European rescue mechanisms therefore cannot be increased without the authorisation of the *Bundestag*. Third, it must be ensured that there is sufficient parliamentary influence on the manner in which the funds made available are dealt with. The *Bundestag* must therefore be constantly informed of the implementation of financial assistance.[226]

The natural dissatisfaction shown by the *Bundesverfassungsgericht* and possibly by other Constitutional Courts[227] to the erosion of national fiscal competence does not mean, however, that any implementation of the Eurozone budgetary capacity should automatically be shelved. Much will depend on how this tool will be set up in practice. Focusing on the several proposals put forward so far, notably the conditional incentives for convergence and competitiveness, the common unemployment insurance and the 'rainy-day' fund, their creation does not necessarily require a transfer of genuine fiscal rights to the European level. More precisely, as long as the financing and the activation of the additional budgetary capacity respects the following conditions, national fiscal sovereignty will remain unimpeded.

First, the budgetary capacity can't be financed by taxes, but only through national contributions or a new system of own resources. The latter are particularly suitable for the current proposal because they can provide a stable and potentially significant

---

[223] Nettesheim identifies five requirements for the participation in the mechanism: prohibition of external determination (*Verbot der Fremdbestimmung*), determination of the financial exposure (*Bestimmtheit*), calculability of financial consequences of participation (*Begrenztheit und Übersehbarkeit der Folgewirkung*), possibility to manage the participation and withdraw it (*Steuerbarkeit /Umkehrbarkeit*), sustainability of the financial effort (*Verhältnismäßigkeit der absoluten Belastungshöhe*). See Nettesheim (2011), pp. 772–777.

[224] German Federal Constitutional Court, Judgment of 7 September 2011 [2 BvR 987/10], para. 128.

[225] 'The German Bundestag may not transfer its budgetary responsibility to other actors by means of imprecise budgetary authorisations. In particular it may not, even by statute, deliver itself up to any mechanisms with financial effect which—whether by reason of their overall conception or by reason of an overall evaluation of the individual measures—may result in incalculable burdens with budget relevance without prior mandatory consent, whether these are expenses or losses of revenue'. German Federal Constitutional Court, Judgment of 7 September 2011 [2 BvR 987/10], para. 125.

[226] '[T]he German Bundestag participates in the further execution of the statutes merely in the form of giving information to the budget committee'. German Federal Constitutional Court, Judgment of 7 September 2011 [2 BvR 987/10], para. 139.

[227] On the position of other constitutional courts on the matter see Fabbrini (2016), pp. 68–89.

source of revenue, which would bypass the need for proper European taxes.[228] Therefore, as long as national parliaments agree on the payment of contributions to the budgetary capacity or the setup of new own resources, their fiscal sovereignty will remain intact.[229] Evidently, the resources conferred to the budgetary capacity must be quantified *ex ante*.

Second, the activation of the budgetary instrument should comply with technical standards. This means that it should provide resources only once some pre-identified eligibility criteria have come into existence, proving the need for investments or stabilization. Such conditions might regard, for example, the unemployment rate, economic downturns, difficulties with the balance of payments or low competitiveness. Furthermore, national parliaments must be fully involved in deciding the conditions under which the budgetary capacity will operate and resources will be distributed. Once defined the mandate and the rules of procedure of the budgetary capacity, the latter may be either managed by a EU body, such as the Commission or the Eurogroup, and operate in accordance with the technical assessment of an independent authority.[230]

Finally, the decision to take part in the project of additional budgetary capacity must be voluntary. Although the activation of the mechanism will depend on compliance with some eligibility criteria, the disbursement of resources will also need an autonomous and unbiased request by the concerned Member States. This means that European institutions cannot oblige a country to access the mechanism, but only make sure that it respects the rules of participation.[231]

For the moment, the recent project of Budgetary Instrument for Convergence and Competitiveness (BICC) adopted by the Eurogroup in June 2019 seems fully consistent with all the previous conditions,[232] thus leaving the distribution of competences between the Union and the Member States essentially unscathed. Evidently, the gradual development of a fully-fledged fiscal capacity of the Eurozone may instead undermine the conferral principle and make eventually necessary some important constitutional reforms in the Member States.

---

[228]See High-Level Group on Own Resources (2016), p. 27; Fabbrini (2016), p. 164. The German Constitutional Court has ruled out that the own resources are incompatible with the *Grundgesetz*, as they are decided by the Member States and 'art. 311 TFEU does not empower the EU to provide itself by its own authority with the financial means and other resources it considered necessary for the fulfilment of its objectives'. German Federal Constitutional Court, Judgment, 30 June 2009, [2 BvE 2/08], para. 323.

[229]Pilz (2017), p. 643.

[230]A newly European fiscal board, should monitor the effective existence of these conditions and the correct functioning of the transfer mechanism. Cf. Explanatory Statement of the European Parliament Resolution (2017), pp. 23–24. On the role of expert bodies in the economic governance see Tuori and Tuori (2014), p. 221.

[231]This condition is meant to be respected in the project of BICC as resources for investment and reforms will be granted on request of the Member States.

[232]See *supra* Sect. 5.3.3.4.3.

5.6.2.2 What Space for the Incorporation of Intergovernmental Instrument in EU Law?

5.6.2.2.1 The Meaning of Incorporation

The previous chapters have explained how the deepening of the crisis obliged Member States to implement some significant reforms of the governance through intergovernmental mechanisms beyond EU law. This was considered necessary in order to bypass the limits of the legal basis and the political impasse following the unanimity rule in the reform of the treaties. Once the emergency was over, however, European institutions made the incorporation of intergovernmental instruments in EU law a new priority. Notably, the European Commission has proposed a Regulation for the transformation of the ESM into a European Monetary Fund (EMF) under EU law and a Directive transposing some contents of the Fiscal Compact.[233] In order to understand the legal implication of this operation, it is important to provide some clarification of the meaning of 'incorporation in EU law'. The latter process essentially consists of turning a legal provision from a source of law to another, in this case from an intergovernmental treaty to an act of EU law. Accordingly, the obligations coming from a source of law are terminated and they are recreated by another source of law.[234] It is important to highlight that incorporation in EU law does not necessarily imply a genuine transfer of sovereignty from the Member States to the Union. For example, in the case of the creation of the EMF proposed by the Commission, the Member States would remain essentially the owners of the resources and of the decision-making process, even if the Council would be formally involved in the activation of the mechanism in order to comply with the Meroni doctrine.[235] Incorporation clearly aims to reverse the 'flight into international law of the governance', which has caused so far several legal issues, such as the lack of transparency and efficiency of the decision-making process, weak democratic accountability towards the European parliament, weak jurisdictional control of the CJEU, and violation of the principle of institutional balance.

In order to pursue incorporation, the most logical solution would be to trigger art. 48 TEU to start a process of Treaty reform. The measures introduced with the external treaties are indeed so relevant, that they should deserve a full acknowledgement in primary law. Regardless this fact, both EU institutions and national governments have resisted so far the idea of a treaty change for at least two reasons. First, as most measures regard specifically the Member States that have introduced the single currency, it would be difficult to reform by unanimity the EU legal framework in a way as to formalise the special level of integration achieved in the euro area. Second,

[233]European Commission Proposal for a Regulation (2017) and European Commission Proposal for a Directive (2017).

[234]From the point of view of international law, it consists of a succession of treaties relating to the same subject-matter. This phenomenon is regulated by art. 30 VCLT.

[235]See *supra* note 155.

governments and EU institutions don't believe there is at the moment the sufficient popular consensus to call the necessary national referendum in several Member States for a treaty reform by unanimity. In the light of these difficulties, it has been necessary to consider other options to introduce the ESM and the TSCG in EU law.

5.6.2.2.2 The Incorporation of the TESM

Considering the possible incorporation of the ESM in EU law through the establishment of a European Monetary Fund (EMF), the Commission suggested to use the flexibility clause ex art. 352 TFEU.[236] The latter provision notably allows the Council acting by unanimity after obtaining the consent of the EU Parliament to adopt an action, which is not foreseen among the powers conferred to the Union, but is necessary to attain one of the objectives set out in the Treaties. The Commission motivated the choice of art. 352 TFEU on the basis of the Pringle Judgment, which may have implicitly acknowledged the existence of all conditions for its activation: (i) there is no specific legal basis in the Treaty for the creation of a ESM within the EU legal framework, as art. 136(3) TFEU recognises only for the Member States, and not for the Union the possibility to set up a mechanism of this kind; (ii) the measure introduced with the flexibility clause fall within the framework of the EU policies; (iii) the ESM aims to achieve an objective of the EU Treaty, namely the 'stability of the euro area as a whole'.[237]

Contrary to these arguments, the possible use of art. 352 TFEU for the incorporation of the ESM in EU law has been also criticised. Some noticed that art. 352 TFEU requires the unanimity of Member States in the Council and is meant to introduce measures regarding the EU as a whole, while the project of EMF is only relevant to the Member States of the euro area.[238] The criticism is understandable even if it should be highlighted that the stability of the euro area as a whole pursued by the EMF is indirectly also an interest for the other EU Member States, which don't share the single currency. Others criticised the fact that art. 352 TFEU can be used only once proved that EU law is needed to achieve an objective of the Union. As the current intergovernmental framework does already pursue the stability of the euro area, despite all its difficulties, it may be difficult to

---

[236]The Commission noticed that the flexibility clause had been used several times already in the -process of economic and monetary integration: i.e. decisions on the European Monetary Cooperation Fund, the European Currency Unit and the first balance of payment mechanisms. See Explanatory Memorandum of European Commission Proposal for a Regulation (2017), p. 5.

[237]See Explanatory Memorandum of European Commission Proposal for a Regulation (2017), p. 11. In the Pringe Judgment the Court did not exclude the application of art. 352 TFEU for the use of a permanent mechanism. It simply acknowledged that such a decision has not been adopted by the EU institutions. Cf. ECJ Judgment of 27 November 2012, Case C-370/12, *Thomas Pringle v Government of Ireland*, ECLI:EU:C:2012:756, para 67.

[238]Brauneck (2018), p. 83.

explain why incorporation in EU law is necessary to achieve the same objective.[239] Finally, it should be noted that art. 136(3) TFEU clearly affirms that granting the stability of the euro area as a whole through conditional financial assistance is a task for the Member States, not for the Union. If the EMF wants to be the successor of the ESM, it may be necessary to amend the treaty by deleting the express conferral of competence to the Member States outlined in art. 136(3) TFEU.[240] Aside from these legal considerations, the main obstacle to the application of the flexibility clause for the incorporation of the ESM in EU law remains the unanimity rule, which regulates its activation. In this regard, the use of art. 352 TFEU poses the same challenges of a Treaty amendment ex art. 48 TEU.

In the light of these criticisms, other authors suggested to use enhanced cooperation for the incorporation of the ESM in EU law.[241] Unlike the flexibility clause, this provision may be activated by the qualified majority of the Council, thus bypassing the risk of veto rights. Regardless of this undeniable advantage, the use of art. 20 TEU does also present some problems. In the Pringle Judgment, the Court clarified that enhanced cooperation may be established only where the Union itself is competent to act within the area concerned.[242] So art. 20 TEU does allow the application of an existing shared competence in a legislative project involving only a group of Member States, but does not authorise the conferral of new powers to the Union. Even if the stability of the Eurozone as a whole is an objective of the economic union, the EU Treaties seem recognising that only Member States have the power to create a mechanism like the ESM. Schwartz tried to find a legal solution to this problem by recalling that conditionality aims to ensure compliance with the rules of economic coordination, which is notably a competence of the EU.[243] As conditionality represents some form of economic surveillance and pursues the same ends of the EDP, it should be possible to use art. 20 TEU for incorporating the mechanism in EU law. At the same time, as it was already recalled, the ownership of the resources under the EMF would remain with the Member States, thus limiting the risk of transferring sovereign competences.

5.6.2.2.3 The Incorporation of the TSCG

Art. 16 TSCG prescribes the incorporation of the Fiscal Compact in EU law within 5 years since its entry into force. The latter process doesn't present particular legal problematics. Notably the Commission has proposed to translate some norms of the Fiscal Compact in a Directive to be adopted on the basis of the second subparagraph

[239] Editorial Comment (2018), pp. 712–713.

[240] Brauneck (2018), pp. 83–84.

[241] Schwarz (2014), p. 221*;* Lo Schiavo (2017a), pp. 143–144.

[242] See ECJ Judgment of 27 November 2012, Case C-370/12, *Thomas Pringle v Government of Ireland*, ECLI:EU:C:2012:756, para 167.

[243] Schwarz (2014), pp. 411–412.

of art. 126(14) TFEU.[244] The latter states that the Council shall, on a proposal from the Commission and after consulting the European Parliament, lay down detailed rules and definitions for the application of the provisions of the Protocol on the EDP annexed to the Treaties.[245] Accordingly, art. 3 of the Draft Directive aims to amend the SGP by recalling several norms of the Fiscal Compact, which are relevant for the activation and implementation of the EDP. These are precisely the introduction of a MTO in terms of structural balance that is binding in the budgetary cycle, the setup of an automatic correction mechanism, and the creation of independent fiscal institutions. At the same time, the Draft Directive preferred not to recall art. 7 TSCG on the extension of the RMV to all stages of the EDP probably due to controversies on the compliance with the principle of conferral and institutional balance.[246] Quite regrettably, the choice of art. 126(14) TFEU as a legal basis does not allow the incorporation of other relevant provisions of the Fiscal Compact in EU law, such as the enhanced economic coordination between the participating Member States, the setup of the Euro summit, the rules regarding the reduction of public debt. For this reason, it has been suggested the use of a different legal source for an overall incorporation of the TSCG in EU law, for example enhanced cooperation or art. 136 TFEU.[247]

Aside from the discussions on the most appropriate legal basis, the proposal of the European Commission raises doubts regarding its utility. On the one hand, it is clear that incorporation of an intergovernmental instrument in EU law should help strengthening the effectiveness, accountability and internal coherence of the governance. At the same time, the Directive simply replicates some of the existing obligations under the Fiscal Compact, more precisely those regarding the commitment of Member States to interiorise the balance budget rule in national law. As long as the Commission has already confirmed in an official Report issued in February 2017[248] that all participating Member States have already complied (even if in different ways) with the TSCG, it is not clear what new legal consequences, the directive aims to produce on the domestic legal order.[249] The only immediate change is the way obligations can be enforced: rather than using art. 273 TFEU, the CJEU could be referred on the basis of the ordinary infringement procedure under

[244] European Commission Proposal for a Directive (2017).

[245] Art. 3 of the Protocol on the EDP states that '[t]he Member States shall ensure that national procedures in the budgetary area enable them to meet their obligations in this area deriving from these Treaties'.

[246] Cfr. *Supra* Sect. 4.2.3.

[247] Art. 20 TEU may be used as the norms of the TSCG would fall within the *sui generis* competence of economic coordination ex art. 2(3) TFEU. See Lo Schiavo (2017b). p. 215. Another option may be the use of art. 136 TFEU even if the TSCG was adopted by 25 Member States, while this norm applies only to the countries, whose currency is the euro. Ibid. p. 216. The use of the enhanced surveillance or art. 136 TFEU may also help overcoming the unanimity rule foreseen under art. 126 (14) TFEU. See Croci (2018), p. 7.

[248] European Commission Report (2017).

[249] Editorial Comment (2018), p. 710.

art. 258 TFEU. These consequences, however, remain quite abstracts because the Commission has already certified that Member States have respected the obligations replicated in the Directive. Probably, the Commission is expecting that some countries may undo the national legislation introduced to comply with the Fiscal Compact or that a stricter interpretation of the obligation may be necessary in the future. For this reason, art. 5 of the draft Directive states that by 30 June 2024, and every 5 years thereafter, the Commission shall present a report to the European Parliament and to the Council on the implementation of this Directive.

In general, the incorporation of the TSCG would have made more sense, if it became the occasion to modify some of the contents of the agreement in a way to reduce the deficit of effectiveness highlighted in the previous chapter. Assuming that countries are willing to further strengthening European supervision on national public finances, a more reasonable reform would have been for example centralising the supervision on the effective compliance with numerical fiscal rules in the hands of the existing European Fiscal Board, or fixing stricter rules for the reduction of public debt stocks.

As previously explained, regardless the advantages and weak points of the Draft Directive proposed by the Commission, it looks like there is currently no political consensus to turn it into binding legislation.

5.6.3 *Centralisation and the Deficit of Effectiveness*

5.6.3.1 Size of the Instruments

In order to fulfil the objective of the stability of the euro area as a whole, the instruments of the future fiscal union should be able to mobilise an adequate amount of resources. Even if it is not imaginable to reach the size of federal budgets established within sovereign states,[250] it is necessary to put the European mechanisms in the condition to make the difference in regard to both the pursuit of fiscal consolidation and the implementation of stabilisation policies.

Considering the ESM, the mechanism can count at the moment on a subscribed capital of around €700 billion, which corresponds to a lending capacity of €500 billion. It may be doubted that these numbers are enough to take care of the stability of the euro area as a whole. Aside from the fact that some of these resources have already been spent to ensure the stability of Greece and the banking system of Spain

[250]'Even in the most decentralized federations in our sample (Canada, Switzerland, and the United States), the federal government's own revenue and expenditure represent about half of general government final spending (or 15–20 percent of GDP). This is in sharp contrast with the minimal size of the EU budget—it barely accounts for 2 percent of general government spending (1 percent of EU GDP)'. Cottarelli and Guerguil (2014), p. 4.

and Cyprus,[251] what is more important is that the size of the ESM is at the moment far too small to take into consideration a request of financial support coming from a bigger and over-indebted country (i.e. Italy).[252] Even if new capital calls are always possible, they require the unanimity of Member States, meaning that every government shall agree to take on its shoulders part of another country's (enormous) debt.[253] This would clearly represent a difficult choice, as Member States should decide whether assuming the costs of an expansive bailout or letting the country go bankrupt by accepting the (unpredictable) consequences.

In order to avoid this scenario, while it is at the moment unlikely to emancipate the ESM from national contributions or exclude decisions by unanimity, the most effective way is strengthening the preventive side of the governance. An important contribution in this regard should come from the Eurozone budgetary instrument in charge of both promoting economic convergence through the use of common investments and absorbing economic shocks through a stabilisation function. How much resources are necessary to perform these tasks? Most studies on the matter suggest that, at least in an initial stage a transfer mechanism should dispose of between 1 and 3% of European GDP, depending on the stabilisation tasks that it will manage in concrete.[254] Unfortunately the concrete proposals advanced so far are much less ambitious. While the European Commission counted to mobilise around € 55 billion, the informal discussions within the Eurogroup have been targeting an even smaller sum.[255] At these conditions the budgetary instrument for the euro area risks consisting only of a symbolic tool, which is essentially ineffective to ensure the stability of the euro area as a whole.

[251]The ESM has already used 20% of its resources, in particular €50 billions to Greece, €41 billions to the Spanish banking system and €9 billions to Cyprus.

[252]In 2018, Italy had a public debt of around €2.300 billions.

[253]Buchheit and Gulati (2018), p. 66.

[254]On the stabilization impact of a Eurozone budget compared to its size cf. European Commission Staff Working Document (2018), p. 52. Taking for instance the stabilisation function, even a budget between €50 and 70 billion would be able to apply counter cyclical policy only in no more than few Member States. See Wolff (2017), p. 7.

[255]According to the draft MFF 2021–2027, the new delivery tool for the euro area in favour of structural reforms should count on less than €25 billion, while the European Investment Stabilisation Function in charge of stabilising investment levels in the Member States in the event of a large asymmetric shock should consist only of back-to-back loans under the EU budget of up to €30 billion, coupled with a grant component to cover the costs of the interestEuropean Commission Communication (2018), pp. 10–11. The Ministers of Finance of the euro area have considered to provide the BICC with around €17 billion.

5.6.3.2 The Risks of Moral Hazard on the Effectiveness of Fiscal Centralisation

5.6.3.2.1 Moral Hazard and the Budgetary Instrument for the Euro Area

The completion of the economic union will pose new challenges also to the containment of moral hazard.[256] This is a longstanding problem of the EMU, which is essentially due to the contradiction of having a strong economic interdependence between the Member States without an effective European authority in charge of discouraging, stopping or even sanctioning individual misbehaviours. Two reforms will in particular increase the risk of moral hazard: the creation of a budgetary instrument for the euro area and the completion of the banking union.

The setup of a budgetary instrument for the euro area does represent a major challenge for the repression of moral hazard in the monetary union. Indeed, Member States might try to abuse this tool by putting themselves in the position to permanently receive resources from the other countries that are financing the budget. Furthermore, some national governments might feel, they can slow down the process of fiscal consolidation and structural reform by counting on the intervention of the common budgetary capacity in the event that symmetric or asymmetric shocks hit their economy. Evidently, such an attitude would undermine the correct functioning of the mechanism and shake the mutual trust on which the process of fiscal integration is premised. On the other hand, the Eurozone budgetary capacity does have the potential, if certain conditions are fulfilled to reduce the economic misbehaviour of national governments and make European surveillance less necessary. Indeed, in accordance with the paradox of centralisation highlighted by Fabbrini,[257] the shift of fiscal competences at European level may discharge Member States from some of their tasks and automatically reduce the need for public spending at national level. More precisely, once relieved from certain functions such as investing in public goods and absorbing economic shock, national budgets may better comply with the European rules on fiscal stability and focus on structural reforms.[258]

---

[256]On the issue of moral hazard in the EMU see Brunnermeier et al. (2016a), pp. 61, 101; De Grauwe (2016), pp. 229–232.

[257]Fabbrini (2016), pp. 178–179.

[258]The conferral of fiscal competence at European level shall be an effective instrument to reduce surveillance on national parliaments. As it can be noticed in federal countries, which are presenting different levels of fiscal authority, the parliaments of the Member States enjoy some wide autonomy in the management of their fiscal rights, because the federal authority has sufficient resources and the competence to discharge them from several tasks, including the management of asymmetric shocks and the correction of regional imbalances. As noticed by Hinarejos, fiscal federalism protects national autonomy more effectively than strict European surveillance. Cf. Hinarejos (2015), p. 191.

What effects the establishment of a Eurozone budgetary instrument will have in concrete, will depend on the conditions regulating its implementation. In this regard, it is possibly to put forward three proposals.

First, the budgetary instrument should not aim at equalizing income and correcting structural disparities between the Member States,[259] but it should only encourage structural reforms and possibly help the stabilisation of economic shocks within the Eurozone. For this reason, transfers cannot be permanent and unidirectional, but they must be designed in such a way so as to avoid that, 'over a too long period of time, any country is a net loser or gainer from the scheme'.[260] This may be ensured in different ways. Some have suggested that over a certain period of time any recipient Member States would have to return the resources it received. In this way, the European budgetary instrument would have in the long term a balanced net-receipt of transfers.[261] Alternatively, the budgetary instrument should intervene only when national downturns exceed certain levels, thus avoiding manipulation of the mechanism, as well as permanent transfers.[262] This result should be ensured through the provision of accurate activation criteria based on the assessment of effective economic shocks.[263]

Second, the budgetary capacity must count on the strict application of *ex ante* conditions. Member States will receive resources only if they comply with the eligibility criteria that have previously agreed on.[264] The real challenge is clearly to make this conditionality credible, meaning that once a Member State fails to execute its obligations, transfers must effectively cease. In this regard, it is important that transfers are temporary, so that no Member State can count on a permanent flow of resources from the budgetary instrument.[265] At the same time, resources should be

---

[259]President of the European Council, Final Report (2012), p. 12; President of the European Commission, Report (2015), p. 15.

[260]European Commission Communication (2012), p. 32; European Commission Staff Working Document (2018), p. 24.

[261]Such mechanism would turn the common transfer system into a system of implicit debt (without interests). The problem is that in this way the country would do deficit. Genuine transfers would instead better absorb a shock. Hebous and Weichenrieder (2015), p. 15.

[262]See Dolls et al. (2016), p. 13.

[263]Cf. art. 4 of European Commission Proposal for a Regulation (2018b) According to Gros, the euro area needs a system that offsets shocks which are rare, but potentially catastrophic. The small shocks may instead be managed at national level, also through borrowing. The ESM is not currently able to fulfil this function because it only grants loans, while the insurance mechanism should provide transfers. One way to do that would be to create a system of reinsurance of national unemployment insurance systems. Gros (2018), pp. 5–6. Rather than be a rainy-day fund, it will consist of a stormy-days fund.

[264]Cf. art. 3 of European Commission Proposal for a Regulation (2018b). The European Parliament Resolution (2017) mentions instead compliance with a convergence code.

[265]President of the European Council, Final Report (2012), p. 12; European Commission Communication (2012), p. 32; President of the European Commission, Report (2015), p. 15; Explanatory Statement of the European Parliament Resolution (2017), p. 22; European Commission Communication (2017b), p. 14.

provided in instalments, so that the concerned countries are encouraged to comply with European rules for the entire period that they are benefitting from the grants. Recipient Member States should also agree on a clawback clause, according to which transfers must be paid back in case of certified non-compliance with the eligibility criteria.[266] It should be noticed that the strict application of eligibility criteria for the Eurozone budgetary capacity may be easier than the enforcement of conditionality policy for the ESM. While the latter is an emergency mechanism, which provides financial assistance in situations of extreme distress, when the stability of the Eurozone is at stake, the budgetary capacity will operate normally along the economic cycle by absorbing the economic shocks, which are temporarily affecting a Member State. For this reason, it would be easier for the budgetary capacity to interrupt the flow of resources without immediately incurring recoils on the financial gear of the monetary union. In other words, the TINA ('There Is No Alternative') principle would not apply to the additional budgetary capacity.

Third, the application of the eligibility criteria and the supervision of Member State's fiscal policies should be accompanied with the opinion of technical authorities. Despite the efforts to constitutionalize the balanced budget principle and the introduction of semi-automatic sanctions, the Council has always been unable to effectively apply fiscal rules, as its decisions are substantially based on political considerations. For this reason, it may be opportune to strengthen the European Fiscal Board,[267] which should cooperate with political institutions in the management of the additional budgetary capacity. While it should not be able to completely overturn the decision of political bodies, this independent authority should help the correct application of the tool by verifying the fulfilment of the conditions for its activation and avoiding any undue income redistribution between the Member States.[268]

It should be instead refused any proposal, which envisage to create a procedure to exit the euro area. According to some authors, allowing for an exit option would represent an adequate threat for the Member States who don't want to comply with the European rules.[269] A similar option would, however, be in contrast with the objective of the stability of the euro area as whole, which includes preserving the integrity of the euro area, meaning each national membership. Furthermore, introducing the possibility for countries to leave the single currency may trigger a series of self-fulfilling prophecies, giving room for financial speculation to attack the weaker Member States of the euro area in a way to make the entire monetary union collapse.

---

[266] Hebous and Weichenrieder (2015), pp. 14–15.

[267] On the issue see Calmfors (2015), pp. 23–24.

[268] The European fiscal board should provide semi-binding opinions to the Council in the framework of the SGP.

[269] Hebous and Weichenrieder (2015), pp. 18–21.

5.6.3.2.2 Moral Hazard and the Completion of the Banking Union

The creation of a separate budgetary capacity does not present the only challenge to constraining moral hazard. The completion of the banking union is also problematic, due to the fiscal implications coming from the process of risk sharing.

A clear example is the establishment of a European Deposit Guarantee Scheme (EDIS). Rather than pursuing consolidation policies, countries presenting weaker banks may expect that the liquidity problems and losses of the latter are covered with European resources. In order to avoid this risk, the European Commission has proposed some rules to make sure that risk can be shared only once they have been limited. In this regard, the European Commission suggested in 2017 that the establishment of EDIS should be gradual and conditional to the reduction of risks.[270] Notably, the proposal foresees that EDIS should be set up in three following stages: re-insurance; co-insurance and full-insurance. Accordingly, in the first stage (re-insurance), EDIS should only manage liquidity issues and not cover loses. In the event of a bank default, National Deposit Guarantee Schemes (DGS) should intervene, while EDIS should only provide liquidity once national funds have been exhausted. Second, before moving to the actual co-insurance phase, which would imply a partial mutualisation of losses, it may be necessary to perform a targeted Asset Quality Review to address the Non-Performing Loans and illiquid assets. The passage to this stage may occur only once banks have sufficiently reduced the risks in their portfolio. Also in the second stage the mutualisation of losses should not be immediate, but proceed for stages and be conditional to the effective compliance with risk reduction and prudential rules.[271]

Restraining possible moral hazard behaviours is also a priority for the setup of the other missing pillar of the banking union, namely the common backstop. As the previous analysis has already explained, the governments of the euro area have conferred this function to the ESM. Notably, the activation of the ESM follows the principle of conditionality and indispensability, which aim to foster budgetary consolidation and avoid moral hazard behaviours. For this reason, the Member States of the euro area have decided to synchronise the effective establishment of a common backstop with the progresses, they will achieve in reducing banks' exposure to risks with respect to minimum requirement for own funds and eligible liabilities (MREL) and the trend in non-performing loans (NPLs) reduction.[272]

---

[270] European Commission Communication (2017a), pp. 10–12.

[271] Ibid., pp. 10–12.

[272] See *supra* Sect. 5.3.3.2.

5.6.4 *Centralisation and the Deficit of Democracy*

5.6.4.1 No Fiscal Centralisation Without Democratisation

The previous analysis has explained how the European economic governance is affected by some structural democratic deficits, as its functioning is essentially intergovernmental. Even if the EU Treaties provide for a dialogue between institutions in order to increase the transparency of political decisions, European citizens and their direct representatives are essentially excluded from the functioning of the economic governance. The recent reforms adopted in reaction to the sovereign debt crisis have exacerbated this situation by reducing the margin of action for domestic parliaments on the definition of national fiscal policies and excluding the European Parliament from the new procedures of budgetary supervision and financial assistance.

In this context, the reforms of the economic union, which move in the direction of fiscal centralisation (i.e. the additional budgetary capacity for the euro area, but also the ESM/EMF), will make the correction of the democratic deficit even more urgent. In this regard, it is worth remembering that the competence to collect and redistribute resources in Member States has always been a parliamentary prerogative. Notably, modern democracies were born to give the people control over the government's management of taxation. The motto of the American revolution, 'no taxation without representation', synthetizes well the relationship between the citizens and the fiscal authority in a democratic state. This is the reason why the creation of a European fiscal union would definitely pose a challenge to the genuine functioning of national parliamentary democracy and create the need for an effective source of democratic legitimation at the level where the new fiscal power has arisen.

5.6.4.2 Strengthening Parliamentary Control: Short Term Perspective

Finding a solution to the democratic deficit of the economic union depends on what measures will be implemented in concrete and what model of fiscal union will eventually prevail. Evidently as long as fiscal rights will belong to the Member States, the priority should be to strengthen the role of national parliaments. In this regard, the German Constitutional Court has been categorical in explaining that national parliaments must remain the holder of core sovereign rights, including fiscal powers.[273] This perspective, which conceives democracy only as 'government of the *national* people', however, clashes with the difficulty to ensure stability in the EMU.

[273]German Federal Constitutional Court, Judgment of 7 September 2011 [2 BvR 987/10], paras 101, 104; German Federal Constitutional Court, Judgment of 12 September 2012, [2 BvR 1390/12], para. 106–107; the Estonian Constitutional Court expressed a different opinion on the matter and precisely stated that national parliaments can limit their budgetary sovereignty in order to protect other important constitutional values, such as financial stability. Estonian Supreme Court, Constitutional Judgment, 3-4-1-6-12, 12 July 2012, paras 208–209.

As the analysis developed in the previous chapter has explained, an approach exclusively based on the preservation of the sovereign rights of national parliaments may result problematic. More precisely, it would be difficult to take care of the interdependence consolidated at European level if the activation of the ESM or the budgetary capacity will depend on the positive outcome of many national parliamentary debates detached from each other. The use of a veto power from any of these assemblies would be rather likely, especially considering that decisions will be based on a domestic understanding of European issues and the protection of national interest.[274] At the same time, there is also the risk to recreate between national parliaments the same relationship based on political force which characterises the functioning of intergovernmental bodies. In this perspective, it may be possible that the will of citizens' representatives in stronger countries may prevail over the interests and requests of citizens' representatives in smaller and weaker countries.

In order to escape this deadlock, it is necessary to find a balance where national parliaments are definitely involved in the process of fiscal integration as they are still the owner of sovereignty, but they cooperate with each other and with the EU parliament in a way as to balance national means (resources and competence) with European aims (the stability of the euro area as a whole).[275] A possible solution may be to define for the future economic union a double source of democratic legitimation,[276] both national and European. In this model, national parliaments would maintain their primary role, as they would be in charge of empowering and defining the functioning of the common fiscal instruments. At the same time, the European parliament would also play an important function as it would be in charge of verifying that the latter mechanisms are effectively acting in accordance with the European interest. The following analysis will better explain this division of tasks between national and European democracy.

Considering the functioning of the ESM, the GFCC has already dictated what conditions must be fulfilled regarding the role of national parliaments (or at least the *Bundestag*). Notably, they must have the right to approve any major decisions regarding the functioning of the mechanism and quantify the maximum exposure of national budgets towards it. In this regard, it is important to improve transparency and increase the right of information of domestic parliaments. Looking instead at the setup of the budgetary instrument for the euro area, national parliaments should have

[274]It is possible to have some preview of what may happen by considering the role of national parliaments in the ESM. The mechanism can intervene only once received the green card by nine national parliaments, which is not something always easy to achieve.

[275]According to Fasone, the European Parliament acting in coordination with national parliament could re-establish trust between people and the EU. Through inter-parliamentarian cooperation, the European Parliament should push the national parliaments to 'filter' what happens at national level by taking into consideration the European common interests. It is also needed a simplification of economic coordination and a stronger democratic scrutiny. Fasone (2014), pp. 184–185.

[276]Pilz (2017), p. 644.

a say on the size of the budgetary capacity, how it must be financed[277] and what mandate it shall pursue. This would be possible, for example, if the new budgetary capacity was established through a reform of the own resources system as per art. 311 TFEU and the Multiannual Financial Framework (MFF) as per art. 312 TFEU: before voting in the Council in accordance with these procedures, national governments should be expressly authorised by their parliament. Evidently, if Member States opted for enhanced cooperation pursuant to art. 20 TEU or via the conclusion of a separate international agreement, national parliaments should also grant their approval thereto. National parliaments may also participate in the definition of the eligibility criteria, countries must respect in order to access the budgetary instrument.

Coming to the role of the European Parliament in the future governance, several authors envisage a full sharing of responsibility with the Council. This would lead to a restoration of the 'community method'.[278] For example, the Parliament should be able to check on the use of the stabilisation and consolidation tools and make sure that the European Minister of Economy and Finance complies with the mandate received.[279] Considering the functioning of the future ESM, the participation of the European parliament should be formalised in the decision-making process. Ideally, it should be able to vote on the final approval of the ESM conditionality and its representatives should also take part in the *Troika*.[280] On the other hand, the European Parliament should be involved also in the future functioning of the budgetary instrument for the euro area. First, it should ratify the decision taken by national parliaments with regard to the own resources and the mandate of the mechanism.[281] Furthermore, it should be able to adopt and amend the eligibility criteria that countries must respect to access the budgetary instrument.[282] Finally, the Parliament should hold accountable the authority in charge of the actual management of the tool, either the Minister of Economy and Finance, the Eurogroup or the European Commission.

Ultimately, democratic control can succeed only if there is a sufficient cooperation between the European parliament and the national parliaments. The importance of inter-parliamentarian cooperation has been officially recognised by the Lisbon Treaty in art. 12 TEU and Protocol 1 on the role of national parliaments in the Union.

---

[277]This will be particular important to help setup taxes based on revenue, which only national parliaments are competent to levy.

[278]According to some authors the EU is approaching some form of parliamentary democracy based on bicameralism. See Hix (2008), pp. 38–39. Scharpf is more in favour of extending the community method to the functioning of the governance. Scharpf (2015), p. 395.

[279]European Parliament Resolution (2017).

[280]For example the European Parliament should participate in the approval of the MAP.

[281]If the additional budgetary capacity was established within the framework of the EU budget, the ordinary legislative procedure should be used to approve the new own resources system and the new MFF.

[282]According to the Resolution of the European Parliament of February 2017 on the budgetary capacity of the Eurozone, the convergence code fixing the eligibility criteria should be adopted through the ordinary legislative procedure. Cf. European Parliament Resolution (2017).

The Conference of Parliamentary Committees for Union Affairs of Parliaments of the European Union (COSAC, Conférence des Organes Spécialisés dans les Affaires Communautaire) should be the privileged place for inter-parliamentarian cooperation.[283] It is not a case that art. 13 TSCG recalled the organisation and promotion of a conference of representatives of the relevant committees of the European Parliament and representatives of the relevant committees of national Parliaments in order to discuss budgetary policies and other issues covered by the TSCG. Unfortunately, over the last years the Inter-Parliamentarian Conference on the economic and financial governance has met without achieving significant results.[284] Notably, the conference does not have decision-making powers, nor a legal authority.[285] In order to develop real cooperation and dialogue, it would be necessary to set up some more formal procedures of coordination, for example by providing national parliaments with the right of proposal in the European legislative process or a review system on the model of the subsidiarity check.[286]

5.6.4.3 Long-Term Perspective: Building a Genuine European Democracy

The arrangements suggested in the previous paragraph are meant to deal with the contradictions of starting a process of fiscal integration without challenging, at least from a formal point of view, the fiscal rights of national parliaments. This clearly represents a *contradictio in se*: how is it possible to create a fiscal union, without sharing fiscal rights? Evidently, this formula may work in a transitory stage, when Member States have decided to create some common instruments to mobilise resources for the stability of the euro area, but they still refuse to formally relinquish their competence to do that. The paradox, however, will not stand in the long run. Indeed, every process of fiscal integration implies some inevitable erosion of the conferral principle. As it was already explained, who has the control of resources, does also have the control of the policies financed with them. In perspective, if the European budgetary authority gained some space of self-management, thus emancipating from the control of Member States, it would be necessary to strengthen a genuine democratic control at European level. In such a situation, while inter-

[283]On the role of COSAC see Cygan (2016) and Esposito (2016).

[284]According to Fasone, the difficult settlement of inter-parliamentarian cooperation depends also on the fact that the European Parliament doesn't want to be threaten like the other domestic parliaments of the Union. Cf. Fasone (2014), p. 178. On the inter-parliamentary cooperation in the field of the economic governance cf. also Kreilinger (2016) and Cooper (2016).

[285]Chalmers (2012), p. 687. According to art. 10 of Protocol (No 1) on the Role of National Parliaments in the European Union, the Conference can only submit contribution for the attention of the European Parliament, the Council and the Commission, promote the exchange of information and best practice between national Parliaments and the European Parliament, including their special committees.

[286]See Protocol (No 2) on the application of the principles of subsidiarity and proportionality.

parliamentarian cooperation will still be important, the European parliament shall probably rise and become the main democratic authority in charge of fiscal decisions at European level. As a consequence, the transfer of competences triggered by the process of fiscal centralisation, will require that the national parliaments and the European parliament switch their role as masters of fiscal policy.

This is the reason why European institutions have acknowledged that the creation of a European fiscal union will create in perspective the need to establish a political union between the Member States, which will participate in the project.[287] What legal form, this political union may assume, is still debated. Definitely the transfer of fiscal competence and the creation of a stronger democratic representation at European level would be challenging from the point of view of both European and national constitutional law. Definitely, it is not possible to create European fiscal rights without a treaty amendment. What would be more complicated is, however, the reform of national constitutions. For example, the German Federal Constitutional Court mentioned that the transfer of sovereign rights in areas belonging to the constitutional identity of the country would definitely require the exercise of the constituent power of the people ex art. 146 GG.[288]

5.6.4.4 Does the Euro Area Need Its Own Parliament?

Over the last few years, several proposals envisaged to correct the deficits of the economic governance also by creating a separate level of democracy for the euro area.[289] The idea has gained some public attention, even if most academic and political commenters remained sceptical.[290] Despite the collateral risks of fragmenting democratic representation in the EU, the project of *ad hoc* parliamentary scrutiny for the euro area shouldn't be roughly dismissed, as it is symptomatic of the latest developments of the European integration process.

First, the euro area has developed *special democratic needs*. This started since the outbreak of the sovereign debt crisis, when the stability of the monetary union was

---

[287]Van President of the European Council, Final Report (2012), p. 12; European Commission Communication (2012), p. 32; President of the European Commission, Report (2015), p. 15.

[288]A similar perspective would undeniably require not only an overall Treaty amendment, but also a profound reform of national constitutional law. Cf. Calliess (2011–2012), p. 104. See, German Federal Constitutional Court, Judgment, 30 June 2009, [2 BvE 2/08], para. 179.

[289]On the establishment of a Eurozone level of democracy see Lionello (2017), pp. 179–194. In favour the setup of a Eurozone parliamentary scrutiny see: Hennette et al. (2017). Against see: Allemand and Martucci (2014), pp. 115–131; Fabbrini (2015), pp. 823–846; Fabbrini (2016), pp. 208–220. According to Calliess the euro area should set up a separate chamber next to the Council and the European Parliament and co-decide on every policy effecting the governance (i.e. budgetary, social, labour policies). National parliament should be provided with the right to ask for a suspension of a European decisions (red card). Calliess (2016), p. 55.

[290]Even the President of the European Commission Juncker has stated that the Parliament of the euro area can only be the European Parliament President. Jean-Claude Juncker's state of the Union Address 2017.

ensured through the toughening of European control over domestic budgetary policies and national parliaments. Chapter 4 has already explained exhaustively how the reform of the economic governance caused a progressive evaporation of national democracy.[291]

Second, over the last years a fracture has emerged within the Union between the Member States sharing the single currency and those who don't. This division has revealed itself through a diversification of *priorities and needs* within the Union. Issues like the rescue of countries experiencing financial difficulties, the breakup of the toxic loop between sovereigns and banks, as well as the difficult economic recovery after the crisis have specifically regarded the Eurozone and only its Member States have tried to find common solutions to these problems. In the light of this fracture, the European Parliament might not be the best institution to manage the Eurozone priorities, because one-fourth of its members come from countries, which are not directly affected by these specific needs and interests.

Third, the *current composition of the European Parliament* is not able to ensure a genuine representation of citizens. On the one hand, MEPs are still elected nationally on the basis of different domestic laws and without a genuine European debate; on the other hand, the principle of digressive proportionality makes sure that citizens resident in smaller states are proportionally more represented than those living in major countries.

Lastly, the ongoing political tensions between the EU and several governments on issues such as the distribution of refugees and the compliance of domestic laws with the democratic principle, may prevent Member States from reaching the necessary *unanimity* to confer new tasks to the European Parliament.

Considering now the feasibility of establishing a separate level of democracy for the euro area within the current legal framework, the EU Treaties definitely exclude any major institutional reform of this kind. Either such a scrutiny is set up through an informal agreement of the political parties without providing it with any legal authority,[292] or governments have to choose the path of constitutional amendments to the EU Treaties ex art. 48 TUE. Only in the event reforming the EU Treaties by unanimity proved hard to achieve, Member States might set up a separate assembly beyond the EU legal framework though an intergovernmental agreement.[293]

In the light of these observations, we can imagine some possible concretisations of a Eurozone parliamentary scrutiny.[294] One option is the creation of a *Eurozone committee* within the European Parliament composed only of MEPs coming from the countries sharing the single currency. The committee would take part fully in the

[291]Cf. *supra* Sect. 4.4.2.

[292]Within the limits of the existing legal framework the European Parliament has adopted on December 2013 a Resolution to create an informal parliamentary scrutiny for the Economic and Monetary Union on the basis of a political agreement between political groups. Cf. European Parliament Resolution (2013).

[293]Hennette et al. (2017), pp. 41–44.

[294]For an overview of the authors in favour of these three options see Verlhest (2014), pp. 19–21.

Eurozone governance and keep the plenary informed of its decisions. At the same time, the reform should ideally take the chance to also remedy some important deficits of democratic representation in the European Parliament, such as digression in proportionally between the electors and the elected and the lack of common electoral law. Another possible concretisation of a separate parliamentary scrutiny is the creation of a *new assembly* elected by the citizens living in the Eurozone. If the reform passed through a Treaty change ex art. 48 TEU, this separate parliament should ideally become a new institution of the EU. Last, a separate parliamentary scrutiny for the euro area might also take the form of an *inter-parliamentarian assembly* composed of national parliamentarians from the Eurozone countries.[295] Even if this assembly might be less compact, it would offer the opportunity to take count of both majorities at European level and within each national parliamentarian delegation.[296]

References

Adamski D (2018) Redefining European economic integration. Cambridge University Press, Cambridge

Allard C, Koeva Brooks P, Bluedorn J C, Bornhorst F, Christopherson K, Ohnsorge F, Poghosyan T (2013) Towards a Fiscal Union for the Euro Area, IMF Staff Discussion Note 9

Allemand F (2017) More or less intergovernmental cooperation within the new EMU? In: Daniele L, Simone R, Cisotta P (eds) Democracy in the EMU in the aftermath of the crisis. Springer, Berlin, pp 73–99

Allemand F, Martucci F (2014) La légitimité démocratique de la gouvernance économique européenne. Revue de l'OFCE/Débats et politiques:115–131

Andritzky J, Christofzik D I, Désirée I. Feld LP, Scheuering U (2016) A Mechanism to Regulate Sovereign Debt Restructuring in the Euro Area, Working Paper No 4

Andritzky J, Christofzik DI, Désirée I, Feld LP, Scheuering U (2018) A mechanism to regulate sovereign debt restructuring in the euro area Int Financ, 1–15

Arnold N, Barkbu B, Ture E, Wang H, Yao J, (2018) A Central Fiscal Stabilization. Capacity for the Euro Area. IMF Staff Discussion Note, March 2018 SDN/18/03

Audit M (2014) A debt restructuration mechanism for European sovereigns: an emerging idea. In: Paulus CG (ed) Debt restructuring mechanism for sovereigns: do we need a legal procedure? Beck, Munich, pp 213–222

Barbieri Hermitte R (2017) Sovereign debt restructuring mechanisms: mind the trap. In: Paganetto L (ed) Sustainable growth in the EU. Springer, Berlin, pp 105–119

Beblavý M, Maselli I (2015) Reinsurance of National Unemployment Benefit Schemes, CEPS Special Report, No 401

Beck G (2014) The Court of Justice, the Bundesverfassungsgericht and legal reasoning during the euro crisis: the rule of law as a fair-weather phenomenon. Eur Public Law 20:539–566

Bénassy-Quéré A, Ragot X, Wolff GB (2016) Which fiscal union for the euro area? Bruegel Policy Contribution, Issue 5

---

[295] Hennette et al. (2017), pp. 31–38.

[296] This might be necessary if national constitutional courts required that domestic parliamentary representations shall agree on any fiscal decisions made at the European level.

Bénassy-Quéré A, Brunnermeier M, Enderlein H, Farhi E, Fratzscher M, Fuest C, Gourinchas P, Martin P, Pisani-Ferry J, Rey H, Schnabel I, Véron N, Weder di Mauro B, Zettelmeyer J (2018) Reconciling risk sharing with market discipline: a constructive approach to euro area reform. CEPR Policy Insight No. 91

Berger H, Dell'Ariccia G, Obstfeld M (2018) Revisiting the economic case for fiscal union in the euro area. IMF, Washington

Bizioli G, Sacchetto C (2016) European constitutional integration. The case of direct taxation. In: Avi-Yonah RS, Lang M (eds) Comparative fiscal federalism. Wolters Kluwer, Alphen aan den Rijn, pp 11–24

Brauneck J (2018) Erlauben die Europaischen Vertrage einen Europaischen Wahrungsfonds und einen Europaischen Finanzminister. Europäisches Wirtschafts- und Steuerrecht 15:81–89

Brunnermeier M K, Langfield S, Pagano M, Reis P, Van Nieuwerburgh S, Vayanos D (2016a) ESBies: safety in the tranches. Working ESRB Paper Series No 21

Brunnermeier MK, James H, Landau J (2016b) The euro and the battle of ideas. Princeton University Press, Princenton

Buchheit L, Gulati M, Tirado I (2013) The problem of holdout creditors in Eurozone sovereign debt restructurings. Working Paper Durham, Duke Law School

Buchheit LC, Gulati GM (2018) Sovereign debt restructuring in Europe. Global Policy 9(Suppl 1):65–69

Cafaro S (2017) L'Unione Economica e Monetaria dopo la crisi. Cosa abbiamo imparato? Edizioni Scientifiche Italiane, Napoli

Calliess C (2011–2012) From fiscal compact to fiscal union? New rules for the Eurozone. Camb Yearb Eur Legal Stud 14:101–117

Calliess C (2016) The governance framework of the Eurozone and the need for a treaty reform. In: Fabbrini F, Ballin EH, Somsen H (eds) What form of Government for the European Union and the Eurozone? Hart, Oxford, pp 37–56

Calmfors L (2015) The roles of fiscal rules, fiscal councils and fiscal union in EU integration. IFN Working Paper No 1076

Carboni GG (2014) Fiscal federalism and comparative law. Comp Law Rev 5:1–20

Carnot N, Kizior M, Mourre G (2017) Fiscal stabilisation in the euro-area: a simulation exercise. Université Libre de Bruxelles Working Papers, CEB 17-025

Chalmers D (2012) The European redistributive state and a European law of struggle. Eur Law J 18:667–693

Commission of the European Communities (1977) Report of the Study Group on the Role of Public Finance in European Integration

Cooper I (2016) The interparliamentary conference on stability, Economic coordination and governance in the European Union (the 'Article 13 Conference'). In: Lupo N, Fasone C (eds) Interparliamentary cooperation in the composite European constitution. Hart, Oxford, pp 247–268

Corsetti G, Feld LP, Lane PR, Reichlin L, Rey H, Vayanos D, Weder di Mauro B (2015) A new start for the eurozone: dealing with debt. monitoring the eurozone. CEPR Press

Corsetti G, Feld L, Koijen R, Reichlin L, Reis R, Rey, H, Weder di Mauro B (2016) Reinforcing the eurozone and protecting an open society. Monitoring the eurozone, CEPR Press, London

Cottarelli C (2016) A European fiscal union: the case for a larger central budget. Economia Politica 33(1):1–8

Cottarelli C, Guerguil M (2014) Introduction and overview. In: Cottarelli C, Guerguil M (eds) Designign a European fiscal union. Routledge, London

Council (2019) 'Capital markets union: Council adopts new rules facilitating access to pension products and investment funds', Press Release 438/19, 14th June 2019

Croci F (2018) Is it worth the effort? The European Commission's proposal for integrating the substance of the 'Fiscal Compact' into the EU legal order Revue de l'euro, 52

Cygan A (2016) COSAC: birth, evolution, failures and perspectives. In: Lupo N, Fasone C (eds) Interparliamentary cooperation in the composite European constitution. Hart, Oxford, pp 207–226

Daniele L (2009) Le istituzioni politiche dell'Unione europea dopo il Trattato di Lisbona: verso un nuovo equilibrio? Studi Sull'integrazione Europea 4:43–54

De Grauwe P (2016) Economics of Monetary Union. Oxford University Press, Oxford

De Streel A (2014) EU fiscal governance and the effectiveness of its reform. In: Adams M, Fabbrini F, Larouche P (eds) The constitutionalization of European budgetary constraints. Hart, Oxford, pp 85–104

Delbecque B (2013) Proposal for a Stabilisation Fund for the EMU. CEPS Working Documents, No 385

Dolls M, Fuest C, Heinemann F, Peichl A (2016) Reconciling insurance with market discipline: a blueprint for a European fiscal union. CESifo Economic Studies, No 62

Dullien S, Fernández J, López M, Maass G, del Prado D, von Weizsäcker J (2017) Fit for purpose: a German-Spanish proposal for a robust European Unemployment Insurance. Friedrich Ebert Stiftung

Editorial Comment (2018) Tinkering with economic and monetary union. Common Mark Law Rev 55:709–718

Enderlein H, Haas J (2015) What would a European Finance Minister do? A proposal', Jacques Delors Institut, Policy Paper No 145

Esposito A (2016) The Role of COSAC in EU interparliamentary cooperation: an (Endless) Quest for an Identity. In: Lupo N, Fasone C (eds) Interparliamentary cooperation in the composite European constitution. Hart Publishing, Oxford, pp 325–333

Euro Summit (2018) Statement of 14th December 2018, Euro 503/18, Eurosummit 3, TSGC 10

Euro Summit (2019) Statement of 21st June 2019, Euro 502/19, Eurosummit 1, TSGC 3

Eurogroup (2018a) Eurogroup report to Leaders on EMU deepening, 4th December 2018

Eurogroup (2018b) 'Terms of reference of the common backstop to the Single Resolution Fund', 4th December 2018

Eurogroup (2018c) 'Term sheet on the European Stability Mechanism', 4th December 2018

Eurogroup (2019) 'Term sheet on the Budgetary Instrument for Convergence and Competitiveness', 14th June 2019

European Commission, 'EU Budget for the Future', 2nd May 2018

European Commission Communication (2012) A blueprint for a deep and genuine Economic and Monetary Union, launching a European debate, 30th November 2012, COM(2012)777/2 final

European Commission Communication (2015) Action Paper on Building a Capital Markets Union', 30th September 2015, COM(2015) 468

European Commission Communication (2017a) On Completing the Banking Union, 11th October 2017, COM(2017) 592 final

European Commission Communication (2017b) New Budgetary Instruments for a stable Euro Area within the Union Framework, 6th December 2017, COM/2017/0822 final

European Commission Communication (2017c) A European Minister of Economy and Finance, 6th December 2017, COM/2017/0823 final

European Commission Communication (2018) A Modern Budget for a Union that Protects, Empowers and Defends. The Multiannual Financial Framework for 2021-2027, COM/2018/321 final

European Commission Green Paper (2011) On the feasibility of introducing Stability Bonds, 23rd November 2011, COM(2011) 818 final

European Commission Green Paper (2015) Building a Capital Markets Union, 18th February 2015, COM(2015) 63 final

European Commission, Proposal for a Council Directive (2017) Provisions for strengthening fiscal responsibility and the medium-term budgetary orientation in the Member States, COM/2017/0824 final

European Commission Proposal for a Council Regulation (2017) On the establishment of the European Monetary Fund, COM/2017/0827 final
European Commission Proposal for a Regulation (2015) amending Regulation (EU) 806/2014 in order to establish a European Deposit Insurance Scheme COM/2015/0586 final
European Commission Proposal for a Regulation (2018a) on the establishment of the Reform Support Programme. COM/2018/391 final
European Commission Proposal for a Regulation (2018b) on the establishment of a European Investment Stabilisation Function, COM/2018/387 final
European Commission Proposal for a Regulation (2019) On a governance framework for the budgetary instrument for convergence and competitiveness for the euro area, COM(2019) 354 final
European Commission Report (2017) Report from the Commission presented under Article 8 of the Treaty on Stability, Coordination and Governance in the Economic and Monetary Union', C/2017/1201 final
European Commission Staff Working Document (2018) Impact Assessment Accompanying the document Proposal for a Regulation of the European Parliament and of the Council on the establishment of a European Investment Stabilisation Function, SWD(2018) 297 final
European Parliament Resolution of 12th December 2013 on constitutional problems of a multitier governance in the European Union (2012/2078(INI))
European Parliament Resolution of 16th February 2017 on budgetary capacity for the euro area (2015/2344(INI))
Fabbrini F (2015) Representation in the European parliament: of false problems and real challenges. Zeitschrift für ausländisches öffentliches Recht und Völkerrecht 75:823–846
Fabbrini F (2016) Economic governance in Europe. Comparative paradoxes and constitutional challenges. Oxford University Press, Oxford
Fasone A (2014) European economic governance and parliamentary representation. What place for the European parliament? Eur Law J 20:164–185
Forsthoff U (2018) Fünf Jahre ESM – Entwicklungsperspektiven. Europäische Zeitschrift für Wirtschaftsrecht 29:108–118
Fuest C, Peichl A (2012) European fiscal union: what is it? Does it work? And are there really no alternatives? IZA Policy Paper No 39
Fuest C, Heinemann F, Schröder C (2016) A viable insolvency procedure for sovereigns in the euro area. J Common Mark Stud 54:301–317
Gelpern A (2014a) A sensible step to mitigate sovereign bond dysfunction, 29th August 2014. Washington, Peterson Institute for International Economics
Gelpern A (2014b) A Skeptic's case for sovereign bankruptcy. In: Paulus CG (ed) Debt restructuring mechanism for sovereigns: do we need a legal procedure? Beck, Munich, pp 261–278
Gianviti F, Krueger A, Pisani-Ferry J, Sapir A, von Hagen J (2010) A European mechanism for sovereign debt crisis resolution: a proposal? Blueprint Series, Bruegel
Gros D (2018) A fiscal shock absorber for the euro area? Rationale and insights from the economics of insurance (and reinsurance). In: Andritzky J, Rocholl J (eds) Towards a more resilient euro area ideas from the 'Future Europe' forum. CEPS, Brussels
Gros D, Mayer T (2010) How to deal with sovereign default in Europe: create the European Monetary Fund Now! CEPS Policy Brief No. 202
Gros D, Schoenmaker D (2014) European deposit insurance and resolution in the banking union. J Common Mark Stud 52(3):529–546
Hebous S, Weichenrieder A (2015) Towards a fiscal union? On the acceptability of a Fiscal Transfer System in the Eurozone. SAFE, White Paper No. 28
Hennette S, Piketty T, Sacriste G, Vauchez A (2017) Pour un traité de démocratisation de l'Europe. Éditions du Seuil, Paris

High-Level Group on Own Resources (2016) Future financing of the EU, Final Report and recommendations, December 2016
Hinarejos A (2012) The euro area crisis and constitutional limits to fiscal integration. Cambridge Yearb Eur Legal Stud 14:259–260
Hinarejos A (2013) Fiscal federalism in the European Union: evolution and future choices for EMU. Common Mark Law Rev 51:1621–1642
Hinarejos A (2015) The euro area crisis in constitutional perspective. Oxford University Press, Oxford
Hix S (2008) What's wrong with the European Union and how to fix it? Wiley, London
Hofmann C (2013) A legal analysis of the Eurozone crisis. Fordham J Corp Financ Law 18:519–564
IMF (2014) Strengthening the contractual framework to address collective action problems in sovereign debt restructuring. IMF
Ioannidis M (2016) Europe's new transformations: how the EU economic constitution changed during the Eurozone crisis. Common Mark Law Rev 53:1237–1282
Kreilinger V (2016) Inter-parliamentary cooperation and its challenges: the case of economic and financial goverannce. In: Fabbrini F, Ballin EH, Somsen H (eds) What form of government for the European Union and the eurozone? Hart, Oxford, pp 271–288
Lellouch T, Sode A (2014) An unemployment insurance scheme for the euro area, TrésorEconomics, No 132
Lionello L (2017) Does the eurozone need its own parliament? Legal necessity and feasibility of a eurozone parliamentary scrutiny. In: Daniele D, Simone P, Cisotta R (eds) Democracy in the EMU in the aftermath of the crisis. Springer, Berlin, pp 179–194
Lo Schiavo G (2017a) The role of financial stability in EU law and policy. Wolters Kluwer, Alphen aan den Rijn
Lo Schiavo G (2017b) The treaty on stability, coordination and governance and the ESM treaty: intergovernmental arrangements outside EU law, but for the benefit of the EMU? In: Giegerich T, Schmitt DC, Zeitzmann S (eds) Flexibility in the EU and beyond. Hart, Oxford, pp 195–224
Maduro PP (2012) A New Governance for the European Union and the Euro: Democracy and Justice, EUI RSCAS PP; 2012/11
Marzinotto A, Sapir A, Wolff G B (2011) What kind of fiscal union. Bruegel Policy Brief No 6
Mody A (2013) Sovereign Debt and its Restructuring Framework in the Euro Area. Bruegel Working Paper, No 5.
Moloney N (2014) European Banking Union: assessing its risks and resilience. Common Mark Law Rev 51(6):1609–1670
Nettesheim M (2011) Euro-Rettung und Grundgesetz. Verfassungsgerichtliche Vorgaben für den Umbau der Wahrungsunion. Europarecht, pp 765–783
Nunner-Krautgasser B (2014) The importance of being prepared – a call for a European sovereign debt restructuring mechanism. In: Paulus CG (ed) Debt restructuring mechanism for sovereigns: do we need a legal procedure? Beck, Munich, pp 241–250
Ortino M (2018) The case for truly independent EU regulatory authorities in the field of financial regulation. Eur Bus Law Rev 29(3):465–496
Panizza U (2013) Do we need a mechanism for solving sovereign debt crises? A rule-based discussion. Graduate Institute of International and Development Studies, Geneva, Working Paper No 3
Paulus A, Tirado I (2013) Sweet and lowdown: a 'Resolvency' process and the Eurozone's crisis management framework. Law Econ Yearly Rev 2:504–559
Pilz S (2017) Ein Schatzamt für die Eurozone? Überlegungen zu den Vorschlägen des Europäischen Parlaments und der Kommission zu einer Reform der Wirtschaftsunion. Europäische Zeitschrift für Wirtschaftsrecht 28:637–645

Pisani-Ferry J, Vihriälä E, Wolff G (2013) Options for a Euro-area fiscal capacity, Policy Contributions 765, Bruegel

President of the European Commission (2015) Completing Europe's Economic and Monetary Union, 22nd June 2015

President of the European Commission: Jean-Claude Juncker's state of the Union Address 2017

President of the European Council, Final Report (2012) Towards a genuine Economic and Monetary Union, 5th December 2012

President of the French Republic (2017) Initiative pour l'Europe - Discours d'Emmanuel Macron pour une Europe souveraine, unie, démocratique', 26th September 2017

President of the French Republic, Chancellor of the German Federal Republic, Meseberg Declaration. Renewing Europe's promises of security and prosperity, 19th June 2018

Quaglia L, Howarth D, Liebe M (2016) The political economy of European capital markets Union. J Common Mark Stud 54(1):185–203

Repasi R (2013) Legal options for an additional EMU fiscal capacity. European Parliament, Directorate General for Internal Policies, PE 474.397

Reuters (2014) EU should be able to veto national budgets: Germany's Schäuble, 28th November 2014

Rossolillo G (2018) Fiscalità e sovranità: riflessioni sulla ripartizione delle competenze tra Stati membri e Union Europea. Il Diritto dell'Unione Europea, 123–152

Santini A (2015) Il Bilancio dell'Unione Europea. In: Enciclopedia del diritto - Annali VIII, Giuffè, Milano, pp 821–837

Santini A, Lionello L (2018) La proposta franco-tedesca per la creazione di un bilancio della zona euro: criticità e prospettive. Diritto comunitario e degli scambi internazionali 57(3):371–393

Sapir A, Véron N, Wolff G (2018) Capital Markets Union, Making It Reality, Bruegel, Policy Contribution No 7

Scharpf FW (2015) After the crash: a perspective on multilevel European democracy. Eur Law J 21:384–405

Schäuble W (2017) Non-paper for paving the way towards a Stability Union

Schwarz M (2014) A memorandum of misunderstanding – the doomed road of the European stability mechanism and a possible way out: enhanced cooperation. Common Mark Law Rev 51:389–424

Scott A (2012) Does Economic union require a fiscal union? In: Shuibhne NN, Gormley LW (eds) From single market to Economic union: essays in memory of John A. Usher. Oxford University Press, Oxford, pp 40–63

Thirion G (2017) European Fiscal Union: Economic rational and design challenges. CEPS Working Documents, No 1

Tosato GL (2016) L'Unione economica e monetaria: evoluzione e criticità legali. In: Tizzano A (ed) Verso i 60 anni dai Trattati di Roma. Giappichelli, Torino, pp 223–240

Triggiani E (2010) Gli equilibri politici interistituzionali dopo la riforma di Lisbona. Studi Sull'integrazione Europea 5:9–34

Tuori K, Tuori K (2014) The eurozone crisis. A constitutional analysis. Cambridge University Press, Cambridge

Vallée S (2014) From mutual insurance to fiscal federalism: rebuilding the economic and monetary union after the demise of the Maastricht architecture. Int Econ 138:49–62

Van den Bergh R (2016) Farewell Utopia? Why the European Union should take the economics of federalism seriously. Maastricht J Eur Comp Law 23(6):937–964

Verlhest S (2014) The sense and nonsense of eurozone level democracy. Egmont Paper No 70

Weber A (2013) Europa und Völkerrechtliche Elemente der Gewährleistung von Haushaltsdisziplin in der Wahrungsunion. Europarecht, 375–388

Weder di Mauro B, Zettelmeyer J (2017) The New Global Financial Safety Net: Struggling for Coherent Governance in a Multipolar System. CIGI Essays on International Finance No 4

Wolff G (2017) Beyond the Juncker and Schäuble visions of Euro-area governance, Bruegel. Policy Brief Issue 6, 1st December 2017

Wyplosz C (2014) The eurozone crisis: a near-perfect case of mismanagement. Economia Marche: J Appl Econ 33:1–13

Zettelmeyer J (2018) Managing deep debt crises in the euro area: towards a feasible regime. Global Policy 9:70–79

Chapter 6
Conclusions

As it was explained in the introduction, the single currency has been established leaving a fundamental issue unresolved: is it possible to create a monetary union and ensure its survival without providing it with the essential attributes of a state? Even if only time will definitely answer this question, the research developed in the book may at least help giving some possible suggestions.

Chapter 2 started considering the asymmetry between the economic and the monetary union. The latter has been responsible for the development of some chronical fragilities in the EMU, namely the economic divergence between the Member States and their excessive exposure towards economic shocks, which prepared the ground for the outbreak of the sovereign debt crisis. Once the latter spread out, the objective of the 'stability of the euro area as a whole' started to emerge gradually: over the last few years, Member States and EU institutions have been committed to ensuring the survival and the integrity of the currency union against internal and external crisis. Accordingly, the stability of the euro area as a whole has become the primary objective of economic policy, which has been pursued through the use of both consolidation and stabilisation tools.

As the research explained in Chap. 3, the measures adopted in the aftermath of the sovereign debt crisis aimed to contain the several emergencies, which were undermining the stability of the euro area. What the reforms could not do instead was questioning the political equilibria and the legal principles, on which the Member States founded the EMU in the Maastricht Treaty. More precisely, neither the strengthening of European surveillance on national public finances, nor the conditional financial assistance of the ESM, nor the partial establishment of the European banking union have produced any real shift of fiscal sovereignty from the Member States to the Union.

Chapter 4 has deeply analysed the outstanding fragilities of the governance. First of all, due to the limits of the existing primary law, reforms have been adopted either providing an extensive interpretation of the European Treaty or recurring to inter-governmental agreements beyond the EU law: this has undermined the legal

L. Lionello, *The Pursuit of Stability of the Euro Area as a Whole*, Studies in European Economic Law and Regulation 18,
https://doi.org/10.1007/978-3-030-28045-1_6

coherence and the institutional balance of the governance (deficit of legality). Second, the instruments created for the pursuit of stability of the euro area through the development of both stabilisation and consolidation policies are not fully capable of fulfilling their targets. This failure depends on the scarce credibility of European fiscal rules, the weaknesses of the Commission, the limited resources available at European level, as well as the structural inefficiencies of economic coordination in the hands of intergovernmental bodies (deficit of effectiveness). Finally, the limited instruments of democratic control at European and national level have undermined the relationship between citizens and EU institutions (lack of democratic accountability).[1]

Faced with the structural deficits of the governance and the enduring fragilities of the euro area, a new debate has started on the possible reforms, the economic union may need in order to be finally complete and achieve stability. Chapter 5 has acknowledged the numerous proposals advanced in this regard and identified the main challenges for their implementation. Notably, the political and academic debate has proposed two different approaches to the completion of the EMU. The advocates of the existing decentralised model of economic union believe that the latter may be successfully reformed through the creation of a debt restructuration mechanism and stronger surveillance instruments on national budgets. On the other side, the European Commission and most of the academic doctrine have spoken in favour of a process of fiscal centralisation in the euro area. The latter may start with the creation of an additional budgetary instrument to foster investment and reforms in the euro area.

As explained in the previous chapter, while the decentralised model of economic union and fiscal centralisation represent in abstract two opposite trends, it is not impossible to find a balance between them, when the reforms are applied in concrete. The problem is evidently to choose what approach should prevail, meaning what should be the rule and what the exception. On the one hand, reaffirming the existing model of economic union, regardless the possible improvements, would mean to display common resources for the stability of the euro area only in case of extreme emergencies, while convergence and fiscal consolidation should be normally pursued by the individual efforts of the Member States. Implementing fiscal centralisation would mean instead to use common mechanisms and resources to promote convergence and stability in the euro area, while strengthening at the same time the procedures of democratic control. Debt restructuring should not be excluded, but only in exceptional situations.

While the decision on what model should prevail in concrete will be taken by the political leaders of both the Member States and the Union, several arguments deduced in the previous analysis convinced the *author* that the process of fiscal

---

[1]While the analysis has tried to explain this phenomenon from a legal perspective, part of the economic doctrine has also come to similar conclusions. Snell has effectively synthetized a 'trilemma' of the EMU, according to which monetary unification, national economic sovereignty and democracy can't be realised at the same time, thus making necessary to choose two out of three. Snell (2016), pp. 159–160.

centralisation has better chances than the decentralised model to fix the existing deficits of the governance. In other words, there a number of reasons why the process of fiscal centralisation (and in perspective political integration) represents the best guarantee to ensure the survival and the integrity of the euro area.

First of all, fiscal unions have more effective instruments to encourage diligent behaviours of national governments and contain the risks of moral hazard. By sharing the power on revenues and public spending with the European level, Member States would reduce their chance to hold destabilisation behaviours, as national budgetary laws would mobilise less resources and their targets would focus on more limited objectives. At the same time, common budgetary instruments may provide some significant incentives to encourage compliance of Member States with fiscal rules and the implementation of structural reforms. This result may be ensured through a careful application of the conditionality policy or eligibility criteria to access the common budgetary instrument of the euro area.

Second, the creation of a fiscal union would represent the best shelter for the stability of the euro area against external economic shocks, as well as fiscal or banking crisis originated within the Member States. While it is desirable that national governments remain on the frontline to manage cyclical economic shocks, this being the reason why they should normally pursue sound budgetary policies, a common budgetary instrument for the euro area would be better equipped to deal with economic crisis of significant magnitude,[2] as it could mobilise more resources in a shorter amount of time.

Third, the establishment of a fiscal union represents at the moment the best opportunity to create genuine mechanisms of democratic accountability at European level.[3] Indeed, as long as national legislatures retain their exclusive fiscal sovereignty, even if the latter is more and more constrained by external surveillance, the European parliament won't be able to request a real involvement in the decision-making process. In accordance with the principle of subsidiarity, the transfer of fiscal competence from the Member States to the Union would instead create the need for democratic control at the level, where the new power must be held accountable. Accordingly, even the establishment of a fiscal union has been criticised due to the lack of a common *demos* and genuine accountability mechanisms, the process of fiscal integration in the euro area may consolidate solidarity between European citizens and trigger a real democratisation of the economic governance.[4]

In the light of these practical arguments, the process of fiscal centralisation does represent in principle the best strategy to reform the Eurozone governance and

[2]It should be noted that fiscal federations have less need to apply surveillance on the fiscal behaviours of Member States. In the United States, for example, there is no equivalent to art. 125 TFEU. The no bailout tradition has been compensated through the use of a strong federal budget, which can rescue states experiencing financial difficulties through a variety of transfer mechanisms. Estella (2016), pp. 537–538.

[3]Cf. Crum (2013), p. 623.

[4]Creating a fiscal union would lead to the establishment of a political union. Cf. Véron (2012). On the possible evolution towards a political union cf. Rossolillo (2018), pp. 148–151.

ensure its stability in the long term. Even if much will depend on how it will be implemented in concrete, this approach does offer adequate solutions to overcome the deficit of democracy and effectiveness of the economic union. While the creation of a genuine European fiscal power will eventually require the reform of the EU Treaties, as well as national constitutional law, it is nevertheless realistic to create some common instrument to start the process of fiscal centralisation also within the current legal framework.

Once identified the preferable approach to the completion of the economic union, it is possible to develop some further considerations on the objective of the stability of the euro area as a whole. Notably, the latter has been defined as the 'preservation of both the existence and the integrity of the monetary union'. The analysis of this goal has occupied a central role in the monograph: it worked as a fundamental benchmark to assess the effectiveness of the governance, as well as the quality of future reforms, and it helped to explain why the monetary union needs some form of fiscal integration and democratisation in order to fulfil its needs of stability. In the light of the conclusive remarks on the completion of the governance and the need to balance the asymmetry between the economic and the monetary union, it is possible to deduce some further meanings of the objective.

First of all, the achievement of the objective of the stability of the euro area as a whole should not rely only on the use stabilisation and consolidation tools, but also on the pursuit of economic growth and social cohesion. Real stability can't be achieved simply avoiding or managing situations of financial distress, which may cause a dramatic collapse of the monetary union, but it requires to make the economic union more attractive and protective of the people's interests. This should be done by strengthening the process of convergence between the Member States and democratisation of the governance. The threats of to the stability of the Eurozone don't come only from the risk of sovereign default or the financial collapse of banks, but also from social inequalities, the scarce economic growth and, more importantly, the fact that the euro is perceived as an obstacle to economic and social progress by many citizens. The process of fiscal centralisation should embrace a wider conception of stability, which include the gradual economic convergence between the Member States. This should also fill the deficit of output democratic legitimacy, which characterise the existing governance. The new conception of stability seems be partially acknowledged in the project of budgetary instrument for the euro area (BICC), which was recently agreed by the Eurogroup.

Second, the pursuit of the stability of the euro area has been triggering a process of transformation in the economic union, which is still ongoing. Despite appearances, stability is not a score, but it is a process. More precisely, unlike price stability and sound budgetary policy, the fulfilment of the stability of the euro area as a whole can't be quantified in a specific threshold, but it requires a continuous and overall commitment from both the Member States and the EU institutions. Their effort to the cause of stability has assumed over the last few years different forms, including fiscal consolidation, banking restructuration and the provision of conditional financial support to banks and Member States. At the same time, stability has been also pursued through a process of gradual reform of the governance aimed at excogitating more and more effective instruments of stabilisation and consolidation. Accordingly, the stability of the euro area represents not only an objective of economic policy, but it has also become a general objective of the EU, which follows the goal of creating an economic and monetary union ex art. 3(4). Evidently, the establishment of the EMU has created the collateral objective for the Member States and the EU institutions of conserving it. In order to achieve this result, the governance of the euro area shall be subject to a continuous process of improvement.

Third, if the pursuit of stability takes the path of fiscal integration, the existing governance model based on the commitment of Member States under European supervision (etero-preservation of stability) may evolve into some form of shared economic government, where the Union has its own instruments to contribute to the cause of stability next to those of the national governments (co-preservation of stability). This will happen in particular, if the ESM will be incorporated into EU law and the European institutions will be able to manage the new fiscal instruments to foster convergence and stabilisation in the euro area. In perspective, if the process of integration will continue and establish a genuine fiscal capacity, European institutions will be able to take care of the stability of the euro area as a whole without the immediate support of the Member States (self-preservation of stability).[5] Evidently the impact of the pursuit of stability of the euro area as whole on the principle of conferral is massive. There is indeed a clear assonance between the concepts of self-preservation and self-determination. If EU institutions developed some (fiscal) tools to take care of the stability of the euro area on their own, this may slowly lead to a gradual emancipation of the economic governance from the authority of Masters of the Treaty, which means, in other words, setting the basis for a European political union.[6]

References

Crum B (2013) Saving the euro at the cost of democracy? J Common Mark Stud 51:614–630

Estella A (2016) European Union bailouts and credibility: the constitutional dimension. Eur Public Law 22:507–540

---

[5] In this way, the function of the objective of the stability of the euro area as a whole may complete the transition from 'competence-enabling' to 'policy orientation', thus getting closer to the role of objectives in sovereign states (*Staatszielbestimmungen* and *objectifs de valeur constitutionnelle*). See *supra* Sect. 2.2.2.

[6] It is not a case that the establishment of a political union has been advocated in several official documents issued by the Presidents of EU institutions over the last few years in regard to the completion of the EMU. According to the roadmaps for the completion of the EMU drafted therein, the euro area should be supported with a number of new pillars, namely a banking union, a capital market union, a genuine economic fiscal union and, eventually, a political union. Cf. European Commission Communication (2012), pp. 35–36; President of the European Commission, Report (2015), p. 5.

European Commission Communication (2012) A blueprint for a deep and genuine economic and monetary union, launching a European debate, 30th November 2012, COM(2012)777/2 final
President of the European Commission (2015) Completing Europe's Economic and Monetary Union, 22 June 2015
Rossolillo G (2018) Fiscalità e sovranità: riflessioni sulla ripartizione delle competenze tra Stati membri e Union Europea. Il Diritto dell'Unione Europea, 123–152
Snell J (2016) The trilemma of European economic and monetary integration, and its consequences. Eur Law J 22:157–179
Véron N (2012) Challenges of Europe's Fourfold Union. Hearing at the US Senate Committee on Foreign Relations, August 2012

Index

L. Lionello, *The Pursuit of Stability of the Euro Area as a Whole*, Studies in European Economic Law and Regulation 18,
https://doi.org/10.1007/978-3-030-28045-1

Printed by Printforce, the Netherlands